ALSO BY ANNE HOLLANDER

Seeing Through Clothes

Moving Pictures

Moving Pictures

Anne Hollander

Alfred A. Knopf

New York   1989

THIS IS A BORZOI BOOK
PUBLISHED BY ALFRED A. KNOPF, INC.

The material in Chapter One was originally published in different form as
two articles: "Moving Pictures," Raritan, Winter 1986; and "The
Unacknowledged Brothel of Art," Grand Street, Spring 1987.

Library of Congress Cataloging-in-Publication Data
Hollander, Anne.
Moving pictures / Anne Hollander. — 1st ed.
p.   cm.
Bibliography: p.
Includes index.
ISBN 0-394-57400-1
1. Motion pictures—Aesthetics.   2. Art and motion pictures.
3. Popular culture.   4. Art, European.   I. Title.
PN1995. H614   1989
791.43'01—dc19   89-45323   CIP

Manufactured in the United States of America
First Edition

To T.N.

ACKNOWLEDGMENTS

I received great help in writing this book from conversations with several people. I wish especially to thank Rogers Albritton, Martha Hollander, Rosalind Krauss, and Derek Parfit for their enabling suggestions, objections, provocations, and encouragement.

—A.H.

CONTENTS

Moving Pictures

Introduction

MOVIES, like paintings, are intended for all time. Theater is ephemeral—each production lasts only as long as its run, and each performance is a new version of the piece. But a painting or a movie is an enduring work, subject only to circumstantial injury and decay. Our relation to movies and paintings is one of hopeless inequality: they will outlast us. Our mutability and mortality are weak in the face of those ageless moments they recount, those creatures and vistas unchangingly and forever going through their motions.

The power of moving pictures has been undeniable since the beginning of the cinema. The fascination they exerted when they were confined to recording simple incidents, even before screenplays existed, made them instantly and permanently important to life. What they did not first seem to be was art, at least not in the same universe with the works of Rembrandt and Michelangelo. But anyone could have told, from the kind of force the screen image had, that movies were linked to compelling pictures of all kinds. People's deepest feelings were engaged by the pictures themselves, as they had been by earlier illuminations, paintings, and engravings—by all works that outlast and transcend the viewer. One reason was that elements of those earlier visions lurked in the screen image, exerting their old power in a new form.

It was not just the show. Theater has a different magic, the spell of live performance, which carries audiences away by the immediacy of the event. The theatrical spell may easily be broken, ruined by a breakdown of memory or nerve; and it is slightly different each time. But film shares in the perfect, unchanging action of still pictures, which may be interrupted only if the surface is covered, or melts, or if the light dies. Just as God and Adam perpetually lose touch on the ceiling of the Sistine Chapel, so Fred

home, whether now or fifty years from now. Like all reproductions, they invite private fantasy, private memory and association, not public excitement. The demand of the picture is personal and unmediated; the artist, the performer with all his demands, is absent.

This absence is another feature of much North European art. Although each viewer knows that the breathtaking effect was made by the purposive design and skill of the artist, the impact of a Rembrandt Bible scene or a Vermeer interior is primarily that of the subject, the atmosphere, and the action. In contrast, the initial impact of a painting in the very different classical and Italian tradition—let us say one of Raphael's—is that of a performance, with the subject visibly (and perhaps also breathtakingly) built into it. The reflections on metal and glass painted in a Van Eyck Annunciation or a Kalf still-life seem like spontaneous miracles, whereas the draperies painted by Botticelli seem like variations in a sung aria. Although we know that Van Eyck and Kalf also actually applied a brush, we are not invited to think first of that as we look. The effect of their paintings is to offer the phenomena as freshly springing into existence, the depicted events as natural occurrences. The subject may well be absorbing in itself; but if it is in fact neutral or boring, the medium will force it to be meaningful—without apparent intervention. In the other tradition of art, the classic and modern art that calls attention to itself, intervention is the whole point: the flowers on the table are interesting only because of what the painter has done about them. In cinematic and proto-cinematic art, the flowers are made interesting by a sort of magic that makes their mere visibility seem a significant story in itself.

In the following chapters I explore what looks to me like the impulse to make art of this kind, and I pursue its emergence in the movies, because I think its history is continuous. In the first chapter I try to locate the specific sources for the emotive power of moving-picture imagery. I see it first in the distinctive rendering of light by the painters of the North European Renaissance, together with their ways of composing the space in pictures to suggest and invite psychological motion. But printed graphic illustration was also born in Northern Europe in the fifteenth century, to supplement the paintings and to begin re-creating them in graphic form; and I want to show why the black-and-white media have had a special power to move the world ever since. By harnessing the elements of light and shade, and by making pictures not only repeatable but movable and adaptable, they have shown what is essential for getting images to do their deepest emotional work.

The rest of the book follows the history of Western painting and graphics from the fifteenth to the twentieth century, reading the work of certain artists as attempts to make narrative out of a particular kind of mobile-seeming imagery. Whatever the theme of the picture, proto-cinematic imagery sets the viewer's psyche in motion, reveals arbitrarily rather than describes thoroughly, disturbs more than it satisfies, and strongly suggests the impossibility of seeing everything at once. I contrast such pictures to the classic kind, which create a fictive world where completeness is the aim and the true subject of the narrative is the artist. Such classic art often uses carefully wrought beauty as its vessel of comprehensiveness: painters invent visions of color and order that make delicious whole sense out of the unpalatable, indigestible world, especially out of our partial and often incomprehensible views of it. The aim of such pictures is to embody an ideal of art itself as a force for order, with reforming and elevating power.

The point about movies is not just that they move, but that they move us. And the chief way they do that is by offering sets of partial and puzzling views, just as life does, and making art directly out of their arbitrary, unfinished nature. The world is presented in a fluid medium that depends on incompleteness, quick change, and often on ambiguity. Cinematic art therefore engages our anxiety and empathy first, and allows beauty to arise from the very quality of contingency that informs the images. Before the camera existed, many artists in the still media tried to do the same thing, to create beauty the same way, and indeed to create narrative, revealing a story in the unpredictable flow of visual life and seizing the viewer's soul with it, rather than preparing tableaux that exposed their own mastery.

Many of the artists I discuss here followed the original example set forth in the Northern Renaissance, directly or derivatively or obliquely. At the same time they seem to a modern, post-cinematic eye to have prefigured the way movies work as pictures in the modern world. I see the rise of film as a natural continuation of their special kind of illustrative impulse, which appeared in serious painting of all kinds as well as in less serious graphic work. When movie-makers came to create their own lifelike fictions, they went right on following the same example in the new language of the camera.

The desire to make pictures in this way, using certain optical effects to appeal to unconscious feelings rather than to the conscious intelligence, is essentially romantic in the deepest sense, committed to the personal in its very form, even if the topic is general or noncommittal. If the topic is itself romantic, the cinema is now a better medium than any other for carrying it forward in the modern world, more serious and more potent than prose fiction or theater. Movies continue to expound specifically romantic themes— varieties of obsessive passion, the monster creation, the spiritual quest—with greater seriousness than any other current mode of fiction; and indeed with the same seriousness visible in the works of German and English Romantic painters and some of their later followers in the United States. Such paintings are now in fact being taken more seriously than ever: they are sharing in our new self-aware passion for movie romance. The vitality of cinematic imagery for conveying romantic myths resides in that same ancient reliance on atmospheric lighting and arbitrary composition, on fidelity to shifting visual circumstance, however minimally suggested, rather than to fixed, known pictorial expectation. Pictures in this mode, now presented in movies in dramatic sequences that perpetually promise still more revelations cast in the same mode, grip and draw the private imagination—in fact "romanticize" any material.

They do this especially with material that might be considered the most objective and detached. Allegedly neutral themes, those that were once thought to underlie the Dutch genre works of the seventeenth century, are often the ones that grip most effectively; the viewer feels magnetized, not pressed or pushed. The more the painter or movie-maker working in this psychological mode seems *not* to be making a point, the more we feel like seeking for one, looking longer, guessing what it is or will be. On the other hand, if the visual material in the picture is fashionably stylized, as in 1930's comedies or 1950's melodramas, the effect of rendering it in the essentially unsleek cinematic medium increases the emotive power of the result. Dutch painters had already discovered this point, too: ideally exquisite satin dresses and invented perfect furniture look pregnant with drama, if mobile lighting and composition charge the atmosphere with feeling and invite the viewer's projection.

Everyone knows that bad movies can be thrilling and have an appeal beyond their defects. This is usually because of the visual thrill built into the medium, the light-borne picture that transcends bad acting, bad writing, and bad editing. Any picture is better than no picture, whereas an embarrassing live performance is much worse than none at all. A dull lecture or a comic speech may be excruciating; but any slide show or classroom movie—however grimly instructive the material, even graphs and cell structure—has its array of irresistible prizes.

Visual illustration, without the imposition of a present performer or an insistent artist's hand, fills some obviously deep gap in our inner lives, beyond the desire for entertainment or the quest for knowledge. Life seems to need illuminating through the eye, whatever other benefits are gained from reading and learning; the soul needs its own window. Dramatic printed captions, voice-over comments in slide lectures and later in movies, and background music are all reinforcements for the illustrative, or what might better be called the illuminative mode as a direct channel to the individual psyche. On the stage this was first suggested by the famous dioramas of the early 1800's, which produced dramatic narrative out of large pictures lit from behind and unrolled on a stage to musical accompaniment; and the music dramas of Wagner later took up the idea of speaking to the unconscious by fusing living pictures and meaningful thematic sound. Supertitles projected over the proscenium arch during a performance confirm even more strongly the relation between opera and film; and music video further reinforces the connection between cinematic visual imagery and music's power over the psyche. Lately art museums have seized on the cinematic trick of providing canned audible captions to go along with the pictures, furnishing continuous commentary on tape with earphones, a moving track of sound that speaks personally to each visitor and turns the whole gallery into a movie house. Soon one may well have a choice of speech or music with the show. The disembodied voice keeps the event well away from any awkward performance by a living guide, and makes the paintings seem comfortably like filmed reproductions of themselves.

Cinema is the newest form of illustration. It encapsulates the whole history of figurative art, helping itself to that history's most effective devices, continuing the special triumph of art for the public that was begun by prints and engravings and continued through the dynamic agency of the camera. Public exhibitions of paintings that are now possible on an international scale, with works of art traveling all over the world to be seen by people who might never hope to visit them, are only one part of the way art has become part of public consciousness. The other way is through its ghostly existence in the graphic world, the king of which is now the movies.

Now only books for children are consistently illustrated; books for adults are not supposed to need pictures. Magazines and newspapers make up for that lack in adult life, overlapping inspired advertising photography with glossy photojournalism so that together they deliver a single glittering cinematic montage of lifelike fantasy. Other graphic material, also conceived by imaginations trained in the cinematic style of allusion, makes narrative out of visual situations that reveal and suggest without explaining. Television does the same. Cinema, that great infant, has demonstrated to other media how to use past art to suit the present eye, how to respond, absorb, reflect, and move on, seizing what is needed and eating it without thanks, flourishing with ungovernable energy on mixed garbage and gourmet fare. Film and television frames are stuffed with material grabbed without ceremony from Manet and Goya, from Velázquez and Vermeer, from Turner, Church, and Bierstadt, just as commercial photography also is. All of these are filtered through graphic conventions that may modify but cannot obscure the sources or mute their effects. The whole makes a modern illustrative art of incomparable richness, even though it lacks coherence. Meanwhile the original Manets and Vermeers are still with us, glowing like live coals in the galleries, but also winking in miniature from millions of postcards and posters.

In any age and any medium, most art is bad. This is just as true of painting in the Renaissance as it is of movies in the twentieth century, and no truer of commercial art than of serious portraits; but we are now more awake to the badness in certain genres than to that in others, because our present ranking system is retroactive. We are more inclined to see all Renaissance frescoes as better than all nineteenth-century fashion plates, because we have come to believe in the superiority of both fresco and the Renaissance to any sort of commercial fashion art. But in fact good frescoes are proportionately as rare as good fashion plates. So, of course, are good movies.

We have come to believe, moreover, that a work of art may be good only if it has some kind of artistic integrity, that it must display some obedience to the self-perpetuating laws of art itself rather than smack of greed, opportunism, and exploitation; and so we are inclined to value those artistic media that make such integrity easier to maintain in our own society. But good art has had a way of appearing in allegedly debased genres, and the bad examples in lofty ones have been mercilessly shown up during both the nineteenth and twentieth centuries, sometimes obscuring the good altogether. By such means nineteenth-century academic and narrative painting was discounted for most of the twentieth, all of it rated at the low level of its obvious disasters. Hollywood movies were once considered that way, too. Lately we have thrown all painting from the past into one basket, not trying to distinguish good from bad in case we might be proved wrong later on, and preferring to assume that everything is good for something. Current painting receives the same enlarged acceptance.

In the allegedly low media, the same lack of discrimination seems to matter less, but it also works to obscure differences of quality and make good judgment all the harder. Yet the differences are still there between the few good things and the huge number of inferior products, just as they are in any epoch and any form of art. Fine works live surrounded by shoals of noble failures and basely corrupt projects in the same medium, lamentable botches and slick bags of tricks, things flawed, dull, shallow, false, or crazed, or just untalented efforts—and, of course, things made up out of stolen parts, the bad, sad, mad, and moving Frankenstein monsters of art.

But in much bad art there is often real satisfaction for its time, sometimes for all time; and it acquires a sort of provisional goodness that resides in its ability to move and please, that makes it hard to give up or throw out altogether, in fact that often makes it endure. So the difficulties of judgment about artistic authenticity are further complicated by the question of authentic response. There is even an element of the moving and the pleasing that can make good works of art seem questionable, just because tawdry ones share in it—and it is that element that made all movies seem suspect at the beginning. The medium flowed too readily in the emotional vein, which was then rapidly losing prestige among the fine arts.

The distinction between high art and low art has been vexed by the difficulty in making these other distinctions. The temptation has arisen during the course of modern history to think that anything intended to make money or otherwise succeed by working directly on our feelings—pornography is the most extreme example, advertising art is another—must be bad in itself and therefore low by nature, especially when the normal badness common to most art is considered to be a quality of the genre itself. This situation once applied to novels, which were considered a debased form, partly because of the pleasure they gave, their obvious link to private fantasy. It took generations of great works to transcend the normal badness of most novels, and make an acknowledged fine art out of prose fiction. Though bad religious art of the past is still given more credit than bad advertising art of this century, the badness is quite similar. Good pornography is unfortunately not so clearly recognized to be better than bad; and there is so far little stimulus to raise the standard and make the distinction more noticeable.

It is well understood that bad art relies on good, raiding and degrading the carefully balanced effects of talent and skill, making crude versions of refined achievements. Some of this process in fact can have great value, can in some cases enlighten later perception of the original by subjecting it to selective brutal usage, can even seem to improve on it by remodeling it in a harsher form, a dumber mode. The "improvement" is a trick effect; the original retains its superiority, which is nevertheless enhanced and enriched by bad treatment—not by contrast, but somehow by a combination of sordid attrition and added emotional freight, like a ruined statue.

Less obvious but no less common is the reliance of good art on bad for certain cheap effects or crude details, for clever ways to take shortcuts or use filler, for sure-fire banal motifs. Such larceny works both ways, so that the bad source can also be enriched by being robbed. Visual artists have in fact all been stealing from one another for centuries across all boundaries, and they are aided in this by the fluid graphic media, which put everything indiscriminately up for grabs. The movies in this century represent a magnificent compendium of all such thievery and its enormously satisfying and profitable results.

The most commonly stolen goods are the arrangements that guarantee emotional responses. That is why camera art can do the best stealing, since its form depends on the light and dark that create feeling through pictures by unconscious means, and thus hide the very fact of theft perhaps even from the thief. Only when the images hit the screen do the effects become visible, as they begin to feed the visual habits of future generations on all the varied and accumulated treasures of the past.

ONE
Moving Pictures

Light and Vision

A MOVIE is a sequence of pictures made with a camera and projected on a screen. Since the camera defines the medium, movies are part of the history of all camera art; they are heirs to the claims staked by photographers at the very beginning of the camera's life. But photographic pretensions were formed against a background of concern for the proper character and function of painting. The far-reaching possibilities shown by the early camera were perceived by eyes trained in strategies that painters had worked out for rendering reality inside a frame; and such artistic strategies were known, at least by artists themselves, to have evolved from earlier painters' methods. Whatever the camera could do as illuminator of the visual world was first seen in painters' terms, backed up by centuries of painterly tradition. Today the movies, as they continue to further camera work in the mode of realistic pictorial sequences, are still engaging with certain painters of the past.

Photography itself soon escaped painters' terms. The still camera established and expanded its own separate empire of the eye and eventually, as a reproductive agent, turned back to conquer painting itself. But the link between the new pictorial scope of the camera and the long history of painting was authentic, and certain painters in the later nineteenth century, such as Manet, Degas, and Caillebotte, responded to the camera even more creatively than photographers could at the time. Painters were even able to take the camera beyond its immediately apparent possibilities and project it into the cinematic realm—to make paintings that look not like photographs but like frames from hypothetical movies.

To do this, they drew not just on the newly revealed capacities of the still camera, but on an existing painterly tradition that history-minded artists could see was already aligned with camera vision. This was the tradition of

North European realism, which nineteenth-century artists saw most vividly flourishing in seventeenth-century Holland, but whose sources lay in the Flemish art of the fifteenth century. That tradition was continued and modified throughout the interwoven history of European art: many painters shared in the particularly Northern proto-cinematic impulse without being themselves Nordic, having absorbed the original Flemish and Dutch principles. Velázquez, Chardin, Turner, and Goya had affinities with Dutch and Flemish art; and their works contributed to this pictorial tradition, which I think led to modern cinema, even more than to the opposing classical one, which inexorably led to modern painting.

For five centuries realistic painting in Northern Europe was expressed in what Kenneth Clark calls the Alternative Convention—a mode of rendering visible reality in art that was fundamentally different from the classicizing tradition established by Italian Renaissance artists and theorists. One way to describe what Northern artists did is to say they invented a cinema in painterly terms. There was more to this than telling stories and rendering natural appearances convincingly—Italian Renaissance painters were very good at both of those. But a cinematic art also invests natural appearances with their own absolute meaning, and then incorporates the viewer into the universe these appearances create. The viewer's own immediate visual experience is evoked by the visual world inside the frame, so that his responses to the picture can be direct, not mediated by a tacit acknowledgment that the artist's style is what really conveys the picture's meaning. Such direct effects were managed by many painters of Northern Europe, beginning with Van Eyck.

The classical tradition in art, founded on ideals attributed to a revived antiquity, embraced what was believed to be a higher aim than a simple grip on the beholder's soul through his naked eye. A painting could be a microcosm, an independent perfect universe; and the terms on which such a vision came into existence had to be those of an acknowledged creator, implicitly modeled on the divine creator. Acknowledgment of the creator had to be perpetually demanded, so that every stroke of the artist's brush, his every minute disposition inside the painted world, said to the gazing eye, You must know that I have made this. The appeal was to the viewer's appreciation of the way the painter brought the universe inside the picture to completion. Linear perspective, the learned discovery of the Italian Renaissance, was one excellent device for promoting the sense of the artist as inspired interpreter and technician. In this tradition the painter performs for the viewer; his act (not his subject) is what you see.

When the camera first came into use, it seemed to destroy or at least to sidestep this function of the artist as vicar of our responses to the visible world. Between the actual scene and the eventual picture came only some mechanical magic. No forming hand showed the force of a transforming mind and will; the whole thing was a trick of the light, arousing cheap wonder and stupefaction. Henri Focillon wrote in his 1936 essay on "The Artist's Hand" about "the cruel inertia of the photograph, attained by a handless eye, repelling our sympathy even while attracting it, a marvel of light but a passive monster. Photography is like the art of another planet. . . . The hand never intervenes to spread over it the warmth and flow of human life."

The spell of photographs is certainly different from the one that movies weave. Passivity is one of photography's strong points, and detachment is one of the most resonant notes it can strike. The belief is widespread that the camera is a neutral observer, which makes the photographer a super-human creature who can turn the same cold machine on human pain and shame that he turns on buildings and waterfalls—a witness-bearer, not a creator. Much of the fascination of the still camera comes from its function as official voyeur for the squeamish public, its role as professional spy on the secrets of life, death, and unliving matter. And a quite natural opposing desire has also allowed the photographer to imitate the classic painter, so that his vision and technique dominate his subject. But still another view envisions the camera as an artistic tool that can engender its own myth, ro-mance, and drama as painting and poetry do. Considered that way, the still camera is a stage on the way to the movie camera. In order to engage the viewer with the haunting kind of narrative suggested by Rembrandt and De Hooch, by Turner or Manet and Degas, there had to be movies, not just photography.

Movie-goers know that human warmth may seem to flow straight from the eye of the moving camera itself, without the intervention of "the artist's hand." Movement and light create cinematic drama when the movie-maker's narrative will turn his eye on the world; and in this way they bring it closer to certain painters' work than still photographs can ever be. A pho-tograph may indeed repel and fascinate, but the images on a movie screen engulf and transform; and modern responses to movies, not to photo-graphs, are more like what certain engulfing painters of the past were ob-viously after. The effect of a "handless eye" was one of their secrets.

The greatest secret in the engulfing effect of modern cinema is the pro-jection of the film image so that light pours through it onto a screen, and cancels other sources of illumination. In the dark room, the light comes only from the moving picture, so that it alone makes the world. The painters in the Northern tradition often tried for this effect, too, aiming for a jewel-like transparency that made the picture seem to be conducting light through it, rather than reflecting externally applied light from its modeled surfaces. Many works in the Northern style show an illuminating door or window at the back or side, as if to signal this aim to be a source of light and not a scheme for its refraction.

Today, in the Museo del Prado in Madrid, Velázquez' celebrated painting *Las Meninas* is exhibited alone in a dark room and lit invisibly from the side, so that the distant open doorway and tall windows inside the painting seem to be lighting the room in the museum, not just the room in the picture. The picture seems projected—it is set up to look like a film shot, and there is even a barrier keeping the audience from approaching its surface, just as in a movie theater. What this arrangement in fact does is to show how much like a film shot the painting already looks; and it only takes a moment to imagine certain other works displayed the same way: Vermeer's and other Dutch artists' interiors, for example, which also have light-filled windows and doors, or Velázquez' other paintings showing the same kind of ambiguous action and illumination—*The Forge of Vulcan* or *The Spinners* —or a Degas view from backstage or a Caillebotte street. The quasi-projected mode of display reveals what *Las Meninas* (and its kindred) is really like: not a photograph, which may sit frozen on the page, but a cinematic fragment, an engulfing, light-made, passing moment.

Long before photography, chiaroscuro modes of realistic picture-making had been developed in Northern Europe, where light itself is a precious source to be carefully tapped. The greatest North European painters, beginning in the fifteenth century, used light as if it were alive, inviting it and coaxing it to expand and create its own visions. For Italian painters, on the other hand, it was as if the pervasive sun needed to be kept at bay, mediated by art, diffused into colors, and tempered by modeling into refined shapes. The artist's skill intervened to modify the crude glare that made phenomena too harsh for a direct gaze. But in paintings in the tradition of Van Eyck or Vermeer, the "reality" of the image depends on the sense that the light of the moving eye has been directly engaged by the moving light on separate phenomena—by each illuminated thing itself, not by an idealizing version that manages the lighting so as to harmonize each thing with other things. Painted light, imitating the action of seen light, can give this sense that the world of the picture is momentarily actual and in uncertain motion —becoming seamlessly part of our own shifting world, even while remaining a painting in a frame. It does not fool or please the eye; it is like part of the eye's usual experience. Whether applied in paint or by the movie camera, this "photographic" method gives a peculiar atmosphere to the phenomena it records—a presence, the look of having a distilled meaning.

A painting made this way does not primarily display its forms outlined and then modeled by a painter's learned and informing hand, whipped into shape by the brilliance of a tutored brush; it does not show color seized away from nature to be a formal tool manipulated into leading its own autonomous life. It does not show a cleverly created artificial space populated by ravishingly believable fictions. It seems to be something the artist has momentarily conjured, not wrought. Light behaves inside the frame just as it does outside it; and the artist seems to stand back saying, like the camera, Behold what there is. Scrupulously hard-edged details are quite unnecessary to this effect—it can be created entirely by tonality rendered with flecks and smudges, as in a Rembrandt or a Goya, and even with awkwardly applied ones, as in a Manet. But it was probably the exquisitely meticulous Van Eyck who first achieved entire success with rendering natural lighting. His own understanding of its effect appears in his inscription on the Arnolfini marriage portrait—*"Johannes de Eyck fuit hic,"* or "Jan van Eyck was here"—not only witnessing the wedding but "seeing" the scene into existence for us, just as if paint had nothing to do with it.

In the fifteenth century, one aspect of the Northern use of light was the illusionistic rendering of surface. In the great Flemish paintings the textures of fur and glass, cloth, gold, and skin were famous in their time for their extreme distinctiveness; they even produced a certain discomfort along with admiration. And here is where the psychological dimension of "cinematographic" image-making first appeared. The "handless eye," impartially and relentlessly focused on the variable appearances of things, seems to expose not just the phenomena but the viewer, too. Naked representations of separate objects, using light effects apparently unedited by an ideal of visual or ideological harmony, have an unsettling effect. Things that look too individually real force a relation to *us,* not to each other. What are we to make of them? Their perfection and their totality seem to charge them with meaning: but what do they mean? And what are they asking of us? It is as if the artist had left the meaning to be provided by the viewer. And indeed, allegorical significance has been energetically read into many paintings in the Northern tradition as if it had been pulled into them, snared and tugged by the sharp hook of the charged atmosphere. The presence of objects and persons manifested by Northern light is a steady invitation, sometimes an imperative demand. Ambiguous genre works in the seventeenth-century Dutch tradition have needed elaborate moral meaning attached to them in this century, partly because of the familiar feelings of mysterious awareness and expectation they generate in our cinematic age. Movies have taught us to recognize the presence of meaning in uneventful scenes full of vivid objects.

In classical Italian Renaissance art, on the other hand, phenomena submitted to the sovereignty of creative will served by a trained hand; and its descendants have flourished in Baroque rhetoric, Rococo elegance, Neo-classic and Romantic dramaturgy, Impressionist vibrance, and modern formal abstraction. The meaning of separate phenomena in a classic picture primarily nourishes the internal coherence of the whole. The artist conducts the painting like a symphony, standing up in front; all the parts serve one artistic purpose, however arbitrary their choice and arrangement may appear. The painting holds itself and its meaning together in the net of its harmonious form. If it is realistic, any strange action on the part of pictured figures, any violence, any cryptic arrangements of landscape and objects—as in Giorgione's *Tempesta*, for example, or Botticelli's *Primavera*, or some Pre-Raphaelite narrative works—may invite study, philosophical or theological speculation, and historical interpretation; but they are not directly unsettling. The subject itself does not make uncomfortably direct psychological demands—although the *painter* may, on his own behalf. The composition, the palette, the crisp or fuzzy rendering, all the carefully achieved unity of paint and surface keeps the subject inside the world of paint and keeps the viewer safe—safe from uneasiness, and safe to feel whatever pleasure and profit that unity itself affords. No matter how turbulent or peculiar the action inside the frame, it cannot get out. What does get out is the message of art itself that carries any subject in solution. Strong emotional demands are made, but indirectly by the artist through the paint.

Actions and objects in movies get straight at the viewer in a way that is at odds with these classic aims of painting, even before we have considered the difference between a moving and a still image. In their essential looks, films move us with a kind of pictorial demand that many painters do not ever wish to make—an unmediated appeal that goes straight through our eyes to our feelings first and leaves the artist's artistry aside. In any realistic image, light and shadow do this work better than line and color, or even explicit story and action. Almost a century of black-and-white cinematography has proved this, even more than still photography; but painters, and especially graphic artists working in black and white, knew it long before.

For human creatures dependent on the sun, the action of light has an obvious primal drama that compels the human imagination. The universal dramatic relation between light and vision has forced the metaphors for achieving redemption, for gaining understanding, for acquiring knowledge, for all transcendence. Consequently, light in figurative art, as Van Eyck discovered, has an edge over any other formal element. If the dramatic action of ordinary light can be accurately represented in a religious picture, for example, the image can manifest spiritual transfiguration simply by showing the real light of day on the right group of common objects. They will seem to fill with meaning, just as the world seems to fill with it when dawn breaks. And so an ordinary stable can effectively be shown as the sacred birthplace of the Redeemer, not by applying stagy spotlights or supernatural gold rays, but just by showing exactly how thin daylight filters through the uneven timbers of a broken door. Two centuries later, a similar rush of human meaning seems to fill the room where a woman is standing at her kitchen window and nothing at all is happening, except for milk pouring out and light coming in (1.1).

1.1 JAN VERMEER, *Woman Pouring Milk*

Light does not stay still. The movie camera by its very nature engages our feelings about our relation to the movement of the earth and sun, simply by making art out of the constant action of light, even without showing any other kind of movement. The quality of movement in Vermeer's still kitchen is carried not in the rendering of arrested human action—it is in the surge of feeling that attaches to the perception of light's motion. In a picture, the offer of light's action to the gazing eye is like an offer of enlightenment: the picture is a discovery. But at the same time, the still image is a lesson in contingency. The discovery is not one instant, but a dip into a flow of light that must keep changing, that shows what both is and is not a present moment, a moving present that is always full of both hope and loss. And so the Vermeer is like a sequence of movie frames, not like a photograph that tries to freeze the light. The still image is laden with constant shift, like still moments in life itself.

The passage of every daylight hour changes the relationships between light, shadow, and color in the seen world. Everything directly seen is also seen in motion, since light itself moves; and so not only does nature never stay the same, it never stays *looking* the same. Any mode of visual art, like Vermeer's or like the movies, that makes this point about light in terms of personal experience is bound to be very affecting. It engages our deepest feelings about our relation to time, vision, and material things, our sense of transience. Movies do just that, whatever style of film-making they are cast in and whatever else they do. And so the dialectic of light and dark ensures the emotional potency of any movie—even without an exciting scenario or good acting and editing—just by representing the mutable chiaroscuro that makes us see and know the mutable world. Recent advances in color cinematography are in fact largely a matter of improvements in lighting. In early color movies, the color tended to flatten and deaden the natural chiaroscuro of the camera medium, and as Stanley Cavell points out, they seemed unreal and inexpressive in consequence, less rather than more like nature.

Movies redouble the effect of light's motion by actually moving. The picture never stands still, just as light never does—and just as the eye never does. The moving eye is the other half of moving light, the analogue of the individual desiring heart and searching mind. The fixed gaze is the property of death; the living eye is in motion, always ranging for food. Again, modes of art using human experience for their subject that both engage the scanning eye and suggest its analogy to the inner life can rely on a raw emotional pull. In movies the camera itself is the seeking gaze, demanding enlightenment, and its choices can demonstrate its superior insight: good cinematography and editing give the effect of satisfying the eye's immediate prior longings at every instant. Ideally, the camera unerringly finds what the bodily eye and the mind's eye are both unconsciously lusting for, or perhaps dreading.

The moving eye is open, and it signifies openness to experience—the constant susceptibility of the individual inner life, which in a sacred context used to be called the soul. Imitating the movement of light and eyes, films work directly on the modern psyche in the same way that Van Eyck's religious pictures once worked on the fifteenth-century soul. The Flemish paintings were famous for arousing pious feeling almost too sensationally for Italian views of artistic propriety. They did it not just by shedding light on the break of woolen folds and the wrinkling of knuckles (striking the soul with truth as the eye is struck with phenomena), but by putting the soul itself into motion. In art, for the soul to be moved, the eye must move; and so, quite apart from the light, the painting must move.

To make this happen, the picture plane, the effect of a flat, fixed, and containing surface, must seem to disappear. Natural lighting goes a long way toward creating this illusion, but it is not the only thing that does. The forms inside the frame can be so arranged that the frame itself seems to be moving through space and the action inside it perpetually going on. The eye may move over it, or even in and out of it, with the random scan it uses on real life. This sense of the frame potentially moving from side to side or up and down is given by compositions that are deliberately made to seem arbitrary—that are made so that the painting seems to say, If you look at this scene from just here for a moment, everything arranges itself like this; but you can plainly see that a slightly different view would do just as well. You could obviously shift a bit to the left, or climb up on something and look down: you might just see some more of the horse over here, or less of the shrubbery over there, more sky or fewer townsfolk. Maybe you will in a minute. The visual field is offered as subject to rearrangement, just as it is in the daily life of the eye, and of the attention, and of the feelings.

Paintings that suggest this turn the plane into an empty screen where action in and out and to and fro is always imminent, and the floating eye and soul are exposed to unknown possibilities. This effect appears in Hugo van der Goes, but it shows up much later in Goya and many others well before movies. Such art unsettles rather than pleases, and raises expectations rather than satisfying them. Like film it suggests a great deal more than it states and makes strong, if unarticulated, demands on the individual viewer.

All these effects are naturally stronger when the subject matter inside the frame is familiar and conventional. The possibilities suggested beyond the frame, or in a differently chosen frame, can make a sacred or a trite subject ambiguous and suggestively incomplete—they make a Flemish Annunciation, for example, into a scene of present expectancy rather than ritual mystery, or a Degas nude in her bath disturbing instead of pleasant. The "fixing" of the image has been done so that it keeps our private feeling on the move; the demand on the viewer is for a vital sort of meditation, a condition of steady psychic action—as in dreaming, fantasizing, or in ordinary seeing. By painting of this kind, we are never really taken out of ourselves; we are meant to stay in ourselves as we participate. And the picture seems to keep shifting to include our inner movements in its own motion, to allow room for our unconscious lives.

There are more ways to make a still painting move. A painter may avoid familiarly stylized cadences for the figural poses, and so achieve the look of unfinished progression. This means insisting on a slight ambiguity of human forms, so that the shapes taken by moving bodies become abstract and unfitted to standard notions of proper pictorial action. The kneeling and the marching, the registering of grief or surprise cannot be immediately "read": they must be *watched*. Georges de la Tour, like Rembrandt, was very good at this—it is an anti-classic strategy of great force. Similarly, by tipping down the pictured floor, a painter can keep the frame moving toward us, mysteriously enlarging so that we feel invited to move into the picture. At the same time the reverse motion occurs: in the small Dutch interiors with visible distant openings, the picture is both coming to enclose us and retreating, drawing us with it after the light. This is the engulfing effect, a cameralike movement that comes to claim the viewer, acknowledging no barrier between the action and his inner life.

The effect is the opposite of the one that stays at a fixed distance inside a still frame and weaves its pictorial spell to entrance us into stillness before it. That is the effect of pictures by Leonardo or Rubens, for example, at which the eye tends to stare as at a whirling gold watch, and the feet to stand rooted—or even to back away in awe. The perfect perspective in a Piero della Francesca has a similar effect. The movement inside such a picture is autonomous, the vibrations self-generated. It is an incantation, humming with the interplay of color, the accord of shapes and volumes, the poetry of line, or with the dazzling array of visible strokes dealt by a masterly wrist, tracks that the ensorcelled eye cannot resist tracing in their dance around the confines of the plane. Realistic narrative couched in such terms exerts an enormous power: the action has been woven like a charm and seems like fate. But it is a general fate, never connected with our own private destiny as we can feel it.

Gazing at some great paintings in that mode can turn you to stone or stop your breath. They invoke the artifice of eternity and transcend the common business of living, even while they may portray it. But the "moving" picture invites the eye both to move into the picture and then to stay free inside it, free to scan, to pause, to close in and move back, to find its own path. The uncertain path of private feeling is correspondingly opened up, and so we project the motions of our own souls into the picture to engage with the action.

In paintings by Rembrandt such as the very late *Conspiracy of Claudius Civilis* in Stockholm (1.2), for example, or the 1646 *Adoration of the Shepherds* (1.3) in Munich, inspired lighting puts the atmosphere into motion, so that it overflows the space and reaches toward the viewer; meanwhile the figure style and compositional mode suggest continuous behavior in a shifting frame. The result is moving drama without strong color, vigorous action, or surface detail. Its motion moves us, whatever Rembrandt's subject; and we answer with that emotional response which automatically follows the response of the eye to light. The narrative action inside the picture is psychologically freighted in advance and needs no theatrical emphasis or conventional rhetoric. Gestures and postures, facial expressions and drap-

1.2 REMBRANDT VAN RIJN, *The Conspiracy of Claudius Civilis*

1.3 REMBRANDT VAN RIJN, *The Adoration of the Shepherds*

ery movements are muted, unstylized, and unfocused, and yet achieve maximum impact.

Using almost no figures at all, Turner achieved a similar charged emotional effect with landscape two centuries later by using light as if it were the agent of physical turbulence and cataclysm. The great Turners are cinematic because of this method—the light works directly on the feelings, so as to render wind and water in its distinctively emotional terms. No detachment about the scene portrayed is permissible or even possible. You are there.

Motion and Narrative

Because they are made out of forward movement, as well as out of the fundamentals of light and shadow, films are essentially dramatic and not theatrical. Drama orders action as meaning, and experiencing the movement of time is necessary to it, whereas theater can be static like an emblem or an epiphany—the significant action may all be simultaneous, and may consist of some timeless and constant interaction. Botticelli's *Birth of Venus,* for example (1.4), like many Italian Renaissance paintings, is a piece of theater—an apparition, not a dramatic scene. Even though it purports to show an event, everything is present at once and all relationships already completed, only waiting to be deciphered by the viewer. The pictured movements of waves, limbs, hair, fabric, and wind go nowhere but remain stationary, standing for the eternal, celestial mosaic that holds all things in orbit, here shown fixed and recycling forever.

By contrast, movies, like Shakespeare's plays and Greek tragedies, are always going somewhere unknown and taking us with them. Drama demands this device. Nevertheless they also remain pictures, even if they do not fit into Botticelli's pictorial universe. They do fit into Rembrandt's and Goya's—that is, into a scheme of expression founded on the dialectic of night and day, and the progress through them that produces the next day and night, and the next. In this pictorial tradition, all other seen movement is subject to the intractable movement through time—the movement expressed by the motion of earthly light and its corollary darkness. In still pictures, that motion is perceptible only through the fluid action of the eye, which also mirrors the uncertain journey of personal experience—the inner state, subject to outer circumstance. Pictures that appeal to this connection between time and consciousness point up the fact that the timeless universe is an absolute void, outer darkness: there is no cosmic harmony that we can actually see. Human seeing means only seeing *something,* never ev-

1.4 SANDRO BOTTICELLI, *The Birth of Venus*

erything; the view is subjective, always from here—as the light shows. This is the fundamental stuff of drama; and the cinematic kind of art demonstrates it, using chiaroscuro pictures to engage us in it. In film art, it puts the pictures into an actual moving sequence.

Even if the movie camera sits on a motionless subject, the film is still moving and we are still waiting, expectant and responding, our eyes and spirits in motion. Movies that end with fade-outs on continuing action, or more recently with freeze-frames, show how *endlessness* is at the core of the medium—no tableau can put a true stop to visual flow or to the flow of time and feeling. The drama itself is propelled by editing and montage that make direct shifts from one moving picture to another without waiting for any closure or cadence inside the frame to signal the completion of the message. This situation is in fact what makes film part of an old artistic tradition, a modern development in the history of infinite pictures rather than of finite theater.

Anything can be a story in film's distinctive pictorial mode, where meaning is alive in the very medium and feeling is *de facto* engaged. Inevitably, movies became a popular narrative form, and they seemed to be aimed in a different direction from the one taken by modern painters. Especially in the United States, movies naturally allied themselves with the persuasive arts of entertainment and propaganda, during the same period when modern painting was succeeding more and more in detaching itself from those things. Still photography also became a form of modern art directed away from sensationalism and toward a formal seriousness that ensured an accompanying high esthetic status. Only photojournalists and certain photographers in the documentary style, developing their medium at the same time, showed an affinity with cinematic illustration. Movie-making became show business, carried on by a huge industry mounting vast collaborative efforts to please the public and make a profit: whereas paintings, and artistic photographs, were perceived to be the inspired works of single individuals pursuing esthetic goals in preference to worldly aims. The dramatic pictorial narratives of film art flourished for decades in Hollywood, far away from modern painters' studios. The brilliant art direction and cinematography that created the visual flavor of popular movies operated in their own separate universe.

As art critics of our own time began to view painters of the past with modernist and formalist eyes, movies lost their connection not only with modern art but with art history. "Fine Art" could be referred to in movies only by making use of visual allusions to a known work of art; but these allusions explicitly sought to suppress the cinematic nature of film, instead of demonstrating constitutional affinities between earlier pictures and the art of movies. Meanwhile an independent art of cinema was generated, as film-makers developed the medium on its own terms, referring and alluding to the works of its own past, and its distance from painting seemed to increase. By our day, film is thought to have more affinities with the whole history of literary fictions, novels in particular, than with painting. The steady engagement of common fantasy and the multi-layered character of film art give it an obvious poetic dimension; to scholars of poetics, movies seem like models of modern poetic consciousness, and by now the entire corpus of film history may be viewed in the light of such an awareness. But the actual pictorial vessel in which it is all carried has its own significant aptitude for this poetic and narrative work. The power of the cinematic method of picture-making, already established during centuries of realistic painting in the tradition begun by the Flemish, never lost its hold. Its ability to engage, mystify, and unnerve the beholder now serves the art of movies in the same way it always did.

It is sometimes said that movies carry on the tradition of spectacular historical narrative and fictional anecdote in painting. With respect to subject matter, they certainly have done so. Costume epics are supposed to correspond to the history paintings of Delaroche, Meissonier, and Gérôme, or of Lord Leighton, Poynter, and Alma-Tadema. By the same token one might argue that film melodramas and domestic comedies carry on the narrative art derived from the descriptive and somewhat coy Dutch genre scenes of the later seventeenth century—those by Metsu, Netscher, and Van Mieris—and continued during the eighteenth and nineteenth centuries when translated into the language of Greuze and Fragonard, or of Wilkie, Faed, and Frith. This descriptive style was the mold in which most historical and anecdotal painting of those two centuries was cast; but except for the themes, there is hardly anything cinematic about the way any of it looks.

Lawrence Gowing has pointed out an important difference between what Vermeer does and what Dou and Steen do, when they paint a woman working in a kitchen or a group sitting around a table. It boils down to the difference between letting us see something and carefully describing it to us. Any Vermeer scene, like a film shot, is rendered in terms of revelation through light, the constant agent of possibility. It avoids the clever manipulations of drawing and composition that govern a Steen or a Dou, whereby our eyes and minds are pushed into accepting a preconceived shape, a way for things to look that we expect. The subdued drama between men and women in Vermeer appears to be unfolding and even escaping the frame as we watch; but in Steen and Dou the scene is ostensive, complete within the frame, unveiled as on a stage, and accompanied by an explanatory gloss.

The gloss is pictorial. It is the visible choice made to expound a scene according to a set of stylistic rules for composition, modeling, and delineation, a scheme that the painter knows the beholder has previously assimilated as a language suitable for carrying the intended meanings. Thus knowing comes before seeing, not during it; expectations are satisfied, not mysteriously raised, and so a comfortable relation between picture and viewer is maintained. Thousands of nineteenth-century narrative paintings devoted to startling incident or heroic action have this textual flavor—and such works are basically at odds with cinema, no matter how meticulous and naturalistic the historical details or how sensational the subject. They are always more like the lucid theater of Botticelli or the spectacles staged by Rubens than the ambiguous drama of Rembrandt.

The narrative meaning in cinematic art is discovered by absorbing the sequence of pictures directly, not by reading them and understanding them. Watching a movie, you have no time to read; you are immersed in the pool, not looking at its surface, and you must swim. Such unmediated vision is also offered by many painters, but not the ones giving the leisurely entertainment provided by Frith and Meissonier, the sensuous pleasure produced by Titian and Delacroix, or the intellectual exercise afforded by much Pre-Raphaelite art. Good movies, and what I am calling proto-cinematic paintings, sustain a drama of imminent disclosure and incipient revelation. The story is not explained to an audience but revealed to a participant. The scene of expectation is uneasy: what is going to happen? Not in the plot, but simply before our eyes. It will not necessarily be terrible or wonderful, just something not yet seen. Such an atmosphere can invest a neutral or tranquil scene with meaning when there is as yet nothing obvious *to* mean—the sense that it is about to mean something. Paintings that convey this feeling tend not to repay a minute, satisfying study of many details. They seem to demand glancing at, glancing away, and then glancing back, as if the eye had missed something it might yet apprehend the next instant. They bear watching. Details may indeed abound, but no study yields an obvious relationship among them, only the strong sense of imminent meaning for us.

The great scenic painters of the eighteenth and nineteenth centuries produced something less like movies and more like the sensational historical novels of Walter Scott, which were very theatrical in conception and visual detail. The stage of Scott's time followed a reciprocal pattern when it adapted his books, using tableaux and theatrical arrangements taken from historical paintings. The literary ground on which most historical narrative paintings stood and the language-like mode in which they were often set forth gave them a staged flavor to begin with, and they were often founded on respected models derived from the classic Renaissance "theatrical" style.

Nothing is more unsettling than to look at some significant-seeming communication and feel, I can't read this. What is it about? Yet much movie power is generated by that very circumstance—maybe I'll get it in a minute; I'll keep watching. Other cognition comes quite easily; only logical or "textual" comprehension eludes. Watching movies is in fact accomplished in these conditions, with ambiguity as a given, each shot full of what hasn't yet happened, may happen, may be actually happening but be inexplicable until later, or may be present but never need explaining. This is characteristic of the cinematic mode. Any unfolding drama may contain the presence of phenomena that contribute mightily to the audience's engagement in the action, but also fail to convey any readable meaning.

Material objects—cars, buildings, trees, chairs—are poetic in purely pictorial ways: they are themselves potential characters in the cinematic drama, not inanimate properties invested with meaning from elsewhere. Paintings in which ordinary objects are filled with their own self-aware

breathing life, and seem independently to claim a share in the drama's unknown further developments—not obediently to support its patent certain-
ties—are the forerunners of film. The objects in Van Eyck's marriage
portrait are like this; so are the ones in Manet's *Luncheon in the Studio.* So,
too, are the buildings in a street scene by Berckheyde or the parts of church
interiors by Emanuel de Witte, or the water and fire in Turner's visions.
These paintings are not anecdotal, but they are infinitely dramatic, full of
promise and continuous suggestion.

Painting became deeply divided and sharply compromised in France
after the middle of the last century, soon after the camera made its appearance. The new fundamentalist Realism propounded and practiced by Courbet and other painters of his generation demanded acute currency of
subject and unrhetorical honesty of execution, instead of established
themes suavely rendered in standard artistic terms. The new ideals of
French Realism were later refined by the Impressionists and expanded by
Symbolist painters seeking to render imaginative rather than optical or political realities. In part inspired by the advance of science, Realism led still
further, to an extreme concern with ultimate structure; and advanced
painters took a narrowing path toward a realism expressed in the abstraction and reduction of form. In this long process, avowedly narrative and
illustrative painting lost out and lost caste—lost "reality" of a kind—
without, however, losing any power.

Both the showing and telling of stories never ceased being done in pictures, but their continuing life was nourished in the graphic arts, where the
narrative tradition had great cumulative force and all the unbroken authority of popular art. These printed media, however, had many of the same antecedents in the great "cinematic" art of the past, and a similar license to
concentrate on an economy of emotional effect. I will eventually try to show
that there is much more formal affinity between movies and dramatic
black-and-white nineteenth-century illustration than between movies and
most narrative Salon-painting of the same period.

The swift establishment of the camera could only complicate the progress of mid-nineteenth-century Realism in painting. Peter Galassi has demonstrated how a generation of painters in several traditions had been
experimenting with new ways to convey visual actualities and had created
an artistic climate for the camera's invention and acceptance. As early as
the late eighteenth century, casual views, ambiguous scenes, and unpre-
possessing subject matter viewed from odd angles had begun to concern
certain painters, almost as if the scanning or tracking action of a possible
camera were more interesting than an ability to fix details. More than anticipating photography, they seemed to have been searching for a cinema-

tography that could at that time only occur in still art. The camera itself had to catch up only in this century.

Even though the first photographs were monochromatic, the new pictures made by "the pencil of nature" were unanswerably "real" when it came to the look of light on surfaces and the random look of natural things —the action of water, the clustering of branches, the flow of hair and cloth, and the minute details of faces. Despite their veracity, however, early photographs were hard for some art-trained viewers to "see"—one lady spoke of leaves resembling "bits of tin." Then and for a long time afterward, the mechanical camera eye seemed to many to be obviously soulless and detached from feeling, and only the creative artist's eye could still claim to be imaginative and personal; and so camera art early on became commonly associated with heartless and chilly academism. "Photographic" came to mean congealed in an aspic of perfect details, not informed with a new dimension of light and motion.

But the poetics of camera art developed quickly enough, and much intercourse with painting began to occur as both painters and photographers responded to emotional flavors in the formal properties of photographs. It was then, in the 1860's, that Vermeer was rediscovered and revived, the work of Frans Hals was first exhibited in its own museum at The Hague, and many painters paid new attention to Dutch art because it seemed to prefigure modern artistic concerns, now that the camera had come to add to them. I would claim that a future cinema seemed to lurk in these old works, and that painters could see it there, even if photographers had not yet gone so far.

But the camera sat uncomfortably between high and low art, where it still remains. Photography might propose a new set of possibilities for painting and itself draw upon old ones; but at the same time it was simply the newest and most mechanical graphic art, obviously open to corruption, clearly ready to become a tool, like many others, to be used mainly for commercial purposes. Among the several nearly simultaneous inventors of photography, some in fact came upon it while searching for an improved reproductive method that might increase the commercial scope of all picture-making. Although the engraved reproduction of paintings had been an established branch of graphic art for centuries, it was exclusive and expensive. It had much more importance for artists and connoisseurs than for the public at large, who were consumers of all the popular political, commercial, and crude religious imagery flooding Europe since the invention of printing itself. Cheaper, more generally accessible, and more accurate reproductive methods were constantly being sought and tried; but it was the camera that made the greatest leap.

The most important result of the camera's development was a kind of synthesis of high and low art. Through photographic reproduction, great paintings could be instantly transmuted directly into popular imagery *as photographs*. Their real looks, their basic beauties and virtues could be exposed to everyone, in the same medium that exposed the beauties of the cityscape, the half-open blossom, or the neighbor's kids—and the same one that also entertained and swayed the eager public with all kinds of crude, slick, funny, or sentimental junk. And so the *Mona Lisa* and Vermeer's woman pouring milk could become part of everyone's visual consciousness, and influence everyone's unconscious idea of how a picture of a woman looks—or can be made to look for certain reasons—right along with Garbo and Grandma, the girl in the beer ad and the stricken widow in the newspaper.

Movies are the richest art that grew out of this synthetic vision created by the camera. Film-makers can now draw directly, even largely unconsciously, on the great art of the past, because the camera itself has long since taken possession of it all. Movies have built on the visual past, using old artistic means and translating them directly into film—an activity quite distinct from the mere allusion to actual paintings. The best film-imagery, the stuff that makes movies the art they are, derives its power from the expressive methods used for centuries in the kind of realist art devoted to evoking subjective experience. The camera, being both a popular graphic medium and a reproductive mirror through which such art became accessible, has allowed the movies to carry it on.

Black and White

Because it is both "reproductive" and "creative" and may copy or fake as easily as invent, graphic art is situated at a crossroads, a meeting place for the most refined and the crudest aims. It is the largely unacknowledged brothel of art, to which high thought, low feeling, and commercial interest all resort, to make use of the same commodities on an equal footing. Popular graphic art, which everyone sees without looking at it, gave direct underground nourishment to all the flowers of fine art achieved at a carefully great distance from it, and also provided most of the visual education of the audience for fine art. Meanwhile the world's great paintings and sculptures were gradually transmuted by reproduction into popular graphic art themselves, entering the stream of public consciousness and plunging below that into the public unconscious, to help nurture all visual life. For centuries, this reproduction of great art, like most popular art, was realized in some kind of black-and-white medium; and consequently the language of monochrome vision has been the great *lingua franca* of Western art.

"Graphic" means "like writing"; it now also means "like truth." These two meanings combine and diverge when pictures are the issue. From the early sixteenth century until well into the nineteenth, most pictorial reproductions of both sculpture and painting were black-and-white prints done by professional engravers, who copied onto metal plates from drawings, which had in turn been copied by a hand still different from the one that had made the original works. The outlines, spatial arrangements, and tonal modeling of any work might be fairly well conveyed by such reproductions, but they were essentially "written" versions, translations through several stages into a purely graphic language remote from paint or marble.

The black and white that gave them life was the same kind that vivifies words printed on paper. All the old engraved emblem-books carrying significant pictures inseparable from texts only confirmed the sense that an engraving of a painting was an especially meaningful "reading" of it, as if it were a text itself—perhaps even a clearer reading than the direct gaze, dazzled by color, could rightly apprehend from the original. Many paintings reproduced as engravings were accompanied by verses printed underneath that expounded or described them (sometimes wrongly, as in the case of the famous Terborch brothel scene called *Fatherly Advice* only in reproduction). Printed versions of paintings were thus rendered authoritative by association with printed words. With the spread of illustrated books in the sixteenth century, black-and-white pictures also became tools of instruction, some of them diagrams and maps. These were offered in the same clean and regular lines used to shade the curves of realistic botanical specimens, or to clarify the walls of pictured fortifications. Similar crisp lines would march alongside, in platoons of words formed to escort the images with all the strength of printed type straight into the viewer's understanding.

These early combinations of printed words and pictures helped to form the association between black-and-white printed representations and unadorned truthfulness that gives the term "graphic" one of its meanings. We have built on this association the idea that if a picture is in black and white, it can be apprehended more clearly, even though it may be enjoyed less. By extension, photographs and movies in black and white are considered good because they are so true, not because they are so real. Their often brilliant beauty rests on this. "Living color" may be more lifelike and more delicious, but, like life itself, it is also more distracting, entrancing and misleading. We are back to Rembrandt and the power of chiaroscuro to invoke the soul rather than please the senses—and thus to stand for unadorned psychological truth, rather than the abstract fictions made possible by the limitless orchestration of color.

Graphic and photographic modes here overlap. In pictorial illustration or narrative art, photo-graphic black-and-white rendering (the chiaroscuro mode, whether done by a camera or etching, lithography or ink and wash) has the power to suggest both the objective truth of printed matter and the subjective truth of feeling, which is signified by the image of presently falling light that must always illuminate one particular point of view. It has a distilled intensity that carries over easily from the etchings of Rembrandt, Piranesi, and Goya straight into the documentary style of photography and on into *film noir*. Circumstances and events offered in this pictorial mode have double impact, given the interaction between their two ways of being "graphic."

All this is leaving out drawing, the truly "written" pictures done by the flexible hand and wrist that draw a story for us as we watch. This is truly "descriptive" art, personal and spontaneous, with the air of being improvised for present company. It has a great theatrical fascination, akin to what enchants in classic art. In the comic vein, Wilhelm Busch, Al Hirschfeld, and Daumier draw like witty conversationalists, even more like jugglers or dancers; the hand keeps moving, as we watch open-mouthed and laugh and marvel. Such cursive comic art, moreover, now gains its real power from being printed immediately in the thousands for everybody, and appearing in new daily or weekly versions that urge no pondering and demand no study. Such art looks swiftly done, dashed off like a brief note to the whole world while the thought is still occupying the artist—and through the modern print media, the entire public may get it at a glance. Black-and-white expression delivers laughs widely and fast, as it does all other emotional freight. The reading eye is ready for it, just as it is for printed type, and nothing impedes the swift flight and sharp dig of graphic wit. Nothing in color is ever so funny, even though it may be more fun.

The black-and-white mode remains the vehicle of a truthfulness that is temporally conceived and notated, and that deals with the drama of subjectivity. Color, working directly on the senses, affects independent responses of mood much more than it urges sympathy or promotes thought. However important its sensory impact is, color is unnecessary to significant narrative, as comic strips show. In colored popular art, the color serves the interests of pleasure, not meaning; and in Expressionist art it has sometimes served the interests of anxiety and pain. Color may be more effectively used for neutral meaning in a code or diagram than for narrative meaning in realistic representation. Whether "written" (like calligraphic cartoon art and

line engraving) or revealed (like Fritz Lang movies, newspaper photographs, and Rembrandt etchings), pictorial narrative in black and white
has a satisfactory completeness of emotional impact and a higher speed of
effectiveness than anything in color. It moves, and it is moving. Generations of art lovers hung engravings and, later, monochrome lithographic or
photographic reproductions of great paintings in their homes—moved,
through arrangements of tone alone, by the works of Raphael and Reynolds, of Murillo and Guido Reni unsupported by the beauties of the spectrum. Such reproduced works, although they look obviously incomplete as
paintings, nevertheless look powerfully real as pictures. They have a force
not unlike black-and-white sensational illustration.

When the photographer joined the painter as a fellow artist, he also
joined the graphic artist, sharing not only in painters' serious aims but in
the essentially underground movement of popular commercial art, with its
traditional aim to stir the public with comedy, sex, violence, and sentiment.
The camera could now convey these things in the potent chiaroscuro rendering that in the fine arts had long since established so firm a grip on the
feelings. The camera was thus assured of a potential force as a popular
graphic medium greater even than that of skillful drawing. Meanwhile it
could reproduce great paintings in that same chiaroscuro, and share in the
traditions of great printmaking. As a new form of black-and-white expression, the camera was supported by a formidable history of persuasive colorless image-making, endowed with mythic possibilities and associations as
well as ordinary appeal.

Movies took that history to the next step. Eventually, film-makers could
combine the familiar themes of popular graphics with the accumulated
emotional flavors of reproduced painting and the directly powerful graphic
beauty of photography, the legacy of Rembrandt. They performed the great
synthesis foreseen or envisioned by the nineteenth-century Realists, with
Baudelaire as their spokesman, to create a new history-painting in genre
terms, making universal myths out of everyday material.

The old reproductive graphic arts were the means of moving the fine arts
into the world, of getting them to do their broader cultural and emotional
work, and the camera soon came to do the same job. Goltzius' glamorous
sixteenth-century engraving of the Farnese Hercules, for example (1.5),
rendered with glistening musculature and shown admired by up-gazing citizens, is echoed by the glorious modern photographs of Michelangelo's
sculptures, which caress and exalt his works with seductive lighting and
bathe them in dramatic luster for everyone's eyes, so that Michelangelo may
touch everyone's heart—even those who can never get to Rome or Florence.

Monochrome sculpture yields naturally to enhancement by the black-

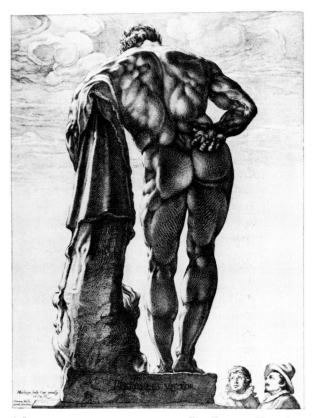

1.5 HENDRICK GOLTZIUS, *The Farnese Hercules.*
Engraving

and-white camera, just as it did to the suavities of engraving; but paintings also took on new qualities under the camera eye that sees beyond the colors. What the black-and-white camera does to a painting is not to give a reading of it, as an engraving does, but to make a movie of it—to plumb, as it were, its cinematic heart. It tells the "story" of the painting by translating it into the graphic medium of unmitigated drama.

Thus painting was gradually transmuted into popular graphic art in the emotional medium of light and shade, not just in the intellectual terms of engraved lines—which have, as William M. Ivins has repeatedly demonstrated, their own editorial effect on any original. Nineteenth-century black-and-white photographs of paintings began to share in the uncanny emotional atmosphere of the *carte de visite* portraits and topographical studies being purveyed by professional commercial photographers. The black-and-white reproductive camera seemed not to take something away from paintings but to add something, as the engraving techniques also had done—only this time it was something directly optical and directly emotional, the truthfulness of light, not written language.

"Cinematic" paintings of the later nineteenth century, the works by Manet and Degas or by Homer and Eakins that seem most pregnant with possibilities for movie-camera art, tend to be subdued in palette. They diverge from the Impressionist way of using dynamic color itself to produce the light and unify the surface. Similarly, in the contemporaneous works of Adolph Menzel and in much Scandinavian painting the relationship between the tonal system and the subject matter gives the paintings their atmosphere, just as in films. It is not the vibrant relationship among the colors that primarily counts, nor the interaction between colors and composition that creates a subject, as in Impressionist works. The general impulse of most avowedly Realist painting in the middle of the century was toward monochromy; and this retreat from color suggests an awareness that approximation to a graphic mode might be appropriate to both psychological and social truth-telling, even without anecdote.

The suppression of color in painting apparently guaranteed the look of both subjective engagement and detached observation. Concentration on dynamic color relations, on the other hand, as in Impressionism or Expressionism, produced a vivid sensory milieu in which the subject, whatever it was, could be dissolved or sublimed, and where the artist's fundamental skill and choice still formed the most noticeable elements of the picture, just as in the Italian Renaissance. A pure energy, a self-perpetuating life, is generated by the interaction of the colors the painter deploys; and their beauty (or, as in Van Gogh, their unbearable vibrancy) ravishes even before the subject registers. Ambiguous feelings, uncomfortable facts, or uncertain circumstances may be apprehended only through a sensory veil woven by the color, which then gives the subject an extrinsic measure of stress or delight.

Color proves the painter. It definitively separates him from the workaday graphic practitioner and raises his efforts into the sphere of arcane understanding. The alleged "secrets of the Old Masters" were all about the control of color, which meant the control of natural forces, and color supported the idea of the artist as analogue of a divine creator with a divine plan. When painters such as the Impressionists wished to reassert the autonomous sovereignty of the painter's art, they naturally used color to contain and elevate their new vision of the painter's reality—perhaps particularly to distinguish theirs from other, etiolated or degraded modes of showing it.

But Manet (by contrast with the later Monet), Degas (by contrast with Renoir), and Vuillard (by contrast with Bonnard) often waived this divine prerogative: they frequently withdrew from the intoxicating sensory possibilities of color, choosing instead to work with the psychologically suggestive possibilities of tone. They also worked in print media, often experimentally, as Rembrandt had done. In the tonal paintings of these artists, color is extremely potent, just as it is in Vermeer; but what predominates is the emotive flavor conjured by the dialectic of light and shade. Tonality unifies the muted palette, just as it does in Velázquez—and the intermittent vivid color works all the better as the servant of tone. This tonal predominance produces the "graphic" look, graphic in the sense of being psychologically realistic: the subject is perceived and rendered as contingent and ephemeral, immediate and somewhat ambiguous rather than timeless and remote, beautiful and clear. A perfect balance of color regardless of subject, on the other hand, as in a painting by Matisse, produces a satisfaction unclouded by the drama of emotional circumstance. The web of color holds the woman on the sofa and inside the room forever; and we are not forcibly engaged by her momentary inner state. The artist is seen to master and subdue the subject through the medium, and so to master us.

In portraiture, the subject must ideally be shown to master the painter to a certain degree—to have his or her own emotional valence and temporal importance. That is why Velázquez', Van Dyck's, and Rembrandt's tonal priorities made them unsurpassed masters of the portrait genre. Manet and Sargent continued their program, and the movie camera is final heir to the method. The most beloved modern screen performers are spoken of as being "loved" by the camera: their inmost souls are drawn out by its fleeting, contingent, tonal mode of rendering, and so they draw the viewer to them. There are people who cannot allow the camera to love them—perhaps they should only be painted by Matisse or Modigliani.

It is now commonplace to see the deliberate use of Hopper and Eakins in the production design of current movies, even when they are not directly quoted, although they often are. But it is also noticeable that such particularly *cinematic* painting is the only kind that translates well into actual film. Attempts to suggest Raphael and Botticelli or Poussin look contrived, whereas the Caravaggesque frames in *The Verdict,* for example, blended unnoticeably and effectively with the modern subject. Goya has been very well and also unnoticeably transferred to film, since in both painting and graphic art his fusions of tonal abstraction with emotional content are so complete, and his temporal sensibility is so keen. Goya's sense of fashion, for example, was clearly as acute as his sense of horror or irony; and all his works record agonies and ambiguities in process, not frozen moments.

Modern eyes and minds trained by movies have learned to appreciate certain artists of the past in preference to others, who were more admired before the ascendancy of camera vision. Many of the painters I will be discussing later on were only considered great in this century, at least partly because their cinematic style of genius now seems congenial, whereas it used to be more perplexing and less effective. Guido Reni and Raphael have lost some of their supremacy to Vermeer and Chardin. Piranesi has appealed profoundly to cinema-trained viewers in the twentieth century, just as he did to Baudelaire's prophetically cinematic soul more than to the general nineteenth-century public. Caravaggio and Velázquez are now preferred to Rubens, whose huge painterly talents led him to emphasize a cursive and chromatic flow of form rather than to tap the flow of light. In Rubens the unmediated eye is always less important than the mediating, life-giving, and ennobling hand. But Caravaggio and Velázquez show the alternative preoccupation with tone and its capacity to suggest the mystery in appearances. Their interest in the direct links between light, vision, and feeling strikes a more sympathetic chord in the modern film-goer than Rubens' robust and brilliant idealizations ever can.

Caspar David Friedrich, the effect of whose work depends greatly on dramatic arrangements of tone, especially back lighting, has achieved a great vogue in our time. His way of centering an image is in fact like the use of a moving camera gradually homing in on an object, to invest it with meaning by fixing it in the center of the frame—a tree, a person from the back. Movies now allow us to respond willingly to such tactics, rather than reject them as too blatantly "romantic." The American "Luminist" landscape painters have come in for a similar new respect, now that film-makers have shown us not to fear artistic compromise in their lighting effects.

The American Romantic painters' view of nature had strong ties with Germany, and their techniques of landscape painting show this: the same back lighting used by Schinkel in 1814 (1.6) was employed in 1860 by Frederick Edwin Church. Modern echoes of this relation resonate in the influence of German film-directors and cinematographers who came and made American movies in a German Romantic-Realist genre—the *film noir,* where lighting matters so much. They bequeathed a distinctive kingdom of cinematic reality to the American imaginative life. These German film-makers were themselves natural heirs to the old Northern artists' mode, which uses light as the primary animator of feeling. Their movies helped later generations of American film-makers to transmute the "graphic" pictorial mode into the basic stuff of modern vision, modern feeling, and modern fantasy. In part through them, we can now "see" Friedrich, Schinkel, Church, and other painters using similar Romantic methods deriving from the Northern tradition.

1.6   KARL FRIEDRICH SCHINKEL, *Gothic Cathedral by a River*

Our modern difficulty in actually "seeing" what many people originally found so dreadful about Manet's *Olympia* (1.7) in the 1860's, or Sargent's *Madame X* (1.8) twenty years later, shows how much the camera has changed our vision. Although it was the harsh, realistically erotic impact of these female portraits that actually gave offense, the voiced objections were about the technique—the application of paint, the color and the modeling, the unprecedented details. The unbearable sexiness of these two very different women is conveyed not only by their unequivocal postures, accouterments, and expressions, but by the way they are lighted—the up-front, flash-bulb directness in both paintings. The lighting *exposes* the women, and so seems to expose the unqualified vigor of their sexuality. The veil has been lifted: they are too "graphic." The very lack of flattering tonal gradation—flattering, that is, to the viewer's artistic and erotic expectations— gives the portraits life in a new dimension of artistic reality. This is not just

the new world of modern painting, but the suggestive photo-graphic world
that the movies later expanded.

Another cinematic and initially unacceptable element in these two paintings is their offer of both graphic realities and conventional erotic material
closely linked in one image. They combine the kind of thing that was common in stylized, cheap erotica (Madame Gautreau's corseting, cosmetics,
and originally slipped shoulder strap; Olympia's slippers, pussycat, and
neck ribbon) with the established components of serious Realism (the look
of muscle and bone, to say nothing of will and character, on the faces and
bodies of both women). These same combinations now produce the whole visual flavor of the movie-star image—the piquant details of a woman's actual personal quality are fused with a slick, eroticized version of current
fashions in desirable appearance. Movies get much of their visual potency
by following *Madame X* and *Olympia* in feminine imagery, linking the
greatest painterly traditions with the popular graphic mode that includes
both tawdry prints and salacious photographs.

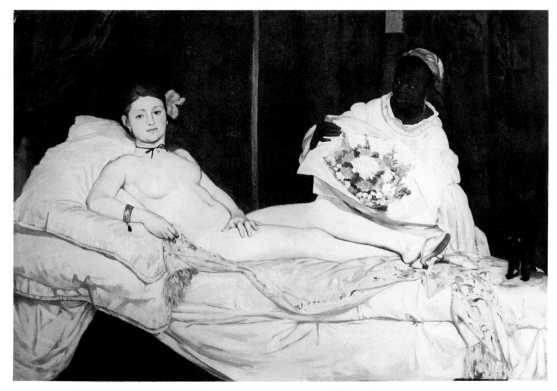

1.7 EDOUARD MANET, *Olympia*

1.8 JOHN SINGER SARGENT, *Madame X*

By the beginning of this century, a whole generation after *Madame X,* eyes conditioned simultaneously by monochrome reproductions of paintings and by black-and-white commercial art were bound to be well primed for the visual poetics of black-and-white movies, even as they were finding modern painting increasingly difficult. "High" and "low" art thus began to split even further in the general awareness: painting came to be seen in modernist terms, and the painterly antecedents of movies lost artistic credibility.

Color and Reality

Authentic illustration is not the same as narrative art. The best illustrations give the sense of an instant full of the possibilities of the adjacent instants, a vision of the phrase in process, not its cadence. Narrative painters who freeze a moment, like photographers with similar aims, make a static memorial out of a fleeting second—an artificial cadence. The graphic kind of illustrative spirit, on the other hand, never tries to eternalize an instant but rather to suggest (not narrate) a whole event. Rembrandt did it in both painting and graphic work; modern photojournalism does it; and the comic graphic art that does it best is not the kind by Daumier or Busch, which shows a sequence of funny poses described by the artist's hand, but the kind done by Feiffer or Schulz, which shows only the same two people talking or one person thinking in each frame. The words may appear to be the point; but actually the graphic vision of developing emotional confrontation or inner state is what gives life to the text. The monochromy of such imagery aids its veracity, and our satisfaction with it comes from our cinematic understanding of life.

Movies turned popular graphic illustration into poetry and continued the process of turning certain kinds of serious figurative painting into graphic art; and so they produced a synthesis and a modernization of both. Figurative painting has come back into favor partly because of our cinematic awareness: movie vision has made it possible to find a way toward a "post-modern" realism in painting itself, to form a bridge with all its old realisms, partly because of the fusion that the popular graphic art of film has achieved with traditional painterly methods for appealing to the modern soul.

Old-fashioned graphic illustrations, such as Sidney Paget's "Sherlock Holmes" pictures for *The Strand Magazine,* compare both with certain painters' sketches and prints and with the continuity sketches (or storyboards) made in designing scenes for movies. There is an affinity among

1.9 EDOUARD MANET, *Au Paradis.* Lithograph

1.10 WILLIAM CAMERON MENZIES,
continuity sketch for *Gone With the Wind,* 1939

1.11 ANTHONIE VAN DYCK,
Christ Carrying the Cross. Sketch

some of Van Dyck's preliminary sketches in ink and wash, Goya's *Capri-chos,* Homer's and Paget's magazine illustrations, Manet's small lithographic urban scenes, and the surviving sketches made for scenes in *Gone With the Wind* or Hitchcock's *The Birds* (even though those movies were in color, the storyboards for them significantly did not need any) (1.9–1.13). The pictorial method consists mainly of massing figures and objects both near and far in deep back-opening space, and rendering them in patches of light and shade for maximum emotional and kinetic effect. All such works show an arrangement of light and shade governing the "ordinary" disposition of significant elements. We therefore may not easily "read" the event in terms of composition, as we can in a tableaulike painting, but we feel plunged into it with one glance. To understand it, we must "watch" what is happening, try to feel it out; the composition itself does not give away the story. In addition there are no linear caresses of the artist's hand to emphasize and direct the flow of meaning, no "writing" to help us, and no "beauty" to distract us, just as there is no color to swamp our attention.

1.12 SIDNEY PAGET, "His eyes fell upon the stick in
Holmes' hand." 1901. Illustration for Conan Doyle's
The Hound of the Baskervilles

The common factor among them all is the sovereignty of chiaroscuro vision as the essence of meaningful illumination in pictures. And this leads to
the idea that even movies in color are *graphic*—that is, essentially in black
and white. In the same way, Manet's *Olympia* also is, and *Madame X,* too.
The color in many color movies is a pure amenity, a modern luxury and not
a necessity. This shows most when they are perpetuated on black-and-white
television, like the mobilizing black-and-white photographs of great paintings. The current process of "colorization" used for old black-and-white
movies does nothing at all for their narrative impact; but it serves to give
them an updated look and the air of general opulence audiences now expect
on the screen as a matter of course. Colorized movies don't look more realistic, they just look more lush, delicious, and expensive and therefore more

familiar to new audiences. To a certain extent, color has remained irrelevant, as it was in the beginning, to the profound effect movies have on modern life.

I noted earlier that the advent of color for movies in fact created a set-
back in the quality of their realism, not an advance. The advance was in the
unalloyed pleasure and excitement early color gave to the sequence of
images, despite its fruit-salad, Currier-and-Ives look. Efforts at cinematic
unreality ironically looked "realer" in color: musical comedy, historical
pageantry, nature-adventure, and the more ritualized and operatic Westerns. The pleasure these gave was the same provided by N. C. Wyeth and
Maxfield Parrish figuring forth legend and fantasy in rainbow hues. But
true "graphic" realism remained in the rich range of black-and-white imagery used for urban and suburban melodrama, the fables of organized crime,
psychological thrillers, or the *Grapes of Wrath* forms of rural grimness,

1.13 FRANCISCO GOYA, *Mala Noche.* Aquatint
from *Los Caprichos,* 1799

which derived most directly from Rembrandt. Color made Monument Valley more beautiful in Westerns, but not more dramatic.

The realities of both wild nature and the unruly distant past are made easier to take in color, which mollifies and beautifies the unfamiliar, the harsh, and the dangerous. Modern horrors submit to the same beautifying effects, as in *Apocalypse Now.* Color keeps them, as it keeps the Middle Ages or the Sahara Desert, unreal enough to bear. Spilled blood is much more baldly horrible in black and white, although it is more exciting in color—and of course more beautiful.

The flavors of the psyche are echoed in colors, and consequently color has a historic connection with symbol. In art, a realistic image using colors may trade simultaneously on their symbolic meaning and their direct sensory effect, as when red is worn by a dangerously attractive woman or white by a young and pure one. Creative perversity may have enormous play and produce considerable tension if impact and meaning are made to diverge, as when Expressionist painters use green for skin or red for grass, or when an evil woman wears white, as in the movie *Fatal Attraction.*

But color seems to float free of realism in art anyway, even while enhancing it. Rather it is conventional color relations, which have their own perceptual reality, that artists fuse with realistic composition and lighting in order to make realistic images look right. All color in art is a code, as Gombrich has said, not an imitation. The colors in color photography and cinematography are no "realer" than those of paint, which have long adhered to artistic conventions independent of nature, and to the technical limitations of the medium. Printed color, just like painted color, is a technical matter of great complexity, and the photographic color-reproduction of paintings is a well-known technological pitfall. Usually no two color photographs of the same painting are alike, and few are like the painting itself, which in turn is often not much like nature. The "reality" of color in photographic reproduction or in direct photography and cinematography is a fiction we all accept, because the relationship among the colors looks acceptably real, and the total result is often very beautiful.

Color also now has a new role in cinema like the one played in avant-garde twentieth-century art. It is the basic sign of the superior artist who transcends narrative and illustrative goals to push the medium itself into fresh territory. This continues to expose the independence of expressive color from narrative meaning and from successful realistic drama. In documentary nature films, on the other hand, color has its own abstract "realistic" beauty, which has very romantic overtones. We love to see the vivid desert flower blossoming against the drab sand, the glistening emerald insect in the harsh crevices of the bark. The sensuous power of color photography helps to emphasize the distance between wildlife and our life; and color now elevates Nature into the highest sphere of Art, to distinguish it from Man, especially modern Western Man. This is another way that color can suggest the celestial plan, while black and white stands for mundane arrangements. The gaudiest Western films (*Shane, Days of Heaven*) have always insisted heavily on this conventional Romantic division between scenery and humanity.

Apart from the issue of color, old nineteenth-century Romantic-Realist terms defined ordinary popular movies as a pictorial genre and created their artistic landscape in the modern imagination. The chiaroscuro film medium, like painting in the Romantic-Realist tradition, fused Romantic ideals about the sovereignty of feeling with details of acute visual currency. That is how movies could give romantic narrative a modern vitality, just when modern painting began to find it useless and passé. Painting became acceptable as legitimately abstract; but deliberately abstract or surrealistic film was apt to be experienced as a disturbing departure from the romantic standard set by the great popular masterpieces of melodrama, comedy, documentary, adventure, and crime caper that gave movies their generative place inside the world's fantasies. All these genres take pictorial realism for their starting point. They proceed by calling attention to the extraordinary in the ordinary, and they unfold a romantic tale made entirely of realistic pictures containing that same paradox—a continuous flow of directly presented actualities, but each pregnant with possible meaning and each giving birth to the next, a sort of perpetual Vermeer or Manet, an ongoing Goya, an endless Hopper, but used to create a fairy tale not much different from "Cinderella" or "Jack the Giant Killer."

Other kinds of film strain against that standard. In *Passion,* Godard specifically brings up in the dialogue the avant-garde film-maker's struggle against the force of "the story" in modern cinematic expectations— although it is a legitimate force in expectations about graphic art, which film is by definition. But graphic "story" need not be a melodrama or a true-to-life narrative, only an emotionally satisfying dramatic sequence, like a myth—an emotionally realistic drama such as the great photographic illustrators like Rembrandt offered, or the great illuminative painters like Vermeer. Film-makers need only do that, as Antonioni does, especially in *L'Eclisse* and *La Notte* (both, naturally, in black and white), and no plot more elaborate than the story of inner states is required to satisfy the need for "story." But without *emotional* continuity, a film becomes disjointed and irritating and easy to forget, however beautiful. This is because the very nature of the chiaroscuro mode sets up the expectation of recognizable psychic movement.

Since cinematography is only one part of movie-making, what the audience eventually sees is the result of a good deal of random circumstance intermixed with the result of careful effort. Movie-making is intrinsically somewhat aleatory, partly because it represents the combined efforts of diverse practitioners who are not all aiming for the same thing, are not even completely aware of each other's aims or sometimes even of their own, and are not in complete agreement about immediate common goals. One single, absolute controlling artistic purpose was impossible for the popular movies that have shaped consciousness. Moreover, the movie-camera eye itself can only come to some agreement with the phenomena under its gaze; it cannot totally control or shape them, having no hands. The human hands and eyes that help the camera to give us its final results, especially those of editors, must work with the fundamental arbitrariness of film footage itself. Ultimately the viewing eye allows for and comes to delight in the flux of chance in any shot, and that very arbitrariness becomes part of the stuff of the myth itself, the romance as well as the reality.

M E Y E R   S C H A P I R O   speaks of all art fusing through hindsight after the Armory Show of 1913, to create a modern criticism that could account for the art of both present and past. The gradual ascendancy and pervasiveness of movie-camera vision has also done this to us, although without our actually knowing it, creating both a movie-goer's response to past art and an art viewer's response to movies. We did not know this was happening, because for a long time the poetic character of graphic film-imagery was not so consciously perceived as were the things that linked movies to theater. Movies were allowed to be emotional *entertainment,* but art was supposed to be judged by modern standards that precluded putting their emotional, illustrative, and dramatic qualities first. But movies stirred up responses that had already been schooled by the absorption of old pictorial cues, transmitted through illustrations that used the old formulas and through the graphic reproduction of past art.

Many early movies were stagy. Vaudeville turns and other theatrical material were presented as if seen inside a stage frame, not a picture frame. In those early days, movement was the point, not camera imagery. But the more the medium advanced, the closer it came to its dramatic pictorial ancestors and the further from the stage. Authentically cinematic motion is comprehensive, surging in and out of the frame and back and forth in time like psychic movement. It is quite unlike the temporal language of the theater, which moves along at a fixed distance from the watcher, with conventional stage rhythms governing its phrasing, the stage space enclosing the action, the stage time forcing the issues, and the live performance itself invoking the concept of sacred artifice. But true cinematic drama in movies and paintings follows a movement similar to Diderot's sense of his own soul as *"un tableau mouvant"*: As Michael Fried says, it works as the reflection of "integral yet constantly changing being." And that is the story.

The camera, which in still photography can look so objective, in motion is the narrative vessel of subjectivity itself, like the dreamer's eye, or the painter's eye in the idiosyncratic tradition I will later be tracking. Not detached observation, not lively commentary, but total engagement is what it offers—a persuasiveness of seeing, not as understanding or as knowledge, but as being itself. The work of seeing is rendered so as to signify the image of time and our movement through it, as we all try to find the correspondence between our inward journeys and the march of outward events.

TWO

The Fifteenth Century

By THE BEGINNING of the fifteenth century, European painting had vanquished space and freed itself from obedience to the flat surface that had dictated the rules for five hundred years. The boundary of a picture thereafter became a gateway to another world, rather than a box for treasures that might be contemplated while they kept their place, embedded in gold or fixed in abstraction. During the previous century, when sculptors and illuminators as well as painters struggled to recapture the spatial illusion practiced in antiquity, progress in such effort was internationally shared. Jean Pucelle, painting manuscripts in Paris in the 1320's, could use material developed a decade before by Duccio for his two altarpieces in Siena, or by Giovanni Pisano for his relief sculptures in Pistoia. French, Italian, and Burgundian artists freely learned as much from each other as different localities and different media allowed. And gradually solids again emerged from the plane, sculpture again stood free, and pictured man cast his shadow.

After the common battle was over, individual interpretations and celebrations of the shared triumph of illusion inevitably appeared. Flemish, Dutch, and German artists came to pursue visual goals different from the one Italian classicists sought. The revival of antiquity was an Italian preoccupation, and the idea of it was seized on as a means to create a version of cosmic order in the world and in the mind by means of art. Panofsky and others have described the connection between an idealizing Renaissance Neoplatonism and the idea of order in Italian art—a link that contrasts sharply with the connection between Gothic Northern art and a medieval nominalist philosophy that sees fundamental meaning in discrete phenomena.

Apart from the idea that minute particulars have infinite significance, the primary influence on the fifteenth-century painting of Northern Eu-

rope was the illustrative impulse that created the great manuscript illuminations from that region. In both the fourteenth and fifteenth centuries,
illustrated books were more common in France and the Netherlands than
at any other time or place; and by the 1390's the artists who made them
were pushing pictorial limits further than anyone else, Italians included.
The aims of illustration, as modern eyes conceive it, are certainly well
served by the idea that universal meaning dwells in casual actualities, in
specific examples rather than in one ideal form, in specific time rather than
eternity. Such assumptions permit the provisional framing of scenes and
the opening up of possible space around the action, and also the use of random phenomena in sacred images to suggest the sacredness of the random
in life itself.

Book illustration, in which such visual notions were first set forth, was
an intimate art seeking direct impact on a single viewer at close range. The
appropriate pictorial "ideal" for such a situation, for so private a relation
between the painting and its viewer, is obviously not one that removes
beauty and meaning from casual particulars and locates them in a search
for general perfection. On the contrary, the particularity of things is the
governing principle for devotional book illumination. It pointedly shows its
encompassing value, for example, in pages where the pictures are embraced
by borders of carefully specific beasts and flowers. Such pages suggest that
in sacred art, direct access to the individual soul is best achieved through
images expounding the minuteness of God's attention, not His larger
purpose.

The divine plan is patent in the divine subject matter—the Fall, the Incarnation, the Passion, martyrdoms and miracles—but its personal meaning, such as a Book of Hours for private use would properly convey, is
embodied by the piercingly specific pictorial method. In the illuminated
works of the Boucicaut Master at the turn of the fifteenth century, for example, each sharp bend of the arm or angle of the furniture, each fold of the
robe or swag of the canopy clamors for individual attention. No rhythmic
harmonizing and focusing technique enables the eye to slide over tributary
material to a central icon. Newly developed perspectival arrangements give
the setting a spatial conviction that allows the scene to be open-backed,
open-sided, or set at an angle, so that the space stays in motion. Feet point
in slightly different directions, each hand has a separate notable gesture,
heads are at different levels and tilt or turn at what seems like individual
will. A corner of the book sticks out over the table's edge.

What unites such scenes for the eye is a new way with light and texture,
an atmosphere, later perfected by the Flemish panel-painters, that gives
the sense of miraculous common presence to many disparate things—the

harmony that the eye automatically creates in actual life. The very disparity of objects meanwhile suggests the idea of subjectivity—the unique soul under God's eye, the unique object under the light. To look is to be personally engaged, and identified with particularity. The sacred story being illustrated is offered in terms of experience, not of eternal and transcendent truth, and so the very forms in which persons and things and their relations are cast must have the provisional and uncertain look of living, which is governed by the nature of chance as well as by natural law.

The Northern panel-painters who built upon the illuminators' discoveries and methods made intensified use of them to the same effect: direct spiritual persuasion and present engagement. The further exploration, beyond the technical scope of the early illuminators, of ways to render light and to order space continued the same attention to intense particularity and eccentric perspective, so that the eye (and consequently the soul) has constant exercise inside the picture. No heavenly repose, figured forth as the perfection of perspectival coordinates, as a cadence of *contrapposto* or a rhyming of folds and limbs, no triumphant summation of the creative power of reason offers a happy refuge for the eye or distant promise for the soul—such as we find it in Piero della Francesca and Botticelli and Domenico Veneziano. In Van Eyck, Van der Weyden, and Van der Goes we are shown that beauty cannot be abstract. There is nothing art can do to fix the universe for us.

This provisional flavor is the fundamental characteristic of all Northern painting beginning with Van Eyck, and it bears a striking resemblance to the characteristics of camera art—especially movie-camera art, which aims to illustrate the flux of experience rather than enclose one event in one frame. Narrative in this kind of picturing is a matter of constant flow, so that what is "incidental" is always the sharp-edged look of the world while something is happening, not the incident itself preserved in a fictional completeness. The artistic form used for the kind of painting that aims to "illuminate" in this cinematic way has to combine a precision of optical effect with a vast lack of fixity or closure in each shape and each spatial relation.

In writing of *The Madonna in the Church* of Van Eyck (2.1), Panofsky has demonstrated that the image shows the Virgin *as* the church as well as in it, her huge size in proportion to the interior being the sign of her filling it as if it were a symbolic niche, of the kind earlier painters used to house her, with the same symbolic purpose, so that she embodies the church she inhabits. In the raised chancel, angels say Mass before her altar. The rays of the sun come supernaturally from the north to strike through the glass and hit the floor in patches with breathtaking naturalism, but defying natural law to obey symbolic law. The sunlight stands for heavenly light, here

2.1 JAN VAN EYCK, *The Madonna in the Church*

contravening the normal action of ordinary light that comes from east or west. It penetrates the church without breaking the glass, just as the Holy Ghost entered and impregnated the intact body of the Virgin, in direct opposition to the laws of the flesh.

This image, heavily saturated with symbolic meaning, nevertheless has an airy, natural weightlessness, like a vision in a dream or a sequence in a film. The cathedral interior is viewed at an angle. The perspective and lighting are so natural that the church seems full of moving air, and the viewer himself feels in motion inside it. We feel in particular the steady impulse to shift a little to the left, so that the right side of the nave may appear, the cross and the altar in the sanctuary may arrive at the center of the framing arch, and the Virgin may stand perfectly aligned before it, under the apex of the frame.

The majestic Virgin is meanwhile herself en route across the nave to take her place in the center, gently swaying along as she follows the lateral direction of her own gaze, her mantle trailing behind. Her hair is a cloud in the celestial radiance, wafted in the breeze made by her progress. She has already passed the present central axis of the frame; we must move quickly leftward, to be ready when she turns to stand and face us. This is not a static icon, but the picture of a process in which we share.

The solemnity of the event is not fractured but in fact specifically conveyed by its urgently lifelike and dreamlike ambience. For this sweet-faced and thin-fingered Virgin with her tenderly inclined head, whose crown and cape seem too big for her, is not only walking but growing as we watch. We only slowly realize that she is already fifty feet tall, and soon will fill the body of the building with her miraculous presence, blotting out the cross, the altar, and the chancel with her own body. Her crown will reach the roof, she will become the church, and then we will wake up transfigured and bemused, blinking in the common daylight. This great holy vision into which the watcher is so totally drawn was painted in the late 1420's on a panel a little over twelve inches high, itself an illustrative and technical miracle.

Similar cinematic effects are produced in an entirely different mode by Hugo van der Goes in the *Monforte Altar,* now in Berlin (2.2), which measures roughly five by eight feet and was painted in the 1470's. Here the space seems to tip up in back as if to spill the figures toward the viewer, while at the same time the kings and followers entering at right seem to be arriving from several angles, emerging in mid-step and mid-gesture to form vivid but unclear human shapes muffled in rich stuffs. This whole suite of magi seems to be constantly arriving, pouring onto the scene haphazardly before regrouping for some clear, static, elegant pose that never jells.

These arriving kings seem to be in motion, because the eye must keep

2.2 HUGO VAN DER GOES, *Monforte Altar,* central panel

moving over the figures to seek a harmony for them, to create a rhythm they seem not to achieve for themselves. Only the central figures form conventional images—the praying king, the iconic seated Virgin—and these are subject to the spilling-forward action of the tipped floor. Unmoving, they seem to loom as they sit rather high in the frame. We look at the kneeling king straight on; but the first entering king at the right is seen from below, and we look up under his chin. Suddenly we are kneeling on that floor ourselves, along with Joseph and the first king. The stone, the flowers, the gold gift in the foreground are in sharp focus right under our downward gaze, and the scene spreads up and back in a slightly distorted, fragmented set of discrete images. The perfect Virgin and Baby maintain their fixed beauty in the center of our optical attention—though not, significantly, in the center of the picture.

The visual phenomena invoked in this painting are very like what happens in actual life. There is a focus of attention, and an unstable set of impressions surrounding it that seem to claim our eye, should we let it shift to them; if we don't, they seem to move at us, to seek notice. But the eye does tend naturally to shift, and it will automatically glance over the surrounding claims to its attention even while concentrating, and even if they don't move at all. When the eye does shift, it sees in perfect focus. There is no blurring of the edges in this painting to suggest that anything is worthier of notice than anything else at any given second of scrutiny. The eye is invited to keep moving, as a reflection or an echo of spiritual movement—not to caress the beautiful, still tracery of curves and lines, but to keep on grasping what keeps on happening.

There is also implied movement in and out of the frame, an action suggested not only by the ongoing entrance of figures both near and far, but by the arbitrariness of the frame itself. The boundary is especially arbitrary at the bottom edge, which is the threshold of the picture, the way in for the viewer. In many Flemish paintings and in later ones derived from them, this bottom edge is an ambiguous barrier. It seems to be sweeping toward the viewer's own toes, attempting to scoop him up and engage him as the scene simultaneously slides toward him. The exact distance between him and the action never seems fixed, no matter how still the action itself may be. And as he seems able to approach or retreat from it, so all the other edges marking the field of vision seem able or likely to shift to correspond. So also in this process, the lateral angles, which determine what will be centered in the frame and what will appear to the right or left, become equally moot.

In the *Monforte Altar,* the kneeling king is in fact in the center, but it seems that we might at any moment move slightly to the right, among the other kings' retainers, and have the Virgin in the exact center, while we could see more of the distant landscape—more milling men and horses, more flowers and more sky. The set seems ready to keep revolving under the eye of a circling camera, as it also seems ready to move toward us or away. The "movement" in this picture is complex and dynamic: it is not simply that certain figures are shown in motion, but that the whole picture is kinetic.

These great examples of the Northern uses of realism are essentially *persuasive,* "graphic" in the sense that the word means something almost outside the proper scope of art, a too-immediate rendering, too specific for inclusion in an esthetic scheme. A "graphic" description suggests something not just accurately but intolerably realistic. The Van Eyck and Van der Goes paintings, with their uncanny details and mysterious spaces, are unnerving and unseizable, "graphic" because they are extra realistic in an unstable mode, instead of submitting to the satisfying new Italian laws of pictorial fiction that were guaranteed to produce Beauty. The use by both these painters of compositional methods drawn from medieval illumination also gives their works that air of artless immediacy which is always conveyed by any archaizing style—the effect that once made people call these works "primitive."

Van Eyck's own new method for convincingly showing volumes in space relied on a new use of light that he combined with the old floating look of the manuscript scenes. His reality is both directly optical and emotional because of its clever fusion of familiar unstable material with an unfamiliar new sense of presence and actuality. His works are like old known pictures come to unbelievable life.

On the other hand Masaccio, Van Eyck's great Florentine contemporary, conveyed the illusion of weight and volume and proportionate distances between things in entirely new spatial arrangements, to which light chiefly contributed as an agent for modeling form. The Italian style of optical reality was mainly a matter of space, including newly understandable relations among the bodily parts—a search for clarity and stability, to show how well art could reach the mind through the eye. In such a scheme, emotion is indirectly rather than immediately aroused; it comes from wonder at the achievement of the artist, a swoon of submission to the power of art, a response both to revealed beauty itself and to its abstract power.

But in the Flemish tradition, the artist is swallowed up in the subject as much as possible, so that the viewer may feel the direct impact of the event itself, and only later realize that someone arranged it that way. How was this effect achieved in painting? In Van Eyck's interior scenes, for example, such as the Washington *Annunciation* and the Arnolfini portrait, the defining corners of the rooms tend to be obscured by figures or furniture, as they are much later in Vermeer's paintings. The rooms nevertheless makes perfect optical sense, primarily because the lighting gives the perspective its authority without the need of visible linear coordinates, and renders the textures palpable. Just as in the movies, light really does it all.

In the earlier manuscript illuminations that hadn't the benefit of such sophisticated rendering of light, such as those of the Limbourg brothers, the "naïve," unstable perspective was authenticated by the decorative surface of the picture. In Van Eyck, the surface vanishes. We are brought inside the space, which keeps the tilted floor and ambiguous corners of the illuminations, now so magnificently "realized" that we must admit they were naïve only in the sense of being too directly truthful, not wrong.

In the fifteenth-century Italian art founded on the newly developed rules of linear perspective, optical truth has an entirely different effect—partly one of novelty itself. The surface remains, but it has turned to glass. We see into a framed universe as into a new heaven and a new earth, a vision of reality that apes the unrest and uncertainty of life only in terms of perfection. Nothing moves except in harmony; nothing stands still except in comfort. We stand out here, pressing our faces to the pane and staring, hopeless of entry. The pictured world recedes into the unattainable pictorial universe, and only our desire may follow.

These same effects, on which the power of the classical tradition is based, are what continue to make the ancient statues so fascinating. Bodies and draperies and their interrelations seem right rather than real; they have a way of eluding emotional identification. For architecture and for all forms of design, rightness is what is wanted; but in visions of imagined life, perfect rightness, although enormously compelling, may show a certain aridity and limitation, especially in less than inspired works. Uninspiring life itself is rarely right, and then only in patches.

But classically conceived art may naturally be seen as a corrective to life, and at its greatest it has been one—it has changed things, imposing its superior truth on the facts, standing firm in behalf of our limitless hopes, feeding our longing. Nevertheless it is the broken state of most ancient statues that gives them the pathos of actuality and brings them near us. Unbroken Neoclassic approximations like Thorwaldsen's tend to keep their distance, whereas Michelangelo's delicately unbalanced figures speak directly to our emotional responses, our awareness of all the imbalance in the actual experience of the flesh.

European art was thus roughly divided up during the course of the fifteenth century between those who followed the classical aims that were later to flower in the academies of the next century, and those like the Flemish painters who evolved more slowly out of earlier, medieval modes and finally produced the triumphs of Dutch and Spanish art in the seventeenth century. In the fifteenth century the classicizing impulse was well in the vanguard, supported by both innovative intellectual theory and intelligent patronage. At the end of the century a German artist like Dürer, coming with his comprehensive artistic ambitions out of a regional and medieval Northern craft tradition, had no choice but to visit Italy and lay hold of the new control of visual form engendered there.

At the time there could be a general interconnection among all serious artists, so far as ambition dictated and geographical limitations permitted them to travel and see one another's work; but the character of patronage kept innovation to a minimum (except for the most celebrated practitioners), and that meant no excessive borrowings from heterodox traditions. Thus the individual modes of separate schools and separate studios continued to develop and remain distinct, along with known individual hands. Fifteenth-century Flemish, Dutch, and German artists were continuing on autonomous paths, despite the pervasive and persuasive importance of advanced Italian theories.

Although Northern artists' most startling painterly advance was in the realm of texture as revealed by light, their own conquest of space demanded a variety of perspective no less telling than the scientific, intellectual Italian kind. Not just the Van Eyck interiors but the landscape settings for Petrus Christus' Nativities and Depositions, for example, have a complete spatial authenticity that does not require any tolerance from us for a medieval naïveté. Again, it is still a matter of lighting. It is most especially in these Flemish painters' works that the effective lighting of the setting *behind* a pictured event or personage was first used to give a scene psychological depth—a device that became standard in cinematic painting, as well as in cinema itself.

There is a very sophisticated precedent for such effects in the Flemish manuscript illuminations known as the Turin-Milan Hours, dating from before 1425, some of which have been attributed to Van Eyck. Kenneth Clark has called attention to the emotional responses created by the unprecedented rendering of light on distant water in some of these illuminations—an effect he also attributes to popular landscape imagery in the late nineteenth century, and which has manifestly carried over into the commercial photography and cinematography of our world. He also says of some of the earlier scenes in the Van Eyck *Ghent Altarpiece* that "there is a remarkable sense of our being *in* the landscape—of our being able to proceed smoothly from foreground to distance."

This sense is the direct product of the lighting that serves to unite the scene with the setting and the viewer with the scene. The effect works even when the landscape has been removed behind a parapet, as in the Chancellor Rolin Madonna, or when it appears through a window. The light is made to move, to come pouring down from the sky over the distant and the near scene as well as over the viewer with an encompassing naturalism, a bath of reality that includes the ongoing drama of life in which we, as ordinary beings, are bearing a part. And so, through its realizing agency, we can feel present at the Baptism of Christ, even though the picture of it at the bottom of one manuscript page is about six inches wide and three inches high.

The effect depends entirely on a manifest experiential link between the background and the main action: the opened depths must not form a painted curtain behind what is happening. In the large, august, and mysterious Baptism by Piero della Francesca, for example, probably painted a whole generation after Van Eyck in about 1460 (2.3), the landscape includes the viewer on intellectual rather than experiential terms. The perfect linear perspective joins with the exquisite abstract clarity of each pose and figure—the even hemlines of the angels' dresses, their crisp and level heads and level waistbands, the dish exactly over the center of Christ's

2.3 PIERO DELLA FRANCESCA, *The Baptism of Christ*

head and directly under the hieratic dove—to deny the natural reality of the perfect landscape setting. The riverbed approaches our feet, but the sky and hills seem exquisitely painted on a scenic drop, the distant groups of characters on a sequence of receding scrims that might be lifted or rolled away, the whole perhaps easily replaced by flat gold behind the foremost group. The breathtaking hush in this work is the sudden absence of air: we could not actually survive behind this picture plane.

A *Virgin and Child* by Cima da Conegliano from about 1500, to take a still later example (2.4), shows a woman and baby seated on a marble bench and separated from the viewer by a marble parapet. The distant Italian hills with towns, bridges, roads, river, and livestock might as well be an exquisitely realistic tapestry behind her. Suffused, generalized light and perfect harmony of color unite the Virgin and the landscape in one theoretically outdoor but nevertheless unnaturalistic and roomlike place, where nothing may move casually in or out, forward or back. The Virgin and the backdrop refer to one another as on a stage—they interact concep-

2.4 CIMA DA CONEGLIANO, *The Virgin and Child*

tually and, of course, beautifully, but the drama is enacted only in the foreground, and only between Mother and Son and viewer and painter, whose name appears conspicuously on the parapet before our eyes.

Early designers of stage sets would similarly paint a schematically opened-up backdrop for drama, to stand for the possibility of alternative action without permitting it, and to locate the drama itself in a conventional context—court or village, town or temple. A system of apparently receding painted streets was the earliest method; but distant painted patches of sea and mountains or towers and bridges have since been used for centuries in the theater as background signals, to convey the idea of the larger setting rather than to permit any interaction between it, the present drama, and the viewer. Scenic rather than cinematic painters have long relied on similar devices.

In the little Turin-Milan manuscript Baptism, however (2.5), something else has been set up. Just as in the *Monforte Altar,* we have not only a constant flow of air but an apparent constant flow of possible action both for us and for the players. Christ stands in the water, his legs and genitals both conveniently shielded by the foreground bank, where St. John crouches above him. The configuration of this shore and bank is given the natural appearance of a stream with someone standing in it, if the viewer were approaching the bank from a certain distance. We can't yet see all of him; the grassy bank is in the way. But a party of other figures coming toward the scene from the distant right, and also half hidden from us by the near bank, can obviously see all of him already. We will, too, when we get to the edge. There is some pebbly beach onto which the other participants and spectators will soon arrive, and from which Christ has obviously waded out; but the painter has not tried to show him wading. He gives us everything else: beach, baptist, Christ, water, sky, and witnesses, surrounding landscape, and distant river. But he has allowed it all to exist in the contingent realm of worldly events in process, simply by setting the scene with a lifelike lack of emphasis or symmetry, while arranging the gradual recession of hills, buildings, and water with a perspectival authority confirmed by light.

Then, to show that the scene is in fact the Baptism of Christ, not a water game of some sort, he suddenly produces the gold-shedding dove in mid-flight downward from a benignly bending God Himself. But God is not in this scene; He is enthroned inside the initial letter of the text above. This is a very cinematic sort of switch. God's posture, beard, and robes are also lifelike and asymmetrical, His mood attentive—but His flat gold background shows He lives in Eternity, and only makes an appearance here, fixed inside the sacred text that has revealed Him to us. Meanwhile the Baptism goes on in the earthly sunshine where we live. Above God, another

2.5 *The Baptism of Christ.* Detail of illumination from *The Turin-Milan Hours*

shot from the same film shows a flashback sequence which is the main body of the narrative, the birth of St. John years before. Between them the text, or voice-over, connects the two events.

This arrangement of sacred subject matter was conventionally used for altarpieces with predellas below showing relevant narrative material in small scenes—the events in the life of a saint shown martyred or enthroned above, or scenes from Christ's Passion below the scene of His Nativity. The big altarpieces designed this way have a ceremonial flavor, a way of making pointed references in a dignified manner, deliberately suggesting that the picture itself was a sacred public pageant, the static projection of a mystery play with different acts. But the quality of multiple simultaneous narrative in the Flemish manuscripts is quite different, especially in those done later in the century, after the astounding triumphs of lighting and composition had been achieved in its first quarter. They show none of the austere detachment proper to the large public rendering of sacred material; they are full of private intensity, now supported by advanced technique.

2.6 GERARD DAVID, *The Baptism of Christ*, central panel

The great Flemish altarpieces of the later fifteenth century done by Van der Goes, Memling, and Gerard David maintain the cinematic style first developed by Van Eyck. By 1502 Gerard David could paint a Baptism explicitly showing Christ wading in a shady woodland spring (2.6). It is a cool, elegiac scene atmospherically enhanced by two dim forests, one sheltering the apostles from whom Christ is parting at right behind the foreground scene, and another shading the audience in the left distance, where John delivers a sermon. David was a deliberately archaistic painter; he had no difficulty deciding to combine three scenes from separate times into one landscape setting, as medieval artists had done. But here again, the archaic device is hauntingly realized in modern, subjective, even introspective terms, as if David had decided to make a modern movie out of an old illumination.

The late illuminations themselves are even more gripping in their subjective flavor. These miniature works have close affinities with the panel paintings, and we have seen that some painters did both kinds of work and belonged to the same guild. It is also not irrelevant that Alexander Bening, the great Ghent illuminator, married into Hugo van der Goes' family, or that Gerard David himself married a well-known miniature-painter after establishing himself in Bruges. Manuscripts were done in workshops that aimed to establish a studio style, not to celebrate an individual hand. Individual talents combined to fix the prevailing character of each workshop's product; ateliers would be staffed by family members of both sexes as well as by employees, and would generate basic models, from which a great many slightly varied illustrated books could be made in a comparatively short time—like the old MGM or Paramount, in a miniature sort of way. The studio product had a predictable character, and personal accomplishment was not given special credit for successful effects, even if it was responsible. Just as with the movies, such credit came much later.

These establishments, similarly, became large, profitable, internationally famous, and competitive. Their works penetrated into the private lives of churchmen and merchants, nobles and princes and their wives, daughters, and sisters. Their lack of public existence has since kept them from sharing in the subsequent historic fame of the great panel-paintings, which have entered public collections and been exposed to centuries of public awareness. But their influence has been as great as their impact on their owners must originally have been. That impact can still be felt, because it is still modern. It depends on pictorial cues that are still active and effective.

Emotional effect was important in fifteenth-century Northern Europe for religious reasons. Flemish art was consistently seen by the Italians as exceptionally, even embarrassingly *pious;* and it was in fact religious feel-

ing rather than doctrinal orthodoxy, philosophical understanding, or esthetic harmony that these works were specifically tailored to express—a
new inward, personal, and emotional religious mode that was gaining
strength, and being expressed in new devotional books as well as in art.

The particularity in these Northern pictures reflects a Northern particularity of spiritual desire. Their subjective mood manifests that longing for
personal application and meaning in Christianity which later gathered
power, forced the reformation of the religious establishment, and became
the foundation of Protestantism—demonstrably a Northern phenomenon.
Excessive personal piety seemed a Northern phenomenon even in the fifteenth century.

Thus the psychological depth in the Flemish works had a religious nature; but that same look of depth, achieved by the canny manipulation of
light and a quasi-awkward compositional program, also works perfectly for
rendering the modern inner world, the spiritual realities now called psychological truths. Minute surface verisimilitude can also serve an emotional
purpose in secular imageries, as inanimate things take on moral and psychic rather than godly meaning—as in Hitchcock films, for example.

By the nineteenth century, a good deal of Protestant religious piety had
become transmuted into Wordsworth's Natural Piety—the sense of a cosmic meaning in personal affinity with Nature; and that in turn has become
one of the great internalized pieties of twentieth-century America, where
the movies have so brilliantly flourished. I am suggesting that the perfect
pictorial method for expressing all such pieties already existed in North
European art: it did not need to be invented. When it was translated into
film, movies became the true religious painting of the secular modern
world.

Panofsky defines the secret of Eyckian painting as the juxtaposition of
the microscope and the telescope: "the simultaneous realization and, in a
sense, reconciliation of the 'two infinites'—infinitesimally small and infinitely large." This, he also claims, is a secret that eluded the Italians; and
that is not surprising, since their aim was perfect integration and not reconciliation, which recognizes conflict. This reconciling work is exactly what
film picturing is always doing, blowing up minutiae to huge size and significance while at the same time offering visions of an endlessly proliferating
Beyond, in another turn of the street, a room behind the door, a plain below
the hill.

The private communion each viewer has with a movie has been described;
and it seems uncannily similar to the private communion a single viewer
can have with a very small, very realistic, and emotionally charged picture
—a microcosmic vision that can overwhelm. A large painting invites a pub-

lic audience that is aware of itself as a group, like a congregation. A tiny picture, like a movie in a dark theater, invokes a solitary private dream from each single witness. This kind of effect seems to have been what the illuminators intended. Their rendering of distance and presence and the quality of action is often given an extra emotional sharpness when it is offered in a small format, just as in *The Madonna in the Church*. There is always great force in the intimate treatment of an enormous subject.

Examples appear in certain illuminations that have direct connections with certain altarpieces. Several different versions of the same vivid scene of the Massacre of the Innocents were done for different books by the same studio, possibly the same hand—the Maximilian Master, who may in fact have been Alexander Bening (2.7). Unlike many treatments of this subject, this one has only three or four main figures and one or two subsidiary ones. The wholesale violence and deliberate cruelty of the slaughter are offered with the economy of Goya and the optical precision of a newsreel. No quantity of artistically bared breasts, clasped hands, and the tumultuous piling up of bodies is needed to convey this horror: A soldier quickly reaches out to yank a fear-stricken woman by her dress, before she can slip out of the frame with her tiny baby clutched tightly to her neck. Another woman lies flat on her back, her hair spreading out between the legs of another soldier, whose backside in wrinkled tights is thrust out at us, as he leans over to butcher a baby half hidden by his obscenely awkward pose. We can see only its little legs streaming blood. A third woman faces us, sitting in the puddle formed by her skirt, on which lies the bloody corpse of a swaddled infant. Her hand is helplessly lifted; her jaw drops numbly. It all looks like a newspaper photograph of a modern atrocity in progress. Behind, a simple townscape recedes to merge with a tranquil countryside, past one or two soldiers moving off to the left who stolidly seek prey in other parts of town. In the distance, we can just see Mary and Joseph escaping to Egypt. The three versions of this picture are about postcard size.

A later version of this same composition by another hand forms part of an altarpiece now in Lübeck. But this panel is four feet high, and the tone of the image is altogether changed and somewhat Italianized. The bending soldier's pose and costume have been cleaned up and made graceful, and his victim isn't bleeding. The reaching soldier touches the woman's dress, but he does not yank it out of its elegant shape; her baby is loosely held, not clutched; her open-mouthed face has an air of polite surprise. Present at the scene only by pictorial courtesy, Herod looks on regally from a distant little balcony. There are no patrolling soldiers, no stunned sitting woman: for his large, formal version, this artist clearly renders the horrible event as a kind of dance, so as not to horrify us too much.

2.7 *The Massacre of the Innocents.* Illumination from *The Hours of Isabel la Católica*

The Maximilian Master also illustrated the Way to Calvary twice in the same way, but one version is a close-up of the other. The camera has first caught the whole procession from a distance, and then zoomed in to concentrate on Christ's half-length figure and the faces nearest him. Behind, the very same distant portion of the cavalcade can be seen, now closing its ranks and moving a bit farther on. But these two pictures, being destined for different books, would not have been seen together except by the artist himself, imagining the scene with his cinematic eye.

Miniatures with secular subjects were plentiful in later illuminated books, and in Books of Hours they chiefly illustrated calendars, to show activities proper to the seasons and the months. Such works also gained lifelike actuality during the course of the fifteenth century, so that the miniatures of Alexander Bening's son Simon from the first quarter of the sixteenth century are like little documentaries of daily life, unfocused by tragic martyrdoms or sacred epiphanies, and also unenhanced by the gracile, courtly rendering of earlier days. As always in this tradition, the real drama is in the movement of light and air, as it gives breath and pulse to all these nameless and often faceless busy people shearing sheep, chopping trees, or serving food by the fire on a winter's night while the cat basks nearby (2.8, 2.9).

All the living forms and the action, unlike those in Bruegel's large works on similar themes, are unemphatic, unrhetorical, and unstartling. There is no irony here, no low comedy, no commentary on human folly. The artist and his superior judgment stay out of sight, so we may absorb the quality of these unselfconscious people without absorbing any editorial commentary. This also is a modern cinematic style. It is the seriously romantic documentary mode, used by Carl Dreyer in *Ordet,* for example, as well as Olmi in *The Tree of Wooden Clogs,* that slows down physical action so as to permit the expressive force of light to act instead, to model the bodies and faces and invest them with a meaning that seems to go beyond their behavior.

2.8 SIMON BENING, *Winter Evening.* Illumination from *The Da Costa Hours*

2.9 SIMON BENING, *June*. Detached leaf

THREE
The Sixteenth Century

By THE END of the fifteenth century, print had made it possible for illustrated books to take over part of the function of public sculpture and wall painting, and to begin the almost infinite modern expansion of visual life for ordinary people. The way in which many people could see the same image was individualized—the picture could come to the public one person at a time. This in itself is the beginning of cinematic experience, whereby many people may be gripped by something simultaneously, and yet quite privately. Images designed for such a situation are inevitably tailored to suit it, as they soon were in the arts of the sixteenth and seventeenth centuries. Along with its old purpose as public oratory, visual art became a word in each private mind, a vision in each private eye. The particularity of the Northern tradition lent itself admirably to this new kind of direct communication.

It has become a cliché that the invention of movable type helped to spread the Reformation, by its capacity to move new ideas—literacy itself among them—swiftly through new levels and groups of people. This suggests that print is like Protestantism: it aims to be general, to break down old hierarchies, to offer the same thing privately to many people at once, to ally itself with middle-class ideas of private commerce and private morality. An additional quality of printed *pictures* is that they can do all this while using the direct appeal to the eye used in traditional public art. With the rise of printed books, not just the Reformation—which was in fact more appropriately conveyed through the flexible medium of words than through icons, which were associated with the old order—but all image-wielding enterprises could address the people directly, through pictures designed to seize on the feelings and persuade each soul with independent force. By the sixteenth century internal developments in art lent themselves to the cause of persuasiveness. Advanced realism could be used to editorialize with greater effect than cruder or more abstract medieval methods allowed.

Except in secular calendar scenes, the psychological effects achieved by Renaissance illuminators were created to illustrate known texts, classic and poetic or sacred and Biblical: the fixed subject was deepened but not advanced by the illustrations. The limited audience for these books was visually well educated, able to appreciate the sophistication of the pictures while already having the texts by heart; but literacy, even among those at the very highest level of society who commissioned these exquisite books, was by no means a universal habit. Each book was also unique, slightly different from every other product of the same workshop done from the same models; bookmaking was a custom business for a private clientele. But the emotional range of illustrative methods was thoroughly explored, even though nothing new was added to the content.

On the eve of the great public expansion of printed texts and of commercial graphic art, these advanced illuminations were prophetic, from the expressive point of view, of new illustrative possibilities. Not just rich connoisseurs but everybody could respond to the new personal directness of their visual realities, the new sense of the pictorially possible that they explored. The most original thematic contribution they made was that of the landscape subject, the natural scene void of sacred apparitions but freighted instead with psychological suggestions born of common life and ordinary light. This, too, was prophetic.

The early printed block books, coming into existence in Northern Europe in the fourteenth and fifteenth centuries at a much lower social and esthetic level, had had more motive power with much less emotive skill. In these devotional and didactic works, the pictures, carved on the same block as the text and bearing much of the message, were direct attempts to teach or warn, to harrow up the soul or strike it with wonder. They did not deal with the august scriptural subjects, and their style was as harsh as their themes. But it was such books that made Northern Europe the cradle of illustration, the place where pictures were first most intimately connected with personal experience.

Individual printed pictures were even older than the block books and had served simpler purposes long before the spread of pictorial or textual literacy. Playing cards, which were the first printed pictures in Europe, and simple devotional images were available to the public without having any special persuasive aim in their pictorial style. Religious prints—saints' images, madonnas, crucifixions, and the like—were sold at shrines and fairs and tacked up unframed on walls, or pasted inside box lids and cupboard doors, with the primitive reverence now reserved for wallet photographs or pinups tucked into the mirror frame. Early-fifteenth-century Netherlandish painters such as Van Eyck, Petrus Christus, or the Master of Flémalle often self-consciously emphasized the brand-new realism of their own technique by including such simple prints in their panel paintings of interior scenes, where they sometimes appear tacked to the wall of the room. Although this may demonstrate these painters' own sense of superiority to cruder forms of art, at the same time the motif suggests a certain feeling of solidarity, an awareness that the power of art itself transcends false boundaries between high and low aims, or between old themes and new skills.

The talismanic character of the medieval religious prints (or indeed of playing cards) gave them so intimate an importance in life that there was no need for realism in their style of rendering. It was the later painters of sacred subjects—Van Eyck, Van der Weyden, Van der Goes—who added the persuasive element to the artistic form itself, to bring the standard holy images into sharp visual focus. But these new paintings kept their old numinous life, even while they acquired new material preciousness and worldly reality. Their new realism could not secularize them.

Meanwhile, during the same period and still mainly for religious purposes, pictorial journalism and sensational pictorial fiction were coming to life in Northern Europe. At the time, printed or hand-painted color was a very crude element in early printed pictures; the "graphic" idiom prevailed, and the "color" of black-and-white narrative consistently proved the most telling. The block books flourished in the early fifteenth century, some in comic-book style showing speeches written in banderoles. Themes included crypto-erotic little tales, "graphically" showing the amorous relation between Christ and the Christian Soul, or "graphic" illustrations for the Song of Songs. The *Ars Moriendi* was one of the most popular of these block books, describing the trials besetting the departing soul and illustrated with vivid deathbed scenes showing the dying man tempted by demons, as he lies surrounded by attendants both pernicious and benign (3.1). Domestic details—tables, curtains, vessels, pets—are sharply present along with the devils.

In the 1930's Panofsky described a link between such early graphic works and early silent movies, equating the exaggerated crude lines engraved on wood with the crudity of silent-screen acting, by comparison with the evolved refinements of stage acting or of flexible pencil- and brushwork. One may now go even further, since film has gone so far, and see a comparison between later graphic works of utmost subtlety, such as those of Rembrandt and Goya, with the dramatic and psychological scope of modern film acting, which has departed as radically from stage acting as

3.1 *The Impatience of the Sick Man.* Engraving
from *"L'art au Morier" (Ars Moriendi)*

Rembrandt from crude woodcuts. Even more acutely, Panofsky also called
attention to the "folkloristic" iconography in early movies, especially cartoons, which is similarly shared with the early block books and narrative
strip prints: "sadism, pornography, the humor engendered by both, and
moral justice . . . the primitive and inexhaustible David and Goliath motif,
the triumph of the seemingly weak over the seemingly strong." Such thematic material has not altered during the century-long history of film-
making, any more than it altered in Northern illustrative art between the
Middle Ages and the Renaissance. What altered in both cases was the technique and its effectiveness. The satisfying, popular "folkloristic" themes
remained intact in both.

Later in the same essay Panofsky says of the film medium itself, "The
problem is to manipulate and shoot unstylized reality in such a way that
the result has style." This task is exactly what the Northern painters of the
early fifteenth century first tried to do with the great sacred subjects.

Later, the Renaissance illuminators were able to do the same thing, imaginatively varying the sacred themes for their private viewers and adding unprecedented secular material. But Northern graphic illustrators went further, with a much more flexible range of subjects. These artists, of whom the greatest early-fifteenth-century ones were Schongauer, Master E.S., and the Housebook Master, were able, like film-makers, to use basic popular themes with strong meaning to the public at large, to combine and update them as culture advanced, and to make them increasingly, suavely, and more affectingly "real" as the technical ability to "shoot and manipulate unstylized reality" grew.

By 1500 publishing had become a big international business, and ways had been devised to print pictures simultaneously with movable type on the same page. The appeal of pictures stimulated literacy, and the number of illustrated books of all kinds thus increased enormously and reached great numbers of people. The realism in such illustrations correspondingly underwent swift development in a very short time, especially in the North, where both prints and a "graphic" disposition about reality had already had a long early life, so that there was an unusually large public for such productions. By the end of the fifteenth century, Italian book illustration was also well launched, with graceful editions of Dante and Petrarch as well as small printed editions of sacred plays illustrated with brilliantly stable, clear, and economical little scenes. Savonarola's tracts were also published with the addition of just such pictures; and so the persuasive power of the pictorial medium was established.

Scientific treatises and books of instruction appeared with the crisp and perfect sort of illustration that only print could guarantee, free at last of any hand-copyist's failure to understand or willingness to fudge. Drawings of botanical specimens, for example, now made especially to be printed, could be precise and sensitive realistic renderings, instead of easy-to-copy schematic stylizations. And so the general standard for artistic realism was everywhere raised, and the eyes of all Europe were retrained. Single broadsheets and individual prints also increased production and sales, as illustrated books increased the demand for all pictures.

The fame of individual artists was beginning to be spread by their engravings alone, a fame that has persisted ever since. Hardly anyone knows the great illuminators such as the Benings or Horenbout by name; but everyone knows Dürer and Holbein, not because of their paintings but because, through their prints, their fame had already become part of the whole flow of cultivated life even before their own deaths. Both the literate and the unlettered could know them, artists and their patrons and the public all at once. The images they invented became synonymous with truthful appearance, especially for the portraiture of the great; but by extension, printmakers became responsible for portraits of all reality, mythic or actual: Christ and His mother, angels and devils, Death and God the Father acquired their proper looks chiefly through prints. So did peasants and horses, Apollo and Diana, soldiers and dogs, beggars and emperors, prostitutes and nuns.

In the sixteenth century, printed pictures really established their sway over all visual aspects of common life. Although single-sheet woodcuts had long since found their way into individual hands, the realistic style in such popular works had been fully achieved only after 1500. Much early printed illustration, such as those for the great 1493 compendium of geographical and historical lore called *The Nuremberg Chronicle,* had been schematically offered without apologies: one configuration of walls and roofs would stand for the picture of any city, and one draped figure, with a few changes of detail, for the picture of any saint. But during the 1500's, printed illustration caught up with the extraordinary direct power demonstrated by the illuminators.

Most of this achievement must be credited to Dürer, simply because he did more for the prestige of engraving and woodcuts than anyone before or since. Dürer was also a famous painter and a famous traveler, someone burning to embrace the world with his eye and hand and talent, including the world of other talents in other places. He moved through Europe, and so did his pictures. On his journeys, besides exchanging drawings with other famous artists, he was able to pay his way with his engravings, and so to increase his and their influence and fame, and to raise the acknowledged value of all prints. Dürer is the first great figure in the history of that kind of graphic pictorial influence that persists today in the realm of movies. His prints were not in themselves "cinematic" in the precise way I am using that word; but his use of pictures prefigured the power of cinema. His apparent desire to influence and be influenced through pictures has a modern cast that foreshadows the way film works on modern consciousness.

One reason is the encompassing flavor of German Renaissance humanism in Dürer's whole style of working and living. He was not interested in a carefully built and guarded exclusive product but rather in discovery, interchange, and scope; and so he maintained a free-wheeling mode of being an artist that kept him and his works on the move in his time, and made him an enormous success. For a serious artist at that time, using the business of printed pictures was an obvious new way to become a power in the world, to get in everywhere. And so in fact Dürer's was the first artist's signature to be extensively forged.

Dürer was quick to master and to improve all the extant graphic techniques—etching, engraving, woodcut, and drypoint—so as to lift them all at once out of the craft heritage that associated them with gold and silver engraving or with the crudest kind of popular picture, and to insist that black-and-white prints must register as powerfully as paintings—more, since more people, artists or not, could see them and respond. He connected the medium not only with writing (his engravings are like dense, handwritten epics) but more daringly with drawing, which already had enormous artistic prestige, especially in Italy. He translated his own drawings into even more dramatic prints, saying, "What one artist sketches with a quill in a day may outdo what another will labor over for a year." And then he showed the world how such superior labor of a day could also reach thousands in print form. In the modern world, it is the photographer or cinematographer whose one day's work can bring a world into existence inside the minds of countless others.

But the way to do it, then and now, was to play upon and expand the existing visual furniture of such another's mind. Dürer's *Apocalypse* series, for example, was based on popular Biblical illustrations already familiar for centuries in block-book form, even more familiar than scenes from the life of Christ. Since there was already a public accustomed to the subject, Dürer's new, daring visions of it seemed like half-familiar dreams, something frightening conjured from the back of everyone's mind.

One dazzling invention of Dürer's that ensures the impact of these and his other pictures, and one that is in fact acutely cinematic, is the emotional use of back lighting. Dürer was the first to put a blinding white radiance (actually a blank patch on the page) directly behind a darkly shaded head, for example, instead of simply drawing lines outward from it, to stand for shining. Lines that gradually diffuse the light begin only on the edges of the white space, producing the same effect as when we actually look at a light source (3.2). The modeling gives the head optical credibility, but the white nimbus behind it seems also to give it the unbearable brightness of the sun itself, and we almost can't look at it. Everything else in the picture represents a further breaking up of that white light into the lines that make the image we can see; and so we seem to be vouchsafed a vision derived from celestial light.

Holbein's *Dance of Death* is another example of how an antiquated theme, by taking on a new guise and entering the new stream of printed material, could gain fresh life and immortalize its artist. The medieval image of Death seizing each person indiscriminately had been treated in public pictorial terms early in the fifteenth century in the form of large mural decoration for cemeteries and cloisters. Such life-size works, all now lost, were famous tourist attractions, and there was one in Basel, where Holbein lived

3.2 ALBRECHT DÜRER, *The Resurrected Christ.*
Woodcut from *The Small Passion*

in his youth. The Danse Macabre theme was also rendered in block books, in the stark graphic idiom of the time—and those works are also now forgotten, because they lost both moral and visual "reality" during the great changes of the sixteenth century. Nevertheless the old theme was treated as a cycle or a sequence and conceived in motion, as a dance, with a possible link to staged representations of Death formally dancing with his victims in all the carefully ranged levels of society.

When Holbein did his Renaissance version, he was able to reconceive the meaning of the dance, and indeed to abandon the formal dance entirely for a dynamic new way with "unstylized reality" (3.3–3.6). These scenes are tiny frames from a fluid drama of contingency and chance, a few shots from a larger moral tale. The "dance" is now only the undisciplined stumble and jerk of normal motion, with Death wriggling and cringing, stalking and prancing, stretching and stooping in his naked bones, always a limber parody of the human action that feels dignified by its encumbrances of flesh and cloth.

Glancing reference is made to current living figures—the Emperor Maximilian, King Francis I—and much more to current weaknesses in the social fabric, but all without pointed theatrical emphasis. Death tweaks pretentious characters by parts of their garments, discomposing their physical balance and their social presence like some personification of a sudden qualm. But he cheerfully walks off hand in hand with the little child, who waves insouciantly to its helpless mother; he solicitously guides the elbow of the aged. He interrupts practical commerce of all kinds, honest and dishonest alike, and comes between the miser and his gold no faster than between the bridegroom and his bride.

Death comes decked as a suppliant, an attendant, a crass kind of double; and so he quickens the sense of passing life, sharpens the edge of encounters, adds the flavor of anxiety and inward speculations to solitude. And he is just as cruel to the stupid plowman and the crazed fool as he is to the fat abbot, showing neither more mockery nor more respect to the just king than to the shifty lawyer. These are very modern pictures on a very old subject, so modern that the subject itself seems changed, transmuted by the new scope of the medium into something else. Their arbitrary sequence, whereby the ranks of society are utterly disregarded, is an important new aspect of experience not treated in earlier versions.

This series was published in 1538 with a moralizing French text that had nothing to do with Holbein, who had apparently done the pictures some years earlier to please himself, without a commission and without any text. These tiny scenes, about two by two and a half inches in size, carry a great deal of incidental narrative material packed in each frame. Most of it is conveyed by the angle of vision, the organization of space, and the rather casual jumbling of objects and figures. Each scene seems to leak out at the edges, to suggest rather than describe the whole milieu in which Death's errand is shown pinpointed. There is one person he is sent to summon out of the busy square, the cool arcade, the noisy wharf; we actually see only the moment, but he lets us infer the surrounding circumstances—the stuffy convent, or the endless fields. In its montagelike arrangement, it is all one motion picture, not a set of minatory emblems or a sequence of staged boxes.

Holbein was another commercial success like Dürer; and perhaps at the time that was the only kind of artist who could begin to work in this modern, filmlike way, combining old sure-fire graphic themes with a new idea of personal life that only a new variety of artistic realism could convey, in a medium full of stunning new technical effects. Holbein had become a suc-

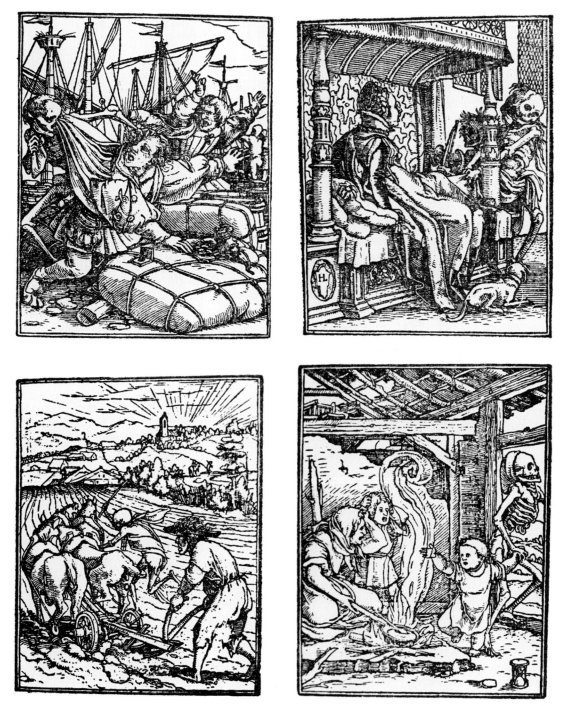

3.3–6 HANS HOLBEIN, *The Merchant, The Duchess, The Ploughman, The Child.*
Four woodcuts from *The Dance of Death*

cessful illustrator before he was twenty, and a practical maker of all kinds of art for all kinds of client. The new publishing business had a lot of work for such a talent, and he did many decorative borders, frontispieces, and ornaments for books besides illustrations. His impact on European visual life was thus redoubled, as in the case of all great painters who were also commercial graphic artists. His graphic work was immediately copied and approximated and alluded to by hosts of other practitioners using print media, while at the same time his paintings and drawings had influence on the work of other painters at the highest level. As with Dürer, it was too late for him to be an illuminator of manuscripts; instead he was among the first to illuminate the whole world through print.

In the sixteenth century, painters began to collect and copy material from original prints, and also to have their paintings reproduced in print form. The international life of art thus began to move along in black-and-white terms. In praising Dürer's original prints, Erasmus conjures all the famous classical praises applied to the painters of antiquity, but he marvels specifically that the modern artist can do it all in monochrome without the blandishments of color. He further remarks that if color were added, it would injure the work—a reference to the tradition of hand-coloring crude woodcuts that had long prevailed. Dürer's prints were obviously in another league. Pure black-and-white expression was thus officially ranked with the power of painting on equal terms; and it was perceived as a modern medium newly improved for transmitting ancient themes. Prints now did what painting had done, but under the dispensations of the modern world, they could do more of it. And in some cases, like movies, they could do it better.

Printmakers copied paintings, as well as other prints; and painters copied prints—not totally, perhaps, but by using visual phrases and tags garnered from various different print sources to fill out original compositions, taking the gesture of an arm or the arrangement of an angel's hair, or a shack on a distant hillside, and reheating them in the creation of a new dish. Really good pictures could now travel to the studios of different artists, who could now learn from them in private, transmuting and modifying and experimenting with another's formal material, working in close contact with another artist's ideas but without needing any contact with the man. Printed type, which now made texts perfectly reproducible—instead of variable according to variations in the skill, brains, or devotion of generations of copyists—did the same for European intellectual life. But in the world of art, the black-and-white medium itself became important as never before, as it became the universal vehicle of visual understanding. Divisions between Northern and Italian vision show up even more acutely in their different uses of it.

The suppression of color even in painting was a long-standing North European impulse, going back to Jean Pucelle's *grisaille* manuscript works in the fourteenth century and continuing with the *grisaille* groups rendered by the Master of Flémalle, Van Eyck, and their followers on the external panels of altarpieces. Going beyond this imitation of colorless sculpture were nocturnal scenes in certain Flemish manuscripts and in the work of Geertgen tot Sint Jans (3.7). Here the moon or sometimes only the divine radiance of the Christ Child illuminates the darkness, and mundane color is washed out by supernal light. This is a very early kind of photo-graphic demonstration, a display of light as a non-mediating vessel, superior to color for conveying truth—especially the truth of spiritual things manifested as material ones, with the Incarnation being the best example.

3.7 GEERTGEN TOT SINT JANS, *The Nativity at Night*

Adrian Stokes has distinguished this Northern way of seeing truth from the Italian in terms of physical atmosphere. He speaks of "the Northern day, whose emphasis is on the transitory or rhythmic nature of light effects. . . . The Northern air is luminous; in the South, the air is clarid, and the stone luminous. Atmospheric effect is solid, tonal." Color suffusion is thus a Southern phenomenon; atmosphere is generated out of form, into which the light has soaked. Tonal gradations, so thoroughly explored by Leonardo da Vinci, had to be entirely encompassed by a given solid form, whereas Northern artists saw tonality as a property of the mobile, light-filled air itself, acting upon solid and colored objects arbitrarily. The light-filled air operates independently of color and form, and so it can seem to stand for the soul moving independently of circumstance, only significantly and occasionally striking against it, as when divinity chooses to inhabit matter.

In Italy the colored object is saturated with light and glows of itself; light, and the soul, have no independent scanning movement. Everything spiritual is captured within the colored mass, and its only movement is its struggle out onto the surface, for which it requires the help of the artist's encouraging and caressing hand. In the North the hand seems absent, and only the eye engages the moving light in its task. The tiny format of Northern illuminations and prints such as *The Dance of Death* aided in the effect of peep-show revelation, the look inside the telescope, the microscope, the viewfinder.

When translating into black-and-white terms, Italian engraving concentrated on modeling. The most famous great practitioner of modeling through engraving was Mantegna, whom Dürer copied, and who was comparable to Donatello in the authority of his plastic vision. Color is irrelevant to both these artists. Mantegna's magisterial prints (of which he made only seven) set the international standard for the form of the classical body in pictures, the desired look of stable grandeur and self-contained ease whatever the personal or mythological context. These austere, crisp works indeed have the look of printed texts or authoritative blueprints, ultimate diagrams from which endless imaginative constructions can be made. Like Dürer's, but in another way, they seem written.

Similarly, the reproductive engravings of Marcantonio Raimondi transmitted the volumetric creations of Raphael and others. Here the shaping hand of the engraver modeled the soft bodies of Raphael's figures as if to transform them into solid sculpture, the better to perpetuate them beyond their fragile, spontaneous first life. Marcantonio worked from Raphael's drawings, translating their fresh roundness into a still clarity, firming up the blurry edges of the cast shadows, explaining all the muscles, using his

graving tool as if it were a pointer—and sometimes adding a few background touches stolen from Dürer, as if to make a little bow to the acknowledged high priest of the graver's art.

Marcantonio and his employees used light and shade to clarify proportion and composition, so that all these reproductive works have the uncanny air of literary criticism. The original text is the point—Marcantonio
is not claiming to be a poet like Dürer or Mantegna—but the construction
put on it becomes a vital part of it forever, and definitively shapes any future direct perceptions. Raphael made his way across Europe in these engravings and into the eyes and minds of the public for three centuries
afterward. At the same time explanatory reproductive engraving was itself
spread everywhere, offering elucidation to everyone in its endlessly imita-
ble textual style. Today our great statesmen gaze back at us from our bank-
notes, trussed up and exposed forever in its satisfying tissue of lines.

Following a parallel textual path, Italian printed book-illustration
sought to integrate picture with text on a harmonious page, to which the
look of the elegant type contributed as much as the elegant representation
of scenes. Both shared the same balanced choreography of curve and return, the dialectic of blankness and blackness, the formal dance of expository line. Similarly, the late Italian manuscript illuminations, unlike the
Flemish ones, are relentlessly calligraphic—it must not be forgotten that
this is a book, and we are always reading, even as we admire.

On the other hand, the blocks of text and the pictures on the pages of
Northern printed books were usually conceived separately, even when they
finally appeared together. Illustrations like Dürer's *Apocalypse* series were
intended to be seen without any text visible at the same time: the appropriate Biblical passages were printed on their backs. In general the role of
words in Northern illustration is more like voice-over or silent-film titles,
something to be absorbed in a separate process—perhaps glanced at,
thought about, or recited inwardly, but not deliberately perused together
with its pictorial complement. On the early German and Netherlandish
printed pages, the eye is acknowledged to be doing two different things
when it reads and when it looks at pictures. The mind connects them, but
the arrangement on the page will decline to let the eye alone fuse them into
one. The pictures are apparitions hanging in mid-air, or vibrating through a
window in the black wall of words. As in a modern newspaper, the pictures
leap out from the type to claim separate attention.

The lucidity of Italian line made it just as easy for pictures to expound
thought as for expository text to look beautiful, a graceful procession of
classical characters. But the density of Gothic script and German type
kept the text packed airless and lightless and unmoving on the page, in

sharp contrast to the explosive brilliance of the lines that made the pictures. Whether or not they appear in books, prints by such great illustrative artists as Burgkmair, Hans Baldung-Grien, and Lucas van Leyden tell their own tales with great insistence. Like movie images, they force their way into the consciousness, bearing far more complexity of meaning with them than the narrative itself calls for, touching on irrelevant associations, and adding ambiguous details to the straightforward facts. As in Northern painting, and as in film, resonant symbols sneak in as customary phenomena, and charge the atmosphere.

This group of Northern printmakers, following Dürer, established for all time the *expressive* authority of black-and-white printed pictures, in a decisive way that could be echoed later only by the camera and the movie camera. Even Mantegna's overwhelming engravings were more expository than expressive, their subjects were traditional, and their form of monochromy has little to do with the movement of light. But the mobile and colorless flickering image, with its distinctive message embodied only in its shifting darks and lights, was a modern contribution unique to Northern Renaissance Europe; it was made available by the equally modern Northern phenomenon of printing that still moves imagery into everyone's head.

The freedom of subject matter for such prints in the early sixteenth century was already enormous, unlike that for paintings; and it was matched by a freedom of treatment with which each printmaker could pursue his private attitudes and obsessions. Hans Baldung-Grien was an artist who took singular advantage of such freedom, allowing his imagination to bound and jiggle and swoop with perverse wayward invention. He is like Jean-Luc Godard or Werner Herzog, or any other idiosyncratic moviemaker, who feels free to push private whims to extremes, to be both comically and horribly concrete, to force emotional and erotic issues, to mystify and disgust, to disturb and enlighten, but never to flatter or elucidate. Stylistic excess becomes part of the subject and propels the narrative. In Baldung, old themes, like Death and the Maiden, are both deepened and jeered at with sharp and nasty new touches. New themes, like The Bewitched Groom or The Wild Horses in a Forest, are wrought out of disturbing old fragments and forced into inexplicable prominence. Religious themes fly off the handle—see the ascending Christ yanked up feet first (3.8), or a cherub crookedly jamming a crown onto Mary's head while the Christ Child climbs into her corsage. Mary Magdalene, raised naked up to heaven, smiles while receiving erotic stimulation from six or eight little angels on her way up (3.9).

Meanwhile the Florentine and Umbrian paintings of the High Renais-

3.8 HANS BALDUNG-GRIEN,
Christ Carried to Heaven by Angels. Engraving

3.9 HANS BALDUNG-GRIEN,
The Elevation of Mary Magdalen. Engraving

sance were beautifully translated into the language of reproductive engraving, so that the link between text and illumination was smoothly
maintained in a new arrangement: the engraving described the painting.
Emblem-books were also an Italian invention arising from the classical notion that one simple static image could fix a complex elusive idea, could
somehow clarify it by submitting it to orderly visual reduction. Even individuals could thus feel themselves "explained" by individually conceived
personal emblems.

The modern ideal of abstraction in art was in part created in this Italian
Renaissance impulse, and first transmitted, like all other European artistic ideas, through the printed imagery of the sixteenth century. It entered
the mainstream of art partly through such illustrations as those for Co-
lonna's cryptic story the *Hypnerotomachia Poliphili* and Alciati's *Emblem-
ata* and its successors. Such books demonstrate how the Italian
Renaissance search for abstract beauty in pictures connected itself to the
desire to embody ideas in beautiful printed language, and to make illustrative pictures seems like visible words transcendently rearranged.

In the first half of the sixteenth century, Venetian prints kept pace with
atmospheric Venetian painting, abandoning line for delicate stipple shading. But the beauty of clear form remained the fundamental principle of
Italian black-and-white art, in original or reproductive works. Ambiguity in
High Renaissance Italian art, conveyed partly in shadowy rendering, consequently looks like a deliberately applied veil, the careful obfuscation of a
clear thought, rather than a mirror of human emotional ambiguity and
non-resolution, such as Northern art is always offering. In Giorgone's
Tempesta, the moist pregnant air and strange relationship among the
characters have suggested not any underlying psychological drama, but a
possible emblematic meaning. The secret of the indwelling light that seems
to irradiate these bodies is the governing and formalizing idea, what Stokes
would see as the glow in the stone, from which Italian art takes its original
impulse.

Meanwhile refined graphic techniques in the North, apart from Dürer's
prodigious displays, began to include the same mysterious stippling for a
different effect. Graphic art continued to be used by various inspired
spirits to do what Northern painting, now burdened by the challenge of
Italian ideals and discoveries, could no longer do with its fifteenth-century
confidence. The Flemish, Dutch, and German painting of the early sixteenth century may have a self-doubting look: even some of the masterly
distortions in the paintings of Altdorfer and Baldung seem to be squirming
under the pressure from the South. But there is no failure of nerve in any
Northern graphic work of the same period, or by the same artists. The keen

modernity of the Northern print medium, which resided in its forceful transfiguration of crude old popular modes, pushed these artists even further into the cinematic realm.

Landscape was the one truly new theme propelling their advance. Except for the illuminators, these graphic artists were the first to render surroundings for their own sake, for their strange ability to carry feeling in solution, even without the presence of any human drama to precipitate it. These sixteenth-century printmakers were the first artists to shift the dramatic focus to a confrontation between the viewer and the landscape and take themselves out of the way. This standard cinematic device for drawing the viewer engages him even without telling him stories and fills him with undefined expectation, urging him to fill the scene with the flavor of his own psychological landscape.

The gradual rise of serious landscape painting during the eighteenth and nineteenth centuries has long been cited for contributing to the demise of the old academic rankings for the artistic genres: while narrative history-painting declined in status as the right vessel of the noblest endeavor, pure landscape (and still-life, too), with its absence of story and its infinite formal flexibility, has been seen as the forerunner of the purely formal painterly concerns that led to abstract art. But non-academic, non-classical, and avowedly subjective art, such as that practiced in the Low Countries, Germany, and later England, had always made use of both indoor and outdoor landscapes as spellbinding devices, rather than as distancing mechanisms designed to keep narrative at bay. Properly speaking, landscape in Northern art also means the landscape of the indoors, because the two are not treated as different in emotive character. The point is made that all surroundings are reflectors of interior states, that both an empty room and a distant valley can be the image of a state of mind. In sixteenth-century graphic art, the fundamental polarity of black and white was manipulated to imply all sorts and conditions of inward gray.

Altdorfer's 1519 etching of the Regensburg Synagogue is ostensibly the straight record of a destroyed building; but like some allegedly topographical photographs of the mid-nineteenth century, it has a distinct emotional dimension (3.10). Here atmosphere has been created by the rendering of muted light, the arbitrarily oblique angle of vision, and by the soft stippled texture—as well as by the suggestive use of figures that pointedly do not agree to pose for a significant tableau. The dimly receding spaces and the ambiguous personages half in or half out the door, half recognizable and half shadowed, portray not just a public structure but a moment of approach to it, full of uncertainty about what is there, where to go, and how to behave. The picture is a little scene of the viewer's cautious visit to the

3.10 ALBRECHT ALTDORFER, *The Regensburg Synagogue.*
Etching

building, not a fixed vista of its public aspect. In about 1530 Altdorfer also
did the very first landscape etching, a distant view of the Danube Valley;
and in the center foreground is a larch tree hung with moss, a tree that has
had innumerable echoes in the history of the emotional arts (3.11). Just
such a tree appears in German Romantic paintings, in fairy-tale illustrations, in Arthur Rackham and in Walt Disney; and it still continues to
spring up afresh in the grounds of Dracula's castle and Frankenstein's
tower, where it has found the perfect home.

Another incidental proto-cinematic feature of sixteenth-century printmaking was the circumstance of its production. Engravings and woodcuts were designed by the artist, but they were cut by a professional engraver and printed by a publisher. Holbein's *Dance of Death* would never have lived at all without the expert and sympathetic work of Lutzelburger, the engraver, and the brothers Trechsel of Lyons, the original publishers. Some later Holbein designs were notably botched by inferior hands, to the extent that it is not even clear that they are by Holbein. A certain risky, collaborative dimension has always prevailed in the reproducible commercial arts, only lately embracing film and television. It has been clear since the beginning that whereas many hands can make a masterpiece, they can also make a mess.

THE FIRST triumphs of secular emotive landscape painting occurred in Dürer's landscape watercolors, which seem to have been intended only for his own eyes. These have another element of proto-cinematic art, that of transparency. Dürer could not try for that in his handwritten woodcuts and poetic engravings, where he used light idiosyncratically, designing his own complex schemes for expounding black-and-white reality, so that some phenomena are described and others are revealed, all in the same picture. But for the watercolors he took up light as the informing source,

3.11 ALBRECHT ALTDORFER, *The Danube Valley*. Etching

the lamp that pours through a tinted film to create a scene vibrating with almost unreal radiance (3.12). These works seem like the first color slides, aimed at generating cinematic power in the capturing of still views. Like Caspar David Friedrich's much later, these scenes seem to have no boundaries. They are not carefully framed topographical views with *coulisses* at each side and *repoussoir* effects in the foreground. The recording eye floats, borne up by the light that holds the world together, homing in now on a tree, now on a house, or backing off to sweep the skyline of a town.

Later in the century Pieter Bruegel, after he had turned from graphic art to painting, made a similar attempt with oil painting to create an incandescent radiance in the sky that illuminates the whole world, and makes it visible as through a colored-glass screen. In the *Fall of Icarus,* the paint film is extremely thin and fresh, so that the sunlight seems to fill the air as if from behind the picture (3.13). The sun comes dazzling toward us across the water, rising as we watch; the shadows cast by the plow seem to move.

3.12 ALBRECHT DÜRER, *The Lake in the Woods*

3.13 PIETER BRUEGEL THE ELDER, *The Fall of Icarus*

We can almost see the world turning; Bruegel has given the horizon a slight curve, and the thinly painted surface shimmers in the morning air. Some of the transparency of watercolor had already been attempted generations before in opaque color by Hieronymus Bosch to help give his unearthly imagery its unearthly glow. Bruegel, who turned to Bosch again and again for inspiration, may also have borrowed this *alla prima* style from him, the "enlightening" mode that also invokes the water-based medium of manuscript illumination where so much light was gathered.

Icarus is small, too, much smaller than many other famous Bruegel landscape works. This is one of the most movielike of Bruegel's paintings, free of any clownish special pleading about human absurdity such as appears in the *Proverbs* or *The War Between Carnival and Lent*. Those works are cartoonlike, harking back, as Bosch did, to the block-book spirit, though with much ironic delicacy of touch. But *Icarus* and the other peasant landscapes —*The Dark Day, The Return of the Herd,* and the beloved *Hunters in the Snow*—share the look of the charged presence of the open air itself, which

emerges from the depths of the picture to surround and invite us. The inviting movement of the air is given practical points of reference, just as in a
Bening or Horenbout picture. The receding procession of trees marking
the descent of the valley moves in counterpoint to the untidy progress of
men and beasts, which casually brings the viewer into the random rhythms
of the anonymous action that ranges over it. Heads are turned various
ways, no one is paying us any attention, any of us may join these villagers
as one of them, shouting to our dog, prodding our cow, following the trees
on our way down the slope (3.14). We do not sit on a gate and regard these
farmers as if they were on a stage, marveling at their quaintness or shud-
dering at their grossness. We are they, various and complex as they are.

The inviting air thus also invites free interchange of feeling. These
works are exercises in the realism of sensibility, where the sense of humor
does creative work. Karel van Mander said you couldn't look at Bruegel's
works without laughing; and this laughter is not a titter of condescension
or a brutal guffaw, but a response to serious wit. There is no visible distancing method at work to keep the peasant remote and picturesque: you
have to take his ridiculous qualities personally, just as in Woody Allen
movies.

In *Icarus,* as in *The Conversion of St. Paul,* a dramatic legendary event is
in progress; and the scene is witnessed as if by a common spectator—part
of Paul's train, or another plowman on a nearer hill, or you or perhaps me
—whose private business and practical worries constitute the real drama
of life. Watching fallen flyers and stricken saints may indeed be intrinsically much less interesting than knowing the right way to plow or how to
ride a horse up a rocky mountain path. The detached commentary on sacred
and classical mythology in these works is subtle, like the use of Alpine landscape: the distance between the peasant and the prophet is bridged by the
mode of representation, just as it would be in film. It is a clear case of "unstylized reality being manipulated so that the result has style." The composition of these works emphasizes lack of stylization in action. Mythological
events are not rendered as part of the dance of the spheres, part of a cyclic
drama with cosmic significance. That is the Italian way, where the controlled disposition of bodily parts and garments and the arrangement of
legendary subject matter conveys the idea that legend itself has a governing power over life. The subject puts a rhythm into the action and interaction of characters, and of all attendant phenomena.

In Bruegel, there is no balletic framework, only the disparate motion of
created things pursuing their own destiny, of which legendary characters
are only instances. Bruegel incorporated the Italian vistas he saw on his
travels into this subjective scheme, declining to classicize or ennoble them

3.14 PIETER BRUEGEL THE ELDER, *The Return of the Herd*

according to prevailing artistic fashion. He would not *design* anything. These pictures have another unity, a sweep and coherence of motion that is like the movie camera's kind of scan. All of them seem to rush out at their open backs, until distant visible objects are lost in ambiguity, even only to the farther reaches of the peasant wedding cottage. A strong current flows fore and aft, flooding out toward the viewer and back into the depths, where Icarus kicks vainly and Paul's collapse has unknowable consequences. That current is their only harmony, like the camera's ranging, and their only narrative device.

As in the case of Holbein's *Dance of Death,* these mythological paintings show the effects of a synthesis. Fusing the old themes of peasant life used for the Books of Hours with the old ritualized sacred scenes, they obliterate the old format for the holy subjects and create a modern subject, the internalization of sacred themes in common experience. Film has been the great engine of this process in modern visual art; and in Bruegel as in movies, the true originality lies in the creative modernization of something very old.

Bruegel was popular in his time and place, partly because he was a successful printmaker. But again, it has only been in this cinematic century that he has been acknowledged as a great painter. We are primed to respond to those breathing landscapes that offer the shifting, subjective view of central events that only movies now employ. The *Icarus* gives a panning shot of the indifferent locale, before zooming in to focus on the thrashing youth; or perhaps we have just closely watched him tumble screaming, and now the camera retreats to show the callous world tending to business. It is like the last shot in *The Clock,* where the camera swings up and back from the poignant, parting lovers to show the desolate girl merging with the rushing millions in New York.

Bruegel died at forty-four and only painted during the last ten or twelve years of his life, having done countless drawings for engraving by Antwerp publishers during his youth. For his prints, he copied the style of Bosch's grotesqueries and did many comic and satiric plates devoid of much poetry. But his sketches and drawings show the same incredible delicacy and clarity, even transparency of the paintings: Bruegel was an artist with both a poetic and a graphic temperament, who clearly would have made movies if he could.

FOUR
The Early Baroque

By 1 6 0 0 , it was clear that art, like Europe itself, had broken up and was recombining. The Northern graphic artists pursued their crisp, black-and-white illustrative path at the same time that the great Venetian painters were saturating their vast mythic scenes with color and shimmer. But Titian also designed some engravings of enormous size that might be *grisaille* Venetian paintings, and Flemish Mannerist painters were attempting bravura renditions of Classical mythology. El Greco's huge, flickering epiphanies were contemporary with Nicholas Hilliard's precise portrait miniatures. Although so various and so national, art was all the more thoroughly internationalized by the spread and prevalence of printed pictures, despite the gulfs between Catholic and Protestant views of imagery, and between views of material life in absolute monarchies and in incipient republics. The printing of pictures made it possible not just for new pictorial ideas but for traditional imagery to proliferate and move through Europe, whereas before it had been static and isolated; and so, paradoxically, art more easily crossed national and religious boundaries that had simultaneously become sharper.

Nevertheless, the Protestant North and the Catholic South continued to develop their differences even as they shared their sources. The Counter-Reformation produced one kind of "realism" in art and advanced Protestantism another. It obviously oversimplifies the case to try to keep them polarized, since so much cross-reference and cross-influence were possible; and yet autonomous traditions die hard. The seventeenth-century art of both Catholic and Protestant Netherlands shows its debt to the Northern past, despite the amount of respect for France and Italy it managed to internalize. In Italy, classical ideals articulated in the Renaissance were held over into the seventeenth century, despite intervening Mannerist distortions or persistent influences from the North.

4.1 HERCULES SEGHERS,
The Mossy Tree. Monotype

Graphic power was now an acknowledged force. Courtly and civil as well as religious propaganda was promulgated by printed imagery, and graphic artists were indispensable employees of kings and dukes, cardinals and abbots. The emotional techniques developed by the book illuminators were joined to the rhetorical skills of public church art and official portraiture in a common, fluid, graphic theater of persuasion, a moving-picture palace without walls. Just as in the modern world, artists could steal from all other artists past and present, and for extremely various purposes. The old hermetic views of craft and art represented by Leonardo da Vinci were exploded. By disseminating both learning and imagery, print broke up their isolation—the keeping and tending of secrets by adepts and initiates. Being "original" came to mean creating a new source instead of searching out the oldest possible one. Movement was forward and outward.

Art was on the move in several ways. The flamboyant overstepping of boundaries was a generally visible and famous theme in Baroque Italian art, but less noticeable kinds of artists were also going beyond old limits. A private artist such as Hercules Seghers (1589–1638) was intensifying both the possibilities of printed graphic expression and the emotional scope of landscape. He made large prints in monotype which could not be reproduced, almost as if he were working in paint. His graphic works took the medium beyond the demands of commercial success into further, purely artistic realms, somewhat as photography has been taken in this century.

The haunting textures and atmospheric qualities Seghers created were not available to commercial graphics until a hundred and fifty years later, with the invention of lithography. In our present climate the inwardness of Seghers' images seem related to modern Expressionist goals, but his use of casual material subject matter, such as books and boats and views out the

4.2 HERCULES SEGHERS, *Distant View with Branch of Pine Tree*. Monotype

window, besides unpeopled landscapes of eerie flavor, contribute to the cinematic view of phenomena. They convey the romantic idea that detached
objects exist to be invested with subjective feeling. Seghers' kind of art,
moreover, shows itself to be a mere conduit for this process, to allow its
functioning in the viewer's experience; the artist is not the one whose emo-
tions are being exposed. Seghers emphasizes this situation by using specific but imaginary landscape, as if reminding beholders of their dreams,
not describing his (4.1, 4.2).

Movement here is not a property of the scanning eye or of the trees and
water themselves; it is the movement of inner response, now totally secular-
ized and individualized. The use of *empty* landscape in particular marks a
deliberate shift away from the demand that spiritual responses be focused
on the Christian myth (or even on Classical myths overlaid by the Christian
one) and toward an unmediated demand for spiritual engagement. Such
themes were thoroughly explored by Romantic artists who, like lithography, flourished two centuries later, long after Seghers (following Altdorfer)
had enunciated them. His work represents another move toward movies,
small but distinct.

Seghers' art was in sympathy with another proto-Romantic and proto-
cinematic artist of his time, Adam Elsheimer (1578–1610). Like so many
others, this painter became known and influential through engraved versions of his works, often done by others. In his paintings he did heroic subjects in a small format, as if to use the emotional resources of graphic art
for painting. He wanted the intensity and intimacy of prints, which had derived ultimately from painted illumination, for large themes that included
many figures and dynamic landscape settings.

Having matured in Frankfurt, Elsheimer worked in Munich, Venice, and
Rome, absorbing contemporary influences from both sides of the Alps, including that of prints from the past. His small works were delicately
painted on copper, and they have the high glossy finish and meticulous naturalism perfected by the Flemish painters in the fifteenth century. But Elsheimer added the mobile compositional effects and solid, easy figure style
of the great Venetian painters such as Veronese and Tintoretto, who had
worked on a heroic scale. The result is extraordinary. Some of Elsheimer's
little paintings—*The Baptism of Christ,* for example—are like Tintoretto
on television. They are like ceiling-sized Venetian paintings miniaturized,
transmuted into the Northern graphic communicative mode for piercing,
instant absorption. Other works, such as *Jupiter and Mercury in the House
of Baucis and Philemon,* have an entirely un-Italian emotional cast created
by the characteristic Nordic lighting that imposes immediate psychic demands on the viewer (4.3). This august Classical myth couched in terms of

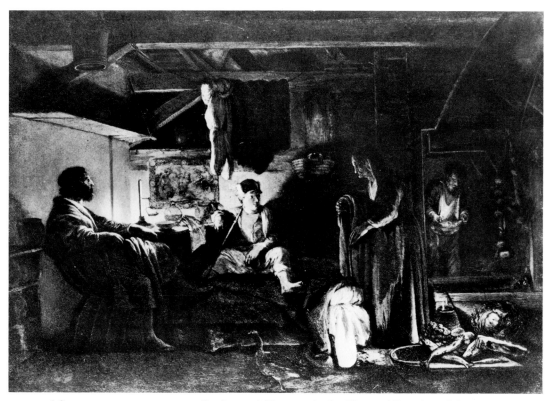

4.3 **ADAM ELSHEIMER**, *Jupiter and Mercury in the House of Baucis and Philemon*

boring peasant life is a perfect example of Northern realism in its revelatory rather than ostensive style.

As in Vermeer, the room is very quiet. There is almost no action or reaction, no bustle, and no pose-holding. All the dramatic movement is in the flash of glances that charge the air already prepared by the glow of the lamp to fill with the awareness of divine presence. But only we can see the alert eyes of the gods, silently blessing the sacred offices of hospitality that are proceeding so slowly and stiffly at the aged couple's hands. This painting, measuring six by nine and a half inches, contains a whole scene from a movie, not one hushed tableau. The old woman shakily folds bedding, and her husband concentrates on safely carrying a full vessel; their eyes are down, they creak and shuffle a bit at their work. Meanwhile in the dim light of their hut, the discreet and watchful gods sit at unusual but unnoticed regal ease, in unnoticed godly dress. We squirm, waiting for the old folks to look up, to feel the divine aura, to notice the strangeness—but they won't, being protected from such knowledge, as they are from self-consciousness, by their perfect goodness. Now the gods and we are secretly witnessing it together—true virtue at work, like two tiny flames in a huge benighted world. Only tomorrow will come the daylight, the epiphany, the recognition, and the reward.

The straightforward details in Elsheimer's little pictures on great themes give them a cameralike flavor that Tintoretto and Veronese, Rubens, Caravaggio, and the Carracci avoided for their large-scale versions of similar subjects. The very choice of a small size for such works, though it may have been dictated by circumstance, suggests a different goal from the one pursued by the great experts at pageantry working at the same period. Elsheimer always avoids the divinely theatrical method in favor of the cinematic style, which depends on the camera's prosaic recording eye even while opting for the sweep of mythic grandeur. In the case of sacred martyrdoms and heavenly visions, he achieves that highly realistic unreality which spectacular films have: Elsheimer seems to have "directed" *The Stoning of St. Stephen,* for example. The massed figures seem real people, their bodies undistorted by any sovereign stylistic mode, only very adroitly placed and instructed (4.4).

Cinema can never do what Tintoretto or Rubens did. Such painters created figure styles and painting techniques and compositional ploys so flexible and interdependent that they may belong only to painting, and the heavenly visions or the allegorical apparitions live only in artistic terms. No photo-graphic material can intrude, or the illusion would be lost. But Elsheimer uses light in the Northern photo-graphic way, to create an earthly actuality for heavenly circumstances, instead of filling the universe with painterly light, like Tintoretto, which needs suspension of disbelief to be rightly seen. He also puts women hanging up their laundry into *The Flight from Burning Troy,* and shows St. Stephen's arms hanging helplessly down, his jaw dropping in stunned, unheroic style after the first stone has struck him, while the man behind him stretches up on tiptoe to crash the stone down again on the bleeding head.

All the figures in these paintings have fresh, natural-seeming bodily deportment, and the lighting has a penetrating flow that is only emphasized when Elsheimer sharpens it for one of his night pieces. There is no insistent theatricality of either light or gesture; but there is also no pointed extra *awkwardness,* such as both Caravaggio and Rembrandt employed. These bodies have familiar ease and proportion rather than any artistic-looking classic grace or anti-classic crudity. They seem simply alive. Viewers need not work to translate their bodily forms and actions out of a poetic language into plain human shape; Elsheimer has arranged it already.

Despite the time he spent in Rome, Elsheimer was a true Northern art-

4.4 ADAM ELSHEIMER, *The Stoning of St. Stephen*

ist, a devoted scion of Dürer and Altdorfer, though one for whom the resources of Italy were easy to assimilate rather than problematic. The small
size, the transcendent use of light, the delicate signs of human interaction
all link him with Van Eyck and the illuminators earlier and with Vermeer
later, but also with the cinematic impulse altogether, despite his capacity to
use Venetian schemes and to encompass classical monumentality. He manages to make Italian elements feed his German need to use the mundane as
the right frame for unearthly truths and spiritual expression. Landscape
served him particularly well for this, on Altdorfer's model with some help
from Giorgone. There he would use separate and specific sources of outdoor lighting: the moon, the reflections on water, the searching beams of
the sun striking from behind the silhouettes of trees, bonfires, lanterns,
and torches—or, in the case of *St. Stephen*, the heavenly searchlight beam-
ing directly from the throne of God. He could unite the characters in his
legendary narratives with the feelings such lighting inspires.

A night scene out of doors, even more than an intimate candlelit interior,
may engage the whole mystery of earth's darkness, which everyone experiences when night falls and lights are lit to fight it. Perhaps the moon lends
its far glow, and sometimes the stars give their distant reassurances. In
Elsheimer's *Flight into Egypt* these phenomena that everyone has won-
dered at contribute both their ordinariness and their magic to the sense of
common life being lived and cosmic attention being paid (4.5). Watched
over by the eyes of night, the fugitive family with its one hopeful torch
makes its way around the moonlit lake toward the safety of a shepherd's
bonfire in the wood. A sense of immediate reality comes from the fact that
the several light sources are also contrasting sources of heat or chill: the
cold lake and moon contrast with the hot fire and torch; extremes threaten
on all sides, protection is uncertain—faith must prevail.

This scene, like many other Elsheimer paintings, has no direct antecedents. His conceptions were unique in their time, prophetic well beyond
any predictable descendants, of which there were quite a few. Rubens,
Rembrandt, and Claude Lorrain, all unique artists, were self-confessedly
indebted to Elsheimer, who died at thirty-two having done only a few small
works. Other great painters thus recognized his intimate and graphic way
with great legends; his paintings were keenly if only privately appreciated
in his day, and much later by Romantic writers. He was clearly attempting
something not then conventionally encompassed by the established rules of
painting, while having no other contemporary channel but through graphic
art, which he also practiced himself. Although his paintings glow with
jewel-like hues, it was his graphic interpreters and reproducers who made
Elsheimer intelligible and famous, beginning with his friend Hendrick

4.5 ADAM ELSHEIMER, *The Flight into Egypt*

Goudt, through whose engravings his works were most widely made known.

The black-and-white medium that made so many painters available to the world intensified Elsheimer's special quality with particular emotional poignance. *The Mocking of Ceres,* for example, known best in an engraving, records an odd episode from Ovid in which Ceres, overcome with thirst and given water at a cottage while searching for her daughter throughout the world, is mocked by a boy for her greedy gulping, and exasperatedly changes him into a lizard. The Elsheimer picture shows the gulping and the mocking, lit by torch and candle outside a hut at night (4.6). The old mistress of the cottage (a relation of Baucis, by her looks) tries to squelch the overexcited little boy, while she herself stares at the thirsty stranger with intense but reserved interest by the light of her candle. A domestic glow comes from the cottage interior; a cool moon looks in from the other corner. Oblivious farm people warm themselves at a small fire in the stable yard at the rear. The tightly composed scene is busy, mysterious, faintly menacing,

4.6 ADAM ELSHEIMER, *The Mocking of Ceres* (copy)

and exciting, like all sudden nighttime activity perceived by children.

Elsheimer has deliberately chosen a subject that is ambiguous and not obvious, and he depends for the picture's effect on its internal emotional relationships—the close, suddenly illuminated encounter of these three oddly assorted characters: the stark-naked pointing boy, the hooded and peering old woman pushing him back, and the strong, beautiful draped goddess, with the light full on her bare throat as she tips up the drinking vessel. You can almost watch her swallowing, and feel the boy's uncontrollable agitation at the sight. Who is she? What will happen? The scene is open-backed, and once again indifferent ordinary life flows around and over the crucial episode in focus, as if to suggest its very arbitrariness.

The *tableau vivant* style of dramatic rendering favored by Caravaggio is very different. Caravaggio also worked in Rome and was Elsheimer's contemporary, and the two artists' work has sometimes been associated. But Caravaggio's scenes take place well downstage, closed off by a backdrop, with a hidden spotlight on the action and the houselights off. The speaking illumination and the monumentally—sometimes elegiacally or ecstatically —awkward figures have a fixed self-consciousness that is infinitely compelling but never natural. Characters often stare challengingly at the audience or engage one another with a keen awareness of being seen. There is great light but no air in Caravaggio's painted encounters; they have a claustral, shadow-boxy, and almost oppressive meaningfulness. In each one, the possibility of alternative circumstance has been renounced: they have a fated look, emphasized by the stasis of even the most dramatic compositions (4.7). Their posing strengthens the erotic quality of each figure, even old and wrinkled ones—they are feeling themselves looked at, they know themselves transfixed by our gaze, forced to experience our sense of their flesh. Caravaggio's paintings are somewhat like photographs made to simulate paintings, with models carefully grouped and lights carefully trained. There is no flow of life: everyone's breath is held, including ours.

There is certainly an intense evocation of truth in Caravaggio's painting, but it is a truth at odds with what the subject invokes. Something is being expounded about the lives of the models, not about the lives of the saints they play. It is their own arresting bare soles or shoulders and equivocal expressions at which we stare, not the saint's or the angel's, and it is their consciousness we touch as our eyes meet theirs or touch their bodies. It is street theater, never film, full of the amateur actor's exhilarating temporary efforts. In these paintings no transformation occurs, as it does in Elsheimer's, of the palpable flesh into the legendary character.

In Caravaggio's works, the insistent presence of the model makes the usual mythic aura impossible to conjure: it is indeed the model's aura that

4.7 CARAVAGGIO, *The Martyrdom of St. Peter*

is being celebrated, and we are invited to share the artist's possession of
another by means of the voracious gaze. We are not invited to tread on holy
ground, but to visit the studio and stare—there is the real shrine. And we
are allowed to come and do it only while the model is holding still and exposed, pretending to be a saint, an angel, or an ancient god. This is a thrilling and disturbing situation, and it exercises an entirely new kind of
sexuality in art, very different from the Mannerist program of surface eroticism used by the previous generation.

In the theatrical early seventeenth century, the alternative cinematic impulse was expressed by Goltzius and Callot, Bosse, Bellange, and Hollar,
the great black-and-white interpreters of the early-Baroque world. They
were the inventors of stylish new public media for transmitting ideas of

worldly power, and of the power of art itself. Callot and Bosse used a fashion-plate figure style, extra tall and slim with nonchalant posture. It was a mode left over from Mannerist painting, but it was most appropriate to the persuasive kind of graphic art devoted to promoting a smooth way of looking at actualities. Traditional sacred themes seem somewhat wrongly cast when enacted by such attenuated and dashing figures, as if department-store mannequins were being used to depict the Annunciation. But illustrations of contemporary life that might describe a military triumph or a local festival look satisfying and reassuring when even ragged soldiers or poor peasants have good figures and a graceful, modish stance and wear their tatters with an air. One aspect of modern commercial films has been a similar way of enhancing realism with bodily fashion. It puts a sexy icing on ordinary events, to make banality attractive and sordid misfortune romantic. Goltzius' engraved classical figures have a similar slick look that has been largely created by the suavity of the lines that model and polish them. In a kind of pop-art tour de force, he even simulated the look of engraving for some of his drawings, as if to show off both his skill and the effectiveness of the commercial graphic medium itself.

Callot had a magnificent gift for massing crowds that, like Elsheimer's, seem directed rather than composed. His big Biblical, military, and festive scenes have a DeMille-like combination of huge scope and small incident, pointed up by the looming *repoussoir* figures in the foreground, who are linked to the action of larger groups receding into the distance. The personnel of each of these is crisply defined, and all milling or marching crowds are neatly distributed among the hills or plains of the broad setting. The sharp black-and-white medium creates a glittering chiaroscuro scrim that incites the eye to motion and to action, bouncing it around the scene, letting it range, or focusing it on one or another vignette, stirring the soul with graphic sparkle. The whole is held together by an exhilarating technical elegance that gives each little figure the dash and finish of a movie actor, a Hollywood-style beggar or merchant. It works similarly to the way the brilliance of cinematography can hold huge crowd scenes in harmony by its own graphic authority, which forbids confusion and boredom in the viewer. There were no painters trying to do just that at the time.

Caravaggio's great contemporaries the Carracci were founding operatic theaters rather than making movies, establishing a stately and glamorous universe wherein epic performances on themes of all kinds might be repeatedly and satisfyingly enacted, by many different artists in many variations. Caravaggio's harsh alternatives went on to influence the Dutch and Spanish purveyors of grim stories, most of which seem no less theatrical than the noble frescoes of the classical school. Rubens shared in the contemporary

sense of theater, but his desire for control of the reproduction and consequent spread of his own works (and his appreciation of Elsheimer) show
him to be among those with a graphic and cinematic understanding—the
sense of that kind of graphic motion which can move the public at large.

Rubens' paintings consistently celebrate the world through the corpore-
ality of paint. The uncanny transparency of earlier cinematic painting—the
thin paint films of Bosch and Bruegel, the glazes of Van Eyck—are at odds
with Rubens' liking for the express tangibility of paint itself. He makes you
feel his hand. The kind of manual brilliance practiced by Callot or Goltzius
in etching and engraving relishes the dialectic of white ground and black
marks—the glowing screen of nothingness, magically broken up by a few
lines and shadows into real-seeming, gripping visions. There is no special
delight in the metal and burin, or even in pen and ink: drawings by Callot
have the same breathtaking bravery that Van Dyck's and Rembrandt's
show, the look of being conjured out of the void and lit by it from behind. It
is quite different from the insistent calligraphy of Dürer, whether etched,
engraved, or drawn.

4.8 JACQUES CALLOT, *The Opening of the Red Sea.* Etching

4.9 JACQUES CALLOT, *Carrying of the Cross.* Etching

The subject matter in Callot's scenic works is seamlessly narrative rather than anecdotal. Drama is seen as a dynamic flow, not a set of well-shaped phrases. *The Opening of the Red Sea* and the *Carrying of the Cross* have a dazzling panoramic integrity beyond any requirements of the story, and free of a painter's need for stable chromatic schemes (4.8, 4.9). His method is related to that of Bruegel, though quite different: related, because these two artists share in the sense of the kinetic scene and the kinetic eye and so both prefigure film; different, because of the different aims and means that made them ancestors of different styles of film.

Callot worked for reigning dukes and princes of the Church in a period when absolute rulers, eager to demonstrate their own power to themselves in cosmic terms, employed artists with a strong understanding of show business to help them do it. In order to sustain the right note, a certain panache, a festive sort of excitement would have to suffuse all kinds of imagery. It would apply to records of grisly executions no less than to descriptions of stage productions, to religious illustration no less than to fashion prints and scenes of military triumph or brutal rapine. Every kind of scene in Callot's oeuvre shows a world with a satisfying surface gloss that flatters the viewer, whatever the subject—flatters him, that is, by suggesting that the universe is rendered chic by his gaze, and that all reality constantly presents itself to be relished as a sort of entertaining tribute.

This was a Hollywood device during the great days of American self-flattery. In the golden age of Hollywood, not a king but a whole nation was served the visible world on a platter, as if it were perfectly baked and glazed. Only the most becoming dishevelment graced the hair of distraught wives and mothers; tenements had laundry as artfully festooned as the draperies of mansions; perfect fit was shared equally by prison garb, office wear, slum and farm gear, campus togs, and evening dress, and perfect figures by all their wearers. It was deliciously realistic.

Callot's scenes are much more like such movies than are most of the nineteenth-century spectacular paintings celebrating French or British imperialism, and that is because of the affinities between graphic media, despite the absence of color in Callot. Only graphic art can keep things moving. Frith's *Railway Station* and *Derby Day* are full of precise colorful details and incidents with a precise anecdotal completeness: Callot lets it all sweep across the plane in streams of energy, with incident barely sketched or skimmed, and precision instead attached to the uniform stylishness of gesture, dress, and setting. Even the *Miseries of War* pictures have a glitter and flicker and a mobile compositional excitement that keeps the atrocities from striking home very sharply. The experience remains scenic, like a filmed engagement between Indians and cavalry. In both, authentic excitement is generated by vivid use of the medium more than by the horrors of the battle. This particular kind of graphic "realism" suggests that the fear and strife of others is wonderful entertainment, but of course only for superior beings, who may view it through the attractive veil (or film) of a highly skilled technical representation. Bruegel, on the other hand, is like a European film-maker intent on verism spiced with cynicism. The world of power and prestige is seen from a distance and perpetually askance, never taken very seriously or very personally, even when great events are afoot. The viewer is roused in his fundamental sympathies and in his sense of humor, not soothed in his sense of comfortable superiority.

In the early seventeenth century, even during the full tide of the Counter-Reformation and the grandiose self-conceptions of monarchs, ordinary secular subject matter had become standard even in Catholic monarchies. This was in part possible precisely because of the penetration of traditional painting by the new force of graphic art, which had been so precocious in exploring secular and genre themes and which had come to form a visual background and representational standard for all European life. Georges de la Tour (1593–1652), like Callot a citizen of the Duchy of Lorraine, where various religious orders had power besides the reigning duke, could produce scenes of elegant chicanery and uproarious gambling, grim portraits of wretched peasants, as well as emblematic Magdalens, saintly martyrdoms, and Biblical groups. There is no irony or sentimentality in his view of one or the other kind of theme; a unifying vision informs both, as if he were a movie-camera subject to the same registration of phenomena, whatever the context. He does not carefully have to paint secular scenes as if they were timeless, or religious scenes as if they were customary sights, because everything is extraordinary under the eye of this artist. Contempo-

4.10 GEORGES DE LA TOUR, *The Angel Appearing to St. Joseph*

rary life is just as bizarre and mysterious as the great sacred tales.

He seems to have developed in isolation and obscurity, and only in this movie-loving century—as with Vermeer and Bruegel—has he been called great. His vision has that same prophetic pre-cinematic look. Most of the movement in his unturbulent groups is the movement of indoor light (usually flame), of breath, and of thought. Eyes slide sideways in an absorbed manner quite different from those in Caravaggio's scenes, quite lacking in audience awareness (4.10). Children have a bright self-contained solemnity devoid of coyness. The practical lighting effects seem related to Caravaggio's style, and De la Tour may have known engraved paintings by Dutch Caravaggisti such as Honthorst and Terbrugghen, although there is nothing very Dutch about these strict but richly lit interiors. The tavern scenes have none of the raunchy giggle and bustle of Dutch contemporary equivalents, no careful grotesquerie—only a bemused, sour humor and unemphatic movements. The deformed and stupid peasants have no trace of either comic swagger or inflated tragic dignity. De la Tour makes the light show us how to see them plain—them, and nothing else. Surroundings are usually swallowed up in darkness; the point is the human beings and the illumination of their inner lives. Nevertheless the darkness is pregnant rather than stifling, because a cogent visible flame is answering it back, glowing from a single source in all directions at once; and the darkness remains a possible world—the world of Everything Else, which is not immediately important beyond this moment, where life is being kindled in the flame of what is happening. In Caravaggio's spotlit scenes, on the other hand, the surrounding curtain of blackness seems there to prevent spill and close the light in, just as on a stage. It is under De la Tour's lamps, moreover, that small movements of heads and faces produce the sudden gleam of eyes that gives these paintings their living, movielike look, along with the unprecedented semi-lost profiles and the ingenuous hands.

De la Tour and Callot were compatriots and near contemporaries, but they were entirely different in their artistic lives and purposes, which represented two different kinds of "graphic" ideal. Callot was an internationally famous artist who painted nothing. It was his mobile graphic skill that kept him on the move himself, traveling from Lorraine to Rome, to Florence, to Holland, and back to Lorraine, where he did religious works for the Franciscan Order. He worked for Louis XIII and Richelieu as well as the Florentine duke and the Regent of the Netherlands; he knew Rubens and Galileo. His many printed works, entirely in black and white and most of them in tiny format, had enormous effect—visual, psychological, perhaps political. By contrast, Georges de la Tour apparently never left Lorraine and produced nothing but a few paintings. He had no known teacher and

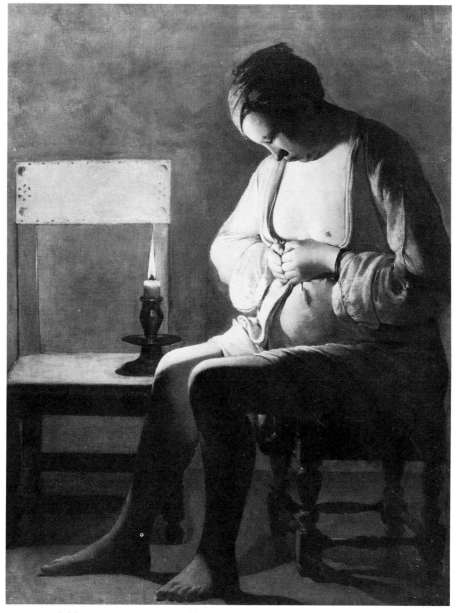

4.11 GEORGES DE LA TOUR, *A Woman Searching for Fleas*

no international connections, although some local fame, including patronage from the duke; and he was reclusive and cantankerous. His direct influence was felt only by his son, who continued painting in the same style some time after his father's death. Later, his very artistic existence sank into oblivion; his pictures were scattered and wrongly attributed.

But De la Tour followed the cinematic impulse even further than Callot: his charged, intimate scenes are life-size. Where Callot collected and choreographed huge numbers on a tiny screen, De la Tour transformed his private scenes of candlelit encounter and spiritual crisis into moments of overwhelming importance, with no Jesuitical zeal and no other rhetorical device than enlargement. These big pictures have small flourish but great intensity, just like movie close-ups. The power of miniature illumination that Elsheimer had continued to make use of is here transcended at last, for the first time: later in the century the Dutch masters would continue the effort. It almost seems natural that De la Tour had to wait for general recognition until the century of the movie screen, where small moments are also made great by light and size, and the stillness is in motion.

Other French painters of the early Baroque period such as Simon Vouet certainly worked large, often with similar subject matter similarly arranged: sacred and secular confrontations of solitary contemplation, viewed from very close. But for the most part such scenes have Caravaggio's flavor of the theater (not the opera stage or the masque, but the street theater of ad hoc performance) or the posed tableau. Theatrical flavor is certainly suited to a large painting: a highly noticeable picture conceived in stage style may politely address the beholder with a proper salutation, instead of letting its heroine just sit there unawares, gazing away into the candle flame or even catching a flea inside her open smock, forcing the viewer to feel uncomfortable for intruding (4.11).

Poussin, another French contemporary, by contrast exemplifies the total painter's view, both anti-graphic and anti-theatrical. Here is the masterly hand in league with the intellect, using the sensory power of color as a metaphor and chief expository medium, as Cézanne later did. The light in Poussin's works is a vibrance induced by the interaction of colors, and the space is created by the management of planes, just as in abstract painting. These works, moreover, try for absolute beauty, like those of Piero della Francesca. And they often win. They have the same enchanting power that is both distancing and elevating, because the painted world is complete in itself, persuasive only about itself and the people in it. The way they are is remote from the way things are, and the way we are.

FIVE
Dutch Genre

SEVENTEENTH-CENTURY Holland made itself a distinctive European power, and its art also had an unmistakable character, no longer very obviously traceable to Caravaggio, Italian classicism, and Mannerism, or even its own Renaissance past. The seventeenth-century Dutch mode has been called one of description rather than narration; but these works somehow do have undeniable narrative motion other than that of an account or a tale. Their descriptive properties are evident, but something is always happening even when there is no event. The greatest of those Dutch artists devoted to the suggestive actualities of life open things to the eye and the eye to things in unprecedented acts of reciprocal revelation. They have a truly movielike style, not attained again until the films of the late twentieth century.

Caravaggio's theatrical effects were made cinematic in Holland. Transmuted by Northern attitudes about illumination and experience, Caravaggesque scenes rendered by Terbrugghen and Honthorst have the ambience of possibility: shifts of feeling and action may really occur, are visibly occurring as we watch. The light seems to liberate motion. Instead of spraying and freezing the moment, as it does in Caravaggio, the light insinuates itself among the characters, demonstrating their relations like the interplay of gazes, or like conversation. There seems to be no sound in Caravaggio, despite all the many open mouths—even the lute playing is suspended; but in Terbrugghen's *The Calling of St. Matthew* (1621), the space is full of rustle and buzz (5.1). In Caravaggio's version of the same theme the moment *strikes,* like the beam of light that seems conjured by the upraised arm of Christ; but in Terbrugghen a camera seems to be moving in on the scene, following Peter's gaze. It turns away from the dark foreground shoulder and profile of Christ, moves over the bald dome of the oblivious old man,

5.1 HENDRICK TERBRUGGHEN, *The Calling of St. Matthew*

wearing eyeglasses and armor as he counts his coins, toward the apprehen-
sive, gaudy boys who flank Matthew, and straight to Matthew's grim and
sentient face. He has already taken up his hat—he knows an enormous fate
is coming at him, and he must make a move. Here, just as in so many Jesus
movies, the Redeemer's power is measured by the reactions of those with
whom he deals. We watch their faces as they look at him, while his figure
remains shadowed and peripheral. Here we can just see his lips open as he
prepares to speak. Meanwhile a bouquet of mobile hands fills the center of
the lighted space; the papers are ruffled on both wall and table, the decorative flaps on the boys' sleeves are agitated—some unearthly breeze is stirring here, causing a chill and some uneasy movement.

Another feature of this painting that is not shared by the Caravaggio
version is the hip-length, life-size view of the characters. Such framing has
long been a cinematic given. Most movie encounters are shown at least once
from just such a distance, without legs and feet but with torsos and hands
for expression, just as we see people when we come near to watch and listen
to them. Film stills showing two or three characters in conversation invari-
ably follow this Baroque convention, which was by no means confined to
Holland and appears constantly in European art of the seventeenth cen-

tury. The more distancing full-length view used in so many of Caravaggio's groups (as opposed to his lute players and grape tasters), just as in many from the fifteenth and sixteenth centuries, is partly what makes them so much like theater. Hip-length views are like life, or more so. The device was another late-fifteenth-century manuscript illuminators' invention, another of their early steps toward emotional immediacy and verisimilitude in personal perception. In the seventeenth century the motif seems to have accompanied large, even life-size format, in a deliberate attempt to draw the viewer closer (5.2, 5.3). He is invited to share in emotional interchanges instead of having to interpret them from a distance, exaggerated by unmistakable gesture and posture as if they were on stage.

Single figures had been shown from hip-level ever since the fifteenth century. This also promoted the sense of personal nearness while displaying the right details of costume and posture to be informative and imposing. But in addition the choice of such a view, whether for a portrait or for the Virgin or a single saint, nicely immobilizes the subject. Without legs, he is seen to be both present and still, rooted in the picture, where he must stay, having no means of escape. He is yours forever while you look at him.

An entirely different effect is achieved by showing a scene among several figures this way, especially if they look at each other. Movement can immediately be attributed to the viewer himself when the group subject's legs are all canceled; we have approached close enough to the scene not to notice legs, just as we would at a crowded informal gathering, but to notice only personal and social transactions, and any physical or sartorial details that have meaning for them—hats, gloves, and ornaments, hair, beards, and breasts, ears but not shoes.

Seating people at a table is an excellent pictorial device for arranging an interpersonal situation, as it is in life. It fixes the subjects even more firmly, not only eliminating their legs but immobilizing their bodies. In art, it often keeps the viewer on his feet among them, moving toward the protagonists and looking down on their business from his upright position. We approach Terbrugghen's Matthew as we approach the villain or hero playing cards in a Western saloon, during the moments when his challenger enters and moves in on him. We see what's on the table as well as on the faces; we come behind one or another shoulder and await the next move. Most of the moving will be emotional, not physical, except for the card or coin turned, the finger pointed (5.4, 5.5).

It seems to have been the Northern painters, following the manuscript artists, who first expanded the emotional dimension of sacred images in just this way, especially that of the Madonna and Child. The beautiful closed system of maternal tenderness never lacked in Italian art, but

5.2 Still from *Perfect Understanding*, 1933

5.3 THEODOR VAN BABUREN, *The Procuress*

5.4 GEORGES DE LA TOUR, *The Payment of Dues*

5.5 Shot from *The Breaking Point*, 1950

5.6 GERARD DAVID, *The Virgin and Child*

Northern painters sought a closer link with the viewer and his own personal experience. Bellini Virgins, however tender, barricade themselves behind parapets; but Gerard David's Virgin sits at a low table feeding Jesus from a bowl right in the same room with us (5.6). Genre motifs here reinforce rather than diminish the supernatural aura: that is the secret of the cinematic method. Here again a table fixes the action, but makes a little scene out of the still image, into which we feel ourselves drawn.

The most straightforwardly descriptive Dutch painters of the seventeenth century have strong affinities with modern animated cartoons, just as they originally did with the moralizing printed picture-books of their own time. They also suggest the kind of ephemeral and entertaining modern movie that creates intentionally crude and glossy versions of realistic material, usually for comic effect.

One very cartoonlike Dutch artist was Adriaen van Ostade, whose villagers and tavern rowdies seem easily translatable into the Disney mode (5.7). The style used for the naturalistic backgrounds in cartoon features of the 1930's and 1940's seems copied straight from the lightly swollen look of Van Ostade's doors, cupboards, and table legs, his squat, rounded, and

mellow shapes for all sorts of humble domestic structures and objects—
and also for humans. The Disney Seven Dwarfs and their cottage seem to
have been invented by Van Ostade, though they and their kin and chattels
had an intermediate incarnation in the work of Moritz von Schwind and
other German Romantic fairy-tale illustrators. But Van Ostade's original,
dumpy vision has a much more accessible coziness than the clear, sweet,
pale efforts of Schwind and his colleagues, who were consciously being antique and folkloric.

The cozy mode was also perfected in the seventeenth century by Gerard
Dou, whose deeply absorbed sages, attentive kitchen wenches, and doting
mothers are also rendered in a rounded, sweetened manner. Their slight
cartoonlike quality is intensified by the paintings' polished surface and
small format. The lighting, however, is sharpened and dramatized in Dou's
pictures. There is no bland flattening out of color through diffusion of
light, to match the comfortable rounding of the shapes, as in Van Ostade.
The effect is shadow-boxy and doll-like, with everyone's forehead shining

5.7 ADRIAEN VAN OSTADE, *Cottage Dooryard*

under the candle glow or the incoming sunbeam exactly like the gleam on
the polished bowl, bottle, or apple. This artist aims to please: the scruffy
qualities of humble life have been subtly made appetizing, without his ever
actually lying. But despite the lighting the Hollywood flavor is still Dis-
neyish, not photographic; the compositions are too pat for the direct eye of
the camera.

Other descriptive Dutch painters have far more straight cinematic characteristics, but also in a Hollywoodish style of realism. In the paintings of
Jan Steen, for example, everyone seems to have the same strongly marked
face with a small smirk, a pointed chin and nose, and slightly puffy, tilted
eyes. This face is in fact Steen's own, and it often appears on the clownish
character who resembles and stands for himself in the paintings; but he
thrusts it on almost all of his other characters, too, and so he also gives his
scenes a touch of the cartoon. Action in these works is comic and a bit
pointed, as in old Technicolor comedies with Doris Day. Like them, it takes
place among prosperous people whose enterprises are made to seem a little
ridiculous while they are nevertheless faithfully rendered in visual terms.
Just as in such films, the textiles, flesh, and furnishings are actual; but the
behavior is slightly overdone, and some excessively. Everyone acts true to
character stereotype, and a general theme of human crudity and silliness
underlies all incident (5.8).

Steen's paintings were linked to the skits done in the same spirit by the
Dutch Rhetorical Societies and, like them, to current proverbs and saws.
But what makes them like film and television, not like theater, is the satisfying natural sheen and common crowding together of real things—the set
decoration, where significant signals are embedded in a random-seeming
collection of stuff under the inclusive, undiscriminating camera eye. The
comic stage of that time and place depended mainly on character and
props. Elaborate stage settings were used only for court masques, tragedies, and operas, and there were no realistic ones at all. Steen's packed
fantasy scenes of domestic rumpus and popular moralistic folklore could
bring the whole rich visual aspect of life to bear on familiar and simple
comic material, just as movies did and do, and as television comedy does
even more.

Svetlana Alpers' insistence on the absolute optical standard of meaning
for this art—to be seen is to mean—is reinforced by the cinematic nature
of its narrative method. For dressing these sets and composing these
groups, the formal language has not been taken down from classic dicta-
tion, to emphasize and seek support from the familiar story of storytelling.
In that method, every object in a picture is offered in a harmonious formal
style that calls attention to its own placement in a traditional scheme, like

5.8 JAN STEEN, *The Doctor's Visit*

the words in a sonnet. The viewer knows where he is, as he "reads" the picture. But here, as in cinema, a great many things are visible just in order to
be so, and only some have direct pertinence to the theme. The jumble of
phenomena defies reading; the picture must be stared at for a long time so
that the eye can gulp one thing after another, both piecemeal and in different combinations, as it scans back and forth. While some of them may
pointedly signify, the elements of the décor seem random and the style of
rendering neutrally photo-graphic. The gestures and postures in Steen's
comedies may resemble the exaggerated comic-acting style of his day, but
for drama done in "takes," as it is in these works, the set has that very in-
tentional casual artlessness we see in modern film. It is the same combina-

tion we see in a Jerry Lewis movie: zany or gross behavior in carefully normal locations, which are then thrown into disorder by the action.

The same idea using different themes is expounded by Metsu, and later by Netscher and Van Mieris. These painters are more romantic, and coarse comedy is subdued in favor of gentle amusement and some sentimentality —nothing is raffish, everything is sweetly respectable, and everyone is very pretty. Metsu offers a great number of rich possessions shown to the best advantage, just as in film melodramas showing Kim Novak anxiously and prettily betraying her husband, but also happily at ease and not at all stifled amid the satisfying trappings of middle-class comfort. Metsu's rugs and jugs and satin skirts, embroidered slippers and glossy lutes are never excessive; as in the most successful film melodramas, they look attainable. Sight is always the point—to see is not only to know, but to possess. A large component in the appeal of such paintings must then have been just this opportunity for studying, savoring, and visually possessing lovely material objects, while being pleasantly entertained by subjects slightly risqué, slightly sentimental, or slightly funny. The moral meanings about the wickedness of sloth, greed, and lechery are neatly folded into a delicious package, just as in "Dallas" and "Dynasty," consisting largely of material things exquisitely rendered to show that their true value is quite detached from the moral of the story (5.9).

There is something not only cinematic (in the woman's-picture style) but positively American about this pictorial mode. It demonstrated the same unstable combination of puritanism and self-indulgence, of prudery and licentiousness that has stamped much American culture—and there are real affinities between seventeenth-century Holland and us, when we are seeing ourselves not only as progressive and prosperous, highly moral, and rather piously materialistic, but also as simple-hearted, unsophisticated, and sexually volatile—as many of our Hollywood films have often shown us doing. There are even more excruciating echoes. With these lovesick maidens visited by pompous doctors, or tipsy housewives about to warm up unbecomingly to dashing casual callers, there is a familiar yet uncomfortable sense of the sexes, one we used to see constantly in films of thirty years ago and before. These well-to-do middle-class women have the kind of freedom that comes with enlightened bourgeois leisure and affluence, that permits comradeship and social parity with men but no practical power or active ambition. They may play around, and also spend money on themselves, and keep the house exquisitely without a husband's or father's supervision; wives and girls have great freedom, but no other work. Tending and brooding about love and possessions—sometimes children—are their preoccupation. The expensive prostitute, the chic matron, and the princesslike

5.9 GABRIEL METSU, *The Musical Party*

daughter are not easy to tell apart—they all wear the same expensive clothes, exchange letters with lovers and confidences with servants, look in the mirror, and practice deception as well as music. Meanwhile, and most importantly, there is no aristocratic standard. These are plain folks, even if they are rich, and there is no tradition of refined, imaginative idleness to support them. Instead, an ideal of virtuous simplicity, industry, and right-eousness keeps these rich and idle people prurient and hypocritical, and produces great ambiguity in pictorial renderings of common scenes. Men have real business elsewhere and are only staying awhile, unless they are just going to leave or just arriving—all these doctors, teachers of music, curled gallants, officers, soldiers, and notaries. Is any of them the hus-band? Women are at home, often fidgeting. Yet sexual equality is supposed to exist, the doors and windows stand open, the street beckons. These women feel free and unfree at once. The happiest, the ones we like best, are those either deeply absorbed in a task or really having fun with the soldiers. The ones being plied with liquor or doubtful propositions, or struggling mutinously with the keyboard, or discussing a clandestine letter with the maid are not much at ease.

It is in fact not peace but unease informed by decorum that makes the greatest of these Dutch works so compelling. The atmosphere in the paintings of Terborch, De Hooch, and Vermeer is somehow immensely freighted, because these artists, unlike Metsu, Steen, Van Ostade, and Dou, have deliberately addressed the problem of ambivalence. In works by the latter group, facial expression is fairly standardized. Three or four conditions of soul are clearly rendered: mothers are benign, urchins giggle, teachers and doctors look sober or affronted. Boors in taverns grimace, young girls are demurely lascivious. But amid the serene appurtenances of De Hooch's universe, for example, the faces of mothers, children, maids, and visiting gentlemen are often carrying somewhat undefined ambiguous expressions that are anything but serene. So, too, are the postures and the physical relations among the visible characters.

One device used by this group of Delft painters is to keep at least one figure with its back turned, or with its face otherwise invisible and unreadable. Steen's characters half turn to the audience, aware of being seen and playing to the gallery: each scene is a prepared comic piece, and we are fixed out front. But in the De Hooch and Vermeer scenes, at least one person is an obvious non-performer, oblivious to observation, absorbed, and emotionally unaccountable—and so the whole picture also is. The exact balance is not made clear. In the great De Hooch *Mother Lacing Her Bodice* (5.10), the mother looks pleasantly stupefied by basic maternal function, still feeling tied to the baby, who is once more swallowed up in its protective cradle and milky dreams. Meanwhile the three-year-old has turned her back in the shadows, and slopes off quietly toward the door. Just what is in her small heart? Understandably, the dog is undecided whether to follow her slow shuffle out to the sunny yard, or stay with the satisfied pair indoors. This is not tranquillity; it is only quiet behavior and orderly housekeeping. The actual emotional circumstance, the "story," is unstated and mutable, still in progress. By contrast, a curtain is drawn up to reveal Gerard Dou's *Mother* (5.11); she smiles brightly, the baby grins, ogles, and flashes its bottom at us, the maid beams, the cradle yawns in luxurious invitation. The maternal breast shines enticingly, and everything reeks of Domestic Contentment, see? But not much of truth.

In the indecorous mode, Steen's comic visions of drunkenness and license are unleavened by any principle of real joy, nor are Van Ostade's tavern brawlers feeling much delight. But the acutely peaceful interiors of the

5.10 PIETER DE HOOCH, *Mother Lacing Her Bodice*

very well behaved are mocked by Steen's fantasy disorders: this is more like what is really going on. And in the low-keyed encounters between Terborch's and De Hooch's ladies and their servants, children, and visitors, there is considerable tension, no matter how smooth the curls and dust-free the windowsills. The tidy and sunlit sumptuousness looks like a firm effort at control, an array of fragments shored against moral ruin.

The theme seems to deepen into the representation of material riches as one kind of spiritual test, a thicket of comfortable circumstance through which, in which, around which the inmost soul must find a way to operate. The metaphor for the soul's flow in and around things is light; the strategy for guiding it aright is perfectly ordered space. In all this material order and comfort there is little pleasurable physical ease, such as Rubens or Italian painters continually convey. Bodily movement and posture is either restrained or awkward, and muffled by the clothes. By contrast, slight ges-

5.11 GERARD DOU, *Mother and Child*

tures of the hand and slight facial expressions are thrown into prominence, again as if to show private spiritual movement finding its way among the heavy furniture and stiffened garments.

Only a few painters attempted to convey this state of inward things in that advanced cinematic style which goes beyond recourse to theatrical or cartoon-graphic tradition, beyond Technicolor Hollywood comedy and melodrama into the realm of seriously poetic film art. De Hooch was a comprehensive master at it. His use of children is especially powerful, and it is often that same three-to-five-year-old girl who focuses the image upon floating consciousness, rather than upon controlled events. This child is often physically separated from adults, and her face and body are slightly indistinct. There are no cute, wistful looks or cheeky grins to emphasize the adult view of children, just as there are no satisfyingly complete, rounded-off formal arrangements in the Dou manner (5.12, 5.13). The dogs in De Hooch are also conductors of emotional atmosphere: they stand and turn their heads attentively to look at something likely to need attention, whether or not the composition of the picture indicates its importance—alert, ready to shift focus instantly, just as we are.

The little girl may be helping with the household tasks in an unemphatic way—no cuteness here either—or just watching them. The scene is certainly peaceable; and yet the idea of inner conditions not necessarily in tune with outward perfection manages to surface in these works and give them their modern appeal. It is a mark of this sophisticated cinematic method that the artist's own feelings are made to retreat, so that those of the human subject engage those of the viewer directly, in fact seem to leap into the vacuum created by that reticence.

The real peace in these Dutch interiors and courtyards is a perspectival authority so perfect that by itself it creates a kind of gratitude in the beholder. Exquisite relations obtain between indoor and outdoor light, between adjacent interior spaces, between human figures and whatever they touch, hold, sit, or lean on or move around among. At the same time, the interesting flow of human feeling is conducted *through* these things, not against a background of them, as it is in a theatrical sort of composition. Here most of the dramatic action is accomplished by arrangements of light and mass that draw feeling out of undramatic objects and circumstances. The withdrawal of rhetoric allows infinite layers of psychological action to pile up; but peace is eternally preserved in the firmness of the table legs and the weight of the jug.

In De Hooch's family scenes, bodily movement is minimal; but bodies are slim, and therefore persons look mobile, because they fill the empty space around them with their possible action instead of using up or weighing down an assigned slot. Faces are full of potential expression, a bit blurred and transitory, ready to compose into a particular mold only in the next, unknowable moment. That there is great deliberateness in De Hooch's cinematic method is suggested by his art-director's habit of editing reality to make it more natural. The look of reportorial exactitude in these courtyards, kitchens, and linen rooms is a total fiction; most of them are made up. Scenes in different pictures apparently take place in the same corner of the same room, which actually has quite different details of structure and décor in each one. The intensely natural, perfectly observed look of casual domestic moments has been deliberately contrived, with a fierce unnoticeable artistry.

The interaction of comfortable if simple physical existence with the na-

5.12 PIETER DE HOOCH, *Child and Mother in a Bedroom*

5.13 PIETER DE HOOCH, *The Kolf Players*

5.14 PIETER DE HOOCH, *Mother Delousing a Child*

5.15 PIETER DE HOOCH, *Couple in a Bedroom with a Dog*

ture of moral and spiritual limits is the theme of this art—"everyday life" in its profoundest sense. Personal and family virtue had long been a conventionally prized value in Protestant Holland; but after the cessation of hostilities with Spain in the middle of the century, artists were increasingly inspired to concentrate on genre subjects that celebrated it, and less on tavern and guardroom subjects, or those showing the military presence in civil life. It was then that Vermeer and De Hooch and Terborch began to refine and intensify the theme, not just of secular and civil virtue but of the inwardness of private life.

In the best De Hooch paintings the theme is concentrated on the domestic affairs of women and children, wherein the fundamental lessons about the relations among things, persons, and feelings are always taught; and the lesson here is that domestic virtue may arise simply out of the true perception of order. The paintings teach that wayward personal feelings will be tempered to manageable degree, and moral weakness given no scope, if everyone is allowed the steady contemplation of clear lines and uncluttered spaces, the touch of smooth surfaces, and the steady breath of clean, moist air. They also teach that life is better when accompanied by little noise and almost no speech. Instead, the dog's feet click on the tiles, and homemade music makes beauty from design, so that domestic harmony has its outward and audible sign. But these children never fall and scream, the dog never barks, the metal vessels never crash down or tumble together, no one jeers or whines or scolds. No one even converses very much. Everything is hushed by the perfect light; imperfect and rebellious souls, unsatisfactory sexual and familial relationships are all comfortably contained in its sovereign equilibrium (5.14).

Morality has thus become a matter of visual esthetics—a very cinematic principle. But such a great investment in visible orderliness as a paradigm of spiritual health means that physical abandon and ungoverned sensual pleasure may not be part of the recipe, but must be opposed to it—fundamentally disorderly and destructive, not capable of refinement and rationalization. Sexual behavior in De Hooch's, Terborch's, and Vermeer's paintings is thus always oblique and ambiguous or plainly crude. There is none of that explicitly erotic delicacy later infused into genre scenes by Watteau and Chardin. In certain De Hooch works the sexual themes are treated as they are in certain modern European films, where the progress of sexual incident is less crucial than the shift of emotional flavor in existing sexual relationships—*La Notte* and *Red Desert*, for example. The several paintings where a man is dressing (undressing?) near a bed, and a woman is making (opening?) the bed or bringing a tray of refreshment, or lacing (unlacing?) her bodice, or adjusting her hood in the glass have great per-

sonal poignance, the greater for the uncertainty about what is actually occurring. Again, faces are virtually unreadable. These may be domestic
encounters, but they might just as easily be venal; in either case, sexuality
has no pleasurable exuberance of its own to assert in these works (5.15).

Terborch is mainly concerned with venal love, and his amorously engaged characters are usually in attitudes and conditions of bemusement
and doubt, or portrayed in moments of slight but pervasive constraint. The
handsome shiny clothes and rich settings seem to produce the constraint
instead of enhancing enjoyment—these brothel scenes look like Victorian
drawing-room assemblies, where personal feeling is under strict behavioral
sanctions and emerges only as ambiguous facial expression or nearly im-
perceptible bodily stirrings. The lesson in Dutch art seems to be that the
life of pleasure is full of constant pressure—a modern American, Protestant sort of lesson.

As Peter Sutton always insists, subjective not objective realism is the

5.16 GERARD TERBORCH, *Woman Peeling Fruit*

keynote of this art, just as it is in film. The picture by Terborch of a woman
peeling apples again makes the action consist of the flow of thought rather
than of behavior, by the adroit placement of the little child (5.16). The
woman in this scene, presumably a young mother, seems to be the same as
the one contemplating an offer of coins from a soldier whom she is about to
ply with drink in another painting, where she apparently plays a harlot
(5.17). The maternal scene is intense; she peels carefully, her eyes fixed on
her work; the boy cares nothing for the peeling of the apple, but tries in-
tently to read her face. What is she thinking? What does she think of me?
Will she show me any approval? This is the same question asked by the
other painting, where the same girl stares at the money and the fat, weath-
ered soldier tries to read her face. What is she thinking? Is it enough? Will
I pass? Do I score? In both, the neat corners of her mouth betray nothing;
her momentary stillness shows only her resistance to the momentary pres-

5.17 G E R A R D   T E R B O R C H , *Soldier and Girl*

sure. At home or in the whorehouse, human transactions are founded upon the same emotional politics.

The delicate brushwork refrains from adding the kind of delicious surface gloss that Dou put on all facts. The faint blur on all edges gives perpetual mobility; total clarity would fix the image. Here, as in Vermeer, the air seems stirred by breathing and slight muscular movement in each figure. Only the satin, where it thickly veils the hips and thighs of Terborch's damsels as they decorously shift their weight, sends sharp answering beams back to the questioning gaze, grasping attention and signaling a wayward vibration underneath the silk, well separated from the impassive face. The movie camera has made full use of such effects, and so has modern fashion geared to camera expression: the mobile, sequined flanks of sullen-faced movie sirens effectively belie their overt indifference. The modern sexual poetry of shine and shadow, so thoroughly explored in the costumes for black-and-white cinema, has its ancestors in the suggestive skirts of Terborch's and Vermeer's well-behaved letter readers and instrument players. Camera sensibility seems already to have been in operation among these obliquely interacting lovers; the paintings are sections of experience without literary or theatrical precedent, exercises in explaining new relations between the eye and the psyche.

The knotty questions about meaning in Dutch genre works done after the middle of the century seem more tractable when they are viewed in cinematic terms, whereby any didactic, proverb-illustrating aspects of personal situation are skillfully disguised, enfolded in the immediacy of contemporary natural appearances and casual behavior. You can understand them without having them explained; you can see them without looking at them. In Emanuel de Witte's *Interior with Woman at a Clavichord,* there is a tension between the muted narrative content of the scene and the dazzling pictorial claims of the interior setting. The set for this shot seems incidentally, irrelevantly, autonomously beautiful; but in fact its beauty is packed with almost unnoticeable contributions to the drama itself that register nearly subliminally, and therefore all the better (5.18).

The woman at the clavichord is showing neither face nor hands nor the title of the score. The man in bed is almost invisible, his clothes dimly bundled on a chair. The dog lies curled in deepest obscurity on a cushion behind the door. The animal sleeps; the man is awake; both are shielded from our scrutiny, almost from our notice, and from the implacably benign sun. But under its fierce, bright touch, the long vista through the rooms to the distant sweeping maid and open window makes a brilliant claim on the picture's center. If we were unobservant, or if we were a self-absorbed child, we would run through the sunlight straight past the real scene, into the far

5.18 EMANUEL DE WITTE, *Interior with Woman at a Clavichord*

room, to ask the maid for a drink. But we are stopped at the threshold,
struck by the looks of that beam of light striking the woman's head. Her
mirror sees it, too. And so, as when the camera rests on the back of Monica
Vitti's head in *Red Desert,* we suddenly know we are in the presence of an
active consciousness, we are looking at a human vessel full of—what? The
vessel on the table, a near twin to the pregnant tankard so near the table's
edge in the foreground of Vermeer's scene with a lady and gentleman and
yet another keyboard, is a rhyming presence (5.19).

It is like a casual-looking foreground telephone in a film shot, where the
camera invites us to watch the people behind it, but we are being instructed
that the phone will significantly ring or be lifted. In these Dutch scenes the

5.19 JAN VERMEER, *A Man and Woman at the Virginals*

tankard fills the atmosphere with an awareness of drinking, what novelists used to call the fumes of wine, even when no one is looking at it or touching it. It contributes to that unique combination of casual phenomena with charged encounter that movies depend on, and that the Dutch seem to have invented. In the Vermeer, the tankard, brimful of traditional meaning, simply sits there; but just by being in the room, where we can see it forming a big third with the couple, it conjures all the old, stagy pictures of amorous folks carousing, and adds a hypothetically turbid past and future to the stillness of this pair.

Emotional action in the De Witte moves laterally, flashing from right to left across the foreground from the window to the bed, through the tankard and the hooded woman, slipping right past the bright vista to the shadowy man, and back again; but the pictorial action is the recession of sun-struck rooms. Like the Vermeer, it is an amazingly modern, cinematic treatment of a classic scene on the ancient, mythological theme of drink, love, and music. Freshly dressed, she plays for him and perhaps sings; but she also plays against him, and for herself. She wants to wake him, and also to tame him. Earlier, they have drunk together, she serving him and playing music then, too; but she has also been urged by him to drink, and more. Her early-morning music now heals him as if it were sunlight; but it also jangles, reminds, and somewhat undoes him: he rests his head on his hand, and does not rise. She, too, is healed, and plays for her own comfort; but she makes some mistakes, and feels foolish. She will shake her coiffed head in a minute. Meanwhile the maid sweeps out yesterday's dust and gets ready for starting again.

None of this is explicit, none of it is anything but fantasy. But all known concatenations of beds and men and women, wine and song and sunlight are nevertheless caught up in this subdued, casual scene—caught and deliberately thrown back, as we are forced to look directly only at a receding view of some invented spacious rooms, rather sparsely occupied in the early hours of the morning. The technical achievement—the perspective and the sun patches—becomes transparent, moreover, as if there were no artist in the equation and only one kind of observer, a single sensitive eye, effortlessly and at once grasping both the private situation and the neutral beauty of the indoor light.

Alpers' formulation that seeing and "picturing" were one activity for the Dutch painters will work for the movie camera, too. A sense of the unedited visible world as the right medium of esthetic and moral truth shows in the way cinema has transmuted old stage conventions, just as Vermeer and De Hooch transmuted stage-style pictorial themes—The Merry Company, The Music Lesson—into what look like casual occurrences in common life. One truth about the visual aspect of real life is that it is always partial. Vermeer's scenes have that spareness of material incident that looks subjectively right, so different from Jan Steen's interiors crammed with an inordinate show of detail. Vermeer seems to be expounding the thought that at any given moment in normal living, most meaningful detail is in the head; the eye as it strikes surrounding circumstance is usually only arbitrarily furnished with significant material, and often meagerly. In Vermeer's works, as in Rembrandt's, what we actually see is quite simple; what is implicit is enormous. It is often made out of assumptions, collections of small visual allusions that the viewer is assumed to understand unconsciously. He needs only the barest hint for the right visual associations to arise and compose in his head, and in his idea of what the picture shows. The less abundant the visual material, the more contribution the viewer feels like making. The light meanwhile stays fluid, striking with stunning indifference; the viewer must use it to interpret personally, to feel let in on things.

But music also fills the void and adjusts the emotional terms, just as it does in the movies. In these paintings music-making and musical instruments also stand for emotional movement itself, like the light. In the many Dutch scenes of affluent life containing music, some doubtless demonstrate polite harmony. But the Vermeer music scenes, just like the De Witte, seem to be using the suggestion of sound to augment the tension, like underscoring, to replace broad gesture and pointed facial expression or a big collection of visible objects.

De Hooch's late works have less light and more music than his great and famous middle-period ones of rooms and courtyards, and even more subtle imaginary settings. The shadows thicken among these well-dressed young people as the music gets louder and the landscape of fantasy expands around them. Formerly De Hooch had invented middle-class houses and their gardens; later he turned the actual New Town Hall in Amsterdam to his own purposes, sometimes pretending it was a pleasure palace full of satin-clad revelers, sometimes rearranging it to give it a fictional though quite plausible aspect, even while depicting it undergoing the scrutiny of visitors and tourists—as if to question the whole possibility of objective vision. Steps echoing on marble floors and the indistinct hum of voices replace the music, and contribute to the effect of suggestive fantasy, conceived in specific local terms.

In the large scene showing visitors to the Hall, the intent gaze of the principal male figure is turned upward over our heads (5.20). He seems to be watching the huge curtain that simulates one hanging before the painting itself, not in it, as if he had a sense of our presence that the others lack. Other disconnected groups gaze in different directions, a child seems to look idly toward us, a dog at something out of the picture. The raised gaze of the solitary man has a strange ambivalence, like so much behavior in De Hooch's work. The man seems about to lower his gaze to meet ours, but he is too entranced by the lifting curtain. Are we in fact characters in the painting he will finally be able to look at when the curtain is fully up?

Something about the arbitrariness of vision and its function inhabits these Dutch pictures. Apart from the great geniuses of genre—De Hooch, Vermeer, Terborch—modest practitioners express the same concern. They show the oddness of ordinary phenomena instead of their beauty and significance, and record dull, unharmonious moments even when ostensibly celebrating the peace and quiet of virtuous existence in prosperous towns,

5.20 PIETER DE HOOCH, *Interior of the New Town Hall in Amsterdam*

putatively a very model of harmony. Jacobus Vrel is such a painter. Like modern town-dwellers who feel that a private sense of psychic emptiness is somehow intensified by perfect domestic surroundings, the personnel in Vrel's works are seen to be somewhat canceled by their milieu.

In *Woman at a Window,* the woman's head is partially cut off from our view by the window frame, and what she is doing is obscure (5.21). Her face and hands are invisible and her body wadded up in her clothes; her avenues of expression are blocked. And yet the moment is expressive. It records nothing of the woman, but rather our act of seeing her lean out that way, as if we were entering and glancing around hastily, registering phenomena without attaching significance to them, but feeling something so strongly

5.21 JACOBUS VREL, *Woman at a Window*

that all visual detail becomes clarified and acquires a false significance. The woman leans out; she does it many times a day, to empty a jug into the canal or shake a mop. But the picture is not showing this fact; it is a scene not of domestic but of visual life, being offered as a metaphor of inner life, just as it is offered in film. The picture shows how such an arbitrary, incomplete, and slightly comic view of a woman in a room can imprint itself on the eye and mind for reasons other than response to the subject.

To show how this works, the painter does not dwell on the intimacy of the scene, nor yet on that intimacy as a distillation of anything else. Its specific small domestic meaning is in fact sidestepped in favor of a peculiar emotional tone that seems irrelevant to the depicted moment. The big and

noticeable woman herself is largely invisible and incalculable; the burden
of the picture is on us, not her. The perspective is a little uncertain, like the
subject, and gives that slight sense of the ground shifting that occurs when
things are seen while one is walking, or by a hand-held camera. The emotional ground shifts to match.

Esaias Boursse and Pieter Janssens Elinga also made paintings showing rooms with seated figures whose personal character is quelled by the
neat surrounding arrangements, including face-shrouding headgear, but
who are nevertheless intensively seen, even while their privacy stays unvio-
lated. We don't catch them at anything, but we are caught by them. In
Elinga's *Woman Reading,* the huge shoes in the foreground are funny and
odd, like the position of the woman's chair (5.22). She sits in the middle of
the room facing the light, which strikes the floor instead of her book; the
fruit bowl placed on the chair seat is another oddity. And yet this is a simple scene, perfectly comprehensible and ordinary: the shoes are clogs, outdoor footgear usually shed in the house; the chair is lightweight and

5.22 PIETER JANSSENS ELINGA, *Woman Reading*

customarily shifts all the time—perhaps she'll move it in a moment. The fruit bowl won't stay put on the domed lid of the nearby chest, and so the maid has put it on the chair, which is a rarely used formal piece of furniture anyway. But why has this picture been painted?

In the case of Vermeer and De Hooch, artists with patently great painterly ambition, the answer to that question may usually be that the picture represents the effort to solve an artistic problem, or several overlapping ones—a master painter's exercise in further mastery. Shoes, bowl, light, and chair would be rung in to serve a large artistic goal, to help the painter extend his strategies. In this division of genre art, the themes are comfortably limited: women at home, engaged in music, needlework, and correspondence, flirtation, cookery, and childcare, or combinations of them. But as soon as a great painter has chosen any one such subject, everything else can be construed as a record of his personal artistic journey, conveniently made in a familiar vehicle to amazing new places.

But Elinga was not very talented or ambitious as a painter. His works

5.23 ESAIAS BOURSSE, *Interior with a Woman Spinning*

have considerable modesty, like those of Vrel, who may even have been an amateur. Yet their choice of specific view within a general subject is just as arbitrary-seeming as De Hooch's or De Witte's choices, without the support of these artists' clearly deeper aims. Boursse's *Interior with a Woman Spinning* also has curiously effaced characters, a man nearly vanishing out of the left margin and nearly resembling a pile of folded bedding or curtains, and a dim, faceless woman. Most of the picture is floor and window, and the muted light penetrating and reflecting off these two planes is one actor in the scene (5.23).

The other is the viewer who is crossing that floor, heading for the distant room beyond and taking in the fireside scene en route, out of the corner of the eye without focusing on it. The picture records that unfocused moment —unfocused but lighted up, like the white wall and wooden window frame on the neighboring building seen blurrily through the glass. Atmosphere is generated by the moving eye and mind of the beholder, not by any interaction between the two inert persons in the room. The composition and the arrangement of light bypass them, and instead invite us. The picture seems to have been painted to show how, as we pass by them, circumstantial phenomena are invested with meaning only by our expectant glance, which is ever open to association and unconsciously charged with projected drama.

Vrel and Boursse do not use strong sunbeams or even strong contrasts; these glimpses insist on engaging the eye unassumingly, as if only making suggestions. There is nothing really there to see after all, and no brilliant signals are arrayed to catch needless attention. These works are records of subjective vision in the commonest use, painted to remind us of how the experience of seeing most commonly works.

Dutch scenes at home or in fictional palaces have a certain physical suavity and comfort, if not mental ease; men and women are well dressed and many are elegant. But other scenes depict the rougher world of guardrooms and taprooms full of soldiers in the same charged, subjective way. The theme itself is as commonplace and nearly as old as that of home music and vinous flirtation: soldiers conversing together, whether on the eve of battle or after victory, are the stuff of much anecdote and secular mythology.

All over embattled Europe in the first half of the seventeenth century, military demeanor and costume were obviously a large fact of visual life; and for the first time European male and female dress began to demonstrate strong emotional contrasts, not just formally balanced differences. Swagger became a large element in male chic, while demure refinement and a high degree of stasis increased in bourgeois female dress. Dutch genre scenes show how flowing hair and expressive hats and sweeping cloaks were masculine privileges, especially among soldiers, while women wore smooth caps and neat chignons, stiff bodices with thick sleeves and heavily falling gathered skirts. Men stuck out their elbows at sharp angles constantly throughout the century, to rest a hand on a hip or sword, to pour a glass; women's dress confined the upper arms and shoulders quite tightly, so that elbows tended to stay close to the body. Under military influence, the male body was extended by big mobile cuffs and flaps and and tapes and straps of all sorts, so that it took up a lot of room and made a lot of motion and noise, especially with the addition of sword, cape, spurs, and those enormous boots. Women kept their mobile adornments to a minimum—a curl or two, pearl drops in the ears. Female elegance appeared in a restrained clarity of line and great richness of fabric: what moved was the light on those glorious skirts. Scenes with soldiers and women together, especially Vermeer's pair in the Frick Collection, frankly play up these contrasts, which were new elements in the visual character of love play, as they must have been in general sexual awareness. In the Frick couple, the soldier's big blotlike hat and big dim elbow in its loose, sloppy sleeve are almost all that convey his sexual flavor—beyond them we have only his nose and a few blurry fingers. Her crisp body, head, and arms are in sharp contrast, as contained and defined and lucent as the glass her hands protect, or as the map above her head (5.24).

In this art, scenes without women are quite different from those with caps and skirts. Male behavior is full of the material quality of male accessories, the constant sense of kit and gear that one can see in military group portraits as well as guardroom paintings. Even civilian portraits share the hat-and-sweeping-cloak theme with the military man. These seventeenth-century male bodies have no line and hardly any clear shape, except that occasionally given by a partial breastplate or unusually tight sleeves. Their erotic effects must have arisen out of sartorial assertion, also manifested in baggy breeches and bunchy shirtsleeves, and in big collars or ruffs. Willem Duyster's *Soldiers by a Fireplace* shows a central figure with a huge fur-brimmed hat, a star among the other hats that fill the scene with their looming and tilting. The card game at the back and the storytelling at the fire have a nonchalance and lack of social tension dependent on a noticeable lack of women or drink or, for that matter, danger (5.25).

These men are smoking and speaking in low tones in a clublike ambience; a purely masculine, low-keyed interplay is in process. The glance of the standing man takes neutral cognizance of our presence—we are a man and a member, too. Chiefly, the system uniting the pools of light also unites these quiet men, making two palpable communities within the picture but creating one gracious milieu for the interchange of calm chat and complex

5.24 JAN VERMEER, *Officer and Laughing Girl*

comradely feeling. Action and passion are at a distance; so are folly, shame, strife, and bravado. The light heals and sustains. These men wear shoes, not boots, and their big hats have a benign protective look. Swords are not in evidence. Are they indeed soldiers? If so, they are not insisting on it at this moment. The foreground boy offers the *repoussoir,* the silhouetted figure against whose awareness the lighted scene exists. We cannot see his eyes; but his parted lips show his absorption in the fur-hatted speaker's words, perhaps in his unusual face and dress, and the boy's satisfaction at being among these glowing beings who take their ease and admit him to their company.

5.25 WILLEM DUYSTER, *Soldiers by a Fireplace*

Restraint is the note struck in this and other Duyster soldier pictures. The viewer is permitted to enter its community and feel out its emotional temper by degrees, as in film scenes where the action consists of just that —the gradual exploration by the camera of a roomful of men slowly unfolding a situation to the viewer's consciousness. It was done in *The Right Stuff* and many others. In Terborch's painting called *The Dispatch,* the action is clear but the situation is made muted and resonant; we are invited to consider what is going on, not told. The standing trumpeter averts his gaze from the seated writer exactly as Vermeer's standing maid does from her writing mistress in the Alfred Beit Collection painting (5.26, 5.27).

5.26 GERARD TERBORCH, *Officer and Trumpeter (The Dispatch)*

Love is apparently the subject of these screeds, which will be delivered
by these subordinates; but it is the psychological complexity of love that is
suggested with precocious modernity in such simple situations. They are
like the paintings of Hopper, or like scenes in films where the camera
watches the members of a group or couple, dwelling at length on each without comment, letting possible changes of inward state suggest themselves
without the need of overt action or expression, and without speech. Such
dramatic devices were only gradually appropriated for cinema, after it had

5.27 JAN VERMEER, *Woman Writing a Letter, with her Maid*

obviously transcended the theatrical conventions with which it had started; but they had been exhaustively explored by Vermeer, De Hooch, and Terborch in paint as they, too, steadily recast old themes in new terms of subjective experience.

While the eyes of these writers are lidded as they bend over their work, the eyes of both maid and trumpeter are wide and full of consciousness. Both gaze out, but not at us. Their understanding is their own, and we can only observe it, empathize, try to interpret. They could speak, but of course they won't unless spoken to. Both have jobs that take them around and about among folk of superior rank, whom they may assist and observe but not address as equals. They are, however, painted as equals; our attention is drawn as much to their possible feelings and knowledge as to that of these correspondents—as much, but not more: these are not romantic pastoral scenes elevating the lowly. The big dog in Terborch's painting, like so many Dutch dogs, is also a channel of pertinent feeling, more uninhibited than any human actor. He is the officer's dog, but he sniffingly attends on the messenger, whose restive attendance on his master alerts him to the emotional stakes. He nearly treads on the fallen ace of hearts.

In both Duyster and Terborch, the male world is treated with as delicate a sensibility as any shown by Vermeer and De Hooch in the reading of encounters between the sexes or generations. These painters never leave men's expressiveness to the dash of their garments, as Callot so brilliantly did. Despite their emphatic clothing the Dutch men in these genre paintings have no *systematic* elegance, no form with which they present their clothed persons and their feelings and intentions together in a harmonious formal whole, like a mask. The women do. The men are more artless, loose, fragmented, and unbuttoned, like their clothing and hair, and so they seem more emotionally unguarded. Their feelings are not transmuted by either dash or decorum into suave, formally realized modes of expression; but neither are they crudely expressed. These men have a Gary Cooperish simplicity of manner, the sort of quality originally associated with Protestantism and later with America altogether—uncourtly, but not ungainly.

Pieter Codde's *Young Man with a Pipe,* from about 1628, already shows how a stiff and formal old fashion in dress may be engagingly mobilized in the new masculine style (5.28). His wrinkled stockings, tousled head, unfastened doublet and collar are new loosening effects, "a sweet disorder" applied to the same tight and formal garments that are familiar from the rigid Jacobean miniatures and portrait engravings of around 1615. The light, moving across the still wall and catching all the bumps, echoes the theme of mutability that his costume states. His still pose is similarly washed with the motion of his thoughts. He looks very appealing in his unarrogant dishevelment, a seventeenth-century James Dean. We are drawn by his solitary, ingenuous, and unselfconscious charm; he seems to be setting the right masculine tone for the advancing century.

Metsu's *Interior of a Smithy* is an example of Dutch male interaction very different from Duyster's and Terborch's meditative groups, or Codde's boy. This scene, like so many of Metsu's, has a pointed, Norman Rockwell–like cast, so that it is not surprising to learn that it was once thought to represent the fleeing Charles II discovered by a blacksmith

5.28 PIETER CODDE, *Young Man with a Pipe*

5.29 GABRIEL METSU, *Interior of a Smithy*

(5.29). It looks invented, artificially realistic instead of naturally conjured, stagy rather than cinematic, and in fact like certain scenes from stage-minded movies. Contrasts of costume, age, and facial expression are stressed by being typified, and contrast of occupation by careful props and posing. There is no room for psychological or even physical motion—it is a tableau, horse included.

Terborch's soldiers, like his other figures, are rendered in the provisional figure style that avoids standard poses and portrays even the smallest element of human behavior as pending, so that it never freezes, and emphasis is shifted to the idea of process. In such a style, no single physical arrangement can ever seem "typical," however often it is reused. Each set of choices seems arbitrary, even though they may all be very much alike. The many similarities are not identities, except occasionally in the case of complete objects, such as the yellow-and-black silk bodice worn by five very different women in Vermeer's oeuvre. In Vermeer, each room is made to look painstakingly observed, and yet each is slightly different—and one must conclude that all are invented, just like De Hooch's courtyards. In such a way of doing things, the idea of detached, neutral vision is undermined. Each image is individually "seen" into existence, with all details precisely tailored to the one revealed view, just as in a dream, or in the kind of film that imitates a dream and not a play.

That Vermeer bodice repeated in five different but similar spots raises the question, Did he invent it? Is this garment a real studio prop, worn by a series of models and made to fit each by pictorial tailoring, or did Vermeer "design" it himself only for the paintings, like all these perfect and plausible rooms—ignoring what the girl really had on so as to introduce that brilliant black and yellow? or was it simply always the same model, wearing her own bodice over and over? By 1665 it was out of fashion and appears no more—Vermeer never ignored fashion, whatever other minutiae he transposed.

De Hooch has a sequence of scenes set in what cursorily seems the same room, with a cupboard bed and another room beyond showing a garden through an open door. They very much have the flavor of a recurring dream: each view of the room is the same, but each set of details is slightly different, and each seems authoritative. In one, a child is being deloused by her mother; in another, the same child runs in from the garden while the mother makes the bed. Still another shows a young couple dressing by the bed with a dog but no child. It would be easy to construct a filmlike narrative out of all of these taken together, especially since De Hooch even provided an eerie close-up of the child who enters from the garden, in a separate picture seen as by a zoom lens (see 5.12 and 5.13). But each room, though the same, is not the same. Each picture is its own dream, its own film entire, full of its own complete suggestive movements and situations. The subjective consciousness is invoked anew each time.

And yet this sequential look among the paintings of De Hooch and Vermeer does again suggest a cinematic ideal—not the straight telling of a "story in pictures" one after another, like a comic strip or a suite of tableaux, but the use of constant movement as itself a narrative theme. Seventeenth-century Dutch paintings were in fact often done in pairs or pendants, to show two aspects of one motif, as if to point out the unfinished character of all experience, both moral and material. They aim to emphasize the lack of cadence possible in any single take. Dramatic sequence is expressed not as a row of salient moments, but as the play of the receptive, seeking eye ranging over the material world, weaving webs of meaning and feeling out of the looks of things.

SIX

Landscape; Prints; Rembrandt

L A N D S C A P E setting provides a solution to the problem of showing situations in process; nature never stands still, says Monet. The Dutch landscape-painters put that fact to use with special attention to the constant movement of light and to the arbitrary character of natural phenomena, which are so different from neat rooms. Aelbert Cuyp was a particular master of rendering the motion inside the still moment in terms of life out of doors. He seems especially to have addressed the question of showing the sun actually rising and filling the world with visibility, as if that were the model and paradigm for all action. Almost nothing else happens in his pictures, which show moments filled only with the passage of time, as cows ruminate and herdsmen seem to do the same, anglers wait for a bite, and horsemen sit back and let their horses drink (6.1).

The best of these paintings are mesmerizing for their expectant, pregnant beauty devoid of incident. They are not documents of rural life or harbor and river life, but only of the morning passing. The cows are full of presence, and their slow responses match the pace of the light's slow rise. The paint itself does not move, as it seems so vigorously to do in Ruisdael's and Hobbema's works portraying similar scenes. There, the artist stirs the trees and the sky with his own brilliant talent; but Cuyp withholds that interfering kind of encouragement. He, like De Hooch, seeks to keep anything definite from occurring, so that we can supply all the possibilities.

Philips Koninck illustrates an alternative cinematic mode in Dutch landscape-paintings. His flat panoramas invite scanning and seem themselves to be flowing past under us as we fly over them (6.2). They have no *arrangement*, except that created by the horizon alone. The sky and earth are separate, but beyond that fact everything is in flux; the eye may travel for miles in all directions without feeling forced to rest on any eminence or

6.1 AELBERT CUYP, *Cavaliers Watering Their Horses*

prominence. The ownership implied by the act of looking must stay fluid and keep moving, never fixing the world into a prospect that could be labeled "perfect" or "beautiful" or "typical," and so be possessed like a snapshot. The artist seems to be saying this to himself, too: artistic ownership is a scanning process. The frame keeps shifting, showing that there really can be no frame, no box in which to package the view. Cities in this scheme are simply further configurations of the landscape; and town and country, like foreground and distance, intermingle without setting themselves up in conventional opposition.

The Dutch frequently used the *contre-jour* technique for landscape lighting, whereby the viewer gazes straight at the light source, and all objects in the painting rise up in some degree of silhouette against it. This method could be construed as a pointedly anti-theatrical and anti-classical device, since such effects occur frequently in actual experience but were impossible on the traditional stage. The *coulisses* with the side lighting of stage convention appeared in the landscape paintings that were committed to

6.2 PHILIPS KONINCK, *View of Fields*

classical ideals—the beauty of proportionate arrangement within fixed boundaries. Lighting a scene from the rear, as if to dazzle the viewer's eyes and unman him, shows an opposing interest in recording natural phenomena for their direct emotional claims, expressly to show how different those are from idealizing formulas.

This anti-classical Theater of Nature, based on the diurnal drama of the rising and setting sun, has become a modern classic source for the movies. It derives most directly from the kind of nineteenth-century Romantic landscape painting that put the sun in the center, imitating the way Claude Lorrain had first done it. But the source for these truly goes back not through Claude, who was using the theme for his own luminous version of classical harmony, but through the magnetic visions of Cuyp and Van der Neer; and so it derives ultimately from the aloof gaze of the sun at the rear of Bruegel's *Icarus,* the same relentless eye of the actual that has given the camera its force.

Most seventeenth-century Dutch artists "actualized" legendary themes as Bruegel had done, instead of casting them in the established style of artistic reality—that is, in the poses and proportions, the calligraphically designed draperies and appurtenances that had so long been associated with mythological subjects as to provide a large part of their meaning. The classic method makes obvious art out of old stories, rendering their harsh content palatable just by associating it with the pleasure of formal artistic order.

Such a process fixes the subject into a shape easily contained by the eye and the mind, even if the facts are unspeakable, like the slaughter of the innocents. The contrasting cinematic method is to keep mythic material in unshapely motion, often thus making it unbearable but very immediate— "graphic," in fact. Emotional conditions become visible processes that are uncertain of any absolute ends or outcomes. Beautiful groupings cannot "graphically" convey unsettled states of life, and so figures look not just awkward but even doubtful and provisional with respect to structure and posture. Faces may be quizzical, blurry or even invisible.

The effect of such a method is a psychological reconstruction of the thematic material, in a style that is perfectly familiar to a movie-goer. Instead of elevating and distancing the theme by using prestigious formal language to describe it, so that the action appears to take place in heaven or a Golden Age—or in nothing but paint—the artist makes the ancient tale seem like a rather haphazard modern event, fraught with the same kind of confused drama that prevails in private homes or offices or public bars, among acquaintances, professional enemies, or family members, where it is not always certain exactly what is happening—only the painter makes it take place in fancy-dress, so that we know the theme is legendary.

Legendary material in Dutch art was in fact often taken from Dutch poetic drama, and then rendered as if to record a stage production on film. The staged effects were represented with the disharmonious discrepancies kept intact. Instead of pictorially beautifying, dignifying, and refining the clothed figures and the setting, the artist carefully shows the scene with the modern trumpery stage arrangements faithfully described. The girl posing as Fame or History whom Vermeer's artist is about to paint is just such a figure, her laurels too large for mythic effect, her drape too stiff, her book and trumpet too heavy. Vermeer thrusts the figure of the painter between us and her, to make the point: and we know he will paint her exact looks, not an ingratiated version.

The characters in such Dutch works are often not completely at home in

their pageant costumes, whereas in Poussin's great productions, for example, the nymphs or saints and their companions wear their universal draperies with unconscious ease. Even including some Rembrandts, Dutch
mythic scenes often look a little embarrassing, and are sometimes quite
harrowing. The props and costumes are indeed like the ones used on the
Dutch stage of the time; and these, although they were often costly, did not
aspire to the suave illusionism or unified stylishness of the French and
Italian courtly theatricals that had classical prototypes in mind, and that
led eventually to opera. Emphasis in the Protestant, middle-class North

6.3 R E M B R A N D T V A N R I J N , *Joseph Accused by Potiphar's Wife*

European theater was on the text and the acting, not on significantly harmonious visual beauty—the personal kind of acting that led eventually to the movies. The props and costumes can look any way, except that rich is naturally most fun; the point is the drama among the characters.

Dutch painters of the same subjects as those used on the stage were in fact divided between those emulating Italian painterly methods, consonant with a courtly interest in idealizing spectacle, and those showing how such scenes might actually look if real people dressed up and acted them out in a naturalistic style. The acting in such paintings as Rembrandt's *Joseph Accused by Potiphar's Wife,* for example, is like film acting, dependent on the effective revelation of personal character rather than on skilled projection by a performer. And in much Dutch history-painting, just as in film, personal quality creates the dramatic impact, not theatrical groupings, gestures, or exaggerated facial expressions. The bed in this scene is another cinematic touch, placed and lighted to stand plainly for sex, while the actors continue to equivocate and maneuver (6.3).

Aert de Gelder's *Way to Golgotha* intensifies the same movie-vision of sacred scenes first realized by Bruegel, and for one of the same subjects (6.4). We are watching Christ come up toward us over the brow of a hill with his burden; but the visual material that fills the frame consists of the costumed watchers and marchers and the panoramic setting, as in the movie of *Ben Hur.* Intense pathos is foreshadowed, not directly dwelt on. The psychological conditions for responding to it are being prepared instead of assumed. By the time the distant bowed figure reaches us, we will be ready to shed tears, because we are now being made to consider the long stony path he has trod from the stern city gates, the milling crowd of soldiers jostling him as they scramble up the rocks, the curious onlookers, and the indifferent placard-bearer, whose attention is so easily distracted by a disturbance off-screen. Faces are turned away, not only from Christ's progress but from us, to emphasize the total lack of anyone's personal concern in this drama. A point is made of its slow, increasing desolation as the scene moves out of Jerusalem to the bleak hillside. No angelic hope hovers in the busy cloudy sky; town and countryside are alike forbidding. Christ sinks under it all, almost out of our sight as heaven, nature, and man desert him, and the camera centers on the outline of the grim and distant city wall.

On a more intimate scale, *The Dance of Salome* by Jacob Hogers takes a cinematic view of a much-theatricalized Biblical scene (6.5). In the center of the painting, the huge drapery frames only a nameless courtier, who turns to look at the dance: the whole view is in the process of shifting away from a conventional tableau of the king and queen at table, with the drapery on the left. The camera has backed up and moved to the right, so as to

6.4 AERT DE GELDER, *The Way to Golgotha*

include the floor on which the dance begins, and has begun focusing on the young princess bouncing toward us from the left. Soon the view will shift farther around, and we will have Salome in the center—the opposing tableau, seen between the two royal heads, this time with the drapery on the right.

Now Salome's stiff naked leg with its sandaled foot kicks out, like an awkwardly applied Classical allusion, and also like an indecent display on the part of a child. It seizes the eye—ours and everyone's—because female legs are rarely seen in this heavily clad milieu. Ladies bare only the bosom; the bare leg is for mythical beings or professionals. This stolid young girl has been inveigled into exposing herself unsuitably, and her dancing dress has been designed to allow it; but her wicked mother, so like her in feature, is unperturbed and even eager. Only the bearded courtier lifts an ineffectively restraining hand. Salome's own hands hang straight down: she is powerless. But her face is serene, and her straight gaze at us affirms that her own honor feels uncompromised.

This young girl on the extreme left and this woman on the extreme right are the twin focuses of attention, insisted on by the lighting, but they are in an uneasy equilibrium, because the transitional arrangement gives the scene a constantly moving center. The tableau refuses to jell. The stiff leg declines to make a graceful bend, which in turn would make the costume look more beautiful and legendary, instead of shocking. The widely separated female figures are almost falling out of the frame and can barely hold the dramatic tension together. But the sweep of the drape does that, further suggesting the motion of eyes and feelings, and the swing of the camera in its steady arc around the central group. Eventually its eye will leave the dancing Salome and move again to the right, to stare at the shining charger over the queen's head.

The costumes and props in this scene also have the *ad hoc* look of dedicated college theater, where antique pomp is often minimally conveyed but great emotional intensity is generated by the total conviction of the cast. A similar effect occurs in early historical films (Renoir's *Nana,* for example) made with modest concern for sumptuously accurate period décor but a great deal for effective lighting and brilliant movie acting.

A good example of historical movie-making by a Dutch painter is Nicholas van Galen's *Judgment of Count William the Good* (6.6). The scene depicted actually took place in the fourteenth century, and so everyone is wearing standard "Ye Olde" costumes: ruffs, capes, and berets with plumes, an agglomeration of motifs actually dating from the sixteenth century but which seem to have registered as "medieval" in the 1650's, as they still do. This scene of summary justice is offered, however, as a modern and

6.5 JACOB HOGERS, *The Dance of Salome*

perhaps justified atrocity, portrayed as if by a quick-witted photojournal-
ist. The greedy bailiff who stole a peasant's cow is about to be brutally de-
capitated by a court servant, right before the eyes of the reigning count and
a few of his friends, without due process or public legal ceremony. The
haste of this decisive action shows only in the harsh lighting and uncere-
monious arrangement of the group.

The draped dais for the seated count's throne is difficult to read as such;
the casually grouped courtiers are standing on an undefined floor; some
witnesses' faces are as dim as those of the main actors—headsman, culprit,
and clerk. The star—the virtuous count, the friend of defrauded peasants
—leans to the left almost out of the picture as he seems to speak *sotto voce*

6.6 NICHOLAS VAN GALEN, *The Judgment of Count William the Good*

to the clerk. The odd shapes taken by ordinary things show the photographic mode: the wretched bailiff's feathered hat on the step, the ungraceful hanging, and the lances all take their existence only from the arbitrary fall of light, which is no respecter of intrinsic importance or claims to abstract beauty.

There is no rhetorical fuss made here, no half-draped personifications of justice, no wailing women or pious observers and commentators reacting, only the impassive silhouetted clerk with his record book, and the bemused courtiers watching the thief meet his fate with one efficient swing of the sword. The satin and plumes look grotesquely irrelevant. The scene looks as if it could be occurring in this century, and it even resembles the famous newspaper photograph from World War II showing a Japanese about to behead an American kneeling before an open grave.

The introspective expressions of the onlookers and the shadowed faces of executioner and condemned man suggest an unauthorized view of an expedient political act, swiftly carried out away from public scrutiny, or a scene from a movie about secret violence in high places. The thing will all be over in a few seconds, the mess cleaned up, the headsman paid, the event quietly entered in the record; and then the feathered hats will move on outdoors to some public function, with public faces suitably adjusted. This painting was meant for and still hangs in a public place, like a fixed historical documentary film. It adorns the town hall of Hasselt, vividly showing how things were done under the enlightened despots of the political past. It pays homage to nothing whatever of artistic or decorative grandeur, only to notions of circumstantial power, both visual and practical.

There is an appealing suggestion in these scenes that fancy-dress releases behavior not possible for these recognizably ordinary folks in their usual clothes. The turbans, pearls, and armor are what allow Dutch girls and businessmen, depicted as legendary persons, to enact scenes of rage and jealousy—not as theatrical professionals, like the exhibitionist performers in Caravaggio's works, but as themselves, here simply inspired and dressed by mythic circumstance. Film actors also give this impression. Peter O'Toole as King Henry II or Lawrence of Arabia, or Charlton Heston as any kind of legendary hero, is always *himself,* rising above or sinking under the force of the story in his own person, with or against which we can identify, depending on the role. The more the role demands fancy-dress, the more uninhibited can be the actor's action; but he is the same as we are, only licensed by costume to take extreme paths.

The painter's aim of personalizing the great Biblical legends reflected a general seventeenth-century impulse to de-iconicize religious art, to lift the curse of idolatry from holy representations and insist only on the personal meanings of sacred events, to be personally applied in modern life. Typological and emblematic religious scenes, with many attendant figures and many layers of meaning, gave way to dramatically conceived moments of confrontation and sudden inner change. In tolerant Holland the simultaneous presence of Catholic influence among Protestant and Jewish patronage allowed an especially broad scope for religious subject matter. Similarly, the presence of humanistically educated patrons permitted an admixture of Classical themes, now also treated with dramatic personal simplicity, instead of with the elaborate court-masque-like staginess of the sixteenth century.

The Mannerist style of history painting, founded on Renaissance models and represented in Holland by Bloemaert, Wttewael, and Cornelis van Haarlem, following the example of the Flemish artist Spranger, had produced works filled with vigorously twisting or swirling figures. It had nevertheless held these artists to the old emblematic method of showing everything pertinent present at once. In such a scheme no action, however

6.7 ABRAHAM BLOEMAERT, *The Marriage of Peleus and Thetis*

turbulent, can escape the frame and involve the viewer. Moreover, no really significant movement seems able to occur amid the competing eddies of motion—there is no room for an emotional center, although there may be a central set-piece (6.7). Each dancer or set of dancers in the masque demands equal star billing, and the eye is invited to find the right references and allusions, which are rhythmically distributed over the whole stage at once. The subject must be gradually deciphered, and so the viewer is flattered in his educated sensibilities. The unifying harmony of the scene is conveyed in the exciting style of the dance, shown in the same eroticized torsion of the figures and their identically suggestive semi-nude limbs and made-up faces, not by any primary emotional meaning in the event. From that, artistic distance is carefully kept.

All over Europe this program was later altered, the stage extras banished, the lighting employed only for central emotional emphasis, motion economized, and characters individualized. Some results were even more intensely theatrical, such as those of Caravaggio, as we have seen; but other and mostly Dutch painters took the opportunity to reconceive the whole visual domain in these new terms, not just the acting space. Rembrandt, Vermeer, and Velázquez did this with unprecedented genius, but the Dutch painters I have been discussing found a cinematic way of framing and directing the action in the picture, whether they worked with genre material or holy legends. The visible action is of the same kind, however different the theme: it shows the unfolding of an event in psychological terms, a set of personal situations simultaneously developing that must engage the viewer on the same terms. The larger world is always present—the world that may encroach or distract or claim a character altogether, or form the subject of a new frame an instant later. Persons and objects and surroundings lurk unseen off every edge, proposing possible shifts of meaning and new combinations of fact or of personnel.

Bodies, faces, and material objects may themselves be quite "inexpressive" by stage standards, or crude because of the requirements of the story; but they are not removed from us by painterly stylization or autonomous pictorial decorum, however seductive or pleasing. The earlier need for beautifully orchestrated movement came from the Renaissance sense of the microcosm, the artistic imperative to keep the entire concept bound by the four sides. Conversely, incompleteness marks the Dutch works—the need to be *supplied* from all sides, and not least from ours.

Genre scenes and history painting were deliberately linked in the work of Vermeer, for example, who put pertinent history paintings on the walls of his bourgeois characters' rooms. These are like the scenes in modern film melodramas that take place in a movie theater with a film going on, or in living rooms with the television on as a background, ironic or not, for present events. The Vermeer pictures almost never show an innocuous still-life or a dim portrait—it is usually a legendary scene, a map or a mirror, or possibly a landscape—the television shows of the time, showing the same world in a different representational convention, rendered as a commentary, a warning, or a joke.

Other, less subtle painters did the same. Eglon van der Neer's sober couple in Boston's Museum of Fine Arts sit beneath a lush and life-size Venus and Cupid, installed over their fireplace (6.8). Their walls, floor, and tables are much more sumptuously clad than they are, in their black garments with constricted shoulders set off by stiff white linen. The big naked figure directly over their heads is like a cartoon balloon of their inmost thoughts; and its function is to show that such genre scenes and such history paintings have the common motif of individual inner reality. In the large, airy salon, this Venus is thinking of them, even as they think of her; she looks at Cupid and broods about sex and children, and settles with comfortable nude ease into her frame over the mantel, taking happy responsibility for the realm of pleasure that this pair prefers to project onto their surroundings.

This kind of submerged emotional situation conveyed by an ordinary surface image is a basic element of narrative film art. Settings and clothing have significant emotional charge, rather than detachable symbolic meanings, and they are always *specific*. The complete visual effect is effortlessly naturalistic, with no visible forcing of meaning. The emotional meaning is discharged a little below the optical surface, where only casual appearances are deployed, just as in actual life. Much is offered for psychological apprehension, while straightforward matter is set forth quite plainly. Literalness and psychic complexity coexist.

Interiority, the private application of all general mysteries, is obviously emphasized by showing such an arrangement inside an urban room. Town life means living privately indoors, with a provisional relation to the outdoors and to other lives. Urban interiors in Dutch paintings are made to seem like inward states furnished with containers and conduits of private feeling. And so legends and landscapes are offered by town-dwelling painters to town-dwelling patrons as pertinent expansions of such interiors, alternative fictional vistas of the same private psychic landscape. When the two are shown together and inside one another, the outward-turning but inward-looking ideal is just as noticeable as when larger worlds are suggested through windows. Movement between them is implied in the same way, an interaction through the door frame or the mirror frame, the window or the picture.

6.8 EGLON VAN DER NEER, *Portrait of a Man and a Woman in an Interior*

Vermeer's great *View of Delft* shows a whole city subjectively, like an inner landscape or a room. In this panorama, light and spatial arrangement are disposed with that same intensive particular view insisted on for small indoor scenes. The whole city is one room, or one mind, examining itself (6.9).

Another painter of towns, Emanuel de Witte, one of whose domestic interiors we examined earlier, made similarly atmospheric portraits of the insides of churches and of townscapes that combine genre and architectural elements. The idea that vision mirrors psychological motion appears strongly in these outdoor shots, where people are seen in momentary close-up as they move along a crowded square shopping at vendors' stalls. The sense of significant passage is keen, a passage of glances and responses accompanying the passage along a street, set off by a passing view of an active, neutral urban milieu.

6.9 JAN VERMEER, *View of Delft*

6.10 EMANUEL DE WITTE, *A Market in a Port*

The view of the people in *A Market in a Port* shows them from the knees up, in a standardly cinematic relation to their frame (6.10). We see them as if we were another customer at the fish stall, or else a camera moving in on them from a more emcompassing view—an establishing shot of the harbor a moment before—to focus the flavor of the general scene on the small interchange among these three. The white-bearded man stares at the woman's face, invisible in its hood; the fish seller looks at him across the shiny fish lying in her open hand. Are the two customers strangers? married? father and daughter? clandestine lovers? We must keep watching.

At any moment the camera may move on past them and concentrate on the two men we can see conversing just beyond; but just now the graybeard's hand seems to rest on his heart: this is a tense if fleeting exchange.

The whole painting is a frame from a larger story, a film of urban life in which these fish and that tower and the light on the figures of passersby play parts as dramatic as the actors'. This woman shows neither her face nor her hands, just like De Witte's other lady at the keyboard; but the contents of her mind are made similarly noticeable through the back of her head, while we watch all the other hands, the other faces, and the open-mouthed fish address her. The whole harbor is engaged in the confrontation with this lady at this moment. And so the whole city is now the chamber, the visualization of the inner self; and yet nothing is really happening. Once again it is only the moving areas of light on transitory things (the shadow of the pail on the velvet skirt) and the unfinished relation of these quiet bright figures to each other and to their ground that create the sense of crucial private incident in process.

The more distantly focused city views of Berckheyde have a similar cinematic glitter that keeps a neutral flavor from predominating. The subjective look given to Delft by Vermeer from his contemplative viewpoint across the water is here given to Haarlem in quite another style (6.11). We are

6.11 GERRIT BERCKHEYDE, *The Marketplace at Haarlem*

again moving across the square, expecting a movielike encounter. The city itself is a matrix for unnameable personal drama; its image is like the inside of our head. Whatever happens to us will find a reflection in its physical features. By contrast, the topographical painter Van der Heyden keeps the view a backdrop, and the flavor picturesque. We admire but we are not inexplicably drawn, as we are by Berckheyde's shadows and De Witte's actors, or unaccountably moved, as we are by Vermeer's Delft.

The theme of emotionally charged architecture was transmitted to later epochs through the topographical tradition in other countries; but it was begun by these Dutch artists, who could make the look of a detached perspectival rendering seem to embody a personal condition. It was often most effectively done, as in De Hooch, by inventing the scene so that it looked absolutely real but was in fact a composite or a fantasy. And like the best cinematic fantasy, it has the absolute authority of detail and atmosphere one sees in dreams.

The other kind of staged, or conscious, architectural fantasy was a common enough theme in painting, including Dutch painting; but the satisfaction it gave was usually that of acknowledged artifice. Certain stagelike kinds of movie have used the same device: Hollywood versions of ancient Rome, like *Cleopatra,* for example, have been given that same thrilling look of deliberately extreme invention. But De Witte's church, home, or exterior settings have a total authority that comes from very selective, sensitive editing. They are like Harry Horner's sets for William Wyler's 1949 film *The Heiress,* in which an impossibly arranged and proportioned New York townhouse was built and photographed to produce a completely authentic one for the eye and the mind. This effect was not accomplished by the use of expressive distortion, but rather of cunning placement and lighting, so that the house was more, and not less, plausible for being a fiction, just like certain of De Witte's sets. He naturally did real ones, too. Like any great production-designer, he could both record and create facts.

In Dutch art, even in all Northern art since the fifteenth century, as well as in movies, the aim is not to be purely "documentary," but to use perfect realism specifically in order to create the perfect fantasy space: only there will inner dispositions—to religious awe, to fear and love, to embarrassment, amusement, and sexual excitement—unfold and breathe and come to life as outward and visible situations.

A L P E R S , Sutton, and others have pointed out that few if any preparatory drawings were made for Dutch paintings, no careful studies for their separate parts, wherein the artist could watch himself fashioning the picture into its perfect state, controlling and conceiving it at every stage. The

Dutch works were apparently wrought directly onto the painting surface, just like the quick sketches these artists also made. These sketches are often more like distinct and separate whole versions of the paintings, not studies. Only later, after they were finished, were paintings engraved and expatiated upon in graphic form, often with titles and captions added. Originally, however, they were immediate visions spontaneously realized.

Paintings were made in enormous numbers in the Netherlands at this period. It was an industry like film, unsupported by academic institutions or traditional theories about canonical practice, but instead done by artists profiting from one another's practical example, borrowing each other's themes and effects, and collaborating without needing justification from theoretical sources or ancient prototypes. Like movie-makers, these artists served a market and worked quickly along lines that had proved successful. As with movies, much bad stuff was produced.

But most Dutch seventeenth-century history painting and much genre painting in fact had their sources in the cumulative storehouse of graphic art. The print media had great scope in Holland, where both Catholic and Protestant texts were published during the earlier decades of religious strife. Printed pictures shared in the increasing power of printed material all over Europe. Consequently the many Dutch scenes of household life did not mind showing their debt to Dutch printed illustrations from preceding generations, especially the ones by Van de Venne for Jacob Cats' rhymed homily called *Houwelyck,* or *Marriage,* which was a best-seller in its time. The connection between such popular pictures and seriously thought-out paintings like Vermeer's was easy to make in the Netherlands, where picture-making had no serious philosophical pretensions but plenty of moral and psychological freight, just as film had in the early days of its success.

The refined artistic goals that Vermeer and De Hooch set for themselves were their own business, and no doubt keenly interesting to other artists; but they seem to have been detached from the public prestige of any artist himself. The role of the painter was elevated, but not abstract and conceptual in the modern mode. One sign of this was the vast range of both style and quality in the work of many individual Dutch artists, whose creative pride was not apparently bound up in being poets and thinkers, who might offer self-referential messages about pictorial language, as poets did about language itself. It has been suggested that they were perhaps more like anatomists and geographers, natural philosophers of the eye. But painters were also like plain graphic illustrators supplying an eager, developing market for visual art. Like illustrators at any epoch, they were respected for superior skill and effectiveness and not for dedication to artistic principles that set them apart from their customers.

The great similarity of theme in so much secular Dutch art itself suggests the pressure of such a market, as does the thematic similarity in the hundreds of movies made before television, and in television dramas ever since. The somewhat strict classification of Dutch themes suggests the same thing: still-life, seascape, winter scene, domestic interior, Bible story, all fulfilling expectations the way Western, war film, romantic comedy, caper movie, and historical spectacular do. High standards were developed and serious artists were not unappreciated; but no sharp conceptual division needed to exist between the creative aims of the painter and an effort to please the picture-loving public. Graphic artists past and present were perceived to share in those same aims. Producing pictures meant satisfying certain popular requirements founded on all the earlier pictures that had reached a profitable market. Breaking artistic ground could be accomplished discreetly or indiscreetly within those limits.

But printmaking was now an even bigger business, a collective enterprise organized to produce a commodity. As in the modern graphic modes, including film, different kinds of printed product were aimed at different consumers, and prices and quality varied enormously. Certain painters' works were reproduced, but by no means all, and many reproductions badly debased the pictures even while they spread the artist's fame. Such reproductive prints were often crude workshop artifacts, not sensitive artistic renderings; and they helped to create the uneasy and still-unresolved relation between refined graphic art and cheap commercial printing—a relation that has always been complicated by the simultaneous existence of bad or boring artistic graphics and very good commercial art.

Printmaking was officially done by artisans, and picture painting by artists. But there had always been great printmaking painters, especially in Northern Europe, and very sophisticated reproductive engravers. In the seventeenth century, however, the expanding print-market caused the graphics business to fragment further. Print selling became an enterprise separate from those of artists, craftsmen, and printers, and print collecting itself became a new kind of prestigious and cultivated custom. A separation was thus forced between the excellence of a print's design and that of its execution—a bad or silly picture could make a rare and costly print, and an exquisite major painting could be crudely engraved and cheaply sold, as if it were on a par with a topical caricature.

The same workshop might do occasional and topographical prints recording the looks of events and places for posterity, as well as suave and expensive reproductive engravings or debased stereotypical reproductions and political prints—and there would be no distinction made among these kinds of art object. Serious painters obviously needed to control the reproduction of their own works in such a climate; and their impulse to do independent graphic work of their own was, moreover, encouraged by the general increase in demand.

Rembrandt and Rubens both organized their own printmaking and picture-reproduction workshops. Rembrandt's paintings, with their many daring innovations applied to standard subjects, sometimes provoked hostile or ambivalent reactions; but his prints succeeded very well in the new print-collecting trend that had affected artistic patronage. Prints actually made by known artists themselves, not by professional print-shops, had the special prestige of both rarity and excellence. Rembrandt not only reproduced his paintings but translated his sketches into etchings, thus making acceptable salable art out of them, too. And so he put them into circulation on his own terms, and into the general stream of visual consciousness—the new graphic world, where his paintings themselves could then penetrate even more effectively.

This desire, to make a potent new art that would quickly engage the viewer simply by dramatically enhancing the familiar medium of black-and-white printed pictures, is a cinematographic impulse. It suggests the wish to concentrate on emotional change, to persuade, to exert power directly over the mind through the eye, as Hitchcock says he was so proud of doing in *Psycho* by using the effects of "pure film." It demonstrates the force of art in life, which is very different from expounding its meaning. The appeal and the assertion are emotional, psychological, and imaginative, not ideological, even in the pious mode. Such works need not muster feeling in any special political or religious cause; their business is to show how easily specific and specifically rendered visions may govern the imagination, and illustrate the soul's inner story.

In the different states of *The Entombment,* for example, we can watch Rembrandt changing the lighting and playing with the mood and texture of the same scene, recasting it again and again, as if recording on film the emotional effect of deepening shadow and ebbing light (6.12, 6.13). Such unique dramatic scenes that Rembrandt invented could be published as prints in succeeding generations, and through their powerful use of chiaroscuro and characterization, they could make a direct claim on public attention, and so foster a new visual and emotional understanding of all graphic possibilities—as great movies have done for us. Meanwhile the large body of other prints gave compositional arrangements, topical material, ideas for costume, setting, and gesture to artists less privately ambitious who were eager to sell and succeed. New reproductions of old paintings did the same.

The black-and-white printed world thus came to hold visual art in solution, not just in the North but all over Europe. The sense of graphic reality

6.12   REMBRANDT VAN RIJN, *The Entombment.*
Etching, first state

was enlarged by a new general understanding of graphic poetry. Mindful of Dürer and Holbein, Rembrandt and Rubens were acutely of their own time in seizing personally on the graphic medium to ensure their personal artistic power—this ensured their immortality far more efficiently than their paintings alone could have done. Rembrandt's idiosyncratic narrative methods made him internationally famous because his prints, not his paintings, could go everywhere, including into the incalculable artistic future.

Light and shade, the essential components of photographic and cinematographic art, were first given their true freedom by Rembrandt, their decisive enlargement into the imaginative world. Moving-camera poetry was made possible for future generations by him. He could not have done it without the support of all the other enterprising printmakers of the seventeenth century, partly because so much artistic accomplishment was mortgaged to printmaking; and the future would judge works of art by whatever

6.13 REMBRANDT VAN RIJN, *The Entombment.*
Etching, fourth state

the standards of graphic translation allowed it to perceive of them. But it was Rembrandt who single-handedly raised the stakes, and set the standard the camera would have to meet.

Rubens ran a large operation, training engravers to produce hundreds of reproductions of his works. Many of these were never touched by the master himself, but all carried his authoritative solutions to artistic problems into the studios of countless artists. Rubens was nevertheless not a specifically graphic visionary like Rembrandt, who kept restlessly and recklessly combining and inventing techniques to achieve the desired effect, unmindful of a future life for the plate or immediate commercial success for the print. Rembrandt also owned hundreds of prints himself, and kept reworking the work of others in past graphic history. Some of his translations might well come under the heading of cinematization, within the graphic tradition itself. His *Holy Family with a Cat,* for example, is found-

6.14 REMBRANDT VAN RIJN, *The Holy Family with a Cat.* Etching

6.15 ANDREA MANTEGNA, *The Virgin of Humility.*
Engraving

ed on Mantegna's *Virgin of Humility* in such a way that, in A. Hyatt Mayor's words, "the upward look that Mantegna uses to awe ... here turns into the small child's familiarity with the undersides of chairs and tables. Far from copying Mantegna's image, Rembrandt developed unsuspected implications in its canonized theme" (6.14, 6.15). The implications are in the emotional capacities of the graphic medium itself, not in the Virgin herself—how biting, inking, and printing from a plate can be used to escalate the immediate, personal properties of the hieratic image, and make us forget the "awesomeness" either of artistic skill or of holy persons.

Mayor also points out how Rembrandt gradually intensifies and cinematizes the old theme of Christ Presented to the People. For the first state of his etching, he put in his own brilliant row of the conventional foreground spectators that everyone used to put in; but then he decided to eliminate them entirely for the seventh and last state, substituting dark arches that open into the depths of the prison (6.16). "He suddenly puts opera glasses to our eyes, pulling us into the void over the twin prison inlets to set us face to face with Christ and Pilate. We now live inside the vision, oblivious to the calculations that went into its making, oblivious to the twenty years needed to get to the bottom of two hundred or three hundred words of reporting, oblivious even to the paper and the ink." The truly cinematic artist seems to vanish entirely, leaving us confronting the scene without help.

Rembrandt seems to have felt no sharp divide between painting and graphic art and, indeed, to have been convinced that both were "graphic" in my larger sense, as Elsheimer seems also to have felt. Rembrandt used paintings as if they were super-etchings enabling him to expand his graphic imagination. His combined painterly and graphic effort suggests that he never invested in paint for itself, like Rubens, or in inked lines for themselves, as Dürer did, but rather in that audience-involving kind of picture-making that transcends the medium, and sometimes makes pictures unbearable to look at. *The Descent from the Cross* is one of these, with the painter's own face shown pushed up against the collapsing body's cold, fleshy stomach (6.17). So is *The Blinding of Samson,* where not just the victim's fists and face but his toes are clenched in agony, and we have to watch the stake go deftly into the eye, the blood spurt; and our sickened fascination is mirrored in the faces of the soldiers and servants and in the hysterical Delilah rushing out but looking back (6.18).

The *Samson* is a huge painting on a deliberately overwhelming subject, but the *Descent* is much smaller and cooler, and also a standard subject in any Passion series. Rembrandt's graphic eye holds these different sorts of

6.16 REMBRANDT VAN RIJN, *Christ Presented to the People*. Etching, seventh state

6.17 REMBRANDT VAN RIJN, *The Descent from the Cross*

6.18 REMBRANDT VAN RIJN, *The Blinding of Samson*

6.19 REMBRANDT VAN RIJN, *Joseph and Potiphar's Wife*. Etching

picture to one sort of narrative mode, which is also shared by the tiny etch-ing of *Joseph and Potiphar's Wife*—another standard theme. This intimate black-and-white scene is no less demanding and unbearable than the vast *Samson* with its vivid hues and busy cast (6.19). The woman's hunger-ing, piglike body and Joseph's revulsion have graphic claims equal to those of the *Samson* or the Deposition—there is nothing more intense in the use of one medium or the other, of large or small size. Violent clash or contact, bad moments of all kinds fit equally well into small etchings or large paintings, and into fast sketches, too. All are storyboards, nothing is fixed.

In the painting of *The Raising of Lazarus,* made about 1630, and the etching on the same subject from about 1632, we see one scene from two different points of view, rendered in two different media and lit from op-posing directions (6.20, 6.21). The etched version is also less than half the size of the painting, and yet the grouping and the dramatic conception are the same. It is as if he did two takes with two cameras of the same group of actors, only changing the angle and the light source. Which is best? Both are best; we can move from one to the other.

Classicizing artists tended to save fluidity for sketches, and made mon-uments when they came to paint. The result is a world of expressive differ-ence between Guercino's volatile drawings, for example, and his stately paintings. By contrast, those in love with the feel of media, like Rubens, vis-ibly enslaved them all to the same uniform and conspicuous mastery. But Rembrandt's later painted surfaces are characterized by a great variability of texture, with thick impasto interspersed among areas of smooth glaze. Paint itself is not sovereign; its integrity within the picture is less compel-ling than its flexibility in serving the subject. The consistency of the scene, not of the medium or the style, must be preserved, however grand or mod-est the production.

The invention of mezzotint in the middle of the seventeenth century was a significant step in the advance of photo-graphic expression. This new tonal graphic method freed the reproducing of paintings and drawings from the mesh of engraved or etched lines that had bound it for so long to a "written" style. But since it was dependent on scraping the ink off the plate in varying degrees to produce the modeling, the technique used no precise lines, and it therefore turned out to be too crude for the most subtle reproduction of complex paintings. It served best as a method for repro-ducing portraits, where the tonal gradations of faces and garments could be particularly effective, and it was most extensively used in England in the eighteenth and early nineteenth centuries, where portraiture was a fa-vored genre. Rembrandt did not need to use this method; and his magical

6.20　REMBRANDT VAN RIJN, *The Raising of Lazarus*

6.21 REMBRANDT VAN RIJN, *The Raising of Lazarus.* Etching

way with etching had far more influence on later and lesser artists in the graphic tradition.

But although mezzotint did not immediately become the preferred reproductive technique, nor an instantly important creative medium like etching, it represented a new desire—some new need for a black-and-white medium with certain poetical possibilities different from engraving or etching, something with an emotional overtone beyond the reach of the crisp methods used before. It is not surprising that it found its best scope in Romantic times. Pure tone, mobile and free of line, could suggest what the moving camera also eventually offered: an analogue to pure vision free of knowledge, a leap from reading into unmediated seeing.

Portraits were adored not only in England. In France particularly, engraving techniques were perfected especially for portraiture, so that celebrities and grandees and beauties might all be fixed in slick pictures for the public. These were not just reproductions of privately commissioned paintings, but often done from drawings made especially to be engraved.

Van Dyck made his brilliant sequence of a hundred etched portraits early in the century, and his *Iconography* set a standard that later generations had a hard time matching. These portraits indeed had an earlier precedent at the dawn of the century in the work of Goltzius, another Fleming, whose dazzlingly versatile graphic skills had made him the most influential North European artist of his time (it was his pupils who later staffed Rubens' workshop). Among his other amazing performances, Goltzius made engraved portraits of a startling immediacy that was created mainly by sharp chiaroscuro. Van Dyck took this style further, adding a Baroque panache to the personal black-and-white image Goltzius had propounded. Van Dyck was a sort of double father of the public portrait, the founder not only of a peerless presentational style for the painted images of the great, but also of the perfect graphic mode for the same thing. He invented a way for distinguished printed pictures of interesting people to look that lasted well into this century and certainly influenced the camera, both moving and still, in its own further explorations of reproducible star imagery.

It did not happen immediately. The dashing modern look of his first etched portraits did not satisfy so well as the much silkier engraved versions, more similar to the French style, that were subsequently done from them. But later Romantic taste caught up with the sparkling dramatic style of his first examples. It was in these that Van Dyck inaugurated the method of defining the face in great detail, and then using an increasingly looser, sketchier technique for the clothing and hands and appurtenances as the image approached the edges of its frame. This dramatic scheme focuses attention on the face, just as the eye or the camera eye does, and suggests that the imprecision of peripheral vision is most suitable for everything else about the person. Ingres later used this device with exquisite skill in his finished portrait drawings. The effect is again one of emotional movement, from the hot center to the cooler edges.

Through the seductive graphic media of the later seventeenth century, portraits entered common visual fantasy rather than staying put on private walls. Portraiture took on the standardizing character that the modern famous photographs of celebrities have, their way of distilling personal looks so perfectly that forever afterward the person must resemble the picture in order to look right. Engraving extant portraits was a way of reproducing one kind of work of art among many; but the Van Dyck series suggested a new genre, the picture series of celebrated folk, intended to bring well-known personages to visual life for everyone's edification.

By the end of the seventeenth century, having your portrait painted had become an ordinary bourgeois thing to do, besides being a matter between great kings and great painters; but to have your portrait *engraved*—a much more expensive technical process—meant that a printmaker and a print publisher were prepared to invest in the sale of your image. You were usually an important official or a well-known nobleman or some kind of national figure, even notorious, whom the public might be expected to want to have a look at. Whether taken from a distinguished painting or not, such an engraved view would be rendered in the same sleek graphic language in which the journalistic camera now transmits our public figures, unmediated by an assertive artistic vision: the "art" lies in the editorial talent, while the "technique" is a technological given.

Rembrandt naturally demonstrates his preoccupations in a very different kind of portraiture. His kind makes the picture of a person seem like a movie scene with only one character in it, rather than a more captivating new example in the long portrait tradition. The sequence of nearly a hundred painted self-portraits shows this quality in particular; and the small one in Boston showing the young Rembrandt in his studio makes this point especially well (6.22).

The picture's small size draws the viewer, as it always does; but the curiously angled composition draws him further still into this scene inhabited by both the small, distant painter and his large, near easel, on which it is strongly suggested that the same self-portrait stands. This is a psychologically induced suggestion—the size and horizontal frame of the invisible painting make a self-portrait unlikely.

But the intense bond created between the man and his canvas in this little composition relates it in our minds to that endless and also somehow unbearable procession of self-portraits that seem like Rembrandt's autobi-

6.22 REMBRANDT VAN RIJN, *The Artist in His Studio.*

ography, full as it is of so many versions and guises and settings for one man's face. Each one of these, large and small, is like a whole scene. Something is going on inside the man's mind, inside the room, between the man and his audience, or the man and his conscience, or his memory, or his sense of humor. Or his art. And so this canvas must be this very painting, and we, the world, are only a great sheet of mutable reflecting glass.

The third principal character in this little group is the pool of light that vibrates in the space between the painter and his easel like an angelic presence. The painter stands back to allow it room, his own eyes in shadow: the painting holds up its face to receive it. This is not a simple painter's self-portrait but a moment full of sacred expectation.

The door at the right is another character. Like all the doors and beds and telephones in movies, it is there to suggest its possible use, before or even without its being used. If we are allowed to watch it like this, that means that sooner or later it will open—or perhaps it has just closed, or will soon be knocked at or hastily bolted from the inside. At this intimate artistic moment, the door suggests interruption. The client, the apprentice, the wife, the maid, the dog—something may at any minute disturb this silent colloquy between the artist, his light, and his surface: his shadowed eyes are wide open, partly with apprehension. Meanwhile we are also free, under the bright gaze coming at us from the back of the room, to believe that we are simply the model ourselves, syndics or burgesses locked in with this close-knit triad, waiting to make a fourth.

The zoom effect in this painting, like the one in Vermeer's *Officer and Laughing Girl,* is a device for extending the use of standard perspectival methods and insisting on optical depth. It keeps the action from looking as if it were staged at a fixed distance, and instead indicates that we must be included in it, by invoking the way our eye would grasp it if we were actually present. Although this picture is small, and even because it is, we are drawn first near to it, then into it: the picture plane seems to vanish. The Dutch peep-boxes designed in the seventeenth century by Hoogstraten and others produced the same in-drawing effect by mechanical means, for the same sense of exciting entertainment that early peep-show movies offered. The ordinary world drops away; one is rapt inside the tiny illusion. It is not surprising that pornography should be shown this way. Cinema altogether, however large the screen, issues this same personal invitation to each viewer, isolates him and captures him.

In Rembrandt's famous portrait etching of Jan Six reading at a window, made twenty years later in another medium and another city, we get the same sense of scene rather than setting, with light as one of the characters (6.23). The man's open collar invites the incoming air and so also seems to invite the inward flow of the daylight he is seeking by the window. We can see that nothing else but light is out there; indoors is where all the thought, feeling, and action dwell. But unless light enters, the page is unintelligible, the room is full of nameless obstacles, the relations among creatures are reduced and primitive. The ease of the man's attitude as he stands enlightened in his window corner shows him to be a confident light seeker, much at home with printed matter—the searching light finds another open book nearby, the mere topmost of a whole pile.

But earlier moments in this very same scene were recorded by Rembrandt in a sketch full of busy strokes (6.24). Here Jan Six is playing with the dog, moving gradually back up against the window ledge to resist the dog's happy advances; and here the sketch shows that light matters very little—the encounter is swift, basic, and tactile. Soon, however, the servant

6.23 REMBRANDT VAN RIJN, *Jan Six Reading.* Etching

calls off the dog, the relieved Six settles more comfortably on his elbow and
picks up the pamphlet. He begins to concentrate, and the waiting daylight
responds promptly with a knowing caress. Under that touch sound dies,
steps and barks recede, attention turns inward, and the eye alone moves in
the room. The one picture is not a sketch for the other, but another frame
from the same episode, just like many Dutch drawings related to paintings.
Moreover, the different moment from the same event is conceived in a different but related medium, as if to demonstrate the mutability that is right
for true visual narration.

And so in Rembrandt portraiture becomes narration, just like self-portraiture, in the cinematic mode. In all his various media the theme is irradiated, mobilized, and made to share in the fluid and suggestive atmosphere of daily living and inward change, or in the hush of holy apparitions, even when there is nothing in the picture but a face. Only Rembrandt seems to have created a body of portraits with this expectant quality. The individuals painted by Frans Hals, for example, are quite different: his works are much more like the brilliant portrait photographs by Irving Penn, where the look of a single personal instant seems eternal, caught forever in one miraculous flash.

6.24 REMBRANDT VAN RIJN, *Jan Six with a Dog.*
Drawing

7.1 JAN VERKOLJE, *An Elegant Couple in an Interior*

SEVEN

French Prints; Watteau, Chardin

Ｂｙ Ｔ Ｈ Ｅ last quarter of the seventeenth century, most Dutch painters had moved away from Rembrandt's unmediated style toward a more suave and elegant tone. French esthetic taste irradiated Europe during the Sun King's reign, and even the painters of Holland were not immune to the impulse, until then lacking in the Netherlands, toward academism and the establishment of rules for art. But the results of French influence among the genre painters were quite haunting and romantic, even while history painters like De Lairesse produced classical machines of entirely un-Dutch sleekness and grandeur. The cinematic vision so thoroughly refined in Dutch art at mid-century was not abandoned, but reworked into a glossier and more self-conscious product.

We have seen that De Hooch's genre scenes in the late 1670's and 1680's, after he went to Amsterdam, were often removed from the lifelike domestic settings he had favored in Delft. He now sometimes made them occur in fanciful palaces, as if purposely to reveal the kind of elegant idealization he wished to describe—a Hollywood-like luxury world, looking perfectly real with real shadows and highlights, real dogs and musical instruments, but only convincing because so perfectly fantasized. And as movies remind us, the point about fantasy is the perfect details. The moody lighting and equivocal action in the late De Hooch works sustain his cinematic style in their new luxurious milieu, but they acquire a new emotional dimension that conspicuous leisure permits: physical self-awareness, the sense of playing a role and making an appearance. For this, one needs models.

Other painters seem to have emphasized this very possibility in late-seventeenth-century affluent life by referring to earlier, unselfconscious ways of living. The scene, for example, by Jan Verkolje from 1674 called *An*

Elegant Couple in an Interior looks like a Hollywood film version of a Vermeer or a Terborch (7.1). This pair see themselves romantically in such old-fashioned terms, while at the same time they like to enjoy the new refinements of upper-class life that improved on the older simplicities. She wears a gauzy veil around her head and shoulders, to mystify her beauty and complicate her movements with a feigned impediment to true perception; the window has draped curtains for the same purpose, to embellish, romanticize, and pretend to impede the light.

Just as in Hollywood, the figures of these two are rendered especially attenuated and crisp: their hair is an attractively neatened version of the artless curls in earlier modes. Fashion itself, if art may be the witness, was creating these very refinements in late-seventeenth-century dress—shortening the sleeve, tightening the waist, editing the coiffure for both sexes. For men the result would soon be the great periwig that was to put so vivid a stamp on all male looks for more than a hundred years. Verkolje's gentleman, besides his newly neat leg and neat waist, has much more beautifully articulated curls than any similar gallant in Terborch's cast of characters.

Both puritanical and military modes are out. The new fashions initiated at Versailles were having their effect on everything, and details not only of dress but of erotic manners seem to have been sharpened up. As the lady picks up her instrument, she momentarily rests her knee on the chair—a more indecorous and also more artful gesture for legs than formerly. Now he actually takes her hand to make her turn her elegant neck (how seductively the veil moves) and overtly points to his viol, suggesting a—er, duet. These two are both less sexually discreet and less naturally behaved than Terborch's couples. They dispose their legs with artificial abandon and part their moist lips while they lift their eyebrows slightly, studying one another's style. As usual, the dog feels the tension and questions the action, here perhaps puzzled by the lack of straightforwardness. In this encounter, there is not much spontaneous feeling needing strict control; the scene is a studied exercise in amorous good form.

The indication of a carefully schooled leisure is the right note to strike, the flavor of court etiquette governing the discovery of love and all subsequent pursuits of pleasure, and importing a modish whiff of rarefied depravity. Since the painter uses the props and setting and narrative form of earlier and simpler Dutch lovers' meetings—musical instruments fingered in a lofty daylit chamber—we are free to see this as a pointed nostalgic reference, on the part of both the director-painter and his actor-lovers.

Gotfried Schalcken was another late-seventeenth-century genre painter who liked to refer to earlier themes in deliberately romanticized style, as if making a historical movie. In his work the effect is quite poignant, never stagy, only heightened, refined, and self-conscious. In Schalcken's small paintings, and in the genre works of Van der Werff before he began to do classical history-paintings, the characters often adopt a new kind of amused and conscious smile, which is quite different from Jan Steen's salacious grins of earlier days, as well as from the straight and radiant smile of Vermeer's girl. In *The Doctor's Visit,* however, we have tears, daintily dabbed with an apron (7.2). Schalcken was a pupil of Gerard Dou, as the small format, delicate lighting, and sweeping drapery here demonstrate,

7.2 GOTFRIED SCHALCKEN, *The Doctor's Visit*

but much more cinematically inclined. These two figures look away from
each other, the slender girl moving off in distraction, the doctor concentrating on the urine in the flask. He is speaking, gravely and ruefully; she
clutches her bosom, her lips tremble, and her eyes fill, for all the world like
Lana Turner in a 1940's woman's picture, as she discovers she's pregnant.

The Doctor's Visit had been a standard comic and moralizing theme for
Dutch painters earlier in the century. It was used by both Dou and Steen,
often to poke fun at the pompous doctor character (who was also a familiar
stage figure) or to giggle at the signs of female licentiousness (see 5.8).
Here, however, we have a bit of authentic sentimental drama with no snig-
gering, a small middle-class tragedy actually in process. The girl is sweet,
the old doctor wise and sober, the situation very sad in the best romantic
style. The framing, grouping, and lighting have the arbitrariness and immediacy of film, different from Dou's staged tableaux or Steen's
bumptious farces. The feathery technique gives a play of possible movement to the figures, the look of breathing that Dou's smooth paintings lack.

Another Schalcken, now in Florence, is one of several fashionably erotic
fantasy portraits he painted, the kind of thing no Dutch painter would have
done in earlier years (7.3). Here is the modern smile that is almost a
simper, a come-hither glance cast in a new romantic style of sexuality, a Rococo vision enhanced by the candle flame that dances suggestively out from
behind the little hand with its crooked pinky. And yet the lighting effects,
derived from Honthorst, Elsheimer, Rembrandt himself, give her real life
and freshness. The "graphic" ideal is intensified: the candlelight is there
to reduce other colors and focus the feelings, in this case on mystery and
intimate excitement. She is a synthetic vision, like a pinup, a long way from
Vermeer's *Head of a Young Girl,* and moving closer to commercial art, popular illustration, and the movies.

In fact, not just earlier artistic themes but the influence of fashion art
apparently intervened between Schalcken and his model, and between Verkolje and his lovers. It placed a filter over the direct rendering of human
situations that would permanently complicate and enrich the cinematic
view of things. By the 1680's, series of *figures de mode* were a standard
feature of graphic art, and they must have been an important element in the
subsequent sense of personal looks. Such fashion prints are not to be confused with commercial fashion plates intended to encourage sales—these
were not in existence until the late eighteenth century. More important,
they are sets of typical figures exemplifying fashionable dress among certain groups, including fancy-dress and theatrical character dress expressed in modish terms. They gave a presentational style to what was
already worn, rather than suggesting what might be worn next (7.4–7.6).

7.3 GOTFRIED SCHALCKEN, *Lady with a Candle*

By the end of the seventeenth century, with the institutionalization and academization of French crafts, and especially with the raising of engraving itself by edict to the rank of liberal and not mechanical art, the French were by far the best designers and reproducers of such costume prints. Not only were French personal luxuries the most refined and desirable in Europe, but their superiority was confirmed by the superior French version of complete personal chic, purveyed in superior fashion prints, portrait prints, and prints of fashionable life.

In the first three decades of the seventeenth century, Jacques Callot and Abraham Bosse had fixed the international image of elegance as essentially French, well before Louis XIV instituted the economic policies that fixed its practical reality. By the time the elaborate rituals of noble idleness had been organized at Versailles, and all the luxury goods used there were manufactured in France, and the academies had been founded, French engravings—which also came to be strictly regulated as to printing, publication, and sale—had long since established their absolute authority as images of

Above left: 7.4 J. D. DE
ST-JEAN, *Suit Worn with a
Sword.* Fashion print, 1670's.
Formal courtly elegance.
Above: 7.5 J. D. DE ST.-JEAN,
Lady Walking in the Country.
Fashion print, 1670's. Stiff but
sprightly leisure clothing.
Left: 7.6 J. D. DE ST.-JEAN,
Gentleman of Quality.
Fashion print, 1690's. Casual
Rococo style

Right: 7.7 JACQUES CALLOT,
figure of a nobleman from
La Noblesse lorraine, 1624

Below: 7.8 ABRAHAM BOSSE,
Shops under the Law Courts.
Etching, c. 1640

sartorial elegance. No prints of modish life by Van de Venne, Jost Amman, Caspar Luikon, Wenceslaus Hollar, or even Goltzius, charming and informative as they are, can possibly match the bravura and suavity of Callot, Bosse, or Jacques Bellange. All these registered in black and white the French genius for picturing fashion long before Louis XIV consolidated French power and caused French fashion itself to dominate Europe (7.7, 7.8).

By that time, a true fashion art, which can coerce the perception of desirable clothed appearance by the sheer force of graphic authority, had already been invented in France; and the later spread of actual French fashion was undoubtedly helped by the pictorial standard it had already set. Not only was an elegant French style of engraved portraiture ready to create the world's vision of great people's faces, but an elegant French engraved figure style also existed to create the visual style of life among them.

The graphic arts thus expanded in different directions and were more variously influential. A new understanding of their serious poetic possibilities, so astoundingly opened up by Rembrandt, now coexisted with new developments in reproductive techniques, but also with an increasing market for glossy fashionable imagery for its own sake. This last was something new, just as Rembrandt's graphic vision had been new; and both gave the public new styles in which to visualize the world and the people in it—in their own sphere, in the wide world, or in all imaginary universes. The way in which movies have done this in this century is well understood; but even with much more limited scope, prints clearly began to do it in earnest in the seventeenth century. The imaginative advances made by such superior artists as Elsheimer and Rembrandt, as well as those of Terborch and Vermeer, could be transmitted to future artists and to their public through the graphic media, where visual ideas mix together and do their most potent work on the imagination and the common sense of reality. Fashionable looks on the French model were now added to the mixture.

During this same century, pictorial journalism increased. While French fashions in engraving and in dress spread notions of elegance, the Dutch graphic artist Romeyn de Hooghe, for example, was also recording Louis XIV's persecution of the Protestants in dramatic broadsheets that show the influence of both Callot and Rembrandt. Printed broadsheets were appearing on all sorts of political and moral subjects, most of them in Northern Europe, where the graphic impulse was so strong and where the overlap of high and popular art was already considerable. Film and television now continue what was begun there and then: the marketing of topical, sentimental, comic, or sensational themes, in graphic media that freely borrow from the whole range of previous visualizations—high and low, rough and sleek, ancient and recent.

Such popular media create visual *assumptions,* after original painters or printmakers have created new visual ideas. The repetition, reduction, and reuse for popular themes of borrowed original motifs transmute them into habits of the eye, so they convey their impact almost unnoticeably, even subliminally, to the picture-viewing public—artists included, of course. Original artists of a later day may then make unconscious use of these same assumptions, besides deliberately learning from earlier artists and consciously inventing new motifs. The new and exquisite fashion prints of the seventeenth century contributed to the figure style of serious painters, not only at the time but eventually in the eighteenth century, when the cumulative effect of such prints, good and bad, had succeeded in redesigning bodies in a new style. There was a new agreement about clothed appearance in both art and life that only print media could have created.

It was serious French style rather than serious French art that had affected Schalcken and Verkolje. Their themes and idiom were firmly Dutch. More relevant to the development of painting was the influence in the other direction of that Dutch idiom on French art, which in turn was to be so powerful in the future, not the least because of the French reproductive techniques that made it famous.

The assimilation of Dutch art by French painters produced those two great favorites of modern taste, Watteau and Chardin. The works of both were quickly and comprehensively engraved, with titles and captions added to reinforce their appeal and ensure their influence in their own time. Watteau's short career was thus immediately extended well past his death in 1721, so that he now can seem to embody the entire eighteenth century, even though he died well within its first quarter. This is partly because his instigation of a new kind of French painting coincided with the shift in French civilized life that began near the end of Louis XIV's reign and continued past the middle of the century.

Paris, not Versailles, became the center of culture and fashion; smaller ducal and princely courts near Paris, more chic and much more liberal than the royal court, made more use of Parisian talent. Urban taste developed in opposition to official court style, and increasingly represented variety, pleasure, and vitality as the rigid courtly modes congealed further. Watteau, for all his outdoor settings, was a wholly urban artist. The milieu for which he painted was a mixture of cultivated financiers and industrialists, lesser nobility who had escaped from court life to Paris, and the artistic, literary, and theatrical people who gave city life its newly acquired refinement. The dreams in Watteau's art are city dreams. They consequently come true in terms of constant personal encounter, individual feeling, and the certainty of nothing but the uneven movement of experience—that is, in the urban imaginative mode. They are set in the kind of outdoors dreamed up (and often arranged for) by city-dwellers to seem as much as possible like overlapping sequences of intimate rooms—a suburban and not a rural paradise, where elegant clothes may be worn to advantage while behavior may nevertheless be spontaneous.

These parks are not imaginary. They are probably modeled on the grounds of the actual suburban houses of Watteau's friends and patrons, where informal costume parties, amateur plays, and concerts of the sort he shows did in fact take place. There people could combine and recombine in small groups or couples in a new style of comfortable upper-class pleasure that was quite refreshing, after the long ascendancy of formal public entertainment at Versailles. In cities, the pursuit of personal relations for private satisfaction may be the acknowledged aim of leisure, whereas at court, court politics and court etiquette and constant visibility must combine to govern the forms legitimate recreation may take. Privacy has no priority.

In Paris, but not at Versailles, pleasure could now be openly sought in refining new styles of intimacy; and for rendering these personal themes in art, the Dutch mode was obviously the most sophisticated. The genre mode in art had lately been brought to a higher pitch in Holland than ever in France or elsewhere. The realm of the personal had been thoroughly explored, partly because most purchasers of paintings were both urban and private, neither courtly nor ecclesiastical. Religious art had acquired the same personal, experiential style—the cinematic disposition—that Watteau could now exercise on his cast of city characters. His significant park statuary is analogous to the significant paintings hanging on those Dutch walls, as delicately ironic comment about the progress of personal life became the right note to strike in France. Patronage was now often in the hands of enlightened private connoisseurs who followed their own taste, rather than an academically controlled official enterprise. History painting was losing its supremacy, and within the Academy, "Poussinistes" were losing out to "Rubénistes" in the current argument about truthful representation. "Naturalism" was again admired, and the value of emotional impact in works of art. "Sensibility" became a virtue.

W H I L E the Dutch were learning erotic and sartorial crispness and systematic art theory from the French, French collectors were beginning to appreciate Dutch and Flemish art more intensively, and French artists to profit from studying them at first hand in private collections. Watteau became acquainted with Dutch paintings, prints, and drawings in his patron Crozat's collection, besides being able to study Rubens' Medici cycle in the Palais de Luxembourg. The delicacy of touch, the famous light-bearing brushwork of the Northern painters, like their subject matter, was beginning to look better to the French than the sober clarity of the Baroque classical school. The kind of art with personal meaning began to appeal more than heroic themes. The secularization of culture was an added element in this shift of French taste as the eighteenth century advanced; and so in Watteau's art, borrowed from the Protestant North, the personal realm was shown extended not by a religious or mythological dimension, but by a theatrical one.

Watteau shows how theater can be an analogue for religion and mythology, a psychological rather than a spiritual domain within which the meanings of personal life may be perpetually enhanced. Such a function was in fact being partly fulfilled by the actual theater in Paris at the time, providing a stylistic center for the city's new cultural life; role playing, the exercise of wit, the pursuit of personal drama, and the display of personal attractions could all be fostered in the atmosphere of a stage tradition newly liberated for the purpose.

There were only two officially recognized and subsidized stages in France, the Opéra and the Comédie. These two performed the classical repertoire. But private companies had long been in existence, appearing in comedies and farces both in traveling shows and at the twice-yearly fairs in Paris for extended runs. The Italian comedy, which had been expelled in 1697, returned in 1719; and out of these eventually came the Opéra Comique. They all tended to parody the serious stage, to mix stock characters from the old Italian *commedia dell'arte* with distinctively French popular characters, and to combine romantic or comic drama with dance, song, mime, and acrobatics.

The world of such a theater became a kind of salon, a gathering place for intellectuals and artists and for the fashionable and intelligent rich, a milieu where the stage could be not only watched but written for, designed for, and appeared on, where actors and musicians were the valued friends of their cultivated audiences. Performers were not servants or playthings, nor were they remote creatures only to be courted and adored. The stock characters of the old scenarios were easily conceived as real people, momentarily dressed in stock costume as we see them in Watteau—to point up the fact that everyone, not just actors, may have many layers of being in a shifting urban world.

A theater of fashionable everyday living was thus being fostered in Paris; but Watteau's art suggests that it was perhaps more like the cinematization of leisure, the view of life as a continuous flow of suggestive, overlapping costumed scenes, in which no vulgar confrontations or dénouements disturb the sense of endless possibility. All this was based on an improvisatory sort of theater, in itself a reflection on the unforeseeable character of city life. The Fêtes Galantes were arranged in suburban parks, where amateurs might participate in performances and also be entertained by professionals; the "embarkations," "pilgrimages," "sacrifices," and "promenades" were got up to mix people together and create unexpected encounters with ambiguous meanings.

Fashion prints undoubtedly had a part in this scene-playing, style-conscious manner of elegant living. The costume plates of Picart, St.-Jean, and others had continued the tradition of Bosse and Callot in setting a uniformly elegant tone for sequences of very different figures. Watteau also did two series of them, one of *figures de mode* and the other of *figures de diverses caractères* (7.9). These were theatrical or regional or humorous figures with the same dashing style as those in the fashion prints. All such series had their original source in the sixteenth-century costume books, which showed class or regional distinctions for anthropological purposes; but the French engravers of the seventeenth century had gone on to create *stylistic* models, so that the figures' common style, and not their different costumes, came to be their main theme.

The academic, rule-making climate of culture under Louis XIV had fostered such an impulse, and many of St.-Jean's figures, for example, display a certain formal stiffness despite their elegance. But Watteau, with the influence of the Northern style at his command, continued the theme with new conviction. The extremely casual figures he sketched, apart from the ones published as prints in sequence, have the same sort of compelling chic as those created by modern fashion photographers who use the device of casual and even awkward action for their artificial arrangements. The men in Watteau's drawings and prints have an incredibly elegant length of leg and torso, a graceful gangliness of pose, and a magnificent nonchalance in the nice disarrangement of their clothes. It even improves on Callot in the quality of its apparently unstudied ease. Some of this Watteau undoubtedly learned from Van Dyck, whose drawings he copied—and it was this synthesis of Northern realism and French stylistic clarity that was one of France's most influential contributions to international fashion: the look of the total figure in its clothes, rendered (in a graphic medium that could be reproduced and eventually popularized) as both ideally elegant and perfectly natural at the same time.

The fashion camera and especially the movie camera have created the ideal anew in this century. Ever since Watteau, it has been something to

7.9 ANTOINE WATTEAU, *Man Walking,
Seen in Profile*. Etching, second state

live up to, a focus of aspiration; it has looked perfect, but *attainable*. As the prestige of courtly fashion gradually lost its importance, the capacity of graphic media to spread (among other things) an accessible-looking ideal of dressed elegance became obvious, and commercial fashion plates came into existence; but the visualization of the figure on which they depended had been invented by certain figurative geniuses of earlier days—Callot, Van Dyck, Watteau.

The women in Watteau's works show a particularly distinct shift from those in the fashion prints of a generation earlier (his elegant males are closer to their prototypes), and one particularly connected to Dutch art. Here again the movement of female sexual feeling is expressed through the excited play of light on satin skirts, through the slight tilt or dip or stiffening of the exposed neck, and through small gestures of the hand. The female figure is thus very eloquent when viewed from the back, where all these elements are more revealing without the face, which may deceive, as necks and moving skirts cannot.

Vermeer and Terborch had worked all this out long before, but it had never been seen in French art until Watteau reworked it in Rococo terms. Unlike the Dutch painters, and unlike Rubens, he makes feminine garments seem to weigh very little and to consist only of delicately bunched and wrinkled yardage—loose-sleeved and indistinct robes hitched up, pulled together, or drawn back, anchored only to some firm stays around the rib cage, which smooth it out to produce a well-defined bodice and décolletage. The waistline matters very little, the nacreous bare chest a great deal. And through the lightweight skirts poke the knees, constantly shifting position to catch the light and call attention to the agitation of hidden thighs and hidden responses. People of both sexes are only precariously and provisionally upright; they may loll and sprawl and lean at any moment, and then spring up again to dance (7.10).

The casual model for deportment set in Watteau's works has had a lasting effect. The unaffected quasi-awkwardness of all these refined movements gives them great appeal and, again, makes their world of leisure and

7.10 ANTOINE WATTEAU, *Peaceful Love*

pleasure seem accessible. This is partly because nothing much happens; nothing is very serious, exciting, or funny, only very suggestive and inconclusive while seeming very human. It is *in motion,* a realism of the feelings that dwells on transition and ambivalence just like the one De Hooch created for his late paintings.

Watteau's theatrical costumes, shown mingling with ordinary clothes and unaffected gestures, bring up the modern idea that all clothing is costume, permitting people to fancy themselves playing various parts for each other, and for their own private satisfaction. Sexual life is here visualized, as it was for the Dutch and as it is for us, in terms of fashion. This kind of art provides a sartorial expression of physical pleasure that deliberately stresses the uncertain character of sexual feeling—specifically, its "this-moment" character, which is linked to temporary guises, passing fads, perverse fantasies, and extreme whims, like fashion itself.

It is from these early days of the eighteenth century, perhaps from Watteau himself, that this idea springs—that fashion is itself the mobile vehicle of an equalizing eroticism, no longer just of class distinction. Popular theater helped to confirm this notion for him, as the movies have confirmed it for us. It does not mean that fashionable clothes must be conventionally sexy, with a lot of flash and exposure; on the contrary, fashions themselves may be simple and muted. But since they constantly change, it is the following of them that suggests sexuality, a subversive love for the richness of fantasy life, and a concomitant belief, perhaps inarticulate or only partially conscious, in the abiding importance of erotic feeling.

In seventeenth-century France, and in other absolute monarchies, it might be easy to see the following of fashion as another aristocratic pastime, a perverse sport of kings invoking not the crude display of rank or riches, which is unnecessary for royalty, but of imaginative self-definition, like the court masque. It might seem to be something geared to the special needs of aristocrats, including the formal restraint of their public sexual manners. The late-seventeenth-century fashion prints had supported the idea, with their elaborate details and stiff figure-compositions. But in Holland, Vermeer and his colleagues had shown how urban fashion in dress infuses private bourgeois feeling and defines the middle-class sexual self, not just its social pretensions. The specific details of fashion, whatever they are, become the conveyors of a changeable personal atmosphere, and hence of mutable sexual possibility.

This has been an important function of fashion ever since, a view patently argued by the whole history of popular movies and now by television, where the dress of people whose sexual feelings we are meant to take seriously is always a perfect example of a particular fashionable ideal. Their perfection is like that of a Watteau sketch or fashion figure, offering a completely current physical ideal of form and dress, whatever the social or occupational sphere of the character, conveyed in a graphic medium that can suggest absolute reality, not artistic license. Clothes are part of all ordinary sexual drama in movies; and it was Watteau, copying the Dutch, who inaugurated this way of using them.

Watteau's whole career has the flavor of unresolved movement that cinema promotes. His paintings were done directly, without plans or cartoons, and often so hastily that the paint failed to adhere and maintain a surface; but they were also slow to develop, inefficiently conceived, put together with that same chancy method now used for film, whereby there are many takes, much extra footage, and editing creates the final outcome. Watteau made thousands of quick sketches and then quickly cooked them into paintings, which nonetheless never seemed to get finished. He had begun as a hack, copying small Dutch paintings for the popular market. Later he lived in a marginal way in the houses of friends or patrons, and he left the world early, having always been surrounded by other people but remaining quite solitary, never settled or stable, as if he needed to keep moving on to the next scene. The screenlike veil of paint in his works is a refined version of Dutch chiaroscuro, a new fluid, almost moist atmosphere where living and feeling go on.

CHARDIN followed up Watteau's themes in new guises, still copying the Dutch and this time very openly. As a French painter, Chardin took a risk by sticking to genre and still-life themes without any allusion to the classical vocabulary even ironically, or through the theatrical metaphors employed by Watteau. It was nevertheless a timely move; his works satisfied the new desire for informality and were very well received. Children and adolescents frequently appeared as central characters, and their presence suggests an even stronger version than Watteau's of the new unaffectedness and mobility of physical being, the love of growth and change, even in a soap bubble.

One more feature of the late-seventeenth-century fashion prints that found its way into later French art was an extremely youthful facial style for both sexes. Smooth round cheeks, small chins, wide-open bright eyes, short noses, and fresh expressions pervade the paintings of Watteau, Chardin, Boucher, Greuze, and Fragonard: these are the same babyish French looks that revive in the works of Renoir and ultimately in the films of Brigitte Bardot. Chardin was prepared to show them as the property of actual children; but in his and some other French painters' works, the facial traits of extreme youth conveyed not only the quality of *douceur,* the gentle gravity associated with unselfconscious innocence, but also conveyed pure fashion, an echo of actual fashion art. And this echo also helps make Chardin's work moving, although perhaps covertly.

The childish facial style supports a stimulating look of chic in scenes of emphatic bourgeois simplicity, while on the surface it only suggests the slightly conscious artlessness for which Chardin's personnel are so famous, and that makes them seem so human—the little girl stealing a glance in the mirror, the boy gazing at his hat as it's brushed by his nurse. It's no wonder his genre paintings were well loved. They contain a double truth: the basic one about color, light, and feeling purveyed by Rembrandt, with whose name Chardin's was immediately associated; and the other, pervasive, but often unacknowledged one about the satisfactions of being perfectly dressed, which may go even deeper when carried in solution in a medium of unimpeachable realism. This is a main component in popular cinematic imagery, one of the things that make movies so inescapably riveting in their basic visual quality, before the acting and directing, the music and the editing even register.

Every single one of Chardin's characters has the straight, almost arched back of current fashion, a perfect figure, and a perfectly groomed head, perfectly fitting clothes (worn with stays even by humble women and girls), and extra-long legs (7.11). All are youthful and good-looking, whether they are laundry maids and cooks or ladies of the house and their children, whether well-to-do or very much less so. All deportment is graceful and becoming without exception, not just decent and circumspect: the lady examining embroidery with her daughter crosses her high-heeled shod feet with the aplomb of the Marquise de Pompadour (7.12). Faces have that same bright-eyed but restrained expressiveness we see in those of Watteau's silken revelers, and the same round cheeks and small chins from the engravings. No one is fat or bony, tired or overexcited, as people often are in Rembrandt. But the atmosphere has that truthful character Rembrandt conjures with his revelatory light, making unphrased action create an emotional presence, instead of describing the complete details of an incident. The modishness, too, is a matter of revelation; we are not belabored with description but made to swallow sartorial perfection in whole gulps.

Chardin's palette, like Rembrandt's and Watteau's, is essentially monochromatic, with strong color appearing only in ravishing patches, while tonality is really doing all the work. Single figures often gaze out of the frame, or turn their heads to prevent a direct view of the face, notably the celebrated little girl with a shuttlecock, whose face is also shadowed (7.13). Her features are quite dim, while her eyes are very wide. Any expression rendered with wide-open eyes in a shadowed face seems more appealing

7.11 J.-B.-S. CHARDIN, *The Return from Market*

ily living. It was ackno

versions of Chardin's c

which had rhymed capt

were often cast in amor

ness of these simple sce

This internalization o

dinary realism so as to e

characteristic of French

movies. It came about i

quisite French fashion p

of these earlier enterpris

to the classic and acade

but the supremely origin

were inspired to create t

or aristocratic patronage

Chardin invested his

emotional presence and i

groups. Personal charact

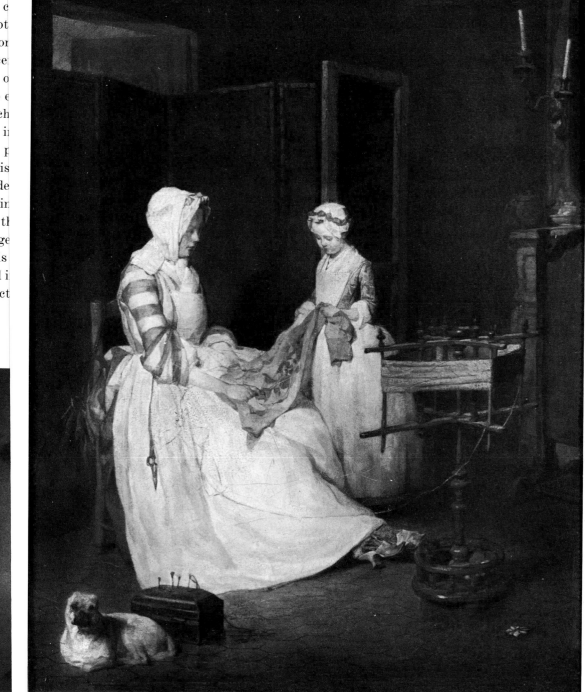

7.14 J.-

7.12 J.-B.-S. CHARDIN, *The Diligent Mother*

7.13 J.-B.-S

7.15 J.-B.-S. CHARDIN, *The Governess.* Engraving from the painting

than a brightly lit grima
in the Studio in Bosto
view, personal awaren
face, and finally show
(7.14). The little girl tu
moving across the roo
sight, and not obedient
her.

All the corseting an
whole fashionable dime
dertone that is well sub

as it is in dead ducks and eviscerated fish. The effect also arises from the cinematic impulse to register the movement of feeling in the process of recording motionless phenomena. These things make claims, they don't just sit there passively waiting for human lives to give them a point. They engage with one another like family members, and with us like fellow beings: This tiny onion, what is it thinking? How does it feel to sit alone, bathed in the light of this incandescent tumbler (7.16)? The odd choices and juxtapositions create such responses, since it looks as if the objects had all secretly agreed to meet, in defiance of the customary rules for gatherings on kitchen tables. The recently shot rabbit and partridge lie together in death like Romeo and Juliet. This easy use of the same atmosphere for domestic scenes and inanimate groups makes Chardin a magical painter; and the same quality that endeared him to the prophets and architects of modernism, that formal neutrality that first made painting seem to transcend its subject, is exactly what also makes him cinematic —or modern in the Alternative Convention, which can mythologize the whole world simply by putting a few phenomena in the right light.

7.16 J.-B.-S. CHARDIN, *Glass of Water and Coffeepot, with Onions*

8.1 G. B. TIEPOLO, *Apotheosis of the Pisani Family*

EIGHT
Tiepolo, Piranesi, Canaletto

I N   O R D E R   to explore the new emotional and formal possibilities
for French art suggested by Dutch painters of the past, Chardin rightly
forsook the grand themes of the Grand Siècle and confined his painterly
universe to the comfortable domestic interior or the artist's studio, where
he could concentrate on specific phenomena. He pursued his proto-
cinematic experiments without resorting to the mythic subject matter most
common to French painters of the past, or developing the modern myths invented by Watteau. But at the same moment and in the same cinematic
mode, the old mythologies were being reinvented in Italy by Giovanni Battista Tiepolo, who seems to have assimilated the Dutch example into the Venetian idiom. This artist is another, like Chardin, who was instantly
appreciated in his own time and much admired in modern times, with a
brief eclipse during the period of Romantic Neoclassicism.

Far from the secular tradition of portable paintings that could enter the
public awareness in a personal way, through gallery exhibition followed by
the sale of captioned reproductions, Tiepolo worked mainly in fresco on the
walls of palaces and villas, or else he did altarpieces for churches. Such endeavor continued the somewhat passé Renaissance tradition of public art,
which requires aggrandizing the image of a noble, civic, or ecclesiastical
patron, using the whole familiar lexicon of Classical, allegorical, and religious terminology.

Tiepolo used only the terminology. His formal language is resolutely un-
classical, specific, and phenomenological. Dramatic immediacy is guaranteed to all the scenes he directs, because he uses the optical mode,
perfected by Vermeer and his compatriots: Tiepolo's allegorical groups
aloft in the firmament have the same look Rembrandt managed, the look of
miracles recorded by an eyewitness; and again it's no wonder his empirical

age adored him, as our movie-loving age does, too. He brings fantasies directly to believable life, sidestepping the most handy, old pictorial tropes.

Unlike Rembrandt and Chardin, but just like Hogers and even Watteau, Tiepolo helped himself to specific theatrical usage to make his epiphanies credible. He offers both old-days clothes and pageant draperies, but they have not been fashioned according to time-honored fresco modes; instead, they are painted as if they were painstakingly built by the tailor's apprentices to last through a long run. The clothes in Tiepolo are palpably made of intractable taffeta and brocade—hemmed, lined, and interlined, and obviously quite heavy to handle while flying in a high divine wind or balancing on one inch of lintel (8.1).

Similarly, poses struck by intertwined beings perching on a tiny vertiginous molding right above our heads have the scrambled look real bodies might have in like circumstances. Their limbs form a jumble difficult to read, their torsos are compressed, and often only bits of a person appear—a shoulder and some hair, a chest and a hand, most often an isolated knee or kicking leg. Their garments also puff out and bunch up to form the ludicrous, somewhat abstract shapes loose cloth really takes, which are at odds with the poetic action of fabric so familiar in the classical phrases refined

8.2 G. B. TIEPOLO, *La Fortuna* (detail)

by Tiepolo's predecessors (8.2). You can see the air whipping under the stuff, just as you can feel the silken billow of it against the thighs and bellies of these actors, along with the moist condensation of the cloud into which the cherub's head is plunging.

Using obvious theater props and costumes creates a personal rapport between subject and viewer, as the Dutch artists knew; but Tiepolo disposes these hefty drapes and appurtenances in the eternal sky, still adorning fashion-bound and modern-looking bodies and borne up by the only truly realistic clouds in the history of ceiling art. As much as the effortless perspective, Tiepolo's clouds are what make the active air and light in his fictions so effective. Their verity alone authenticates the visions, in more than one way. There is always a large amount of formless empty space in Tiepolo frescoes, just as there so often is in an actual cloudy sky. Water vapor takes various forms, often several at once; and the satisfying cumulo-nimbus formations that many artists have thought best able to support plump figures in flight are, in real sky, often interspersed with large areas of uninteresting mist. Sun-struck and glittering fluff must, moreover, have a shady side, which soaks up color as it floats across our view. Tiepolo seems to have been unique in making dramatic capital out of boring meteorological facts. His clouds seem to be undergoing commonplace changes as we watch—not just moving like vehicles, but dissolving, dispersing, transforming themselves in the immemorially unpredictable sky style. Darkness in the mature Tiepolo's works is also a matter not of the night but of moods in the daylight sky; and the unstable arrangements of figures he puts in it have the same quality of happy submission to an absolutely neutral nature, over which the mythologizing artist has no control, and in which ordinary myth-seeking humans can find no message. It is not the portentous Nature of significant stormclouds and pointed lightning flashes, which are caused by painters and poets to match mythical events, but the unanswerable nature denoted by the dumb sky, which puts only its own antic disposition into steady play.

There is consequently something hilarious about Tiepolo events. The drama of Iphigenia's sacrifice, for example, is given a vigorous new emotional charge partly made up of pure laughter at the near apparition of the deer on the cloud in front of the column, or at the funny single hand that grasps another column hiding the rest of the figure, or at scared Agamemnon unceremoniously hiding his face like a little boy. Tiepolo is here advancing the movielike form of realism, which depends on recognizing the emotional potentialities in all the odd arbitrariness of visual life (8.3).

The effect is not theatrical. The theater is by nature sacramental, even in the extreme comic vein, and during performance the audience is first of all respectful of the occasion itself. But Tiepolo produces the responses people

8.3 G . B . T I E P O L O , *The Sacrifice of Iphigenia* (detail)

have at the movies, where you can shout and guffaw simply at the outrageous and delicious extremity of everything, the wonderful stretch of belief they can make you feel, whatever is otherwise happening. The extras in Tiepolo are notable individuals, with their postures and costumes sometimes likely to make them ridiculous, but with their faces full of good will and the honest effort to earn their pay as angels or personified continents or whatever, and also of a certain amusing and not unpleasing complacency. They have the final effect of making the event more and not less believable, even while we giggle at them.

Tiepolo was another kind of cinematic artist, too. Apart from the huge mythic and religious repertoire, he made amazing little graphic works in black and white. These are small fantasies done in the etching medium, which best preserves freshness of vision, showing bizarrely casual groupings of symbolic or occult figures and things. But even though they use the romantic rhetorical trappings invented by Salvator Rosa—skeletons, snakes, owls, old magicians, nude youths, and tender maidens—these pictures have the same attention-getting quality achieved by Rembrandt. They share that look of being storyboards, sketches that convey an event uncertain of outcome, fraught with not yet enunciated problems and not yet clarified meanings (8.4, 8.5).

The chiaroscuro is brilliant; sunlight sparkles on the witches and owls; all elements have a quick optical naturalism, especially the figure groups. These are devoid of posturing, just as in the frescoes, and instead show the odd way bodies look in actual groups, with only an arm showing, or a head blocked off from sight. They seem like news photos of backstage gatherings before a variety show. As in Rembrandt, the lighting manipulates attention with great skill. Near the center, the eye is forced to focus on some clearly detailed objects shown in brightly contrasted patches of light and dark; but when the viewer does look, he is not enlightened, only captured; and his eye is made to keep ranging toward the more diffusely drawn edges of the picture, to find out what else is happening, to discover what is really there, to get the picture.

Both the frescoes and the etchings are lacking in artistic self-display. Even with an extreme degree of spectacular talent exercised expressly for spectacle, Tiepolo never once shows off. His characters sometimes seem to do so, and so we smile at them; but the flavor of his own performance keeps an amazing modesty among the audacious clustering of the personnel. We

8.4 G. B. TIEPOLO, *Death Gives Audience*. Etching

8.5 G. B. TIEPOLO, *Two Magicians with Punchinello*. Etching

never gasp at him, only at it. One reason for this is that same reticence that keeps much of the sky blank and the *staffage* economically small, the invented views of heaven or Egypt or Tauris rendered with very few token props, and the clothes rightly created according to true sartorial possibility.

This is quite unlike Tintoretto, from whom Tiepolo learned so much. There seems to be no break at all in Tintoretto's heroic compositions, and no space for the surging figures to use—every inch is taken up with Tintoretto's genius. Tiepolo instead makes a screenlike transparency predominate. Like a watercolorist leaving a lot of room for the light of the paper to assert itself, he leaves the sweep of ceiling free to be a pregnant space into which we may stare, expecting yet more gods to appear. The result is much less apparent assertion on the artist's part and much more on that of his rising, looming, floating figures—and more, in turn, by the viewer's imagination, which leaps to people the void. On the ceiling of the staircase at the

Wurzburg Residenz, Apollo only fleetingly and ultimately shows up on the huge screen, where we keep searching the dim sky for him as we walk up the steps.

The perspective of Tiepolo's small elements is so perfect that it holds true across empty air unpunctuated by any clouds, buildings, or bodies. The big flat areas of mauve-and-gray fog on the Wurzburg staircase ceiling read effortlessly as real places in the sky, because the allegorical groups sitting miles away on the edges are so comfortably situated in their little spaces. Their very ease creates believability for the sparse and episodic action in the skyey center.

Tiepolo made complete oil sketches of his ceilings before he painted them—not drawings for the separate parts, but whole preliminary versions, which might turn out differently when fully realized *in situ,* where he worked directly and as if spontaneously. This also is unlike the painstaking cartoon method of exact preparation, and more like a Dutch painter, or Watteau, or an art director doing sequences of continuity sketches. The haphazard look of the final event is supported by whole-scene preparation —the moment is never still, each view of it must be a new one.

The atmospheric presence of architecture in Tiepolo's frescoes makes a large contribution to their cinematic flavor, just as architectural ambience has so much power in film. It is buildings and parts of buildings, rooms from inside and out, streets, stairways, and hallways that fix movies inside the soul, far more than any of these things have the power to do for plays on the stage. Stage sets have an acknowledged independent magic, however effective they may be for the drama. They are often admired for themselves, and applauded before the action begins. But in movies, only natural scenery can have such independent claims and can seem so arbitrary and detachable. Man-made places are inescapably bonded to the human feeling and action they surround. They share and often create the menace and tension, the grandeur and euphoria, the banality and slackness of scenes, chiefly because we ourselves are always in them along with the *staffage.* Standard theatrical distance is impossible, except for some of the sunsets and mountains that keep their distance in life as well as art. And so in Tiepolo, a small painted cornice or staircase, one bit of rigging, or one group of columns grounds the whole scene in festivity, archaic solemnity, or coziness.

But the stairs and columns in Tiepolo's works were in fact not done by him. They were provided by an expert in architectural illusionism called Mengozzi-Colonna, one of many in a long Italian decorative tradition. It was these artists of *quadratura*—illusionistic fantasy architecture—who most successfully created movielike fictions out of the whole environment, when they covered the walls or ceilings of real rooms and corridors with invented architectural vistas. It was done not simply to deceive the eye or tell a story, but to set a dramatic mood by insisting on a direct emotional engagement with fictive material surroundings. This is the same thing Griffith did with the famous set for *Intolerance*. Architectural members of great size, unexpected prospects, and steeply rising angles pleasurably unsettle and excite the viewer, especially if everything is in natural lighting, texture, and detail, and also in perfect perspective. Again, as with sci-fi movies or with the heavenly action stirred up by Tiepolo, the response is largely exhilaration at the overreaching make-believe, not solemn awe, even if the structures or the action are solemn and awesome.

The emotional possibilities for pictured buildings were first explored in the late Baroque period by the Bibiena family, who concentrated on stage settings. They invented the *scena per angolo,* whereby the viewer is given an off-center view of part of a palace, street, or temple, and so invited to think of himself as moving toward a door or a gate or toward some possible moment of resolution. Asymmetry was a common Rococo feature, even for small decorative motifs; but when it is used for architectural imagery that is otherwise rendered solid and rational, its emotional charge is very great. The high tension between the unstable angled view and the stable authority of the structure itself generates a nameless excitement that simply waits for a human situation to fill it with significance. Failing that, the excitement stays in solution, ready for any of us to precipitate it. Architectural rendering has ever since chosen the view from an angle that makes one corner loom up and declare an emotional dimension to the school or factory it aims to sell (8.6).

THE ITALIAN tradition for such pictured scenic architecture did have a direct cinematic descendant. In 1911 and thereafter for a few years, several historical spectacular films were made in Italy (and exported to America) that used clear references to Bibiena inventions—but in the film medium they could be actually built sets, photographed with people in them, not illusionistic backdrops (8.7, 8.8). *Quo Vadis, Cabiria, Theodora,* and others made a great impact, largely because of their substantial, authoritative sets, which have the strong operatic power of the historical Bibiena designs. They had an influence on Griffith, and through him on all later spectacular movie sets that have depended on the deployment of heroic, emotionally styled architecture.

Such early movie sets were naturally realized in black and white; but it is an interesting point about actual Baroque stage design that the settings of that time were conceived and executed in monochrome. Illusion was cre-

8.6 GIUSEPPE GALLI-BIBIENA, *scena per angolo* for a *Theatrum Sacrum*

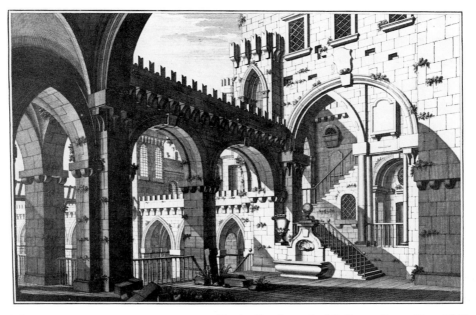

8.7 GIUSEPPE GALLI-BIBIENA, illustration from *Architetture e Prospettive,* 1740

8.8 Still from Leopoldo Carlucci's *Teodora,* 1919

ated by a blend of brilliantly clear delineation and chiaroscuro. This was necessary because stage lighting was achieved by the glow of reflected candlepower, which effectively washed out color. Sheen and glitter were consequently most important for costume, as they later were for film costume; and for settings, drama was focused by black-and-white architectural renderings, still designed to suit the piece according to the Renaissance program for comedy, tragedy, and satire, but increasingly enlivened by dynamic angled views and the sophisticated use of pictured lighting. Color could not carry.

The black-and-white medium in which architectural movie magic was first promulgated thus had a direct predecessor in the Italian graphic mode for monumental stage design. By 1700 European audiences had already learned how the very colorlessness of great visionary structures increases their power to concentrate drama through architecture. The designers of Giovanni Pastrone's *Cabiria* could use this monochromatic storehouse of Baroque scenic effects, and project their influence into our own time in the new graphic medium for drama, where the same methods have since given us overwhelming movie moments in railroad stations, warehouses, stairwells, and sewers. Architectural photographers have shared in the theme; but movie sets in all their possible extremes, and their consequent grip on the inner life, are closer to the Bibienas' dynamic conceptions or to Mengozzi-Colonna's wondrous fresco settings for Tiepolo. Even these tend toward monochromy, as if under the double bleaching effect of ordinary daylight and the hot glare of fantasy.

THE MOST advanced visual associate of the great Rococo scenic designers was Piranesi, to whom the modern movie-loving world so deeply responds. His engravings of magnificent ruins and imaginary prisons daringly offer their lofty antique stabilities as ghosts and dreams, projections of inner states and unspeakable fears, without ever resorting to any standard fantastic vocabulary (8.9). Piranesi worked in the same vein as those artists who designed architectural fantasies to be independent paintings, which might thereafter also be engraved. Many such works (by Pannini, for example) were very elaborate in the received Rococo manner, which lets exuberant ornament stand for richness of imagination. The effect can be charming, a deliberate flirtation with unreality, a rare display of fancy in flight. But Piranesi was a pivotal figure, already looking toward the dramatic simplicities of Neoclassicism, and even beyond them to the radical temper of modern design. We find his fantasies all the more effective for their decorative restraint, which lends greater force to the play of light and shade on primary architectural form. His first prison prints show

8.9　G. B. PIRANESI, prison view. No. 15 from *Carceri d'Invenzione,* 1745

the influence of Tiepolo's strange little graphic works, but instead of the odd disposition of ambiguous characters, Piranesi groups huge interior spaces in the same inconclusive and suggestive manner.

The effect of a screen of flickering atmosphere infuses these black-and-white works, rather than one of solid form rationally illuminated and articulated. The look is not that of abstract pattern on a surface, but of a painted veil lit from behind—the same paradigm of personal consciousness that makes the illuminated manuscripts, watercolors, and the movies so psychologically penetrating. The effect lends vast presence to sparsely peopled architecture and makes us mentally fill it like a screen with possible conflict and passion or accident and incident, all nebulous and unrealized.

C A N A L E T T O was the other eighteenth-century Italian creator of screenlike scenes admired in modern times. This artist operated in a mode quite different from Piranesi's, and his topographical works held a far different sort of artistic status. Piranesi shared in the international, universal prestige of architecture, archeological study, and fine printmaking, all of which stood higher than the kind of local topographical painting in which

Canaletto specialized, which was chiefly marketed to English tourists in Venice.

Piranesi was an academic theorist, learned and directly influential upon the Neoclassic and Romantic movements to come, as well as upon the next trends in the history of design. Canaletto was officially trivial, pleasing and successful but without any acknowledged intellectual or esthetic resonance for the future. And yet Canaletto could also create that same cinematic expectancy out of nothing but the flickering light and its answering shadows on masonry, the look of assorted idlers passing who are nevertheless all equally apt for dramatic encounter. Berckheyde and De Witte had done it in Holland fifty years earlier; but Canaletto, like Vermeer, could do it out of flecks of paint, as if insisting that an emotive force dwells in the sheer *opticality* of visual experience, not its intelligibility. The eye drinks up the scene and the psyche manufactures the drama out of it, below the level of conscious thought.

Canaletto did do a series of magnificent topographical etchings that plainly link him with Piranesi's kind of suggestive graphic poetry, which is founded entirely on the simple realities of an architectural milieu (8.10). Such early-eighteenth-century explorations into the poetic possibilities of

8.10 CANALETTO, *The Portico with a Lantern.* Etching

city views and those of other groups of buildings large and small, crumbling or glittering, presage the importance of topographical art for Romanticism, and eventually for movie romanticism—which both have the same origins in North European art. The Vermeer *View of Delft* and the Berckheyde views had set the standard for deliberately non-fantastical, non-picturesque, quasi-neutral renderings of buildings that nevertheless invite subjective engagement through the use of light. The Italian contribution was the elegant Bibiena formula for putting classic architecture into dramatic motion, using its elements to urge the play of fantasy. Canaletto and other Venetian view-painters created a synthesis of both, which culminated in the German Romantic landscape-painters and the English watercolorists. These both used plain topography for an accumulation of poetic ends that have had their most recent effect in modern film.

Piranesi and Canaletto were both trained in set design; but both, like Tiepolo, too, turned the themes of stage setting into that charged simulacrum of the real environment which film sets now offer. Groups of real and solid architectural forms, like those often actually built as well as painted on backdrops, are transmuted by these artists into momentary, shifting, movie-camera-like views. Everything is clear and in perfect perspective, but it only exists now, as the sun strikes, and we look and wait to know more. In a moment it will dissolve, or we will move, and another will replace it; the flecks on the screen are in perpetual motion. In Canaletto's Venice, just as in Piranesi's colorless Rome or Hopper's New York, the atmosphere crackles with possibility. There is no need for artful gloom, mist, or dramatic distortion to produce it—it is in the crisp shadows cast by the daylight on the cornice, the window ledge, or the angle of the balustrade.

Admirers of serious painting have tended to prefer Guardi to Canaletto. Guardi's works, many of them tiny vignettes, have a fresh painterly economy that makes them seem like much better works of art than Canaletto's straight and thoroughgoing views. But whereas Guardi gives a good sense of the painter's mastery, which always provides a certain emotional completeness, Canaletto instead gives the perfect sense of place, which ideally remains incomplete, as: We can see that we are very much *here*—but now what will *happen* here? As in Tiepolo's ceilings, the disposition of empty space helps give the Canaletto scenes such expectancy, especially in *The Thames and London from Richmond House,* and *Whitehall and the Privy Garden,* which come from his various London sojourns (8.11). The open sky, the smooth water, the empty roadway draw us on, and cause possible meanings to coast across their flat expanses, gathering momentum and waiting to discharge themselves.

These and other Canaletto townscapes seen across water contain an echo

8.11 CANALETTO, *The Thames and London from Richmond House*

of a Dutch artist from even earlier in the seventeenth century than Berckheyde and De Witte. Esaias van de Velde's *View of the Zierickzee* was
painted in 1618, thirty years before Vermeer was to paint Delft; but it
shows that the source of pure topographic poetry had already been tapped
in Holland (8.12). The Dutch city, like Vermeer's Delft and Canaletto's
Venice, seems already posing for Wordsworth, "all bright and glittering in
the smokeless air," with the sweep of bird and cloud ready to move us
across the view, and pull out of us the surge of feeling—"Dear God! The
very houses seem asleep."

8.12 ESAIAS VAN DE VELDE, *View of the Zierickzee*

The total flavor of Canaletto's oeuvre is in fact uneven and untrustwor-
thy, as if each picture, instead of being a complete example of a painter's
general onward struggle for perfection—a performance, as Guardi's are—
is rather one of an endless series of rehearsals, experimental frames of
which many come out brilliantly and some seem dead. A number of them
are also imaginary. The eighteenth-century Italian development of the architectural *capriccio,* or imaginary ideal view, indicates a new focus on the
independent emotional flavor of buildings, apart from their embellishment
of the landscape, their practical interest as landmarks, or even their traditional theatrical uses. By the time of Canaletto and Piranesi, buildings had
become characters—as the Dutch had seen them, and as Chardin had seen
the objects in the kitchen. The consequent impulse to reshape and regroup
the real ones, and to make up new ones real enough to convince and to
charm, is a branch of imaginative skill akin to the new style of invention for
literary characters—buildings are not just *dramatis personae,* but more
like the people in novels.

Like Clarissa or Madame de Merteuil, Canaletto's *Palace with Clock*

Tower is alive (8.13). The cool interior waits behind the shutters as the leaves cast shadows on the hot stuccoed wall. And yet this is a total fiction, a movie set built out of the designer's head and brought to life in sparkling sunshine only on Canaletto's screen. This kind of *capriccio* has an environmental authority lacking in the invented stage sets that serve as painted backdrops to live action, or lacking in any deliberately fantastical, ornate confection that you can look at, but not be in. Here, as in Piranesi's prisons, the fictional building and people are living together, forming an entire possible world, including the undertones and overtones of transience that can be felt in the looks of any real building, fresh or faded.

Buildings attempt to defy time. Certain pictures of buildings, by showing the light in motion on their faces and forms, bring up this aspect of their purpose, especially if structures are shown in a state of decay. Time is often shown to abrade the bodies and claim the lives of buildings only a little less quickly than it sets its mark on humans. But in such visionary form, in a fleeting picture, an imaginary building lives forever like a Tara or a Manderley, where groups and crowds may always be gathering in solid halls and porticoes that never were.

The people in Canaletto's scenes are related to those in Piranesi's, and both show connections with Watteau's personnel, especially his *figures de*

8.13 CANALETTO, *Capriccio: Palace with Clock Tower*

8.14 CANALETTO, *View of the Bacino with the Bucintoro Arriving* (detail)

mode and *figures diverses.* The insouciant brilliance of rendering is the same; and so is the graphic quality, the fashion-art immediacy of the figures (8.14). Peasants drawing water and gentry in wigs have equal panache, shared with Piranesi's archeology-minded gentlemen gesticulating over unearthed shards. The figures in Canaletto's scenes are all energetically alive, wearing their "characteristic" or "typical" costumes with brisk grace. None has Hogarthian grotesqueness or overmannered prettiness. There is no comic exaggeration, only a high-comic, slightly ironic charm. Like Watteau's garden groups, they have the ideal urban look, even in the occasional country-house setting: variety of civilized movement, diversity of class and function without unwonted extremes. Poor and rich are present, but no one is misshapen or covered with sores; nor is anyone overdressed or overweight.

This moderation in Canaletto's vision of population gives it a far greater degree of optical truth than does the kind of panorama insistent on noticeable contrasts; his tempered, quasi-Dutch approach to street scenes echoes the true harmonizing action of the neutral scanning eye. A false "reality" of egregious skeletal beggars and bloated grandees (both of which undoubtedly existed in eighteenth-century Venice and London) would in fact be an idealization (or ideologizing), a stylization of what is known, rather than a true mirror of what is seen.

If you look closely at some of Canaletto's poor, you can see that they might be sick or wretched or crazy, or the rich depraved, if you could approach near enough to examine individuals. But the light here reserves its own excitement. It shines indiscriminately on human life, as if to suggest an equal dramatic potentiality in any small part of it, a sparkling, general potentiality created by the sky itself. The camera may at any moment move in on this poor gondolier or that rich statesman, or sharpen the focus on this group of basket-bearing gossips; but the clouds sweep, gather, and disperse without favor over them all. Palace, tenement, and church expertly receive sun and return shadow; all façades show an equal skill in the task. We are moved by the democracy of light that governs cities, showing what they are made of, testing and embellishing, exposing and rewarding them, keeping time alive in them.

NINE

Hogarth, Greuze, Goya

WILLIAM HOGARTH, born the same year as Cana-letto, is adored by the English because he seems so free of continental influence, so deliciously indigenous. The vigor and beauty of his painting actually owe much to the French Rococo manner, but certainly nothing to any obsession with classic greatness—he pokes satisfying fun at Old Masters—and his illustrative method shows a perfect British independence of the Dutch genre style. Hogarth in fact removes the Dutch optical element entirely from his paintings: they are full of obvious conscious superiority and artistic intervention.

They are also infused with the strong literary tenor that characterizes so much English creative talent, and that has made the dramatic stage and the novel such brilliant English media. There is nothing cinematic about Hogarth pictures, because there is very little in his work that corresponds to the sting of direct vision. For Hogarth, the truth in pictures is best conveyed by working on the viewer's previously digested visual assumptions, as cartoon art and the satiric stage always do. In Hogarth's graphic works the imagery is jammed with meaning and crowded with incident; everything is demonstrated and explicated in successive paragraphs of witty pictorial prose. The spatial arrangements are made especially for such a purpose, and have that showcase, stage-picture look, the familiar shadow box in which the eye is primed to find clues, tags, and keys in an accustomed array. Hogarth is much praised as a portrayer of individuals, beginning with his portraits and ending with the famous engraved scenes about the rake and the harlot, the apprentices and the ill-matched spouses. Such vivid individuals as he created, however, are not shown inside a believable visual field. Even the famous composite portrait of his servants shows the faces in isolation, each a masterpiece with no milieu.

Whereas the total mise-en-scène in a Hogarth engraving reads like spirited prose, the slight exaggeration of every figure gives each personage the specific effect of a declaimed verse, wherein pertinent details, many of them stupid and messy, are described in clear and clever rhymes. Hogarth was a self-confessed moralist—the believability of his pictorial declamation depended on his brilliant use of parable, where the characters are all examples.

His rendering of situations, however, does not rely on revelatory power, the truth of apparition. The movement of light has very little force in his schemes. The grouping is done with contrasts of delineation—the fat juxtaposed with the thin, the stiff with the loose, the hideously distorted with the pure and simple. Faces are reduced versions of the program. Hogarth's approach to us is made as if to readers of Augustan poetry, which wraps and pins the brutal absurdity of life into stunning couplets, rather than to sympathetic observers eyeing the difficult world. Hogarth's engraved stories show how a picture can be deftly filtered through the familiar language of printed lines, the same one that purveys moral tales and expository verses, so as to indicate by the picture's very form that it, like them, is to be read through—perhaps aloud or set to music—not grasped at one glance.

Hogarth was a great absorber of European artistic styles through the medium of engraved reproduction, and he was very good at quoting them. The refined languages of French engraving had, moreover, become well known in England by his time, and Hogarth himself was a friend of the French engraver Gravelot, who lived for years in England and had a deep effect on English graphics. Book illustration was a French luxury product available in England, and Shakespeare illustration was already an English speciality in this French medium; the English public for art was well accustomed to beautifully engraved picture-stories, offered in a lofty literary context. Hogarth's transformation of exquisite engraving into a medium for the kind of crude morality tale formerly confined to cheap broadsides was thus a stroke of publicizing genius; but it also kept his narrative imagery firmly inside the sphere of literary form. It was only in the portraits, including that of the anonymous shrimp girl, that Hogarth used a truly painterly eye, even a cinematic one, which sees the process of experience at work, not just the chain of circumstance.

Joseph Highmore's paintings that illustrate Richardson's *Pamela* come much closer than Hogarth's to Chardin's groups and even to Watteau's, and to Dutch genre art, especially in the use of light to produce the sense of motion and the process of feeling. Highmore also learned the French lesson of using modishness for figures that are to look satisfying while they tell a simple moral story. Highmore's portrait called *Mr. Oldham and his Friends* has a movie-frame look akin to Terbrugghen's *Matthew*, where some odd-looking men are shown interacting ambiguously around a tabletop, and we feel drawn into their company to find out who they are and what's afoot (9.1). The people in this painting seem naturally funny; Highmore doesn't push their comic features at us, we are free to see them for ourselves, and feel spontaneously disarmed by them. They make Hogarth's comic turns like *A Midnight Modern Conversation* seem all the more stagy, because Hogarth pointedly urges us to laugh at his topers and smokers with superior detachment (9.2).

But Highmore's group, like his *Pamela* and *Clarissa* series and Hogarth's oeuvre, mainly underscores the new secular and illustrative turn taken by painting altogether, which represents a giant step along the route of cinematic representation. Recounting contemporary moral tales outright without any Biblical or legendary guises has been a primary movie task from the start, as it was the task of fiction in the nineteenth century; but film has been especially good at working in the opposite direction, creating

9.1 JOSEPH HIGHMORE, *Mr. Oldham and His Friends*

9.2 WILLIAM HOGARTH, *A Midnight Modern Conversation*

myths out of new material and hiding evidence of old sources, even while
making use of their abiding power. Panofsky connected this impulse of cinema with medieval stories in pictures; but the true cinematic visual *style,*
not theme—which can convey the direct sense of personal feeling (or personal fantasy) even while it illustrates an edifying modern parable and
draws secretly on an ancient myth—was only really perfected by the late
seventeenth century and refined in the eighteenth. It goes with a combination, apparently, of ascendant Protestantism and capitalism, such as prevailed in seventeenth-century Holland, eighteenth-century England, and
eventually in America, the natural home of the movies.

In such works of art in Highmore's and Chardin's time, the clever combination of natural appearances with figures inspired by fashion art gave a
modern interior that same look of a lived-in dream that movies now purvey,
while they deliciously transmit their modern homilies of ambition and duty,
love and betrayal (9.3). This device makes narrative into two things at once,
as movies do: one is the sequence of events, the plot; the other is the sequence of our personal experiences that accompanies the plot, consisting of
apparently irrelevant phenomena, the precise flavor of physical atmosphere, and the engagement of private memory and fantasy. In present-day
modern film, as in modern fiction, such material may in fact constitute the
whole of the narrative, and be satisfying and comprehensible. De Hooch

9.3 JOSEPH HIGHMORE, *The Harlowe Family*

had long ago created the same effect with imaginary palaces, and without using any anecdotal content; Schalcken had been more of a storyteller. Highmore produced natural-seeming moments in poignant middle-class stories with fairy-tale overtones, just as Dutch religious painters in the previous century gave the legends the flavor of middle-class confrontations and dilemmas.

By the eighteenth century the visual form of modern narrative had the advantage of the cameralike, subjective expressiveness that the Dutch had perfected, to create direct emotional pull. But Hogarth didn't use it. His work is more like the medieval carvings or the earliest *danse macabre* prints, before Holbein, where the form itself has its own vigorous authority, and the moral meaning is thrust home through that. It is not Tom Rakewell's plight but Hogarth's mind and hand we are forced to confront, and feel, and take personally, almost physically; we get his wonderful way with description, like Dürer's, not the sense of witnessing the living of Tom's increasingly desperate life. The force of art prevents the picture's harsh content from reaching us directly.

Unpretentious popular illustrative graphics were already a medium perfected for secular thrills all over Europe by Hogarth's time. Along with the torture and execution of heretics and the horrors of religious war, broadsheets had illustrated the exploits and punishments of thieves, kidnappers, and murderers as sensationally as possible, and had recorded amazing and awful phenomena. Domestic morality had also long been a theme for popular prints, although popular pictures dealt with moral life in a more allegorical than personal way until the late seventeenth century. Before that, instead of a tale about a real young man, prints would illustrate the fate of the Prodigal Son—in modern dress, perhaps. Later on, a modern tale would hide the Biblical one under appealing current detail and dramatic circumstance. By the eighteenth century, when Hogarth's great scenes were painted, engraved, and published, both the English and the European public were accustomed to straight realistic melodrama and modern anecdote, appearing in the form of printed pictures and being used as media for general moral themes and current events.

David Kunzle has shown how popular picture-stories of the mid-eighteenth century began to concentrate on the psychological background of crimes, and not just on their shocking details and grisly punishments. The personal character of criminals became interesting, and the romantic criminal came into existence—the dashing pirate and highwayman, the jolly if larcenous woman of pleasure, all precursors of the movie gunslinger, bounty hunter, and crime czar, the sympathetic vamp and tramp. At the same time, the study of physiognomy became an important influence on popular picture-stories, allowing them to dwell on the perpetual comedy of individual looks. Caricature developed quickly in this new climate. It was also in the eighteenth century that emphasis in popular pictures shifted from a delight in horrors to a horror of abuses; they began to express the sense of crime and its suitable punishment as a social problem, not as straight sensational entertainment.

Hogarth seized on and expounded all these themes at once, and he made money—but in the most sophisticated artistic media of the time, that is, French-inspired painting and engraving. His pictures are not internally cinematic, but he foreshadowed that synthesis of high and low art only lately accomplished in film, where references to lofty prototypes and low-down modes of current expression are fused in the telling of gripping human stories aimed at all classes. At the time, such a synthesis was newly

possible in forward-looking England, where classes were on the move, public opinion was becoming a recognized force, and it became clear that public
feeling, urged by pictures, could give such opinion its shape.

With all this, history painting was declining, if not in status, at least in
importance. Modern subjects became appropriate for serious painters, not
just for popular graphic artists, in the same period that novels were becoming serious literature and newspapers and journals common reading. Individual personal feeling evolved into an avowed theme for serious art, not a
covert one. Graphic skills and techniques inevitably took a corresponding
leap forward.

Aquatint, which had been invented in the seventeenth century, was a
graphic technique using the etching method, but creating the transparent
effect of a wash drawing by letting the acid bite the plate through a porous
ground of granulated resin. The medium was now further developed to permit authentically tonal printed pictures and ensure greater naturalism for
chiaroscuro effects, especially when used in combination with etched lines.
Goya's great *Caprichos,* made at the end of the century, demonstrated the
triumph of that medium as a means of original expression, but it had come
to be used in England to reproduce illustrative and topographical watercolors, to preserve their atmospheric immediacy. The invention of lithography in 1798 by the Bavarian commercial artist Aloys Senefelder also
offered a new field for spontaneous expression in directly reproducible pictures. Works with the transparency of watercolor and the strong chiaroscuro of ink and wash could be directly captured and soon seen by
thousands, without being first netted in a web of lines. Graphic art could be
more "graphic" in the sense of "truthful," less so in the sense of "written."

News, commentary, and narrative, both pictorial and literary, found a
ready public in England; but for the French public, official Academy exhibitions and constant critical attention gave serious paintings a much
greater prestige and acknowledged importance. Chardin's paintings were
sold as engravings only after they had been known in Academy exhibitions.
Greuze (whom the French called "The French Hogarth") owed his fame to
Diderot's emotional response to his works, expressed in lucid articles that
instructed the viewing public how to react. The prints were sold accord-
ingly. Hogarth received no such critical enhancement in his own country:
he promoted his own pictures, and his publisher sold them—or they sold
themselves, even commented on themselves in the comic and violent manner lacking in Greuze's works.

B O T H   Greuze and Hogarth were popular artists who were essentially
serious history-painters. Both came eventually to use their painter's classi-

cal, art-historical knowledge and training for material that had formerly only been vulgarly portrayed, in works that pleased the general public much better than any strictly popular artists had done. It was a time when art—good art—began to penetrate and inform life, when more people could see and know and have it and be changed by it unawares, so as to see things on its terms. Movies have confirmed this process as a law of modern life; and these two artists were among those who began it, in the century of general enlightenment. Black-and-white reproducible images, needless to say, were its chief medium.

Although Greuze's emergent Neoclassic sensibility makes his graceful scenes of moral life very different from Hogarth's fierce and chaotic ones, both share the idea of theatrical exposition that appears in modern musical comedy rather than in movies. The music that seems to infuse all their scenes is expressive song, not emotional thematic background sound, the underscoring by which movies are so well nourished. In both artists' work, everyone seems about to sing or recite, not to speak. The very aspect the characters wear, as we have suggested, is conveyed in self-evidently poetic style. So is their behavior. The parted lips and extended hand of Greuze's fraught son or parent signal the start of a touching ballad, just as Hogarth's nervous quack or notary seems about to arrange brilliant rhymed couplets into a comic patter-song, to explain his business, his troubles, and his views. For a modern opera based on *The Rake's Progress,* Hogarth made a natural third in the Neoclassic combination of Auden and Stravinsky: they, too, modernized established modes by adapting them to the ironic vein, instead of maintaining a reverent posture toward them, as Greuze kept trying to do (9.4).

Greuze was already in reaction to the Rococo spirit, which in England still ensured that even Hogarth's most horrible scenes might keep a light touch. But Greuze did take up the option to use the appeal of current fashion for injecting serious genre subjects with an immediate eroticism. His fancy-portraits of modishly disheveled sinful girls, swooning with the pleasures of remorse, have a very familiar look; they resemble the modern icons of commercial art that deliberately show no personal character but only an ideal fantasy quality—the thousands of indistinguishable moist-lipped and intensely gazing faces selling the erotic element in all forms of goods and services, as Greuze's demoiselles sold sensuality and morality at once.

Both Hogarth and Greuze were moving, with their century, toward demonstrating the excruciating pleasures of strong feeling. They wished to make outrage or remorse, despair or panic deliciously *noticeable* and perhaps even desirable conditions of the soul, right along with serenity and ex-

9.4 J.-B. GREUZE, *The Chastised Son*

ultation, or extreme pride, brutal lust, and smug complacency. All these
had first of all to *show,* far more than any plot had to be clear—or than the
really ambiguous texture of feeling as it is experienced had to be dealt
with.

Hogarth, and Diderot on Greuze's behalf, also advocated deliberate
asymmetry in composition, to convey the sense of emotional drama, but in
their works such arrangements seem to stand for emotion rather than generating or reflecting any. In the effort not to be decorative and frivolous,
and to insist on the moral meaning of the total scene, both these artists also
forced all inanimate objects to serve the theme. This means that the things
in the pictures have none of that passionate independent character that invests Chardin's domestic gear. They are all overdetermined; and so they do
not create the aura of free psychic movement that gives inanimate things in
movies their important power.

Michael Fried stresses the aim in Greuze's art, as Diderot saw it and
wanted it, of making the characters ignore or even shut out any possible beholder; and yet they do seem ready, absorbed as they may be, to burst into

rhymed soliloquy or a solitary meditative aria. The intense absorption of these characters, like the venal aims of Hogarth's people, needed in fact to be palpably overdone so as to entrance an audience, in the ancient stage tradition. The viewer is not encompassed and drawn in as a possible actor, as in Vermeer and in the movies, but left staring and transfixed outside at a given distance. He can't escape; and so the moral can't escape him. Both these artists are spellbinders and mesmerizers, weaving a net of faces and gestures demanding the kind of attention the stage gets, entrapping an audience in the bewitching rites of live performance.

The eighteenth-century illustrator who more closely followed along the path that leads between Rembrandt and the movies was the Polish-German artist Daniel Chodowiecki, born the year after Greuze. He was not much of a painter; but he, too, did graphic sequences showing the contrasting effects of vice and virtue in modern life, besides satirizing social and esthetic pretensions and illustrating works of fiction. His works are in tiny format, late echoes of the personal mode that had been invented for the medieval illuminations and so strikingly promoted in print by Holbein for his *Dance of Death*. Two and a half centuries later, Chodowiecki did his miniature scenes as illustrations for printed almanacs, for a middle-class audience this time directly concerned with wealth, sex, and morality, rather than with the meanings of sacred legends to a feudal hierarchy, or with the Renaissance view of an old didactic form. But the amount of drama Chodowiecki, like Holbein, could stir up in a two-by-two-and-a-half-inch space is astounding, although Chodowiecki himself was consciously borrowing from Hogarth.

He was encouraged in this by the German critic Lichtenberg, in whom Hogarth's works eventually found their own most penetrating commentator and enthusiast. But Chodowiecki had a far more subjective approach to narrative pictures than Hogarth, especially with regard to facial expression. Lavater's huge illustrated theory of physiognomy, published between 1775 and 1778 and quickly translated, was encouraging many artists to consider faces with new attention; but Lichtenberg and Chodowiecki both found Lavater's basic concept—that the original and God-given shapes of heads and faces are absolute indicators of character—to be both superstitious and ridiculous. Lichtenberg urged Chodowiecki to demonstrate the opposing modern idea that character gradually shapes the face. One of his sequences shows the progress of depravity and virtue in the face alone, with very little other narrative material in each picture. They consequently have a cinematic, close-up look, immediate and personal (9.5). On the other hand, Hogarth's faces, unaffected by theory, are in harmony with the well-developed English theatrical sensibility, and the artistic sources are

French Rococo in a detached and refined tradition. Chodowiecki's faces follow a program to disprove Lavater; but his emotional and dramatic sources are in Rembrandt—the aim is to render the *unconscious* look of psychological states and inward change, rather than the acutely *communicative* look of conscious feeling.

Chodowiecki's faces are devoid of grimace; the settings are simple but suggestive; the composition and lighting carry the real drama. There is very little gratuitous riot among subsidiary characters and material trappings—the artist, like Greuze, was at work in the Neoclassic ambience of the century's second half. But he was also a Northern artist. The story of a rake's ruin or a dissolute woman's downfall is told in small moments and encounters rather than scenic set-pieces, and variable ways of opening up the space inside the little frames give mobility and possibility to the understated action—a street leading back, with a carriage in steep foreshorten-

Opposite above: 9.5 DANIEL
CHODOWIECKI, two pages from
The Progress of Virtue and Vice, 1778.
Above: 9.6 DANIEL
CHODOWIECKI, *Thirst for
Knowledge of the World.* Scene from
The Life of a Rake, 1774.
Right: 9.7 DANIEL CHODOWIECKI,
Usual Refuge. Scene from *The Life of
an Ill-educated Girl,* 1780

ing, an open door or window, and visible light in motion to give the scene a psychological unity (9.6, 9.7).

These printed narrative sequences of the eighteenth century were attempts at realistic storytelling frame by frame, the creation of *romans muets,* as the French called Hogarth's works, to parallel the plays and novels of the same period. Graphic expression suited the new secular narrative mode; it used old popular traditions as a source for new artistic insights and a base for new artistic ambitions. Themes carried out in graphic form, not in painting, by a first-rate artist with first-rate training, could be all the more humanly universal without being religious. They could also be all the more liberated from the solemnities of official high art as well as from the perceived follies and impersonal amoralities of official decorative art—that is, naked nymphs in the Boucher mode. Graphic art offered a new way for an ambitious artist to be serious in a secular vein, as genre art had done for the Dutch; and a similar way to be successful, in the absence of patronage from nobles or an established Church. Film art has done the same for the graphic talents of this century, allowing them to build a great new secular mythology and a new universe of narrative vision on an old popular form, and to be hugely successful at it.

I N   M I D - E I G H T E E N T H - C E N T U R Y   England, the most economically advanced nation at the time, such a commercial turn for art to take seems a suitable sign of those ambitious times. In France and Germany, producing narrative material in popular printed form may rather be associated with fresh ideals of freedom, and of artists as exponents of free expression—personal or political—and as the only proper critics of society. In Spain, on the other hand, one of the most backward countries in Europe by the end of the eighteenth century, Goya nevertheless came to use graphic media in ways that were liberated from recent formal artistic languages, popular or lofty—although not from past popular themes. Goya's graphic art is emancipated but certainly not divorced from traditional popular subject matter; and yet at the same time Goya was a court painter on the most traditional model. There was very little "public" in Spain of the sort to which Hogarth, Greuze, or Chodowiecki could appeal, and Napoleon came to eclipse the court Goya served. It was perhaps inevitable that he should gradually become a privately preoccupied artist in the tradition of Rembrandt, with a coterie of admirers rather than a public. And, like Rembrandt, he eventually spoke to the whole world through the originality and power of his graphic works.

Fred Licht has called Goya the first modern artist, showing that his disturbing and unflattering visions of his royal sitters, for example, demonstrate not a caricatured version of them, which would imply an ideal from which they departed, but a new "alienated" view that the artist shares with his portrait subjects. Such a view portrays royal beings no longer supported by the structure of human faith in God's will, which keeps them and the artist and the beholder alike convinced of their divinely ordained superiority. It instead shows each one thrust alone into the void, facing only himself. Each prince or duchess appears to know the same existential loneliness that artists in various media have since shown is the common lot, and thus the proper common denominator in all portraits—self-, royal, or otherwise.

Goya as artist thus always presents himself as *fellow sufferer,* not as interpreter; and his works, especially the graphic sequences both early and late, both the *Caprichos* and the *Disasters of War,* are very basic documents of the cinematic ideal: the absolute subjective view. The viewer is engaged by the subject itself, never by art's traditional view of it or by the artist's power over it, which stands in for God's power over the ordering and meaning of human life. It is basic, because Goya came more and more to work only for himself and less for any contemporary public, so his uses of currency in visual material became more and more devoted to the currency of fantasy, rather than of common visual facts (9.8). For the *Caprichos* he often used common fantasy material from known tales and plays, but in private visualizations, and not for the Hogarthian kind of public commentary, which relies on quick audience-recognition of visual cues. The cues he instead wants us to recognize may well be the worst aspects of the inner life, delivered in the same "graphic"—that is, unbearably immediate— style of realism in which he recorded (in aquatint) the horrors of the Peninsular Campaign, its instigation and its aftermath, or (in paint) the physical looks of the royal family and the interior of a madhouse.

Goya was a herald of modernity, as Licht persuasively demonstrates, but he does rely on certain formal precedents, chiefly in Northern art, that long before had staked out some of the same terrain. Goya was only more unreservedly committed than some of his contemporaries to exploring further that graphic universe of the psyche which had already been occupied by Altdorfer and Seghers, Elsheimer and Rembrandt, and those honorary Northerners, Tiepolo and Piranesi. Since he was not copying the *forms* of popular art for his serious purposes, Goya could keep relentlessly to the point, which was the psychic illuminations that are possible to the artist who works in light and shade. "In art there is no need for color," he is quoted as saying; "Give me a crayon [that is to say, chalk], and I will 'paint' your portrait." He might also be speaking for Dürer and Rembrandt. The primitive side of man's nature, as Licht points out, is what Goya unflinch-

9.8 FRANCISCO GOYA, "Wait till you've
been anointed." No. 67 of *Los Caprichos,* 1799

ingly portrays, unredeemed by belief. And the "primitive," if by that is
meant the most basic psychological dispositions of the human animal, is
best evoked in the primitive terms of night and day, as the great black-and-
white movie directors have continually evoked it for us.

Line as well as color is demonstrably irrelevant to the kind of vision
Goya proposes. The aquatint medium that he used for the *Caprichos* and the
Desastres can produce imagery entirely with areas of gray, white, and
black, defined without drawing them in lines, which tend to dignify and
tame even the most crude and terrifying subject. Goya uses lines not to delineate shapes but to scratch forms into existence and then to splinter
them, as a squinting, half-blinded eye might apprehend them, to create the
distorting visual detritus that shudders around the edges of things seen in
agonized haste or in semi-conscious distraction, in fear or self-disgust.
This "graphic" kind of clarity can be most sharp when it is most jagged.

Blake and Füssli were contemporaries of Goya's, and their graphic
works of extreme fantasy show the uses to which exquisitely applied linear-
ity may be put, to keep scary and sordid material from being overwhelming

by lodging it firmly in the safe citadels of beauty and rhythm. Goya apparently wanted the overwhelming to overwhelm; he shuns the calligraphic mode even more than Rembrandt, who hadn't the resources of aquatint. Licht shows how much like modern news photographs his war etchings are; but one could go further and say they are more like newsreel footage, as the *Caprichos* are like film frames. The glare in these works and the uneasy, nearly undecipherable surroundings give the strong sense of continuous change and flicker, rather than of a burst of revelation fixed forever on the retina.

Reportorial or fantastical, Goya's frames, even those of the portraits, keep us full of dread and the sense of more to come, just as much film footage does and as the visual experience that is undergone in difficult moments usually does, too. A great deal of what commonly passes before our eyes is unreadable and virtually meaningless, only laden with possible meaning if we had time to stop and make it out. What it carries in its inarticulated mass is an appeal to our faculty of projection, which is sharpened under slight stress—and just such stress, a sort of diffuse agitation, is what pictures in the cinematic style are bent on stirring up.

Goya follows the path of those cinematically inclined artists who want to convey the limited character of individual vision. He is interested in the confusing and fragmented way that seeing is accomplished in the uncertain lives of men and women, when it is not being guided by expectations made familiar in traditional art. The subject then becomes truly subjective, and therefore partial and contingent; the artist becomes unnoticeable; the beholder therefore sees and participates simply by seeing. This method of creating total engagement sidesteps the element of commentary, which requires that the artist first demonstrate his qualifications for commenting by showing his rhetorical skill. If, instead, he can give a direct sense of what it is like to be there among the faceless enemy, the nameless flying monsters, the crushed women and dismembered men, to be oneself a wretch and a ghoul and a panic-stricken brute, then he also effectively shows that any further comment would be monstrous (9.9, 9.10). These things happened; I was there; so are you. So. And the note is struck even for the wildest of grim fantasies—the Colossus, the Saturn, the unconscionable creatures in the *Caprichos.*

The art of central Spain had had a strong debt to Dutch and Flemish art ever since the fifteenth century, when royal patronage first favored the style of Rogier van der Weyden and the Master of Flémalle, and the sixteenth, when Philip II imported Hieronymus Bosch. Goya's art continued to reflect the North both directly and indirectly. Rembrandt was his acknowledged precursor; but so was Velázquez, whose own style of Spanish

9.9 FRANCISCO GOYA, "All this and more."
No. 22 from *Los Desastres de la Guerra*

9.10 FRANCISCO GOYA, "One cannot look at this."
No. 26 from *Los Desastres de la Guerra*

mastery had an international flavor more North European than Italian, especially for court portraiture. The emphasis on monochromy, the retreat from line, and the insistence on aerated light as the sign of psychic movement are Northern qualities common to these and other Spanish artists; but by Goya's time the legacy of Northern realism in Spain had reached a certain finality. He founded no school and had no pupils, and his inspired new versions of old themes could be understood and carried on only after a big gap in artistic time and space. His direct heir is Manet, who, in the 1860's, the first decade of the instantaneous camera, took up the themes of fragmentation, optical ambiguity, and the basic emotional authority of "graphic" painting—and who also sought help with these from Dutch models.

Fashion in dress had a large place even in Goya's most extreme visions. It stood for an aspect of psychological truth, just as it later did in Manet and had done earlier in Chardin and Watteau. The use of acutely current fashion in any realistic mode of art conveys the sense of currency in the wearer and appeals to it in the viewer, especially the sense of sexual immediacy, and the sense of the constant *readiness* of all fantasy. Both movies and television have lately gone very far with this point, showing how important current fashionable ideals are for intensifying the appeal of any strong or violent depiction of life. "Miami Vice" is only one in a long sequence of melodramatic television series that sensationalize the seamier side of life with the help of high fashion. Nineteenth-century stage melodrama had certainly done this; and Hollywood historical films were given a better emotional texture through their incorrect use of modern style for old-fashioned or ancient-world clothes. Characters in grim dramas who are dressed in some version of high fashion appeal not to audiences' sense of reality but to the same underlying fantasies to which extreme fashion itself gives expression.

Certain of Goya's female court portraits exaggerate the skinny arms and torsos and the huge fluffy coiffures of the 1780's. The result fails to show the harmonious and beautiful aspect of that period's fashionable dress—which Vigée-Lebrun and J. L. David were so expertly conveying in France, along with Reynolds and Gainsborough in England—but instead points up its extreme quirkiness, and thus its clear foundation in unconscious fantasy (9.11). We are not given, as we are by Rubens or Ingres, for example, and by most classicizing artists in all periods, the pleasant vision of an elegant lady made beautiful in her time by her attire, a reassuring vision in which artistry triumphs over fashion's peculiarities. Rather, we are shown how the awkwardness of extreme modes truly works, how the distortions of the head and body, the inflations and strangulations of fashion arise in the

9.11 FRANCISCO GOYA, *Portrait of the Marquesa de Pontejos*

soul to give a psychological dimension to the visible body—make it, in fact, into a visualization of common fantasy, a proper product of the wayward and incalculable inner eye.

Such imagery, the kind that insists on distortion instead of tempering it, calls out directly to the corresponding fantasies in the contemporary viewer; the viewer from another time, naturally enough, cherishing quite other fantasies, sees only the oddness. The fifteenth-century Flemish masters (as opposed to Raphael and Leonardo) did the same thing as Goya in their portraits. There, too, are the huge heads and tiny arms of that moment, whereas a later Italian Mannerist artist like Lorenzo Lotto, committed to the workings of fantasy in all physical dispositions, insisted firmly on a modishly monstrous hugeness of arm and torso and a concomitant tininess of head.

Even some of Goya's harshest visions of war contain fashionable female shapes participating in events of utmost brutality. This sort of grim realism cuts deeper and is more unsettling than the realism that evades the mode in dress or tries falsely to universalize it—so unsettling that it often looks like calculated sensationalism. The graphic media in particular, which are so porous and vulnerable to corruption from below, so to speak, face the artist with the risk of being banal and sentimental or lurid. Goya, however, shares with the Northern artists of the fifteenth century the ability to show fashionable bodies in situations of ferocious extremity without descending into gratuitous thrill-mongering. And so he redoubles his effects by skirting that edge; and we hold our breath. Great film-makers have done the same in this century, from Griffith to Fritz Lang, to Chabrol, to Martin Scorsese and Brian de Palma. Meanwhile both Manet and Degas, long after Goya, had taken up the use of fashion as a good tool for creating sharp epiphanies of the inner life, right in the middle of an alleged context of dispassionate realism.

Fashion, especially extreme female fashion, stands for unaccountability. If obvious current fashion is referred to in the figure style of a serious picture, it automatically brings up the incalculable side of sexuality, the unwarranted erotic flavor that may infuse even very straight and sober motifs in art, just as it can suddenly enter—unbidden, winged, and blind—into some of life's dull and purportedly pure transactions. Classic nudity in art, by contrast, shows a desire to refer to human sexual nature directly, to seize undisguisedly on the theme of sex as a serious, perhaps even a sacred, aspect of nature itself. But if nudity in serious art is deliberately rendered *fashionably,* as in Goya's *Naked Maja* or in Manet's *Olympia,* it becomes disturbing for its denial of any possibility of innocence, and seems like a betrayal.

Fashion itself "romanticizes," because it programmatically suggests the forever unattainable, that which always keeps moving out of reach. Its "reality" is in its acknowledgment of sexual fantasy as a steady force. Used in art, it therefore went a long way in helping to create that Romantic Realism which was so dominant in mid-nineteenth-century painting, and which is also the hallmark of all cinema. Goya, in working with and never against fashion, linked himself with the Romantic temper as well as the modern one, and with modern film as well as modern art. The *Desastres de la Guerra* were not even published in his lifetime—he seems to have aimed them like an arrow into the future. And yet even there, just as in the *Caprichos* (which he did publish, although with difficult consequences) and in the portraits, the women are not neutralized to look as if they stood for Everywoman; they are quickly recognizable as modish for their time and as all the better human examples because of that, just like Gish and Garbo, Harlow and Monroe.

TEN

Watercolor;
Turner, Martin

G OYA WAS a nineteenth-century Romantic Realist half a cen-
tury before his time, but other artists of the late eighteenth and early nineteenth centuries, who followed a less eccentric path toward engaging the
inner eye, began choosing to work in landscape. It was a natural choice at a
time when both secular visualization and psychological conviction were requirements for art. Watercolor turned out to be a perfect medium for adding a sense of *enlightenment* to these. What Canaletto had suggested in oils
and Piranesi in engraving was developed further in topographical watercolor, especially by English artists, during the same period that Goya was
expanding aquatint in Spain, for analogous reasons but with different
subjects.

Topographical art was in the greatest demand in England, since the
English were the century's greatest travelers; and the English were the
most appreciative employers of Canaletto and admirers of Piranesi. It was
likewise in England that the atmospheric and creative Dutch topography of
Vermeer, De Witte, and Berckheyde was most imaginatively developed and
transmogrified, chiefly in watercolor. England is famous for its eighteenth-century Gothic revival and its love for extreme picturesqueness, both
kindled by English perceptions of French and Italian art; but it was still
the beauty of red brick with pale moldings that remained constant in the
English contribution to architecture, the Wren vision from the previous
century that owed as much to Dutch simplicity as to Classic prototypes.

Dutch esthetic schemes were similarly inherent in English portraiture,
in marine and landscape painting, and in much English popular illustration, even while Italian taste was ostentatiously governing the style of

grand ceiling frescoes. The Dutch sense of phenomena was as congenial to hard-headed England as the French and Italian styles of emotional expression were attractive. Imported Dutch, German, and Flemish artists, from Holbein to Van Dyck, from Gheeraerts to Zoffany, had virtually created English personal imagery, which was only thereafter confirmed by native talents. England's debt to Northern Europe for finding ways to picture the ordinary world was equal in size to its conscious admiration for Italy and France, which contributed so much to the more deliberate flights of English imagination. Despite English respect for Canaletto and Piranesi, English topography was a direct legacy from Holland, consonant with an empirical spirit and a secular taste. William III, after all, had been a Dutch English king.

During the eighteenth century English travelers in Europe had crystallized the idea of the picturesque in order to make alien lands intelligible and pleasing—at least to the eye. The tourist could countenance the forbidding terrain if he saw it conforming to notions of how pictures look, especially those of Salvator Rosa and other continental Baroque specialists in the rugged and the ragged, or of Claude Lorrain, who was such a master of out-of-door visual poetics. By participating in picturesque ideals, English landscape art could tame natural disorder into orderly beauty without sacrificing any of its specific character. "Nature wants cooking," said the drawing master John Varley—but as if nature were like boiled eggs or steamed green beans, better for the palate if cooked, but not adulterated or disguised. It was only necessary that the elements be rearranged.

The picturesque ideal for landscape and topography was elaborately fostered and even virtually created by many writings on the subject, not just of painters and teachers but of collectors and cultivated travelers, poets and professional essayists. The whole enterprise was conceived as instructive, an aspect of proper imaginative education analogous to acquiring a literary sensibility so as to gain the right sense of life. The formal order of the painted landscape corresponded to the formal power of poetic expression; the free strength created by Wordsworth's controlled diction for "The Prelude" matched the organic vigor of landscapes distilled by Gilpin, for example, into visual coherence out of an uncharted sweep of impressions. The idea took shape that art is essential for rightly processing visual experience, and that visualizations of natural phenomena are essential to the appreciation of them, and so to the acquisition of taste.

The existence of topographical renderings and landscape art became an indispensable part of travel. Pictures were not just to be acquired afterward as souvenirs and commemorations, as they had been in the early part of the century, but to be absorbed beforehand, so as to adjust the visual disposition of the traveler and by extension his spiritual readiness for the undertaking. And only then could travel become a refined pleasure, another field for actual cultivation and not just an occasional and dangerous necessity. Amateur sketching and watercolor painting became the appropriate corollary to appreciative traveling, not just for producing correct records but to show how well the viewer had responded. The practical interpenetration of art and experience seemed an enabling condition for the right exercise of the senses while on the road.

All this is very familiar. Echoes of this early-Romantic idea continue to resonate in modern commercial and documentary landscape photography, which is notably the only kind that influences the camera-carrying traveler. Ever since Claude's own black-and-white reductions of his paintings, the famous *Liber Veritatis,* were reproduced in mezzotint in 1777 and made generally available, the reproductive media have readily lent themselves to selling the right view of nature and showing how to get it. Readers of magazines and watchers of television are still responding to picturesque ideals originally realized by the enlightened English pleasure seekers of the eighteenth century.

The picturesque ideal is essentially static, however; it aims to freeze and contain. Claude's beautifully composed scenes had been part of the great classic search for perfection in terms of visual beauty. He further announced this aim by embedding legendary themes in his carefully arranged visions of nature, so as to associate his way of rendering it with the comprehensive myth-making that seeks to enfold human experience into a cosmological whole. But the picturesque English landscape-making of the eighteenth century that derived from this august precedent aimed chiefly to please, and so ultimately to flatter. It showed how the new consumer of Nature might triumph over the hard challenges she offers and so possess her wholly.

He could benefit, first from the pleasurable exercise of forcing a given view into submission, and then from knowing himself to be appreciative, a lover of beauty and therefore worthy of its surrender to him. The satisfactions of being a sensitive person were blended with those of being master. It then seemed not just pleasant but praiseworthy and therefore good for the self-esteem to travel among rocks and waterfalls and make acceptable sketches of them; the process is now being repeated everywhere with the camera. Picturesque landscape, old and new, makes Nature look attainable, and an attainable art looks like the best tool for capturing it. The appeal is usually to the desire to think well of oneself, and not to the desire for testing and changing oneself, which tends to demand some doubt and pain.

For the treatment of landscape in English art, the picturesque ideal was eventually superseded by the Romantic notion of the sublime; and the sublime has been the appropriate mode for cinematic landscape ever since. The philosophical and literary idea of the sublime acquired an esthetic existence in England through Burke's 1756 essay on it; and for art it was well suited to late-eighteenth-century aspirations toward a new form of expression that would demonstrate a sense of imaginative freedom. The expanding soul now needed expanding vistas detached from the old dispensations of art and religion, both of which had purveyed certainty. No comfortable fixity of subject or style could properly carry the burden of new emotional aspirations, now becoming revolutionary in various senses of the term.

The idea of being ceaselessly drawn by the always unattainable and the forever incomprehensible is what the sublime mode in art tried to convey. It is a cinematic ideal, because movement is implicit in it—a perpetual movement outward and onward toward something that will always be beyond present boundaries of vision or understanding. In the landscape painting that aims to express this idea, framing and *staffage* serve quite different functions from the ones they fulfill in picturesque art; the look of incompleteness and the sense of a personal attention unaccountably *in motion* are more important than balance and containment. A detached ideal of beauty no longer governs the harmonious arrangement of foreground, middle ground, and distance. The aim is no longer to show a "prospect," with a tree or two as *repoussoir* and a few typical inhabitants farther off, being viewed at leisure by someone visibly reposing nearby, who stands in for the viewer of the picture. Such a figure contemplates the scene as a whole and always includes himself as the key to it: perhaps he is composing a poem on it, or sketching it, consciously fitting it into his prior awareness, in some way finishing it off so as to be finally in charge, and thereby making us so. These are the components of picturesque landscape, according to which the viewer feeds on the cooked scene, and it becomes part of his unchanged substance.

The sublime landscape, rather, may seem utterly remote from any human consciousness, even any artist's. By "remote" is not meant necessarily exotic or difficult of access; the view may be of an ordinary shady pool, just as in Dürer's watercolors. The remoteness lies in the scene's visible retreat from any claim to entire comprehension, by anyone's eye and mind, of even a small fragment of the phenomenal world. Even a specific and immediate scene is forever partial, forever escaping and spreading out beyond understanding, beyond an artist's ability to box it in with his skill, with the force of his contemplations, or with literary associations. It may at best be only one frame in an open-ended, unpredictable sequence. Painters who try for this effect do not seem to be eating nature, but showing how nature eats them. They do not speak about the rocks; the rocks speak, like Marabar caves, and everyone is somehow moved and changed forever.

When the picturesque ideal governs the landscape in movies, as it frequently does, the result is often jarringly anti-cinematic, although pleasing in itself. Lush landscape in movies is often non-dramatic, sometimes bootlegged in as a convenient substitute for real drama, instead of informing the theme itself with a larger meaning by visibly enlarging its emotional scope beyond pleasure—perhaps beyond bearing. Picturesqueness remains an enemy of serious film drama; but sublime landscape can be its best servant.

The flexible watercolor medium, which could be thickened and shaded and made richly rhetorical for picturesque effects, could even better convey a transparency that suggests the blank infinity behind phenomena. The landscapes of J. R. Cozens and later of Thomas Girtin and J. S. Cotman, for example, show how rendering the simplest forms in the very thinnest layers of unshaded paint conveys the sense of an endless light that stretches beyond all seeing, but that at the same time precisely illuminates everything near and familiar. Cotman, in true Northern style, used an arbitrary-seeming, casual method of framing and choice of subject matter, the better to give the sense of motion among endless possibilities. While the sky shines blindingly through the taut veil of paint that creates shrubbery or masonry above, the stony foreground is sweeping toward us across the bottom edge. But we are not waiting. We float forward in mid-air, advancing swiftly to merge first with the rocks and the water, then with the tree, and finally the unending sky. The near pond reflects the high clouds, opening another gate to boundlessness right under our feet (10.1).

Cotman's greatest pictures, like Goya's, have been seen as forerunners of modern painting, partly because of their strain toward abstraction, toward a detachment of the forms from their subjects. But just as with Turner, that particular leap is never made. Cotman has greater affinities with the romantic subjectivity of modern film, which can so intensify the way things look that they also seem to strain at their self-contained existence, to leap at us out of their context and into ours. Cotman shares with film-makers an artistic ideal that demands perpetual movement. Under this law of art, resolution is always artificial. Frames can be arbitrarily frozen or the scene can be made to fade out; but the real truth is continuous movement onward into the continuous unknown.

C O T M A N ' S , Girtin's, and Cozens' watercolor subjects were modest by comparison with the scope of Turner's; and Turner in fact seems to have extended the domain of watercolor to swallow up that of oil painting, and

10.1 JOHN SELL COTMAN, *Shady Pool*

also vice versa, as if refusing to distinguish between them. But the work of all these artists has that engulfing effect also realized on the movie screen, where we are drawn in to participate without preparation, not urged to stand back and gaze in a state of schooled understanding. The thin air surrounds us, conveyed in screens of paint that seem to float by themselves. We can feel no guiding hand ordering the direction of our eye; we must move into the picture to seek completion of the view, its meaning, and its next revelations. Cotman's pictures suggest serene possibilities beyond their present surface; Turner's suggest reaches full of dread.

Fear was an important element in experiencing the sublime. It was the sort of fear that is like both awe and anxiety, and that oscillates between the two. The sublime required a large rather than a small fear, never merely a scare, whereas the picturesque often dealt in the pleasures of fright. Greater actual safety in late-eighteenth-century travel made it possible to begin enjoying both—to feel a pleasurable shudder at the precipice, but also a nameless, almost spiritual danger in all nature—and to welcome works of art that deliberately evoked the effect. Among modern movies, *L'Avventura* is an excellent example of the method. There the look of barren hills and houses, illustrating a personal doubt-ridden search for retrieval, continuity, and comprehension, manages to place the viewer at the mercy of the hero's anxiety, to fill the watching consciousness with the same driven, uncomprehending, and hopeless hope.

To be scared in this way without being physically threatened feels like a challenge, a chance to strengthen spiritual muscles, to pit the tiny self against vast forces, and so to feel its tininess respond, begin to refine, to harden and shine with reflective power: this is one of the strongest human pleasures. It can further lead to the sense of being filled with true virtue, if you believe that the fear you are feeling is a proper awareness of God's immensity—or nature's. Rather than flattering the beholder's vanity, by urging him to take personal satisfaction in encompassing nature with the power of his own gaze, the artist of the sublime offers him the pleasures of feeling undone and overwhelmed, raped in the highest cause, and so perhaps changed or changing into finer stuff. The strongly erotic thrill of fear is included in the best strengthening medicine for the soul, with landscape for the binding elixir.

Turner's mature works have the sense of danger in them. They also have just as much of the specific as Cotman's, despite the blur. When there are persons in Turner, they are not detached onlookers or decorations devoid of consciousness; they are dramatically engaged, even if we can hardly see them. We are made to consider the combined external and internal circumstances that swamp them at a critical moment. Turner's characters may be ordinary fishermen or antique heroes, or they may not even be people— they may be buildings, trains, or ships apparently endowed with human sensibility, like *The Fighting Téméraire*. But as in movies, that makes no difference to the way our eye is made to confront what is perpetually escaping, the natural whirl and lurch of the local phenomena that surround the subjective consciousness at intense moments.

This same optical blur, reflecting the vibration of psychic unease, upholds the sense of actuality in any Turner picture, whether it shows a modern fishing boat trying to operate in a storm or Ulysses taunting Polyphemus while escaping with his crew. Similarly in cinema, real rain or fog, or perhaps only the indistinctness of swiftly offered optical impressions, is made to have the same effect in historical movies as it is in films of contemporary life. In movies the subjective viewpoint is always supported by the Turner-like universality of emotional eyesight trying to grasp the world. Ruskin was right to say that Turner showed nature most truly, if the actual flavor of experience is the chosen theme. When there are no dramatic characters, we are invited to be one, to scan the empty ocean or the looming fog, to let things take us as they flow past.

Like Rembrandt, Turner produced an uneven surface, even for his watercolors, thick and thin or rough and smooth on different parts of the same picture. He apparently worked fast, blotting and scraping and scratching at the surface with his fingernail, refusing, also like Rembrandt, to be governed by the material. Such a fluctuating plane imparts an uneven motion to the image, along with a motility to the shapes inside it. The color, too, is "immaterial," never local, always of the air, or of the light, or of the inner eye itself. The prismatic effect is not directly relevant to these hills or that water in particular. The scene reflects the way things go in and out of focus and the eye constantly adjusts and readjusts as it struggles for its life.

Turner's form of indistinctness described the truth dwelt on by the proponents of the sublime—the human inability to fix and wholly understand the energy in the universe. Cinema is devoted to the same idea; the psychological condition that underlies the right perception of film is *uncertainty,* openness to opening views, awareness of the incomplete. The emotional satisfactions movies offer are provisional—perhaps that is what makes them modern, a basic necessity for twentieth-century romanticism. Michael Wood has pointed out that movies raise questions they don't try to answer, and that that is a reason for liking them. We are stirred up; that is our pleasure; and we feel that that is necessary and even enough for authentic narrative in this medium. Any path the story follows through a movie bypasses the countless possible others: What happens to the other car that drives off? The other man walking by? The rest of the clouds? Movie scenes of resolution and dénouement must close in, and so must close off those suggestions made, elsewhere in the film, of all we were permitted to glimpse and feel but not possess—the unresolved residua that have moved us from the start to keep watching, eager for revelations and meanings small or large. The final fade shuts them all down, also provisionally. There may—must—be a sequel.

Turner's urban scenes and much rarer interiors similarly echo the scanning gaze and receptive consciousness and ready emotion required of the modern romantic movie-goer (10.2). People glimpsed in the fantasy drawing-rooms of Petworth or on the Oxford High Street seem dynamic, ready for unknown emotional shifts and discharges, unforeseeable regroupings. *Two Women with a Letter* is an extraordinarily cinematic vision, a genre scene unlike almost any except in movies, yet with the flavor of a Terborch (10.3). We see one woman facing us, her body almost hidden by the nearer one, behind whom we are standing, and who has the letter behind her back. We are very close; we ourselves may even have just secretly given it to her. The woman she faces suddenly looks past her shoulder and straight at us, with parted lips and a face full of possibility—an interesting face, not pretty. Nothing is explained, no emotional or social circumstances are described. We are being forced to participate, perhaps improvise in a pressing moment—the scene will shift in a second, someone will speak or laugh or something else will happen.

Here Turner, who is said to have been no good at figures, does show his unmistakable understanding of fashion, the true sign of sexual understanding. The woman with her back to us shows us her emphatically bared

10.2 J. M. W. TURNER, *Interior at Petworth*

10.3 J. M. W. TURNER, *Two Women with a Letter*

neck and shoulder blades under a high topknot trimmed with a comb and flowers. Her neckline and sleeves sit to perfection. She is a sleek example of fashionable taste for 1835, when the rear view of the female neck, preferably plump above sloping shoulders, was an important focus of sexual charm. Curls descended right and left over the ears and temples, producing a frame for the face in front (Turner's other figure shows this) and for the naked neck in back. Erotica and fashion plates of the date insist on these effects. Turner's scene, like a film shot, enhances its drama with the extra sexual freight carried by modishness.

The atmospheric charge in this scene, also intensified by placing the two figures one behind the other to give a participant's viewpoint, shows that Turner (like a modern film director, or like a Dutch artist) understood the expressive power of modern dressed bodies engaging in small gestures, but he was not much interested in exercising the art-historical terminology of the figure, nude or draped, as a main means of expression. Given the sexual energy in his oeuvre, and the pornography he is known to have done, it may be that his feelings about bodies were too strong to permit it.

Critics have remarked on the stiffness of Turner's figures, when they are present—a stiffness which has an affinity with the same slight awkwardness in both Watteau's and Goya's renderings of bodies, or indeed of Rembrandt's. Turner reveals a disposition again related to the Northern tradition, even further suggesting the slim and slightly tilted people in De Hooch's works. Such a style of corporeal being for people in pictures seems designed deliberately to keep the flavor of unguarded feeling stronger than that of pleasure in normal physical grace. A figure style that dwells on bodily coordination makes any picture easy to look at and identify with in comfort, even if the theme is rape or massacre; the effect of physical imbalance make it feel uneasy, even if the theme is courtly pleasure, or happy love in a peaceful setting.

The link between Turner and Dutch art is consequently emotional, apart from the usual influence of Dutch sea-and-landscape painting on English artists, an affinity that comprises genre and legendary themes besides. For landscape, Turner went beyond Claude in the same simplifying direction as Cuyp and Philips Koninck, who were obviously painting the sublime *avant la lettre*. Like Turner, they painted as if to suggest that only the movement of light, weaving and casting its flexible net through our space and over our world, creating colors and keeping us alive through our eyes, prevents us from being swallowed up in infinity. These artists turn us loose in the scene to feel the pull of that endlessness almost as a danger, even if the scene is calm. The light-struck mist in so many Turner landscapes further suggests to us not an accurate impression made on the straight-gazing eye, but the effect of squinting against infinite light, when it (and perhaps everything else at the moment) reveals that it is too much for us. The townscapes are like the expectant views of Berckheyde seen through eyes now watering under greater stress.

Meanwhile Turner's legendary scenes are reminiscent of Aert de Gelder's *Way to Golgotha,* similarly conceived on a large screen, across which the action is moving without any emphasis on the looks and behavior of the central character. The emotional weather is instead being indicated by the sweep of the terrain, as if to prepare the viewer for a subsequent close-up of Hannibal or Ulysses shouting orders or curses, a scene not yet here but to come (10.4). Exactly the same effects are sought in Turner's accounts of storms in the mountains or at sea, involving a few human beings whom at the moment we can hardly make out, struggling against huge odds. Turner often did try personally to reproduce extreme experiences for himself, and to remember the exact effects of similar ones that happened by chance, so as to paint the effects correctly. The feel of the situation is the point—we are forced to enter into it. At any moment we expect another shot of a sailor or traveler caught in the event, as Turner perhaps had been before he made the picture; but right now we are getting the sense of how it all was. Along with legendary titles emphasizing process—*Dido* building

10.4 J . M . W . T U R N E R , *Hannibal Crossing the Alps*

10.5 J . M . W . **TURNER**, *Messieurs les Voyageurs on Their Return from Italy*
(par la Diligence) in a Snow Drift upon Mount Tarrar—22nd of January, 1829

Carthage, Hannibal crossing . . . , *Ulysses* deriding . . . , etc.—Turner ap-
pends lengthy titles to his modern scenes. They read like captions, with
plenty of present participles and descriptive phrases about the atmospheric
conditions ("Typhoon coming on," etc.), or as if they were directions in a
screenplay (10.5).

In all this Turner, like Goya, cinematically pushes the limits of *illustra-*
tion by showing one poignant physical situation in an intense psychic matrix, sharpening the impact of the moment, and widening the scope of its
resonance. These artists often do this by using somewhat ambiguous terms
for the surrounding material, which can then more easily stand for the
vague forces that are driving the human circumstances into conflict (or accord), and by being absolutely specific about one or two immediate facts.
One figure, tower, face, or ship, or a group of two or three will be emphasized in line and form, and then tinted light and shade will conjure the
larger world, where war and weather are as unaccountable as desire, or the
mist of fear may isolate near vision.

The Turner painting of a royal banquet in Edinburgh (10.6) could easily be by Goya, with its stiffish, bright-eyed figures, its odd angle of presentation and large areas of both bright and unclear interior space; the Goya painting called *The Fire,* showing part of a panicked crowd surging away from an undefined conflagration, could be one of Turner's scenes from legendary or modern history—an *Escape from Burning Troy* or a London disaster (10.7). The circumstances are indistinct and terrifying, but what we can see of the people is very specific, the bodies provisional and awkward in a graphic scramble toward us across the foreground. It has Goya's wartime-newsreel look, which Turner also sought for events in peaceful England or in antiquity.

Illustration in this vein is not anecdotal but illuminative, and not of a story but of a situation—and that includes the way the landscape is affecting a beholder or influencing human events. It is the same mode used in the old Flemish manuscripts, where the pictures *light up* the flow of the story at intervals instead of telling it. The story is made to appeal in the form of recognizable personal experience; and so psychological moments rather than objectively described events are chosen for the pictures. In this mode there need not even be a story, only encounters and discoveries forming an

10.6 J. M. W. TURNER, *George IV at the Provost's Banquet*

10.7 FRANCISCO GOYA, *The Fire*

emotional sequence in which we feel ourselves engaged—the kind of story
we feel almost able to complete out of our own imaginative sympathy, supplying background and various possible outcomes.

When there is *also* a known actual story (such as the conception and
birth of Christ), it is told as if tangentially, the way Turner shows Hannibal's trip or Regulus' punishment: this is also the way movies illustrate the
stories on which they are based. In films, sweeping views of the battle, the
ball, the natural disaster, the prison break, are intercut with views of small
groups against an ambiguous background, like Goya's and Rembrandt's, or
with close-ups of tête-à-tête encounters, like Turner's two women with the
letter. Incident is approached subjectively; there is no room for detached
pictorial narration cast in a uniform declarative style, showing everything

from the same fixed distance, episode by clear episode, one tableau after
another, with the chief characters prominent at all times. Rather, the progressive dialectic of near and far, of inner and outer, of private response to
external circumstance is what makes the stories in movies do their emotional work. Turner and Goya, like others following the impulse traced
here, struggled to make the single picture do what film has done since. The
story, whatever it is, is not "told in pictures," like the little scenes on a pre-
della or in Hogarth's sequential renderings; it is "brought to life" as if it
were happening, and not being told at all.

Turner, like many others, was also an actual illustrator, in that he made
pictures expressly to be reproduced in books and expressly to go with certain poems and travel writings. He was one of many to illustrate James
Thomson's *Seasons*, a favorite with lovers of the picturesque, and later he illustrated Scott and Byron, always with pertinent *landscape*, instead of
large figures grouped in a subordinate setting. The human beings in
Turner's illustrations must often be inferred, as so often in his oeuvre, and
for that very reason the human situation is made more acute because we
rush to project ourselves into it. His avalanche painting, for example
(10.8), shows a cottage being crushed under an immense boulder—no

10.8 J . M . W . T U R N E R , *Avalanche in the Grisons*

screaming or gesticulating bystanders, no visible humans instruct us in how to react, as they do in De Loutherbourg's version of the same subject; only a hapless little cat clinging to the roof tells us the house is inhabited. And we feel ourselves creating our own close-ups of the despairing faces inside. The cat claws directly at our hearts across the distance. Like many film shots, this picture is a vivid illustration of a human drama with no people in it at the moment.

In the period just before Turner's career began, landscape renderings were not illustrative at all. They had become more and more transformed into a commodity in England, where landowners liked to remind themselves of their own property and of England's regional glories, as well as of their own estimable travels. There was a demand for picturesque topographical views bound as sets into books, and graceful pictures of well-known sites were reproduced and sold individually as pleasing possessions for those who never left home. Turner's own introduction to art had been through seeing and copying such prints, and becoming expert in current techniques of both topographical rendering and graphic reproduction. An artist could easily make a living providing such pictures, with no pretensions to imaginative greatness or evocations of human encounters with the sublime. Turner continued to serve this market for straight topography throughout his life, even while the terms of landscape painting changed entirely.

During Turner's lifetime (1775–1851), topographical rendering was virtually transformed into art in its most serious form. New notions of Nature, chiefly expressed in poetry, created an enlarged moral and esthetic dimension for what had been a mundane and very limited activity. It was the one area in painting (and its concomitant graphic works) where the imagination had new territory to subdue, where feeling and seeing were perpetually combining to new avail. The field was being cleared whereon the later dramas of modern painting would be enacted; but at the same time the screen was being set up where modern cinematic topography would later be projected. The existence of such an artistic frontier enabled Turner to cast all the great old themes of history painting into the subjective mood, simply by invoking the new power of landscape to embody individual passion and moral significance.

In *The Battle of Fort Rock, Val d'Aouste, Piedmont, 1796,* Turner re-creates an Alpine battle, an episode from Napoleon's invasion of Italy (10.9). But the fighting is crammed against the left edge of the picture, where the tiny opposing armies skirmish on a narrow path and bridge. The camera is leaving them to it, moving back and to the right so that the screen is gradually filling with the image of the big chasm into which all these lit-

10.9 J . M . W . TURNER , *The Battle of Fort Rock, Val d'Aouste, Piedmont, 1796*

tle soldiers are in danger of falling, whatever their loyalties. Wooded crags
rise on either side of the gulf—we can't see the bottom—and the rest of the
mountains stretch back forever. But one wretch has already fallen onto a
narrow ledge near us, escaping the precipice by inches; he is being awkwardly supported by a woman who holds a baby on her shoulder. A camp
follower? A local matron from an isolated cottage? A gypsy? He is our momentary unknown hero, some ordinary man thrust into extremity by war;
and now history is moving on without him, out of the picture, and he is at
the doubtful mercy of this chance woman and this huge landscape, both so
strange and full of threat—What next?

Turner's distinctive style of sublimity could eventually find its way in
book form into people's inward sense of landscape, not just into their public awareness of its power in narrative painting. He helped to change everyone's private idea of how views look, and how it feels to look at them, and of
what they can mean, and so to prepare the way for the personally illuminating function of modern film-landscape. Besides illustrating the Romantic

poets, he published several sets of ordinary English views—Harbours, Rivers, Castles, pictorial accounts of journeys—which also show the magical way straight topographical reportage was being transformed into illustrative art, in an unprecedented kind of emotional collaboration between the artist and his public.

Turner's great contemporary and fellow English landscape-painter John Constable, on the other hand, was the other sort of artist. He was entirely non-cinematic, and helped to change topographical art into transcendent painting. He made no attempt to create an emotional universe in topographical terms; he was interested in the universe of paint itself, using his beloved rural scenery as an enabling system for testing painterly boundaries, not illustrative themes. His works are tremendously exhilarating, but never haunting. He did not "delight to go back to the first chaos of the world," as Hazlitt said of Turner, or ever try to suggest the inward side of visual perception. Constable's brilliant verve remains detached, and keeps him in the company of Rubens and Titian, as his great admirer Delacroix could see—himself an artist of a similar stamp. Cézanne went on from there.

Turner's *Liber Studiorum,* made in direct imitation of Claude's series and published between 1807 and 1819 in several volumes, was not a book of illustrations for anything; it was simply intended to demonstrate in etching and mezzotint how comprehensive his grasp of landscape was. Here Turner was making landscape as a broad idea, rather than as a small pleasure, available to people in intense black-and-white imagery made for private viewing. The *Liber* also showed that monochromy was perfectly congenial to Turner, since light was his true subject. With his superior psychological understanding of color, Turner was very subtle in his use of it. After visiting the Louvre, he is alleged to have said, "Rubens throws his tints around like a bunch of flowers."

Turner's famous and ferocious indistinctness in fact had special importance in colorless works. We have seen that the color he used in painting was never very local—often not the color of particular things but rather of the light around them, fragmented into primary yellows, reds, and blues. When scenes were engraved or rendered in mezzotint, it was the delicate tonalities, the sensitive and floating chiaroscuro, that carried the mood of the place. The psychological freight carried by topographical imagery in monochrome was thus shifted from the interplay of black shadows and light patches set up by Piranesi and Tiepolo to the moving emanations of cloud conjured by Turner. This shift was inclusive: black shadows retained their force. Turner experimented with them, too, in his later set of dramatic mezzotints referred to as the *Little Liber* (10.10).

10.10 J . M . W . T U R N E R , *Paestum*. Mezzotint from the *Little Liber*

The mezzotint, as a medium for translating watercolor into repeatable and publishable black-and-white images, now permitted the movement of light to echo the movement of feeling with much greater sophistication in pictures for general consumption. Mezzotint is an engraving medium. The plate is roughened all over by a special tool to create the dark areas, then scraped and polished in varying degrees in the areas where light is required, and then inked and wiped with several rags before being printed. A print by this method evolves from general darkness to illumination, and may have soft, subtle, and rich gradations of tone. Mezzotint helped to expand the poetry of buildings, for example, to include a larger emotional circumambience reflected in the variable atmosphere cloaking crags or valleys where they might sit, the harbors or crossroads over which they might preside, singly or in urban clusters. They could engage the viewer not just in a generalized state of expectancy and fantasy, but in a deeper condition that embraces nostalgia and longing. Boulders and buildings seemed to develop stronger personalities and larger individual souls, to be enriched by sharing each other's presence in colorless overcast moonlight, in gray daybreak or rainclouds.

In this century the black-and-white still camera has certainly developed these themes. But the movie camera has had the means to extend them indefinitely, using shifting gradations of tone for circumstantial emotional

effect in outdoor settings. The mist in standard thrillers, whether the locale is urban or mountainous, the glowing smoke of battle scenes and
heavy-industry scenes, the glowing dust of desert scenes are all part of
Turner's legacy. They continue the dramatic uses to which he put the ordinary blurring of ordinary phenomena. Movies now show, as Turner did
first, how real smoke and real anxiety may produce an equally real and indistinguishable kind of blur, and at the same moment.

Turner's effects can rightly be compared to those of the camera (in
which he predictably showed much interest at the end of his life) because he
was precise as to space and scale. The vortex of light and the detonation of
atmosphere never dislodge the convincing rocks and water, carriages and
shipping, people and animals, castles and huts. The rigging is accurate, the
buildings stand up. No liberties are taken with their stable actuality, and
so the luminous riot around them gains credibility. Turner remains topographical, only further recording the helpless shudder of desire and apprehension at what might be gathering shape at the turn of the road or across
the sunny water.

THE CINEMATIC impulse appeared among other English artists
of the same period in different ways, but still founded on the desire to
make pictures conform to the extreme emotional possibilities in ordinary
visual experience; light and shade had still to predominate. Size could add
its force to these in John Ward's *Gordale Scar,* for example, and create
dread on its own. The vast chasm, viewed from its floor by us and one isolated bull, is offered in subdued colors on a scale intended to overwhelm us
directly with natural mystery (10.11). The painter is not smiting us with his
esthetic position on Nature; he simply lets the dark rocks loom up while the
black cleft draws us in and the sky threatens. This would be a haunting
image in small format, but at eleven by fourteen feet, it produces the desire
to turn and run.

Large panoramas became popular in the last third of the eighteenth century, followed by dioramas in the early nineteenth, so that painting could
find yet other ways of trying to escape its confining frame and devour the
beholder. When the spectator looked at a panorama painted on the inside of
a cylindrical surface, he created the effect of movement himself as he kept
turning. In 1782 De Loutherbourg's *Eidophusikon* went further, offering a
continuous picture that actually moved across a proscenium to musical accompaniment, attended by shifting stage lights and made to transform
under the viewer's gaze by the clever use of lighted scrims. The depicted
scenes included views of London and storms at sea, with appropriate
sounds; but the effect seems to have remained picturesque rather than sub-

10.11 J O H N W A R D , *Gordale Scar*

lime, theatrical rather than cinematic, and it aroused wonder mostly at the technical feat. A diorama involved lighting a transparency from behind and showing it in a darkened room, varying the light effects rather than moving the picture, which would again usually be a landscape, a seascape, or a cityscape.

All of these were entertainments, intended to be momentarily exciting and not deeply important. They nevertheless showed a Romantic desire to move beyond the conventional theater, with its suitably adorned performances of texts, into a domain where the sublime effects already attained by landscape painters could be recast as show business. They aimed to let an audience feel directly involved in the basic dramas of the physical world, even if only in the form of tawdry illusions, instead of watching rehearsed and dressed-up actors pretending to be so in theatrical action, diction, and surroundings.

The element of show business in rendering the sublime was heavily emphasized by the history-painter John Martin, who specialized in scenes of Biblical catastrophe, including the Deluge and Judgment Day, and significant debacles of legendary antiquity. Martin's paintings and graphic works became extremely successful in the early nineteenth century, not only in England but in Europe and America, and he had a great deal of effect on the public and on painters much better than he was. He is an example of the sort of artist almost entirely confined to film in this century—an inspired special-effects man, a heroic production-designer. He was an original genius who affected the imaginative lives of thousands in his own generation and long after his time; but his productions exerted their influence in a sensational mode that was then regarded as artistically unserious and was

10.12 JOHN MARTIN, *Belshazzar's Feast*

promulgated in popular media. The mezzotints and engravings Martin made of his works had the distinction of being instantly imitated, forged, and pirated; his painting of *Belshazzar's Feast* was illicitly (and ineptly, to Martin's fury) copied for a diorama—so immediately did he satisfy the public's lust for the exact kind of extreme imagery he invented (10.12). Most serious art-critics and academic painters at the time found it indigestible, irrelevant to the development of painting; and even his defenders in the world of art had trouble with his technical weaknesses. The standard history of art has omitted him entirely until lately.

The cultivated men who unreservedly loved Martin's works in his own day were poets, novelists, and literary critics, many of them French—the same sorts of people who in our time first described the artistic valence of modern commercial movies and made them known as more than minor entertainments. Martin satisfied not just the general but the poetic thirst, too, for an illustrative style to match the Romantic sense of restlessness, of a pull toward what is impossible or toward some cataclysmic release. Victor Hugo and Gautier admired him greatly; the Brontës all copied his engravings.

He cleverly worked on the English passion for topography, then being transmuted by greater English artists, and extended the new emotional view of real buildings to include an emotional style for fantasy architecture —the same device Piranesi used first, and the movies use to seize us now. Charles Lamb said of Martin's "towered structures," "They satisfy our most stretched and craving conceptions of the glories of the antique world." But then he goes on to remark, "It is a pity they were ever peopled . . . ," and one can certainly see why.

Martin's grasp of human looks was very shaky, dependent on trite conventions which make his figures look like cardboard characters from Pollock's Toy Theater. He has none of Goya's or Turner's psychological sympathy, and none of Delacroix' sensuous grasp of the living body. It is clear that his fame, unlike that of the superior painters in Romantic times, could not survive the advent of Realism and the swift development of camera vision thereafter. But his architectural imagination was truly prophetic, and remains with us in all sublime movie versions of legendary structures, including not only the great Griffith sets but those for Lang's *Metropolis,* the Noah's Ark and Tower of Babel in Dino de Laurentiis' *The Bible,* and the great bridges and causeways built by the Krel in *Forbidden Planet.* The War Room in *Dr. Strangelove* and all the futurist hardware first manifested in *2001,* and so much imitated since, are all traceable back to Martin's sets for Biblical disasters and his illustrations to *Paradise Lost* (10.13–10.15). His invented crags and plains, sometimes flooded, some-

Above and right: 10.13, 10.14 JOHN
MARTIN, *The Bridge of Chaos* and
Pandemonium. Engraved
illustrations for Milton's *Paradise
Lost,* 1827. *Below:* 10.15
Architectural vision from Lang's
Metropolis, 1927. Compare with
the tower at the rear in 10.12.

times molten and burning, sometimes celestially verdant, likewise prefigure the planet-scape we find in cinematic science-romances that deal in First or Last Things.

Martin was obsessed with architecture and engineering in real life. He spent years perfecting plans for the reform of London's sewers and water supply and for the redesigning of its public spaces. Among these was a Thames Embankment, of which the extant section is only a poor ghost, which was intended to stretch for miles, all the way from Greenwich to past Hammersmith Bridge. Martin sat on various committees devoted to such projects for improvement, and he published, at his own expense and without hope of recompense, many drawings and plans for his ideas. Although none of them was built, they were admired at the time, and they all dwelt on the same kind of esthetic effects proposed for Thebes or Gomorrah in his spectacular paintings—sweeping prospects of heroic masonry lit with rows and rows of lamps, endless terraced colonnades, and massive towers. They were sublime designs for a wondrous movie London, as re-created by an art director of the fortieth century. Some of his practical suggestions about sewage and water supply were actually put into effect after his death; but his unrealized architectural renderings made their mark on the drawing style of later engineers and urban planners—the distant relatives, perhaps, of those future art directors still to be affected by his irresistible vision.

Martin had no good sense of the relative scale governing the way near and far figures inhabit a scene together; the eye is always struggling, for example, to fit *The Bard* comfortably into his setting, given the distance he is from the viewer and the size of the soldiers below him, but it never works: the bard is too large or they are too small. In fact, except for Moses dividing the Red Sea, sticking one or two agitated characters onto a stagy promontory near the front of an epic scene now seems to fail as a convincing pictorial device for a modern viewer, because the movie-camera view of the world has come to govern so much of our extreme imagining. Turner had already presciently rejected the motif for his best legendary paintings, as we have seen, and stirred his Hannibal right into the distant middle of the snowstorm. But while the theater was still setting the standard for thrills, Martin's arrangements were doubly thrilling: the foreground group invoked the best sensational elements of the melodramatic stage, but at the same time the viewpoint was pulled far back, *away* from the actors; and behind the gesticulating hero, the astounded eye was forced to scan amazing vistas from the secret theater of dreams.

Martin's paintings work better if the viewer edits out the nearby, dated-looking characters entirely. In *Belshazzar's Feast,* for example, his gaze may plunge gratefully across a lengthy view of torch-lit banqueting tables where a thousand sit at dinner, just as it says in the Book of Daniel. The nearest group of block-long tables is outdoors, exposed to the acid glare from ten-foot-high Handwriting on the hundred-foot-high Wall; the rest are set up under thick stone vaults between receding rows of squat columns that finally disappear in darkness a mile away, where they are crowned by two bloated skyscrapers high and fat beyond all hope of measurement. Or, in *The Great Day of His Wrath,* he may see entire cities scooped from their foundations and turned upside down in the middle of a blood-red sky, the towers crumbling head first into an ocean surging with drowned souls (10.16). The secret was to be specific—the other (and much easier) way of inviting the cinematic sublime than Turner's use of lucent blur.

Martin was not a very good painter, poorly trained by a provincial drawing-master. When he submitted his grand machines to the Royal Academy, they were treated with condescension and hung in the anteroom—tolerated, not much respected, but loved by the public. Martin could not hope to pit himself, as the Academy-trained Turner did, against the great painters of the past. Instead he well understood and served the longing to have extreme fantasy brought to life, not in tempered and masterly productions but by astonishing magic. This was a thing then beyond the scope of the stage; but it was certainly possible in pictures, if the artist was prepared to forget about Claude Lorrain.

One way Martin fostered the sense of himself as a wizard was by printing thick booklets to go with his paintings, souvenir programs describing all the archeological research he had done on Babylon (or Tyre, or Nineveh), citing exact dimensions and proportions and giving a small outline drawing of the picture, with each building precisely labeled. It was as if to say that his own artistic talent had nothing to do with his results: he had simply taken great pains to find out the facts and then conjured up the city just as it had stood. Then, usually, he would wave his wand and show it in the throes of total destruction, the grand and heavy masonry shivering into fragments or washing away in a flood, right before your very eyes (10.17, 10.18).

In fact he made the cities up, just as he did Milton's "Pandemonium," from verbal descriptions that left ample scope for the emotional style of visual invention, for dramatic renderings of fierce light, vast space, and great size. Many of the paintings were conceived in harsh reds and blacks pierced with white lightning, and Ruskin was right to call them bombastic. The real effectiveness of Martin's paintings showed in the mezzotints he made from them. These were monochromatic versions much larger than ordinary engravings, on which he worked in various inks, using combined

10.16   JOHN MARTIN, *The Great Day of His Wrath*

10.17   JOHN MARTIN, *The Destruction of Tyre*

10.18 Shot from *Samson and Delilah,* 1947

10.19 JOHN MARTIN, *The Fall of Nineveh.* Tinted mezzotint

techniques with great care and at great length, not trusting such work to artisans as many painters did.

The paintings themselves went on tour like shows, as large history paintings often did, sometimes exhibited as private commercial enterprises with tickets sold (in his case along with the explanatory booklets) rather than under institutional auspices, and sometimes for royalty. Martin's lurid paintings were immediate successes, but it was his later, graphic versions that rightly spread his real influence. They are much better and more haunting: even when tinted, as they sometimes were, the black-and-white medium tempers the bombast and reveals the genius. It almost seems as if he was aware that the graphic mode was his true element, the medium that would preserve him in eclipse, and through which he might move to reach the imagination of the future (10.19). The great past masters of painting he could not hope to rival; but he counts among those who pushed the graphic arts ahead to their cinematic destiny.

At this period, just as during the previous century and more, it was customary for painters to "publish" their works in graphic form, and the traveling exhibition of any given painting included raising subscriptions for the promised engraving made from it. The legal and financial aspects of this relation between an artist and his public varied; but it was a customary and even necessary part of a painter's career that he make money from reproductions of his works, as well as from the sale of the original paintings. If he had a serious graphic imagination, like Rembrandt or Turner or indeed like Martin, he would do the reproducing himself, if it was at all possible, and appear before the public directly as a graphic artist *even of his paintings*. His original graphic works—book illustration or single sheets—might then be all the more perceptible as great in themselves.

Other painters, with a purely painterly gift, may well have cared nothing about the flavor of the engravings made from their works, and felt detached from their possible graphic future in the public consciousness. Such painters, on the other hand, often had a supreme talent for the other kind of graphic art—for drawing, which represents the unique moment of creation and stresses its privacy, rather than its public life. Artists of this kind doubtless felt themselves artistically betrayed rather than confirmed by reproduction, except possibly in the form of reverent painted copies. Such an attitude in turn helped to shape the modern view of the exclusiveness of painting, and to divide it effectively from its former audience—the ones who paid to see the Martins.

There is no rule for this; but many of the painters I have called cinematic —those flourishing since the spread of printed pictures—have made no distinction of value between painterly and graphic expression, and also have been deeply concerned with the way their own paintings became graphic. They have kept a sense of the seamlessness of the pictorial world, even a sense of the porousness of visual awareness itself—the way the emotional effect of pictures may be indistinguishable from that of all other kinds of visual experience, the kind in daydreams, dreams, and daily visual life all at once. Many such painters seemed to desire a moving, flexible future life for their works based on that larger awareness, not just on the enduring virtue of the original paint inside its original frame.

ELEVEN

Friedrich, Schwind; Menzel and His Influence

I N   T H E   P A I N T I N G   he called *Peace: Burial at Sea,* Turner showed white sails looking black against a glowing sky, as if they had crystallized out of the black smoke from a cannon salute (11.1). At the time, certain of his critics objected; the effect seemed perverse and shocking. The motif looks natural by this time because we have seen so many photographic examples, especially in the persuasive kind of advertising art that inherits Turner's general aim to evoke raw responses. His painting was a mourning tribute to a friend and patron, but it approaches that subject so obliquely that the chiaroscuro vocabulary of pure feeling drowns out most of the descriptive language in the picture. The burial is not discernible—we need the caption to know about it—but the fiery clouds and the black sails above the burnished sea create a strong elegy without anecdotes.

Turner's picture dates from 1842, only three years after the official birth of the camera, and two years after the death of Caspar David Friedrich. But thirty-five years earlier, in his *Cross in the Mountains* of 1807, Friedrich was already investigating the pictorial method Turner later arrived at for his personal requiem, and trying to create a new form of strictly psychological religious imagery. He was looking for something that would appeal to specifically Christian spiritual longings, without falling back on representing any traditional Christian myths or doctrines. Friedrich's painting was a devotional image, not just a religious picture; it was built into an altarpiece intended to inspire worship. But he used the same terms Turner used and movies now use to evoke religious feeling when it is required for general purposes, not just for epiphanic episodes in Bible epics —the radiant sky, with something significant in sharp contrast against it.

11.1 J. M. W. TURNER, *Peace: Burial at Sea*

Here it is the cross and the pines, conflating nature and religion with perfect ease (11.2).

As in several of Friedrich's paintings, the cross is only a local, modern crucifix, something one might actually see in rural areas, and the trees are perfectly familiar. So is the sky, with its clouds cut by sunbeams. The awe is inspired simply through the psychic movement evoked by the arrangement. The soul feels most drawn by the ordinary made transcendent; and since the biggest and highest ordinary object here is a crucifix, the soul's immediate response becomes associated with the worship of the Christian God. Neither the exposition of dogma nor the narration of mythology is necessary; the delineation of some pure symbol, such as a direct rendering of a supernatural cross, would be lifeless by comparison.

11.2 C. D. FRIEDRICH, *The Cross in the Mountains*

This shortcut to religious devotion by an emotional route also leaves out the artist as the inspired explicator of God's mysteries to men's eyes. It is another case of the "handless eye," the conjuring of the vision, not its creation. Here it is the conjuring, rather, of a *situation:* the mysteries remain mysterious, and the whole relation between God and human beings (including artists) stays uncertain and therefore exerts a formidable pull. Such a picture suggests that divine revelation lurks in views of common things, especially in natural phenomena—but it is the revelation of a constant process, not an answer or an explication. The artist is only another seeker and partial viewer like ourselves, one who puts a frame around some moments of the search and opens a window briefly, like a film-maker. Beyond the frame is only sky and landscape, perhaps some animals or shipping: it is our response, so often urged and focused by a salient foreground icon against the distant light, that makes it the Beyond, the realm of the spiritually unknown.

The crucifix in *The Cross in the Mountains* is made even more cinematic by being shown slightly off-center and at an angle, like the architectural fantasies of the Bibienas. As with those heavy piers and portals, this delicate vision seems to be turning in a great arc. It makes us wish to circle to meet it, to put ourselves at its center, to climb slowly upward around the rocks, to face the rising beams directly, or maybe to face the sculptured Christ at last, to be finally illuminated with it and by it. The firm stones, the enduring pines, the eternal cross are nevertheless unstable, caught in the motion of the earth, its sun, and our moving camera eye, beacon of the aspiring soul. Religion in the movies is also a matter of manipulating the light, whatever else is in the picture—natural wonders, or the interior of a cathedral, or the dramatization of a canonical miracle (11.3, 11.4).

For several years after 1806 the foreground objects in Friedrich's works were often human beings seen from the back, and often already centered to face the moment of truth in the sunrise, the mountain range, or the opposite riverbank. Their central placement works as a focusing agent, not just fixing the gaze and the attention but filtering them and condensing them into spiritual engines. The background landscape may be apprehended only straight through the soul of the man or woman. We move in like a camera on the back of the head, and only then beyond it to the setting, where

11.3 Still from *Jesus Christ Superstar*, 1973

11.4   C. D. FRIEDRICH,   *The Cross by the Baltic*

the light and the mist and the hills may then never be viewed neutrally. The person's private view gets hugely and permanently in our way (11.5).

Meanwhile he does not know we look at all. He himself is not precisely looking; often there is nothing to see. But his experience—whatever it is, and it must be inner—colors ours without his knowledge or intention. The figure in a picturesque landscape, on the other hand, usually stands aside as if purposely appealing to our gaze and guiding our understanding, allowing us a share in his appreciative version of the view. Friedrich's figure is lost in it, and fundamentally not interested in what it looks like, only in what is happening to him.

This is an extreme example of the cinematic approach to landscape. Instead of harsh rocks and cascades standing for human strife and risk, or brilliantly colored meadows for joy and peace, there is often a luminous void or a misty prospect in which an unremarkable sea or field or mountain forms a rather unfinished-looking setting. The hills and water and trees themselves may form unbeautiful, even awkward compositions. But the

11.5 C. D. FRIEDRICH, *Two Men at Moonrise by the Sea*. Chalk and sepia drawing

movement of the rising mist and spreading light draws on the need for
meaning that burns inside our small packed skulls and clenched hearts;
and we are made to feel the pressure of immense desire for a point to
things. The material in the picture may often be unexciting; the picture itself is always intense.

One source of this effect is Friedrich's working method. He worked the
same way Turner and Watteau did, slowly building spontaneous-looking
paintings out of a hoard of many incidental sketches, and using the same
motif several times. This again is the art director's method, whereby the
force of the fantasy makes the photographed result look more natural, more
true to what we want of our phenomena than any straight record can give.
It's not a matter of artistically retouching or exaggerating a plain view, but
of making the whole thing up out of the most effective small elements to
suit a particular emotional idea, and then offering it as an immediate impression. There is a very thin paint film in Friedrich's works, combined
with an occasional uncertainty (about feet or ears or groups of leaves) in an
otherwise precise, even strangled style. These features reinforce the sense
of mobile response, both his and ours, instead of demanding any reverence
for his visible efforts. And again *transparency* is an essential part of the effect, the look of a whole universe held in existence only by the taut and
tinted screen.

Friedrich insists on the concentration of psychic attention, no other kind. When he chooses something objectively spectacular, like a chalk cliff or an ice field, its dramatic looks are not emphasized by enthusiastic brush-strokes and a theatrical presentation designed for impact; its looks may in fact be somewhat sobered. But he places and lights the phenomenon for slow contemplation, often centrally, so that the craggy stone and the jagged ice may not simply sit there and show off, but must develop the kind of humming, magnetic importance he also gives to naked branches, a ruined arch, flat water, a mean shed, or a fishing boat.

Friedrich's basic assumptions were religious and specifically Protestant Christian, but his sense of the human place in the universe seems larger than that. The crosses on seashores and mountaintops, the looming bits of church and abbey seem important but also incidental. It is as if he thought Christianity was only a small device for organizing the huge spiritual desires that surge through human life, seeking some right channel by earnestly contemplating the often meager sum of what there is to see. Friedrich is interested in the large dimensions acquired by the visible world when in the presence of a large psychological eagerness.

Man's passage through his own individual life was an obvious theme for someone with such a questing disposition, and the sense of death as a further journey, even a desirable one. Friedrich's works are full of such progressions, or the suggestion of them; and they are rendered as if the viewer, painter, and subject were together engaged in that same forward movement toward infinity. This is true even if the subject is not human. The great central tree or ship he often shows is a character, undertaking or undergoing some ordeal, and seemingly *in motion,* twisting, drifting, always seeking; the very hillside floats up hopefully, an eager pilgrim following its tide of visitant clouds. The lighting of the *Abbey in the Oak Wood* or the *Solitary Tree,* as in many other Friedrich landscapes, shows a foreground in shadow contrasted to a luminous distance, no matter what else is in the picture—a procession of monks or a family, a single shepherd or a single sail, some horses or some trees. The effect is of light rising off the earth and drawing everything after it, whatever the time of night or day (11.6, 11.7).

Friedrich represents the transcendental view of the sublime that was later to find such effective exponents in America. He is an early example of a specific strain in the development of Romanticism that insisted on the liberation of the spiritual life from old forms of religious constriction, to concentrate on what Robert Rosenblum calls "the search for the sacred in the secular modern world." Rosenblum finds Friedrich's descendants among certain transcendental modern painters, such as Rothko. But the path Rosenblum traces leads away from the realism, even the materialism, that was

Above: 11.6 C. D. FRIEDRICH, *The Solitary Tree.*

Below: 11.7 C. D. FRIEDRICH, *Couple Looking at the Moon*

essential to Friedrich's style of search. Actualities recorded by the movie camera, on the other hand, can offer a suitable vehicle for it.

Friedrich's sketches show that he pored over the exact look of a straw sunbonnet stuck on the end of a railing, or of a woman's empty house-slipper—not, as Van Gogh later did with his own shoes, to comment upon them in expressive paint, or to comment at all, but simply to stare and stare, as at the sea or the sky. The camera, rather than any later school of painting, has specialized in that special kind of stare, which seems to constitute a question and a quest; and specifically it has been the *moving* camera, which can encompass that steady pull, that drag always onward that prompts such staring to start with, the sense of there being more.

In twentieth-century America, the movies have been more significant conveyors of the transcendental impulse than any other modern art, and perhaps all the more for being so long unrecognized as an art with such capacities. Our movies had the advantage of flourishing unselfconsciously for several generations, tempering their character to our psychological needs, as relief sculptures or mosaics did in earlier worlds. Like them, movies were made by many hands and eyes at once, often with both patchy and masterly results, the botches and the glories existing side by side. Stanley Cavell claims film as Americans' necessary art in some way that it is not for others. Indeed our artistic disposition is that of perpetual quest, vision followed by eager revision, a willingness to throw everything out only to scramble for its recapture, to inflate and deflate, to keep doubting and looking again, claiming and reclaiming, going to extremes, making artistic capital out of a colossal lack of certainty. Our ephemera may express us best; and out of transparent film our movies spin and weave a firm cradle for our enabling tales.

Friedrich shows, in its purest form, where we got it, which is to say from Romantic Germany. By "it" I mean the visual means that added its own transcendental flavor to the ordinary or even banal narrative material of movies. Again, the original source is in the Northern pictorial tradition altogether. Friedrich studied the Dutch landscape-painters of the seventeenth century; but still further back, his modern-seeming, psychologically freighted use of pine trees and rocks derives ultimately from suggestions made about them by Seghers and Altdorfer (see 3.2, 4.1, and 4.2).

Art of the Romantic period reconstituted its own terms so as to be personal, to deal deliberately with the irrational and the unconscious elements in life as actual subject matter; in doing so it prepared the way for the artistic concerns of this century. The German way of doing it could rely on a whole range of overtones from the Northern artistic past, not all of them congenial to American cinematic romanticism.

Friedrich's contemporary Otto Runge, for example, invoked the sublime with a panoply of overt symbolism. Runge was eager to demonstrate both his need to brood on unfathomable matters and his capacity to set up a stable visual system for doing it, full of explicit supernal radiance and earthly wondrousness. His art has no descendants in cinematography, only in animated movies. In direct contrast to this, Friedrich sticks to exact reality for his version of the personal sublime, even the reality of boring and unwondrous coastal rocks and dumb trees. He refrains from showing how wonderful his artist's sensibility is; his posture is one of acute humility, but acute attention to the bearing such things might have on the meaning of life.

This is what makes these landscapes rather like the contrived movie sets of the 1930's and 1940's, the backgrounds for the deliberately Germanic-romantic *Frankenstein* and other horror films, and for ordinary melodrama, too (11.8, 11.9). Artificial snow, carefully wrought and lighted dead trees, well-made papier-mâché rocks, or canned moonlight on the water become part of the drama in such films; we are shown them as aspects of the human story, even if nobody is in the frame at the moment. And even if they look strained, made up for the occasion as Friedrich's trees and ruins also do, they still do their work: we are affected in the right way by the authentic emotional and psychological envelope they put around events.

Such material in movies has Friedrich's effect of purporting to be a plain record of the surroundings, not an artistic vision of them. Movies following the Expressionist example of *Dr. Caligari,* on the other hand, often try to show a deliberately confected environment under complete artistic control, with city streets and interiors overtly emotionalized; but the essential Romantic style of the classic cinema follows Friedrich's much more restrained program for nature. In classic popular movies, bare branches and twilight skies and a pebbly beach with a few broken boards on it are made to look the way they really do look; but the intensity of the human situation at the moment, whether it's one person's inner state or a drama among several people, gives them a pregnant character, the look of being heavy with meanings projected into them by human fantasies and perplexities. This look is directly conveyed first by their very existence as products of moving light (that is, as movie-camera phenomena) but also by their slightly stiff look, which reads almost as self-consciousness. This pointedly stark tree echoes what we feel; but it can actually do nothing except keep rather awkwardly standing there with its branches sticking out. And that's enough, somehow—just what we want.

This is a quality very different from that conveyed by an expressive exaggeration of form, or by excessive spectacular effects. It is also very dif-

11.8 Still from *Evangeline,* 1929

11.9 Still from *Tom Sawyer,* 1938

ferent from the look, common in paintings, of a transmuted impulse toward visual abstraction, of the artist showing what great creating Art can do to Nature. The followers of Friedrich tracked by Rosenblum into the twentieth century have obeyed that impulse; but other followers, doubtless unconscious ones, have been the makers and photographers of natural movie-scenery in the classic Hollywood days.

Like Bruegel, Friedrich began his career as an artist in monochrome. His first successes were small sepia brush drawings, and for years he stated his distinctive themes in that limited medium, as well as in chalk, ink, and pencil, before moving on to oils. Later on, in the paintings, he continued and varied the austerity he had achieved in his early, colorless views, often of nothing but empty sky and smooth sea with a hazy sun or moon rising, and perhaps one or two lumpish offshore rocks, or of uneventful fields and groups of dead trees. These muted graphic works have a fully expectant look, the air of being settings for characters' responses, even when there is nobody about and the scene is very dull.

The lighting is doing most of the work, giving these flat phenomena the power to suggest a longing for deliverance in the same way that classic movie-scenery—pertinent settings for cinematic drama, not beautiful locales photographed for their own sake—suggests a longing for resolution, not resolution itself. The sunset into which the lovers ride, the road down which Chaplin and Goddard walk are poignant because they show, even at the very end, the same pull toward the still-unknown, toward something more, that the movie itself has been exerting. Friedrich could do it with an uninteresting low wall containing a half-opened gate, or with the black entrance into a wood just ahead on the sunny path; and like Chaplin, he could do it all in black and white (11.10, 11.11).

His settings are prepared for the presence of plain characters, persons or a person, not for that of a painter or a poet—for us, in fact, as direct participants in an emotional sequence (not as possible artists' models, or sympathetic fellow painters). He often puts himself into the picture, but not as a painter or an artistically detached observer; and the other figures, small as in Turner's works, are also daydreaming and brooding and waiting, sometimes in pairs, but never admiring the specific beauty of the view itself. There is also no private artistic struggling in public, such as Cézanne undertakes. Friedrich pretends not to be a creative artist at all—not a maker and changer, not even a sharp observer, only a contemplator. The painter's hard work has been unobtrusively gone through, the technical mastery is swallowed up by the atmosphere; that is the art director's desired effect.

Friedrich is another, like Rembrandt and Goya, for whom there was no

11.10 C. D. FRIEDRICH, *Early Snow; Entrance into a Wood*

11.11 Still from *Modern Times,* 1936

sharp break in importance and no significant difference of subject and
treatment between small graphic works and large paintings. He, too, shows
that for the subjective visionary, light is so primary that the medium is
always "graphic," whether it is black and white or paint. Color is employed
as a servant, not acknowledged as a master, and subjects are not ranked to
fit an idea of its superiority. To show that a sunrise is compelling for the
way its changing angle of radiance tints the soul, and not for the glorious
tints it lends the sky, a tiny pencil drawing will suffice. Moonlight is a favorite subject partly because it tends to bleach the color out of familiar
things; and its extreme emotional effects, too, may be conveyed on a small
scale and in the most modest graphic media. On the other hand, the bright-
green meadow sleeping in the afternoon light may be brilliantly painted in
one version, and as brilliantly drawn in sepia in another; the glitter of the
sun, a precious and transient blessing, is the same in both.

The double view of Friedrich's two studio windows is a crucial cinematic
work, a private early commitment to the portrayal of inner process. This
pair of sepia drawings, two frames from one film shot, was done in 1805
but not sent for exhibition until 1812; it was as if Friedrich were hanging
on to them for his own contemplation. They are among his most startling
works, all the more for being so spare, lacking arches or crosses, moonlight or sunbeams, mist, rocks, or people, or any hint of ocean and old trees
(11.12, 11.13).

What we have instead is a long gaze out the window during working

11.12 C. D. FRIEDRICH, *View from the Studio Window, left.* Sepia

hours. It is a record not just of the simple river view and its bare domestic frame, but of what the gazer, pausing at his labors to stare out, had on his mind. Once more there is no demonstration of what glories a painter can make out of a mere glance at the French doors, such as Matisse repeatedly gives. Nor is it a *tour de force* of illusionism, such as certain Dutch painters made. This is, rather, an establishing shot for a scene of private meditation on a common enough theme—the passage of time, and the relation it has to the human sense of inward change, the significant passage of an inner life amid the neutral flow of events.

How can a view out the window show all this? It is a film-maker's question. To a modern movie-goer, Friedrich's pair of frames suggests that after we look for a while at these two uninteresting windows, a person, whose head we shall see from the back, will enter the frame and begin to pace between them in the dim room, staring first out of one and then the other at the light, and allow us to help him watch the distant boats crossing the limited patch of flowing water, the far clouds, the nearby mast of the

11.13 C. D. FRIEDRICH, *View from the Studio Window, right.* Sepia

boat that brushes so close. And as we watch him watching them, we will gradually and semi-consciously see the single key on a hook in the wall, the scissors on the other hook, and the cramped reflection of the top of the door and the top of his head in the dim little mirror facing us.

Then we will get it and feel it—the large and skylit outer stream, the small and dim inner trickle, the desire to unlock and merge, the fear of stasis and the hope in motion, the certainty of death. All cues about such understanding are buried in ordinariness and lucidity, perceptible only if the moving camera keeps insisting on this steady double view. The presence of the implied man or woman is not even necessary.

Friedrich is yet another of those artists who use modish clothing to link the fleeting visual world with a condition of inner longing in the cinematic way. Almost all his characters wear sharply contemporary middle-class town dress, except for the odd monk or hunter, or the men in allegedly Old German costume who have caused so much comment. Their caps and cloaks, always seen from the back, are more like references to the general

Romantic habit of fancy-dress, which was an aspect of fashion at the time, than direct statements of alliance with "olden-days" sentiment. The garments are in fact more like conventional student garb (crossed with a suggestion of artists' trappings) than they are like the real Old German costumes the archaizing Nazarenes took up. Friedrich sometimes wore a cap and cape himself, just as Rembrandt did, and perhaps even because Rembrandt did, in sympathy with the idea of the solitary artist as the stand-in for the single consciousness—the responding Man, never the shaping and mediating God. The figures wearing them in his paintings stand for himself and a friend or disciple, shown in a moment of private receptivity; and each seems much more a humble student than a magisterial artist. Most Friedrich personnel wear modern fashionable clothes, just like movie actors, so that we can be sure to identify with their feelings. The women especially (also just as in movies) wear their fashionable shapes of skirt and hair and ornament as inseparable indications of their emotional selves, the signs of present desire and instant psychological readiness. They look absurd on mountaintops; but somehow right.

FRIEDRICH was famous and influential in his time and had a long career, associated primarily with the city of Dresden and its Academy. In general he represents a German way of being an artist during the Romantic period, serving a middle-class and intellectual public and leading a middle-class town life. His travels were modest journeys to and from his childhood and family homes or to scenic parts of Germany. He never went to Italy or France, or even Switzerland, and artistically and personally remained a local phenomenon. He made no artistic pilgrimages to famous centers of antique glory or advanced modern activity, and created all his innovations in the absence of an artistic avant-garde.

Friedrich was not aiming the message of his art at like-minded artists and connoisseurs, either of his time or in the possible future, over the heads of ordinary and presumably uncultivated people. He was consciously and conscientiously serving a present public, even while embedding private fantasies in his paintings. The public in the small autonomous cities and towns of not yet unified Romantic Germany in fact took itself seriously and fostered an interest in the kind of picture that did more than entertain. Besides the academies of art and learning in the larger cities, small civic art-societies collectively commissioned works and set up competitions. The arts were not the exclusive property either of princes in courts or of artistic coteries in a large capital; and art patronage was unconnected with either kind of exclusive prestige.

Artists from elsewhere and even various noble patrons eventually visited

Friedrich, and literary people and thinkers from Berlin, Weimar, and Jena wrote about him; but his pictures, like those of other German painters, were straightforward commodities provided for current customers, somewhat in the old North European craft tradition which had supported Dutch painters in the seventeenth century—who of course influenced these German Romantics. Consequently, their style and subject matter remained for the most part attuned to a general bourgeois taste, and tended not to be esoteric, exclusive, or founded on a classical ideal; and in that way, too, much Romantic German art prefigured the cinema.

But it is the actual visual quality that is similar, not the circumstances. After the austere spiritual visions of Friedrich and his friends Carus and Dahl, and the more avowedly Dutch-inspired interiors of Kersting, came the more illustrative works of Schwind and Blechen, Ludwig Richter and Menzel, Schadow and Rethel during the middle decades of the century. These artists were part of a movement toward even greater naturalism that went on in different styles in different places, but that also included a new interest in folk tales and old legends as well as in the ordinary events of modern life.

Among these painters, the illustrative impulse was usually carried out in the terms of mundane naturalism laid down by Friedrich, not in the idealizing and artificially artless mode adopted by the Nazarenes, who went to live in Rome and copy medieval art, or in the heavy Neoclassic style propounded at the beginning of the century by Gottlieb Schick. Persons, buildings, objects, and natural phenomena were arranged and lighted for maximum psychological effect—an echo of the Dutch idea—not for pictorial harmony, and all themes were given the flavor of momentary experience. The result is cinematic in a more cozy mode than that of Friedrich's exalted scenes, like ordinary movie comedy and melodrama rather than inspired horror films and thrillers.

The look of having been deliberately set up to look natural, only more so —that same look that Friedrich gave his groups of trees and that informs so much Hollywood set design—was part of the effect sought by Blechen and also by Schinkel, both of whom were actual set designers. Paintings in fact gave them the chance to create movie sets, as it were, to use the charged atmosphere made possible by emotional lighting to better effect than the stage would allow, to make more engulfing drama out of stone walls, snow-laden pines, or Gothic tracery outlined against a setting sun than could appear in any theater of the time (see 1.6).

Meanwhile Schwind's *The Morning Hour,* for example, offers a small personal scene with a much more incidental and faintly comic flavor than Friedrich's back views, even while it relies on his methods (11.14). The set

11.14 MORITZ VON SCHWIND, *The Morning Hour*

dressing in this little scene is again realer than real, too good to be true; but it is also washed with moving air and light and framed as if scanned by cinematography, not fixed by a still shot or painted to show off a skill at charming detail. The effect is very satisfying. Everything we want in such a young girl's bedroom at such a moment is exactly right, and yet it seems perfectly casual and in a sense thrown away—the camera is moving in on her, there will be a cut to her face, the scene will begin to develop. But we have absorbed her little slippers and the shoved-back covers, the simple sewing table; we feel her little bare feet on the wooden floor, scorning the slippers in eagerness to let in the light that still pushes against the left-hand blind. She ignores the mirror for the window—a simple girl, handy with her needle, full of enthusiasm, devoid of vanity—we get it almost without seeing it. Instead we watch her and feel like smiling, and applying the adjective "little" to everything about her.

The back lighting in this small domestic painting does the same work it does in the transcendent outdoor scenes of Friedrich, the landscapes of Cuyp, or the interiors of De Hooch. What makes the picture cinematic is the psychological movement set up by the light coming toward us through the picture, drawing us toward what it may next reveal, interesting us even if the subject is silly; and also by the random-seeming frame that cuts off the chair back and exposes so much extra floor, keeping what we see in a state of potential motion. Schwind's picture, with its modest thematic ambitions, its quality of middle-class sentiment rather than larger spiritual striving, nevertheless shows that high visual ideals may be put to use for the creation of ordinary comedy without any loss of authenticity.

This is what the best classic Hollywood movies have done, even just pictorially. *The Morning Hour* has the movie-frame quality one also finds in Schalcken in the late seventeenth century, although he usually used artificial lighting. What is similar and very movielike is the charged quality of the entire image. Such pictures offer the slightly melodramatic, slightly erotic, slightly sentimental comic view of life; but they are cast in the most serious pictorial terms, the ones based on moving light and atmosphere that were originally set up by the first great religious painters of the North and later used by Vermeer. Schalcken's and Schwind's way of conveying humor and sentiment in modern domestic drama is not with a glossy array of stagy gestures or broad caricaturing, but only by putting a background condition of delicious popular fantasy into a very serious Northern rendering of natural appearances, the kind that makes the painter seem to disappear. The faint blurring of edges here again indicates the natural movement of breath, the flicker of actual eyes.

The girl's perfect figure, perfect hair, and perfect bedroom in the Schwind are echoed in scenes from movies like *Laura,* for example, where Gene Tierney's perfect hair, figure, and bedroom are photographed in live motion, so we can see they are actual, even while we know they are dream-factory products, an art director's careful work. We know it, but we don't see it; what we see is Laura speaking and moving; her perfections, arranged and lighted to be seen by that moving camera, make her both alive and a dream. Schwind sets up his maiden in the same way.

In the first half of the nineteenth century the Germans were best at this kind of thing in painting, because they had the most direct access to the old Northern tradition. Romanticism could operate in genre terms, not just for the formulation of heroic or exotic new visions such as Delacroix was creating in France. The German Romantic emphasis on folk tales as a foundation for serious art gave movielike scope to simple stories, and especially to fragments of possible stories not fully told. Genre themes were given a lightly fairy-tale character, that fantasy flavor which makes movies so compelling. For subject matter, a whole world of afflicted or frustrated lovers, highwaymen, ghostly appearances, poor students, wicked huntsmen, honest woodcutters, mysterious monks, and sheltered princesses could be set forth, arranged, and rearranged in naturalistic terms, without reference to specific literary sources.

These "dreams of a people," as Novalis called them, were, as the movies have been for us, the conduits of the irrational, of unconscious wish. To function as such, they did not have to make use of Dante or Shakespeare or Keats or Tennyson, as so much English Romantic art did. In German Romantic painting, fantasy-narrative fragments could, moreover, be rendered in a transient illustrative style that was connected to Dutch realism, not to the idealistic beauty of Italian Renaissance art or to the rhythmic modes of the Baroque, again such as Delacroix used. Camera narrative, in illustrating fairy tales like *Stagecoach* or *It Came from Outer Space,* must also be grounded in the action of light, the record of its movement through space.

Schwind was an ebullient, wide-ranging artist (he was also a violinist) and he did many sorts of fantasy picture, some of them cartoonlike, some very classical and heroic in style with plenty of Renaissance references to both Dürer and Raphael, and entirely non-cinematic. But his *Apparition in a Forest,* for example, could again be a frame from a film—all the more for being a realistic, quite economical, yet mysterious image that suggests a story without telling it (11.15). It could almost be part of the same film of which *Departure in the Early Morning* is another frame. There the young traveler leaves the house before dawn, the moon still up, the old house dark

11.15 MORITZ VON SCHWIND, *Apparition in a Forest*

11.16 MORITZ VON SCHWIND,
Departure in the Early Morning

and silent as he creaks open the little door and casts back a last look; later, in the woods, the moon is lower and redness colors the east as a luminous lady in white drapery suddenly appears to lead him deeper, farther, to some wonderful and unforeseeable dénouement, no part of his plan (11.16).

The "olden-days" flavor of the apparition picture does not inform the style in which it is done, only the subject. The style contains no colorful medieval limitations, no references to stained glass or antique panel. The lady's hair is bushy and ordinary, not sinuous and decorative, her body is palpable and also ordinary, her dress has real weight and texture as the wind stirs it, unencumbered by the careful arrangement of art-historical folds—it is as if the actress had draped on her sheet, brushed out her hair, waited for the light to hit her and the wind machine to work, and then begun to move off as the camera began to turn. The youth comes crashing and stumbling after her in the darkness through the papier-mâché trees.

The scene is remarkably casual in composition, to keep the feeling of uncertain experience attached to the theme of magic—as in the movies.

Alfred Rethel, who came from the Rhineland and began his studies at the rather sober Düsseldorf Academy, was a very different sort of German artist from the light-hearted Viennese Schwind. His reactionary political views did not prevent him, however, from developing a forward-looking style of realism, even for heavy historical works celebrating the glories of the Holy Roman Empire. The oil sketch for one panel in his projected mural series about the life of Charlemagne is another moment from a historical film, quite different in tone from the operatic style usually used for solemn mural subjects.

The *Visit of Otto III to the Crypt* commemorates a pilgrimage to the embalmed body of Charlemagne by one of his successors (11.17). The great emperor was buried sitting upright, and we see the scary, underground cavity invaded by ladder and torchlight as the eager young king seeks inspiration on his knees before the veiled dead figure. His followers are cautious and terrified, he is calm and reverent; and the tension of the scene is well created by the arrangement of the torchlight that haloes the young king's head, the column cutting off our view of one retainer's face, the descending leg of another coming into sight on the ladder.

This scene is "historically accurate": medieval costume is thoroughly insisted on, and dead Charlemagne wears his famous crown. But the angle at

11.17 ALFRED RETHEL, *The Visit of Otto III to the Crypt*

11.18 KARL SPITZWEG, *The Widower*

which we see the scene looks arbitrary, as Rembrandt often set it up, as if we were a camera moving in on it and able at any second to shift the point of view, or a clandestine person coming nearer to crouch behind the column and watch. This is Romantic Realism at its most acute before the movies, here bringing history alive as they were to do, rather than arranging a historical tableau. Once again, the medium is nearly monochrome, and only the lighting makes the emotional terms.

Rethel preferred to deal with matters of national importance, according to his own conservative views; Karl Spitzweg, another Southerner like Schwind, specialized in cute bourgeois vignettes. He, too, worked up a realistic style dependent on tone, and then used it in a Technicolor sort of way, spreading a delicious multicolored glaze over his chiaroscuro compositions. The style of low-comic fantasy exaggeration in Spitzweg's works is affectionate, quite unlike the harsh satirical tone adopted by his contemporary Daumier. He never sacrificed an overall surface charm and comeliness, even for red-faced old soldiers and aged hermits; the truly grotesque did not appeal to him, as it did to Daumier and before that to Hogarth. As a result, Spitzweg's vignettes do have a Hollywood flavor; but his real successor is Norman Rockwell, not the movies (11.18). Spitzweg, just like Rockwell, has none of Schwind's understanding of the pregnant, passing situation: the frames are always of fixed pictures, not whole scenes. Nothing leaks out at the sides, or toward us to draw us and make us doubtful. We are cast as amused observers and the artist is fundamentally a performer, a cartoonist and not an illustrator, despite the wash of color and the multiple details.

The emphasis in Germany on stories, however, along with a long tradition of graphic talent, did make a graphic illustrator out of almost every artist. Franz Pforr did Dürer imitations, Rethel did Holbein imitations, Richter did Van Ostade imitations; but many painters invented their own new way either of illustrating books or of doing graphic series to be published on their own. The greatest of these was undoubtedly Adolph Menzel, whose monumental set of illustrations for a life of Frederick the Great, published between 1840 and 1842, is a graphic masterpiece with a far-reaching influence. Menzel himself acknowledged the influence of Chodowiecki on the style of this lengthy historical sequence, and quite suitably, since Chodowiecki was Frederick's contemporary and Menzel meant to get the eighteenth-century details exactly right.

But although the sophistication and psychological penetration of Chodowiecki's graphic art were probably important for Menzel, he far surpassed Chodowiecki, and entirely avoided any flavor of the eighteenth-century artist in his actual drawing. There is something startlingly cameralike in the variety of viewpoint, the economy and vitality, the sheer dramatic verity of his hundreds of little pictures for this royal biography. They look just like storyboards for a historical movie, with a very cinematic use of depth and angle and lighting for the shots, combined with a sustained ability to keep the period costumes, interiors, and military gear (to say nothing of famous historical personages) totally actual-seeming, as if filmed from various points of view on the spot, with no recourse to copying bits of specific eighteenth-century pictures, which would have made it all so much easier (11.19–11.23).

Each one of these scenes is visualized as part of an event, not as a picture at all. We see it in progress, sometimes from a distance, sometimes from behind the door or through the window, sometimes from two feet away—and we see only a part, we must keep waiting for the rest, another part. There may be several figures in the scene, a crowd, or only one person, who may not be Frederick but a bored sentry or a waiter. Or we may see Frederick and one other in conversation, only they are a hundred feet away,

ADOLPH MENZEL, scenes from
The Life of Frederick the Great:
11.19 *(top left)* Frederick by a river in
consultation about improvements.
11.20 *(top right)* Frederick with his
minister Cocceji. 11.21 *(above left)*
Armed farmers. 11.22 *(above right)*
Frederick observes the enemy position
at Kollin from an upstairs window.
11.23 *(right)* Frederick exercises his
troops in the rain.

and we are observing the windswept plain on which they stand. This kind of device is another reminder of Aert de Gelder's cinematic view of Christ's progress to Golgotha, which ensures our sympathy for distant, unselfconscious actors by putting them into a large, inimical, or simply impersonal setting.

Menzel's achievement was unprecedented at its date except in Dutch art, and quite new in its properly researched historical details rendered not in a drawing style that also suggested their date, but in the Dutch way, as if they were current phenomena. Rethel had done it for his mural crypt scene, too. The Dutch themselves, as we have seen, and Tiepolo later on, had relied on theatrical tradition for their "old-days" effects in order to make them seem immediate, so that everybody would have a present-day look, except got up in fancy-dress. Menzel was able to dress up his characters in authentic eighteenth-century military uniforms, hoops, and powdered wigs and then set them into believable historical motion in believable historical settings. The *visualization* is the great feat: to be able to see the period figures separated from their usual style of rendering, and then to draw them without retranslating them into a conventional 1840's figure style. They in fact look sketched to resemble the effects of cinematography, not drawn, as if Menzel had invented the movie camera, then designed these scenes for it —a graphic breakthrough, well before the practical event.

Menzel, too, had begun life as a graphic artist, and had no other sort of training. His best paintings, done in the 1840's, are very graphic in flavor and mostly of genre subjects with no historical content. A few of these also have no figures either, such as the famous *Room Giving on a Balcony,* and yet manage to be packed with human presence. When there are people in them, such as in *A Room with the Artist's Sister* or *The Interruption,* they are captured in the full flux of their lives, during the course of not entirely clear incidents that seem to be parts of conversations, confrontations, small crises with no obvious resolutions (11.24, 11.25).

Later Menzel persistently recorded imperial life in Berlin, and the character of his paintings became more diffuse, less intense, more public, but less cinematic. With some exceptions (11.26, 11.27), the large paintings he later made from some of his Frederick the Great drawings are unconvincing by comparison with the tiny originals. During his entire life, however, his drawings kept their immediacy and some of the intensity of Friedrich, especially for subjects such as newel posts, rooftops, flights of stairs, views into rooms, and other odd corner-of-the-eye sights which he treated as subjects for contemplation in the true cinematic style.

The Frederick the Great illustrations had a direct influence on English illustrators of the 1860's, most specifically on Charles Keene, to whom

11.24 ADOLPH MENZEL, *A Room with the Artist's Sister*

Menzel sent a packet of his graphic work in response to receiving some of Keene's by way of tribute. Keene was wholly a graphic artist, not a painter. The Pre-Raphaelite painters, although they did many illustrations, were naturally disaffected from Menzel's modern Realist aims and style, since they were interested in pretending to approach nature as if chastely, from early-Renaissance artistic principles, and consequently to be deliberately pure-minded about art and avoid current vulgarity at all costs.

For his own illustrations Rossetti preferred the surface effects of black and white, using it for its decorative authority rather than for any crude re-

11.25 ADOLPH MENZEL, *The Interruption*

alism suitable to political cartoons and journalistic reportage. Rossetti had a stake in linking the whole flavor of his works to literature, and keeping his black-and-white illustrations graphic in the sense of having been *delineated,* or "written out" as drawings—and certainly of having been derived from more august precursors than Menzel. Holman Hunt flatly denied being influenced by Menzel; but it would be hard to believe that Millais was not, given the unusually modern dramatic quality of his graphic work.

11.26 ADOLPH MENZEL, *Frederick at Hochkirk*

11.27 Still from *The Horse Soldiers*, 1959

Millais, although he was one of the founders of the original Pre-Rapha-elite Brotherhood, was also a friend of Leech and of Dickens, clearly more interested than Rossetti was in the visual desires of the general public, and certainly not afraid to be graphic in the gripping vulgar mode (11.28). His illustrations have a cinematic look, although he was never as good as Menzel, chiefly because his sense of humor was less delicate.

One of the strongest elements in Menzel's Frederick series is its comic flavor, which is a matter of considerable subtlety, designed to humanize the great man without detracting from his greatness. Humor seems to arise spontaneously from all sorts of slightly absurd human circumstances as they are naturally revealed by chance, rather than from any emphasis slyly inserted by the brilliant hand of the artist, the way it is in the work of Daumier, Wilhelm Busch, Rockwell, Spitzweg, and many others—the "laugh *here*" effect.

Keene was primarily a mildly humorous illustrator, and perhaps that is why Menzel impressed him so. He was also allegedly impressed by Chodo-

11.28 JOHN EVERETT MILLAIS, *Accepted.* Sepia

11.29 CHARLES KEENE, "Hard Lines." Illustration in
Punch's Almanack, 1869

11.30 Still from *Marty,* 1955

wiecki, to whom Menzel was much indebted for his superb comic discretion. Keene was a straightforward magazine artist with none of the high painterly aspirations motivating the Pre-Raphaelite group, and no high aims for his graphic work (11.29, 11.30). His pictures appeared in *Punch* and *Once a Week* for many years, and bear a resemblance not only to those of Leech and Millais but to the ones of later illustrators such as Du Maurier and Sidney Paget—all these, like many other illustrators concerned primarily with dramatic presentation, ready to sacrifice decorative refinement and abstract harmony for the sake of the impact of the depicted moment. Such an impact, naturally, required perfect mastery of pertinent material detail, with nothing extra to interfere but nothing important left out, and a perfect grasp of dramatic light and composition.

The English mid-century illustrators produced another new development: Dickens and Thackeray and other novelists began to work in close collaboration with them for the first time. The success of a novel as it was serialized in a magazine came to depend largely on the success of its pictures, and illustrators began to have an effect on the actual writing of the story. Thackeray did his own; Dickens had the help of a whole series of artists to portray his work as he went along, to whom he had to give suitably vivid descriptive material episode by episode, so that writer and illustrator could both meet printers' deadlines. On occasion, the picture was done first and the author wrote the scene afterward to fit it. The process of fictional visualization was well launched, and the movies were clearly becoming a deep if unarticulated necessity.

Turner, who died in 1851, had made illustrations for travel writings on the spot, but did so for poetic fictions only at a considerable remove—Scott and Byron, to say nothing of Homer and Virgil, had written the poems long before his pictures came into being. It was the German Romantic habit of illustrating present fantasies as they arose, perhaps, that created a precedent and a background for the rise of English illustration at mid-century—a rise that was followed by a fall at its end, but that in turn inspired turn-of-the-century talents across the Atlantic.

The idea that a story needs constant visualization—that it might even consist of nothing but visualization—was not new, but ancient; but the new possibilities for dramatic realism in art were growing beyond anything comprehensible to ancient eyes. In the late nineteenth century, moreover, especially in England and America, print media were ready to purvey illustrations to a vast public in books, newspapers, and magazines, not just for fiction but for the dramatization of current events and historical moments. Before the camera itself could get around to it, the comprehensive picturing of both real and imagined life was well under way.

TWELVE

English Art and Illustration; Whistler

A STRONG illustrative tradition in England had flourished long before Menzel's works were published, and it had created a public to support the new surge of both book illustration and illustrative painting. Hogarth was the great native forerunner; and most English artists responsible for the new flood of works continued to demonstrate, as he had done, a powerful connection to the stage. Writers of fiction did the same. As Martin Meisel has shown, novels and stories could be dramatized for stage production in terms of their concurrently printed illustrations, or illustrated in terms of their concurrent dramatization, or sometimes written on purpose to provide suitable material for both pictorial and theatrical tableaux.

Practitioners in all these media worked more or less simultaneously, to serve a public naturally eager for such a thrilling overlap in available entertainments. Stories appeared weekly (with illustrations), novels were serialized monthly (with illustrations in each installment), and plays based on them were immediately written and mounted with allusions to known illustrations in the setting and blocking. History painting, revived and now more literary than ever (with more references to Keats and Tennyson than to Homer and the Bible), joined in the same alliance, especially in their engraved and published versions.

Famous scenes from theatrical literature were depicted by painters, and the paintings were subsequently engraved; but in addition, romantic situations in modern life were invented especially for theatrical rendering in paint, as if they were scenes from Shakespeare. Abraham Solomon's *Waiting for the Verdict,* for example, a narrative picture based on no known story, had more than one play written especially to go with it (12.1). In such

12.1 ABRAHAM SOLOMON, *Waiting for the Verdict*

plays, previous scenes led up to the dramatic grouping arranged by the artist and made famous by the engraved version of the painting; and so the picture came to new life on the stage.

But its initial appeal was as a still image, not as a fragment of dramatic action in process. Shakespearean moments depicted in popular paintings were likewise rendered as still tableaux when they were referred to in production, with the action momentarily frozen so that everyone could recognize the source and enjoy the skill in its realization; it was a moment for applause. Engravings might also be published showing moments from stage productions that had no pictorial precedents, but were now being made into pictures. It may have made little difference to the public whether a picture or a stage production or a story had come first. Observing from a later time, we can see that the black-and-white illustrations done directly for fiction, and in close collaboration with its writer, were the Victorian pictures most free of old painterly and theatrical associations, most forward-looking as cinematic prophecy, and most linked to the Northern graphic tradition including Bruegel and Goya as well as Menzel.

The situation with respect to painting was something of a closed system, based on the much older connection between picture and stage picture which had its origin in the Renaissance link between art and spectacle. Italian Renaissance court theater had invented the framed vision, with remote and amazing illusions achieved inside it, which coexisted with a tradition of painting committed to the same thing. On the court stage, the illusion was not permitted to emerge from the frame, and it was composed of shifting spectacles accompanied by music, poetry, and singing. All realistic acting in such a production took place in front of the curtain according to a different time scheme, as a separate kind of entertainment requiring no exciting visual delights and only a minimally appropriate backdrop. Italian Renaissance paintings often refer to this stage convention, either by keeping the action theatrical, which is to say subordinated to overall spectacular harmony, or by arranging a dramatic encounter in front of a setting rather than inside it.

English popular stage traditions, also dating from the Renaissance, depended (like Dutch ones in the Baroque period) on the acting of texts in convincing style, rather than on any harmonious visual grandeur and illusion. Only the Jacobean and Caroline court masque, copying Italy, went in for spectacle; and in later centuries, the two were uneasily combined on public stages. Indeed the English stage continued to make use, until well into the nineteenth century, of a large apron on which the keenest dramatic moments took place, while supernumeraries and distant spectacular illusions were confined to the inner stage, which was framed by the three-sided proscenium.

Although it would seem as if the new popular link between plays and paintings in nineteenth-century England was the sign of a move toward film, the issue of lifelike portrayal on the Northern visual model was not yet joined at all. For staged or painted drama, there was little portrayal of inward movement, of psychological shifts that might be combined with physical action in believable surroundings into one convincing visual scheme, where a viewer could feel psychologically present himself, free from artistic manipulation of his eyes and feelings.

The great Dutch and Flemish artists and their successors in Romantic times had chiefly used light to make this happen, as well as dynamic framing to suggest that the viewer's field of vision was in motion. But Victorian pictorial lighting and framing tended to follow old proscenium-stage effects for dramatic scenes—except in the work of the black-and-white illustrators. Panoramic paintings such as Frith's *Derby Day* or more concentrated groupings such as Solomon's *Verdict,* although they have great entertainment value, have much less immediate emotional effect than

12.2 H. K. BROWNE, "Mr. Pinch is amazed by
an unexpected apparition." Illustration for Dickens'
Martin Chuzzlewit

12.3 WILLIAM POWELL FRITH, "The Arrest." No. 3 from *The Road to Ruin*.
Etching by Leopold Flameng from the 1878 painting

H. K. Browne's Dickens illustrations or Millais' and Keene's pictures for stories in magazines. Browne's little black-and-white pictures more closely resemble Schwind's or Menzel's Dutch-style genre paintings than English paintings of the date, which were still bound to the old Italian idea that creating a lighted tableau (even on Frith's large scale) was the right way to offer drama inside a frame (12.2, 12.3).

Such a lighted tableau would also have painterly antecedents—in Tintoretto and Veronese, or Raphael and Guido Reni—to support the authenticity of the artist's talent and the high level of his training. These would register with the picture-viewing public and further certify the scene in the picture as worthy of portrayal. As "modern life" increasingly became a proper subject for English paintings, not just for graphic reportage and magazine illustration, Victorian painters had to keep their efforts distinct from cruder pictorial associations, especially when dealing seriously with such flaming subjects as adultery and prostitution or gross social injustice.

If a painting smacked too much of sensational journalism or cheap pornography in its very form, the subject could seem debased, not illuminated. A tawdry modern seduction painted with Titianesque richness, the sorry modern poor made to resemble Murillo's beggars, or the modern rake and gambler rendered in the Hogarthian manner made the painter seem free of prurience as he presented such topics dressed in their artistic best for public gaze. Before about 1880, the result was a sequence of unredeemably "artistic" paintings of ordinary life, deliberately made more remarkable and at the same time more emotionally neutral by their allusions to the most august traditions of art. Black-and-white engravings made from them naturally had a somewhat cinematic character, with a larger capacity to insist only on the subject and engage directly with the viewer's feelings, rather than arousing his admiration. Undoubtedly some of the theatrical renditions of them did, too.

In the theater there were often technically arranged ocean waves, lightning flashes, or rises and collapses of structures in the John Martin style to enliven stage pageantry, and cutouts of horses that could be made to race in the distance, or of trains, carriages, and ships that could move on and off the stage, just as they appeared to do in the paintings from which the set had derived. Such arrangements gave animation to pictorial stage settings, but they also helped to give the illusion of life that was lacking in the paintings themselves. It is in part that very lack that lay behind the need to write plays "leading up" to the pictures; the public liked the paintings better after they had been given the rough immediacy and psychological underpinnings of a stage version, however optically awkward or slightly inaccurate it may have been—perhaps even because of the awkwardness, which is more like real life.

The Pre-Raphaelites, as their name shows, were trying to get away from the lighted-stage-with-waxwork-figures school of history painting, or its equivalent in the painting of modern life. They favored some recognition in painting of the actual stream of experience, rather than the image of a terrific moment, fixed for a spectator's pleasure. And they made great strides toward a liberated and cinematic rendering of bodies and facial expressions, because they were working not just in imitation of very early Renaissance models in preference to High Renaissance staginess, but in repudiation of the current theatricalized taste in art.

Millais was the most cinematic painter among the Pre-Raphaelites, partly because his realism has some of the contingent flavor of the early Flemish paintings. His methods contrast with the way Rossetti, Holman Hunt, and Burne-Jones tended to imitate the harmonious linear beauty and theatrical compositions of Italian art. Millais was concerned with the power of color, like all the Pre-Raphaelites, but it is the light in *Autumn Leaves* or in his later version of Keats' *Eve of St. Agnes,* for example, that makes the picture haunting. Millais also used individual models without reducing them to one type, and so his best paintings still breathe and move, while Rossetti's and Burne-Jones' look embalmed in their idiom. Arthur Hughes made similarly mobile and moving pictures infused with light and feeling—both he and Millais had an excellent grip on how to render the progress of personal drama convincingly, rather than how to freeze symbolic action (12.4).

The problem with most Pre-Raphaelite painting was in the esthetic as well as practical moral imperative behind it all. Ideology ruins these works in some way, as it also makes them fascinating to present-day eyes. Because Pre-Raphaelite artists wished to avoid the cheap impact sought by the tableau-mongers of the date, they unfortunately also sacrificed certain basic pictorial virtues. The main good thing to go was believable lighting, which was considered suspect, manipulative, and stagy. As a result, Pre-Raphaelite paintings usually have a uniform colored surface, with delicate modeling and no chiaroscuro, the look of many fruits preserved in aspic, or of a rug or mosaic. This quality may proudly refer to honest medieval practice before the late-Renaissance institution of coercive dramatic devices, and it certainly keeps the pictures well away from the look of *tableaux vivants* and popular stage effects; but it also keeps them from looking credible.

Again, it keeps them very obviously *artistic*. In many paintings by Millais and Holman Hunt and Ford Madox Brown, the bodies and faces them-

12.4 ARTHUR HUGHES, *The Eve of St. Agnes*

selves do have a refreshingly gangly and natural look, especially when the faces are intended to express a state of continuing change rather than one straight reaction, and the limbs are given the slightly jumbled quality that normally informs much inward awareness of the physical self at crucial moments. The Pre-Raphaelite painters studied the Flemish painters of the fifteenth century as well as the Italians, and appreciated the expressive value of bodily disequilibrium in pictures.

But the desperate need for the painter to appear as a large actor in every painting is fatal to their effect. We get no direct access to the event, such as Vermeer lets us have; the artist insists on explaining the point of the picture while we look at it, and so we cannot take possession of what is happening ourselves. Like as not, the thing has even been enclosed in a didactic, moral-looking frame with a superscription, a device resembling the entrance to a private institution with religious affiliations, where we cannot visit without a guide.

Paintings such as *Work,* for example, or *The Last of England,* or *The Hireling Shepherd,* or *The Shadow of Death* are apparently not really made for *seeing,* despite the incredible effort at getting the right clothes for Biblical characters, the right pebbles, the right cabbages, the correct angle of the elbow, or the truthful wrinkle in the shirt, the careful perfection of all the

to try to elevate the public tone of his efforts, and he made a great publicity feature out of the famous painters who assisted him with his scenic designs. He could thus be artistic and respectable, and keep his productions apparently at a great remove from sensational melodramas, even though he helped himself to many of their visual effects along with those of scholarly painters like Alma-Tadema and Lord Leighton. The set and costume designers of the great Hollywood days certainly made use of the same method for historical themes, and also made much, in publicity releases, of the historical research and artistic advice that had gone into their productions, all of which was ignored if the result failed to satisfy. It is clear that the desire to go still further with the possibilities of spectacle, to get beyond the confines of stages such as Irving's, is behind the great sets built for Griffith and Eisenstein in the cinema's early days—they are attempts to overreach the theater.

But Irving's achievement had a more lasting influence on the stage itself than on the movies, especially the operatic stage. His *mises-en-scène* were fundamentally pictorial, in that they were composed to stay inside the frame and keep the spectator breathless outside it, not to enclose him in its living mouth. Irving produced great classical plays, or modern ones made in imitation of them, as if they were operas; and his own acting style was decidedly operatic—outward and rhetorical, not revelatory of inward states. The English painters of historical spectacle such as Lord Leighton were engaged in the same sort of operatic effort at the same time, and the real progress he and they made was toward creating a new sense of continuous action rather than the formation of tableaux. They were trying to make the theater and theatrical painting aspire to the condition of music in a way that Wagner's productions, with the advantage of his new and continuous actual music, in fact achieved.

An exception to the art-historically theatrical style used in England for legendary material was the work of Lawrence Alma-Tadema. Alma-Tadema was a legitimate heir to the Northern tradition, having been born in Holland and trained in Belgium; and he translated his efforts successfully into English without recourse to Italian Renaissance models. He was able to produce a blend of the High Victorian attitudes toward antiquity (which combined archeological passion with a certain gentlemanly fellow-feeling) and his own, truly Flemish imagination about light, space, and texture. The natural-looking flavor and casual arrangement of Alma-Tadema's intimate scenes and public festivals, which take place in a thoroughly realized and optically convincing ancient Greece and Rome, made them congenial to their casually behaved and well-bred English viewers—never too stagy and embarrassing, nothing overwrought. It has also since caused him to be

12.6 LAURENCE ALMA-TADEMA, *Sappho*

called an influence on movies, and for much technical material he actually
was (12.6).

Nevertheless there is no psychological motion in his paintings, no tension and no possibility, despite the chanting throngs, the coy girls, the poetry being recited, the playing fountains. The figures are models, and
unlike Caravaggio, Alma-Tadema seems to have cared little about them.
Nobody is a living, feeling person, either in the assumed antique role
among the marble slabs or in the modern one on the studio pedestal; and so
we cannot care much about them either, and find them false and silly.

But Alma-Tadema had a magnificent power of visualization quite free of
stage habits; and his arrangements for framing his ancient scenes have real
movie-camera freedom, which is well enhanced by his skill in the rendering
of surfaces—fur, wet mosaic, sunlit water, and miles of marble. He put
such environments into motion, even if he had no sense of how to mobilize a
human situation. And he was a devoted antiquarian besides, so that the
"effects" he produced were the result not of scrambled history working on
the beholder's fuzzy pictorial memory but of real light, air, and angles of
vision animating perfect reconstructions. Irving employed him, but often
ignored him. The material in his paintings, with all its optical authenticity,
now looks wonderful in the movies, where it is tempting to think he meant it
to go. It was largely unusable on the stage and has not lasted in art; but in
films, environments such as he created can be brought to wondrous life by
Charlton Heston and Anne Baxter instead of being inhabited by bored and
boring amateurs.

Meanwhile staged and painterly paintings of legend such as those of
Lord Leighton were giving way to the undramatic and unspecific draped
visions of Albert Moore and to the mannered and strange concoctions of
the later Burne-Jones; and full-scale realistically conceived legendary vision in English art eventually ceased altogether, leaving the field to the
kind of treatment given it by Redon and other French and Belgian Symbol-
ists. English straight drama abandoned spectacular kinds of detailed and
elaborate historical setting in favor of simplicity and suggestion, the better
to emphasize the power of the word. But the opera, in England and everywhere else, continued and continues to use them to this day as a fitting accompaniment to the most extreme projects of music's empire.

Victorian illustrators, on the other hand, had all along been making
some effort to visualize realistic fiction in the cinematic and not the painterly or stagelike style. Illustrators had to show a story in progress in such a
way that the plot was never given away in advance by too much visual infor-
mation, but also see to it that the characters, along with their interaction
and its surroundings, were given looks in keeping with the author's style
and plan, even when he had not specified them. The matter of *motion,* impossible to the theater—the important sense not only of the scene's action
but of the viewer's participatory approaches and retreats and shifts of attention and association—was well considered by Browne and his later colleagues, just as it was gradually becoming a more potent element in fiction
itself—the effect of montage.

Instead of the arbitrary frame that cinematic painters knew how to apply
but that theatrical painters avoided, the great British illustrators, like
Menzel, often went further and used no frame at all—a device that keeps
the action from freezing. Their scenes float on the printed page in a void, in
which the viewer also floats, either close at hand or at a fly-on-the-wall
point of vantage that literary fiction itself was now making possible. For
the Sherlock Holmes stories, for example, Sidney Paget's turn-of-the-
century illustrations show their debt to Browne and Millais (12.7). The pictures are dramatically lighted and full of enough action to create suspense
rather than reveal solutions. Paget provides certain details specified by the
author and invents others to harmonize with them, and each picture is
given as one frame from a continuous narrative viewed from different
angles and distances. The frame is sometimes absent or more often partial,
leaving one side or the bottom edge open to suggest fluid movement in and
out of the depicted moment.

In this illustrative tradition even the most sumptuous settings are offered in terms of suggestion, a matter of atmosphere, as in Turner and
Goya, except for what is immediately pertinent. Menzel was the first to use

12.7 SIDNEY PAGET, "Really, sir, this is a very extraordinary question." Illustration for Conan Doyle's *The Hound of the Baskervilles,* 1902

this pictorial device for straight biography, to illustrate a hero's history directly, as if it were a set of events personally perceptible to anyone in terms of ordinary experience, and free from reference to old heroic depictions, even the reference implied by enclosing each picture in four sides.

Such freedom, as the movie camera has been showing all this time since, is always a matter of escape from the fixed framing and stage lighting that most painters and actors used to agree looked right. But it is also a matter of escape from conventional artistic *prestige,* the ancient need to refer to Veronese and company. References instead are obliquely made to the much less colorful Northern painterly and graphic traditions, those of Rembrandt and company, which had dealt in subjectivity and had given up public heroics in favor of showing how things must have seemed to individuals at the time. Some British painters took up this different challenge in the late nineteenth century, chiefly for dealing with modern life rather than staged history or legend.

The Graphic, founded in 1869, was a magazine specializing in current affairs complete with accompanying pictures, and some of the black-and-white artists working for it later made paintings based on their magazine illustrations. Such a process, the reversal of the usual arrangement that caused original paintings to be reproduced in black and white, is significant. "Realism" was a new goal for painting, already in full pursuit by French painters like Courbet, and generally dependent on the old association of harsh subject matter with the suppression of color. Before *The Graphic,* there had been a great deal of topical English journalism illustrated with grim or comic black-and-white pictures; and engravings were generally believed to convey problematic subjects with greater ease than paintings.

But even more significantly, the camera was in existence by this time, making its inexorable and colorless point about light and optical reality. Photography, unredeemably "graphic" in its basic character as recorder and reproducer of phenomena, could not help contributing to all painters' sense of truth-telling, even if they ignored its direct influence. It also revitalized the sense of possibility in graphic and "graphic" art, to remind artists of the colorless chiaroscuro employed in the interest of realism by some of their greatest painterly forerunners. And so the grimmer the aspects of "modern life" that British painters were willing to tackle as the century advanced, the more they depended on monochrome graphic rather than colorful painterly conventions for making them effective, keeping them from being beautiful and insisting on their truth.

Meisel has compared *Waiting for the Verdict,* painted in 1857, with another prison picture *Newgate: Committed for Trial* of 1878, painted by Frank Holl, who was one of the illustrators for *The Graphic* (12.8). This later image of a poverty-ridden family split apart by the law and the police has none of the high-minded staged pathos of the first, and likewise none of its allusions to Poussin. Twenty years have changed the formal reference to that of a photo-graphic and graphic mode of presenting harsh facts, with references to Goya and the possible future of the camera instead of to the classic tragedians of painting. Not just the lighting and uneasy framing but the ambiguity of the content, the uncertain faces and postures and relationships of the personnel, show the artist's aim to find a new right style for rendering a specific but difficult situation, something messy and full of unclear conflict at a moment of maximum difficulty. It has a news-photo look, with nothing harmonized according to classical principles, even the human relations.

The painting also looks back to Menzel's prophetic interiors of the mid-1840's, despite the great difference in the pictured milieu. Whether the scene is middle-class and comfortable or working-class and miserable, the imagery of tense subjective attention has the same flavor. The Holl painting also resembles Frank Bramley's *A Hopeless Dawn,* with its much more explicit and intimate drama (12.9); Caillebotte's *Floor Scrapers* with its

12.8 FRANK HOLL, *Newgate: Committed for Trial*

sensitive reference to modern labor without any other tale to tell (12.10); and Lovis Corinth's *Salome* (12.11), a shockingly graphic German answer to the elegant English school of mythic rendition. Whether the theme is modern genre, the predicaments of the urban and rural poor, or ancient legend, the cinematic eye regards it with attention to the movement of emotive possibility, the shifting aspect of things that conjures associations and a shift of feeling, the strange shapes reality takes under the light.

Pictures in this vein in the late nineteenth century share an emotional cast, an appeal to empathy, an emotional projection conjured mainly by the sovereignty of light over design and the consequent pull on the feelings. The momentary glimpse of an event, trivial or not, that has unknown antecedents and unknowable results is an old theme in art; but the theme becomes part of a movielike effect in such a picture, because it seems to contain not just events we cannot know about, but previous or future emotional states we cannot know about either, a continuum not just of external action but of living that seems to include us.

12.9 FRANK BRAMLEY, *A Hopeless Dawn*

12.10 GUSTAVE CAILLEBOTTE, *The Floor Scrapers*

12.11 LOVIS CORINTH, *Salome*

All sorts of small visual detail become charged with potential meaning, as they always do in attentive moments, so there is no need to give extra noticeability to anything burdened with obvious significance. On the contrary, the irrelevant object takes it on. Caillebotte's floor scrapers have no anecdotal claims to our sympathy, unlike Holl's cast of characters; but the painting, with its lighted patch of empty floor and its unselfconscious struggling figures, has the same ability to yield pathos without seeming to try; and part of the pathos comes from the sharp tracery of the ironwork in the window, which has nothing to do with anything except our eyes, and with our present imagination about life and work and the beauty of floors and railings. The associations are ours; the painter does not point to them.

The emotional charge of ordinary phenomena had been a concern of Turner's in the first part of the century, and later English painters again took up the theme in terms of landscape itself. The new graphic realism of feeling demanded more attention in art than just what could be given to modern human situations, wretched or privileged. The stage of life has many kinds of people on it; but the screen of life has much more than people. Both Turner and Friedrich had long before established a vocabulary of light and motion in paint to deal with the way everything else on the screen besides humans can seem to fill with human significance, even if it has none itself.

The new camera gave artists more scope and a new vocabulary for the same kind of investigation into ways of creating drama without anecdote, declamation, or pantomime. To do this it was necessary at the time, however, to be a *painter* rather than a photographer; unless, as history has revealed, one could have been a cinematographer. Atkinson Grimshaw's nocturnal urban views show no feverish desire to render high life or low life in any particular light, only the life of streets at night glistening with potential event. The potentiality, the look of things happening even when nothing is happening, was still impossible to photography, but easy for painters with a long pictorial tradition to draw on for doing just that, even if it was photography that was currently inspiring them.

Grimshaw's *View of Liverpool Quay by Moonlight* of 1887 shows an om-

12.12 ATKINSON GRIMSHAW, *View of Liverpool Quay by Moonlight*

nibus coach with a green rear light pausing on the damp cobbles to pick up a woman, and several indistinctly identified passersby on the sidewalks lighted by shopwindows (12.12). The moonlight of the title is only a remote glow filtered through smoke and fog, but the streetlights are like jewels, the jewels in the shops are like flames, and the words on the billboards and shop signs glow with all the thrilling non-significance that fills the urban night. We are looking at a prosaic corner of a provincial city, but the scene is laden with a beauty that seems, like so much in cinema, to be truly in the eye of the beholder—the moving eye of the camera that invests so much in so little. The *picture* is not so beautiful; it is the crummy street itself that is made to twinkle and glimmer with our expectations. In a moment a pale gentleman played by Stewart Granger will emerge from the jeweler's shop, look both ways, and stride nonchalantly across the wet street, bent on sinister business among the low life on the docks.

Grimshaw did many paintings of such city streets and waterfronts, most of them not in London, none of them commenting on the specific evils of the metropolis, dwelling instead without comment on the way light interacts with towns so that reflecting surfaces mock each other and themselves, and the streetlamp comments unwittingly on the moon. City living looks hot or cold depending only on which way you face and how fast you move; windows glare like ice or glow like coals in warehouses and shacks and brick mansions; wet pavement and river water are grim or golden depending on which light is striking at the time. It is a new view, a way to be dramatic and subjectively poetic simply by being kinetic and optical.

Whistler was a friend and admirer of Grimshaw, as he was of many other painters on both sides of the Channel and the Atlantic. Grimshaw even gave him some help with perspective; but in other respects Whistler felt himself to be a much larger figure with far loftier artistic ambitions. Whistler's shower of rockets, however, could be bursting over a Grimshaw city, and his views of the Thames by night have a similar suggestiveness, the quality of being settings viewed as if in motion toward something more (12.13).

Whistler found it necessary to retreat so far from anecdote that he insisted on using musical terminology for his titles; but that habit also reveals the kinetic impulse behind them, and withdraws not at all into an objective attitude toward the scene itself—quite the reverse. Whistler created many pictures that have both abstract-sounding titles and very strong emotional presence. In an effort to elevate art and himself along with it, to assert his own independence and the sovereignty of the artist, he preached loudly about how pictures should be recognized to consist only of colors and shapes and tonalities, not the "claptrap" of characters and props; and

12.13 J. A. McN. WHISTLER, *Nocturne in
Black and Gold: The Falling Rocket*

yet his *White Girl* and the portrait of his mother have been loved for generations because of the women in them and their accessories, not for the
beauty of their composition.

Whistler must have intended it so. In emphasizing (in his flamboyant
speech and writings) the elementary components of a painting, especially
its tonal components, he was in fact describing the sources of mood and atmosphere in any picture that has a recognizable subject; and to consider
the power of atmosphere means to acknowledge the contribution of the beholder's fund of personal fantasy to the picture's effect, in fact to depend
upon it. The "story" or the "drama" is just as gripping as in the anecdotal
mode; but it is something half created by the viewer out of the expectations
the painter raises and the psychic weather he whips up. And so, while defining out loud his artistic aims as detached from any catering to ordinary
sentiment, Whistler was nevertheless also defining what largely creates
that very sentiment; and he made good use of it in his art, which remained

12.14 J. A. MCN. WHISTLER, *Study in Flesh
Tones and Black: Portrait of Theodore Duret*

committed to realistic subjects laden with suggestion and potential meaning—real bridges and real people—rather than to neutral props such as
Moore's girls from never-never land. And so he could have it both ways.

When Whistler painted his portrait of Theodore Duret in 1883, he called
it *Study in Flesh Tones and Black,* as if to rub it in that a picture is
only an arrangement (12.14). But the subject (created, of course, *by* the arrangement but by no means identical with it) is what makes the picture
vital, dramatic, heavy with potential "story," a shot from a film. The man in
black evening dress embraces his wife's clinging, rosy cloak as if it were
her body and grips her red fan in his gloved hand as if it were a dagger. His
feet are braced, his face is purpling, and the frown is beginning on his
shiny brow. The moment is both poised and turbulent; we are waiting. And
although they are not the whole story, the volatile purple, pink, and red and
the stiff, dim black are largely responsible for how we understand what is
happening. With his title, more than claiming the picture as nothing but a
group of contrasting tones, Whistler was distinguishing what has since
been recognized to create feeling and meaning through pictures by our
movie-going age, and what once did so in the Romantic age of Turner. But
he wanted to keep it (or perhaps, for the first time, make it) exclusive, a
property of High Art, an esthetic principle at odds with vulgar appreciation. And so the title also wants to keep our empathy at bay, resist our lust
for anecdote, and maintain the picture strictly in the artist's keeping, not
ours. He did the same with the *Black and Gray* mother.

Whistler has been famous as a herald of modernity in painting, an apostle of French artistic gospel to the benighted Victorians; and yet it is clear
that he was also another apostle of the cinematic method before movies existed. He was known to have learned abstraction from the Japanese and advanced modes of artistic Realism from the French, already allegedly free
from illustration and staginess; but he was also a true Romantic, although
he did not wish to appear so. That is perhaps because he was an American
on foreign soil, and his native aptitude for serious romanticism was an embarrassment to him. He had to keep talking to disguise it; and thus he for-
mulated a number of modernist principles, almost out of what seems like
private defiance rather than principled conviction. Degas once said to him,
"You behave as if you have no talent."

Among the other signs of Whistler's cinematic sensibility was his great
graphic talent, which he again exercised with as much flair and delicacy as
he used for paint, with similar tonal concerns and emotional results. His
1860 etching entitled *Rotherhithe* and his painting called *Wapping on
Thames* have the same sort of cinematic disposition. Each shows a free-
floating view of a scene with some people, rather like De Witte's fish-

monger scene from two hundred years earlier, here with the boats and
water and the shaded faces making an ambiguous meeting out of an ordinary if unstable arrangement (12.15, 12.16). Since the people are sitting, it
is clearly the eye that is moving, scanning both the river and the gathering
for some future comprehension of its own.

Whistler was not an Impressionist and also not a Symbolist; his affinities in France were chiefly with Degas, who also had an interest in the dramatic possibilities generated by overall tonality, mobility, and ambiguity,
and no desire to abandon the actual. But in England Whistler was a snob
and a determined esthete, and did eventually abandon the work of consid-
ering how common life looks and feels. He refused to be even as much of an
illustrator as his natural gifts usually made him. He did not move in the direction of abstraction, which was not yet quite available to him, or of the
camera, which he would have scorned to use, but toward ever more ten-
uously suggestive vistas and glimpses. For all their vapor, these lack the

12.15 J. A. McN. WHISTLER, *Rotherhithe.*
Etching, 1860

12.16 J. A. MCN. WHISTLER, *Wapping on Thames*

convinced, questlike thrust of Turner's late works; Whistler was in retreat, not searching further. After his death, "pictorial" photography in the first decade of this century seems to have been trying to show Whistler what he might have done with the camera, along the same vaporous path. But the movie camera, which he might well have adopted with even better results, was not available either. And he would have scorned that, too. He always refused, somehow, to be the American artist he actually was.

THIRTEEN
America

AMERICAN romanticism is always realistic. American Romantic art has blended poetic aspiration with great respect for the specific, a continuous hard-headedness wedded to a not always coherent spiritual desire. This is an esthetic character and stance that can easily seem ridiculous, especially when it is expressed in works of art that are less than excellent, or in works of commercial and popular art. Sentimentality and bombast lie in wait to take over the stylistic government, however earnest the basic aims, if those aims are founded on contradictions that are beyond the scope of the artist or of the medium. The American movies ever since Griffith have often had an aspiring rather than a confident quality, a visual romanticism reaching toward an unarticulated grandeur, toward excess, toward some kind of largeness or sleekness or creative overemphasis, combined with a great straightforwardness of theme and a literal-minded moral flavor. American fantasy has had to struggle for any expressive unity it has achieved, and the struggle has showed, becoming part of the expression and part of the achievement.

In many movies and in some allegorical subjects treated by American folk artists or portraits by untutored limners, the results were ridiculous indeed, untempered by irony or ambiguity, but often appealing for their very unwieldiness. Even in bad Hollywood movies an appeal is generated by the very fact that the hard-headed camera is recording every melodramatic moment, every poetic visual effort, every thrilling effect, even when it fails. The aspiring character remains in the very look of the thing, the flavor of an invincible pictorial romanticism even in the cynical productions of a mass entertainment business, offered without pretensions to high art. Vulgarity and tediousness of theme, direction, and acting can be redeemed by pure camera magic, even the kind that has been unconsciously created, in a way impossible for analogous lapses on the live stage.

The movies in America were carrying on an American tradition of style in visual art that had begun long before. American painting in the early nineteenth century, and even in the eighteenth, had some of the same flavor of romantic aspiration combined with literalness, the same desire that a work of art should be both wondrous and honest, both blunt and transcendent without compromise either way, so that the result is often slightly overwrought, weird, often esthetically insecure, but compelling for that very reason.

John Singleton Copley set the tone for the American arts in his *Watson and the Shark,* a picture that offers a heroic and erotic vision of a frightening contemporary incident and a documentary record of it at the same time (13.1). It is an example of how realism in art may be romantic without the classical vocabulary for artistic excitement, the Baroque lunges and flourishes and attendant sartorial flutter perfected by Rubens and others, but by using the direct pictorial drama best employed by the Flemish, the Dutch, and later the Spanish: light and shade, naturalistically unstable physical action, psychologically accurate facial expression, and rightly constructed real clothes, whether they are costumes or not.

Copley agreed to render a modern event for which he could put the people in modern dress and then juxtapose them to a naked figure in extremity, a device of much greater dramatic power than showing a nude among draped or costumed figures. And although the realistic method he perfected was drawn from Northern models—or from English ones based on Dutch prototypes—he could here combine it with subtle references to Raphael's *Miraculous Draft of Fishes* and still not depart from drama in the direction of theater. The scene is overbearingly immediate, and Raphael hardly shows. The slight classical reference keeps the picture bearable, rather than making it romantic. The romanticism, in American fashion, is in the realism itself, in the lifted hair of the harpoon wielder, the bald man's grip on the other one's shirt, in every actual detail being shown as intrinsically dramatic, instead of having rhetorical devices signal traditional thrills.

The painting is very large for its subject, again in keeping with emergent American esthetic habits. The topic seems more appropriate for a small magazine-engraving like the thousands of later ones depicting sensational current events. But these common sailors in danger are blown up to movie-screen size, with the water and the murderous shark ready to swallow the viewer as if he were another nearby naked boy. This is an example of a picture that seems to be going on, that needs watching rather than study, that refuses to settle comfortably into its frame but continually promises or

13.1   JOHN SINGLETON COPLEY,   *Watson and the Shark*

threatens more than it actually shows. The motion in it is unaccountable, pushing out of the frame and out at us, borne by water and fright.

Copley did the other kind of work, too, in which events are portrayed in The Grand Manner; but those were products of his later years in England. Like Whistler, he eventually found his artistic ambitions compromised by America and sought a more lofty esthetic arena for them. But *Watson* was prophetic, not just of American painting but of American movies. It has the openness to its audience, the engulfing effect of cinema, and it shows a willingness to be extreme, to skate near the edge of banality and sensationalism; at the same time the subject is presented without artistic fuss, in documentary terms as if a camera had been turned on it. It has an unselfconscious seriousness, and an air of thrilling expectation built on the fresh idea that the recording of facts can be used as a romantic artistic device. As film has later shown, the final effect is all in the editing.

American vision in the first half of the nineteenth century continually enlarged, to fill the endlessness of the Western expanses. Landscape could eventually become the proper American religious art, suitable to the idea that God had given this land to this nation, and then come to dwell in it Himself as the local abiding Soul of Nature—a pure spirit, democratic and non-denominational. The group of American landscape-painters now called Luminists did not always work in a large format, but the limitless expansion of vision they registered in their works took that same path explored by Friedrich at about the same period, the path that keeps moving straight at the unknown.

Endlessness can be addressed in a small frame. It can become the stuff of pure subjectivity so that the artist disappears, only the vista exists for the viewer, and he seems to merge with it as in Emerson's famous eyeball. Cinema invites us to be just such an eyeball; and in America, long before the camera, as in Germany and before that in Holland, the way to convey the idea lay in painting the light beyond the horizon (even indoors) as if it were a force coming to claim the beholder—not just his eyes, but his soul through his eyes. The light is also considered as it strikes objects; and they are presented as if irradiated, "illustrated" by light rather than merely lit. Again transparency is stressed, the white radiance that is stained by the world's life, the white screen against which the pictures are projected.

The light in such works of art suggests cinema, because it seems to make the objects in the world important even if they are slack and dull in themselves. Like Friedrich, Luminist painters such as M. J. Heade might show uneventful and boring stretches of marsh and beach transmuted simply by the staring and hungry eye, which summons the light and endows it with a power that stays in motion when once called up (13.2). This state of pictorial things was natural to Romantic America, and it was essentially North European in origin. In America, however, it was combined with the myth-making impulse that wished to leave traditional European religious and cultural assumptions behind and make up something new.

Barbara Novak has suggested that the power of Luminist composition comes in part from its connection to a tradition of folk art—which is also what may have supported it in Germany as practiced by Friedrich, Carus, and Dahl—the slightly primitive cast the pictures have, an unmodulated look. Before the Civil War, American painters were trying to establish a native art that would have a power and beauty worthy of God's primitive American wilderness, but also of American enterprise, unaffected zeal, and practical intelligence—qualities that can also have an honorable primitive

13.2 M. J. HEADE, *Sunrise on the Marshes*

13.3 FITZ HUGH LANE, *Brace's Rock, Brace's Cove*

flavor without borrowing refinements to tone them down or work them up. The need was for something forthright and mystical at the same time, but something well made and technically respectable, too. Crudity was not an ingredient in American Romantic idealism, any more than delicacy; material expression had to have the finish and solidity of inspired works that form new traditions (13.3).

Besides the austere painters of the Luminist sort, there were ambitious visionaries who plunged straight ahead to tackle both the immensity of the land and the need to people it with some version of human glory—perhaps the sense that merely the right response to virgin waterfalls and ancient forests might constitute the better part of American virtue. Thomas Cole was an immigrant from England, but his career took on an entirely American style, combining serious idealism with a steady desire to get ahead. To do that, Cole helped himself to a mixture of Claudian and Salvatoran conventions for landscape, in an effort to subdue the untamed American scene to a visually acceptable condition of ideal sublimity. He was among the first to paint the giant-sized landscapes that later became the speciality of Church and Bierstadt; but the works that made him famous were his two series about human and national destiny, *The Course of Empire* and *The Voyage of Life.*

These two cycles were done after his visit to Europe beginning in 1829, but before he went he had already painted the wonderfully cinematic *Expulsion from the Garden of Eden.* This work looks like one of the sets from the original *King Kong,* an imaginary landscape full of moral import but also realistically overwhelming, despite its obviously designed and constructed look (13.4). The angelic light bursting through the arch, forcing the tiny fleeing pair across the chasm as if it were a wind, gives a force to the papier-mâché rocks that is similar to the excitement generated in that movie by the fake primeval landscape populated by constructed dinosaurs. The vision of First Things conceived in grand and terrible terms is Romantic in an American way, different from John Martin's architectural versions of extreme moments. Here it is the *landscape* that has been worked up to the right emotional pitch to seize and swamp the viewer, expressly to illuminate the moment when Man's Fall is brought home to him, not just to invoke the abstract landscape sublime. It gives the impression that America is too much for its inhabitants; the garden is not a garden but part of an overmastering wilderness, of which even the peaceful reaches are vast and jungly; the outer world is racked by storms. What strength is required of us for surviving here, what ferocity to match the land?

Cole did another Biblical scene before his English sojourn, a vision of *The Waters Receding after the Deluge* which has been almost perfectly repeated in the Dino de Laurentiis film *The Bible.* Here Cole designs a primal view of rock, water, and sky devoid of reference to the painterly wildernesses of French and English art, something harsh and strange and lit from behind like a German vision (13.5). The closed little ark floats almost unnoticed among the eerie emergent shapes of boulders, the dove flutters; only a skull in the foreground reminds us that this is the planet earth after

13.4 THOMAS COLE, *The Expulsion from the Garden of Eden*

a cataclysm, not a world created for a "Star Trek" episode. Even John Martin's extreme rocks for his *Sadak in Search of the Waters of Oblivion* are kept at an artistic distance, like a painted backdrop; they have less cinematic immediacy than these looming monsters, which Cole has made to seem alive.

By contrast, *The Voyage of Life,* however famous, is more amusing than thrilling; the boat on its river is fun to follow, but the element of the specific is missing, from both protagonist and surroundings, so it has none of the power either of the Biblical *Expulsion* and *Waters Receding* or of Copley's factual *Watson* to compel real dread and empathy. The paintings might as well not be realistically done, but rendered in the style of tenth-century mosaic or the crudest Expressionist terms: the realism diminishes rather than contributes to the effectiveness of the theme, because Cole has gone overboard with the conception at the expense of believability.

The Course of Empire is another matter. Here Cole, showing his proto-cinematic soul again, makes landscape and architecture interact in wholly

13.5 THOMAS COLE, *The Waters Receding After the Deluge*

satisfactory ways as metaphors for spiritual striving, overreaching and failure. As his fake-ancient and imaginary civilization rises and destroys itself, the wilderness is never sacrificed. As we shift our view, slowly circling
around them to watch the ferment of construction and destruction, the
mountain and the harbor keep their natural authority, emblems of man's
wild persistent soul that leads him to such excesses. And the excesses are
absolutely specific, as they are in Martin's work and as they are in movies,
improving on the facts by the creation of better facts, rather than by using
fancies special to art. The wilderness again is invented as well as the colonnades and ships; Cole preferred to compose a natural paradise in his own
cultivated idiom rather than to make poetry out of its actual tough prose.

The effect of actuality was sought by Albert Bierstadt in the next generation, after the search for an American form of sublimity was an acknowledged success, and the significant beauties of the continent were
everybody's assumption. Claude and Salvator no longer needed to be sum-

moned to prove them; and so the extreme romanticism of Bierstadt's land-scapes is instead founded firmly on the documentary idea, which is the same idea behind the modern movie view of scenery. The artist needs only to reveal mountains in the sunset or a waterfall at dawn, and we are pro-voked both to gasp and to think of the power in the universe and our own insignificance; also to congratulate ourselves on our dominion over these wonders. The composition is left asymmetrical and full of possibility, rather than festooned in Claudian harmony; and the application of paint is almost undetectable. The painter does not intrude upon our communion with these marvels. The moral message is better conveyed in terms of a di-rect demand: What can you do to measure up? Bierstadt echoes the Ameri-can form of romance, the striving to keep pace with overwhelming facts, to enlarge to meet them.

Bierstadt actually took a lot of liberties with the facts, but not in the form of visible poeticizing in the old European manner. By the time he be-came well known in the middle of the century, the camera was well estab-lished as the purveyor of visual fact; and artists were resorting to it almost as a matter of course, although with a great variation in attitude toward its specific uses. For landscape art intending to suggest the topographical tra-dition, a photograph was no disgrace as an obvious help, functioning as one kind of sketch. Bierstadt took many photographs himself on his Western trips; and his two brothers set up a photography business later in New York, partly stocked by Albert's Western views.

Cole's America had lain east of the Mississippi. The "photo-graphic" look was more acceptable than the Claudian model for the great American West, which lacked a history of literary description and celebration and had to owe its fame to its very actuality, its amazing quality of being There. But at that time the camera was less satisfactory for recording the overall beauty of any big landscape than for recording details. Many of Bierstadt's better photographs are of Indians and their gear, animals, other members of the wagon train, and various vignettes of the surroundings, rather than of great vistas. The staggering vistas were cooked up later in the studio, out of sketches and partial camera views; and it would be correct to say that later photography of the West, especially the inviting kind that found its way onto the great blow-ups in Grand Central Station or onto countless calendars, and then into the cinematography of countless Westerns, owes its origins to the inventions of Bierstadt, who showed what it ought to do. The liberties he took with fact are virtually invisible. Although he offered views that simply cannot be correctly identified, because he combined them out of disparate studies, the authenticity of their general look is unques-tionable; he seems to have made up views God ought to have arranged. They create, with their combination of the factual and the awe-inspiring, a new mythology of the wilderness that goes far beyond old European ideals of the literary sublime and straight into the romantic poetics of documentary cinema that inform twentieth-century landscape imagery.

Bierstadt learned his craft in Germany, and was himself a native of Düsseldorf, where he later went back as a student after his family had settled in the United States when he was a baby. The Düsseldorf Academy was famous for its down-to-earth approach to representation, and many American art-students went there before the Civil War to gain some training in an empirical style of painting sure to be acceptable in America, with its well-known love of the palpable. But the Northern style of realism included, even in prosaic Düsseldorf, that dependence on light that casts its own spell on the psyche and creates romance out of plain facts.

The American cloud-capped mountains and sparkling lakes in Bierstadt's works owe much of their magic to their Dutch pictorial heritage, preserved well into the mid-nineteenth century in Germany, and even more

13.6 ALBERT BIERSTADT, *Mount Adams, Washington*

smoothly portable onto the American Western scene than the elegant Claudian arrangements that had been filtered through England first and used by Cole and his colleagues for Eastern views (13.6). Some of the Luminist painters also owed their greatest debt to simple Holland, only in their modest works it was much more noticeable; Bierstadt went in for grandeur.

His largest painting was not a straight landscape but an imaginary *Landing of Columbus* measuring nine by seventeen feet; but this prodigy has been destroyed. A close second is *The Domes of the Yosemite,* which is roughly nine and a half by fifteen feet in size, and now hangs in the Athenaeum in St. Johnsbury, Vermont, while *The Rocky Mountains* in the Metropolitan Museum is a mere six by ten (13.7). There is something both hilarious and magnificent about such works. They haven't the painterly suavity of Church's similarly grand performances; but they have a marvelous overreaching character, and always much more mobility than anything by Church, whose *Cotopaxi,* for all its finished exoticism, is less dynamic than any one of Bierstadt's Yosemite views, even the little ones. The biggest

13.7 ALBERT BIERSTADT, *The Rocky Mountains*

ones try the impossible, bursting out of their frames in an attempt to emu-
late the vistas they represent, to make what movies eventually made out of
scenic raw material, a contest with extremeness. An essential point about
them is that they look accessible not to exploration or tourism but to vision
itself, again because of the Dutch-realistic, cameralike technique. In contrast, the dreamy veil over much standard Romantic landscape keeps it remote, even the work of the Hudson River–school painters who followed
Cole's example. Although it may seem quite real, you do not seem to be
there yourself: the experience has been had for you by the artist.

Bierstadt was in essence an illustrator, like so many of the best American artists. Topography itself is a pure form of illustration, a mode of rendering that illuminates a physical situation without offering a different
artistic story along with it; and inspired topography can be a tale in itself,
in which the viewer loves the risk of sharing without prior clues. But illustration had acquired a bad name by the end of the century, and Bierstadt's
popularity had waned well before the time of his death in 1902. He was accused of being Germanic in the worst ways, heavy and overdetailed, and he
sometimes deserved it; but such judgments could not fail to be made in the
new climate of respect for Frenchness.

Illustration, however, was the natural wellspring of much great nineteenth-century art, perhaps especially in America, and it provided a way to
make pictures that certainly proved enabling rather than crippling in the
careers of Homer and Eakins and eventually of Sargent and Hopper.
Homer's early career as a popular graphic artist helped to form what can be

13.8 W I N S L O W   H O M E R ,   *West Point, Prout's Neck*

called his cinematic turn of mind. The artistic course of his life exemplified the way illustration could eventually be turned into movies, the way the illuminative function, which had gradually become the property of cheap magazines, could be redeemed to serve everyone in a transcendent new mode, as centuries before illuminated manuscripts had served their limited public. The shift in Homer's career has never been described like that, however, but rather as a rise out of commercial banality into the free reaches of high art. He gave up illustrating for magazines and went to live as a recluse in Maine to paint the sea. But he was a great success besides, with a thoroughly professional view of his own marketability and no high-minded artistic posing. Most of the sea paintings could be film shots, rendered as they are in that cinematic mode that is both neutral and impassioned, both documentary and romantic (13.8).

The most interesting part of his career is the middle one, where the illustrations and the paintings overlap. It was then that Homer allowed his illustrations to become "monumental" and irradiated with atmosphere without allowing their straightforward currency of subject to become diffuse or beside the point. They remain illustrations because they keep their air of personal drama, which is if anything magnified by a use of sun interspersed with black shadow that makes these paintings "graphic" in both senses. In 1866 he painted ladies outdoors exactly as Monet did—the same skirts, grass, and half-glimpsed faces (13.9, 13.10). But in Monet's works nothing is happening except in paint; the whole thing appeals as a new way of seeing, breathtaking and crackling with light and quite void of drama other than the one played out by the glitter itself; the women relinquish all personal importance in its favor. (The famous *Women in the Garden* is only one of several like this from the late 1860's.) In Homer's paintings on this theme, of which there are also several, the personalities retain their individual mystery, and the constant possibility of hidden conflict and alliance, signal and response, drenches the painting along with the pitiless sunlight. They play croquet instead of gathering bouquets, but that is not what generates the tension; the activities could be interchanged and not change the difference between the two.

Speaking entirely about form, Novak remarks that Homer's girls respond to gravitational pull, whereas Monet's float in a new pictorial universe on the surface of the canvas. And that pull of gravity includes the weight of feeling and human connection, the palpable drag of living. It is markedly poignant when he uses young and pretty women, as he so often does. He puts them into very slightly uneasy situations that he does not explain, so that they seem somehow compromised in their chignons and shoe buttons, subtly unprepared and off-balance (13.11).

13.9 WINSLOW HOMER, *The Croquet Game*

13.10 CLAUDE MONET, *Women in the Garden*

13.11 WINSLOW HOMER, *Croquet Player*

In the wood engravings for *Harper's Weekly,* the same flavor is conveyed in plain black and white and small size, only there is usually a title and a recognizable American scene like *The Summit of Mt. Washington,* or *Skating in Central Park.* In these the uneasiness is often suggested in cinematic style by hat ribbons and sash ends whipping up at ungainly angles, and bell skirts swinging without grace under the forces of wind and unexpressed worry. Like De Hooch, Homer will not allow pretty women and pretty children to be the objects of our benign and unimaginative pleasure. We are made aware of their incalculable psychic burdens, even when they are fortunate and good-looking. We can sense, without being told outright, how they feel themselves on general trial, on view under an inescapable huge scrutiny, primed to be done in, no matter how nice the weather or how perfect the attire, by some small slight or failure, some private embarrassment (13.12–13.15).

These flavors exist in the scenes with rural boys and youthful fisherfolk, as well as in the groups of dressed-up summer girls at Newport or Long Branch, and in both the paintings and the little prints for *Harper's.* The young faces are devoid of cute grins, flirtatious simpers, or picturesque pensiveness; either they have the unfocused blurry look perfected by De Hooch, perhaps even a sharp glance or a small unconscious-seeming gri-

13.12–15 WINSLOW HOMER, magazine illustrations

13.12 "Winter—A Skating Scene," *Harper's Weekly*, 1868

13.13 "Our National Winter Exercise—Skating," *Harper's Weekly*, 1866

13.14 "She turned her face to the window," *The Galaxy*, 1868

13.15 "Weary and dissatisfied with everything,"
The Galaxy, 1869

13.16 WINSLOW HOMER, *Boys in a Pasture*

mace of the smooth features, or they carry the suggestive baggage of a "lost profile," like the ones in the works of Georges de la Tour (13.16). Homer does this by pure "graphic" means, using light and dark to illuminate the way life moves, but with special attention neither to its detached visual pleasures nor to its gripping incidents, but to the latent emotional current in it, which can nudge drama into anything if it is put in a certain light.

When he painted *The Life Line* in 1884 and *Undertow* in 1886, Homer used the same sea he later painted for itself; here these rescues of half-drowned women float across the churning water like sequences in a larger movie we can never see all of, and the ocean thunders everywhere, larger still. There is a sharp erotic flavor in these scenes of helpless female bodies being wrested out of the surge by impersonal-looking men, skirts shoved up and breasts molded by wet clothes, beautiful faces still and stark; but nothing is made of it. The illustrative function has to work by itself without a prior narrative. We are forced to make the story up. There are no extras in the picture to suggest more of the plot; we are faced only with a cold set of moments that will soon be over, leaving the water empty once more and the sense of dread spreading (13.17, 13.18).

The graphic skill that made Homer a living for years keeps his shots full of similar intensity, even if the ocean is the only character, and makes vital scenes instead of decorative clusters out of small groups of people seen from a distance. *In the Mountains* can in no way be seen as a neutral, detached view of climbing women, merely an interesting pattern of light and line; it is an illustration with plenty of narrative suggestion, almost like one

13.17 WINSLOW HOMER, *Undertow*

13.18 WINSLOW HOMER, *The Life Line*

of several in a magazine story; but it has been transfigured on a big screen and left hanging in mid-air with no text. The sharp black shadows do it, they are what project each woman's introspective capacity and keep the picture fostering our sense that something is happening to them, inwardly as well as outwardly; the lack of picturesqueness does this, too, the topographical simplicity of their sloping path: neither we nor they are simply admiring the view. A similar scene rendered in the fractured light of Impressionism would keep us happy to stay at a distance from the women and instead to enter the privileged universe of painting itself, where their fate has no meaning and we have no responsibilities.

Homer seems to have created a new seriousness for genre art, as movies were later to do again. He did it using old conventions of commercial illustration (as cinema also did), not pushing the boundaries of painterly discovery (as the Impressionists did). The Impressionists were able to redeem genre art from sentimentality by recasting it in an authoritative new artistic language that fused nature, humans, and artifacts together into one harmonious syntax. Homer did equivalent redemptive work on genre subjects in the opposing cinematic way—deepening their graphic potential and their openness to dissonance. There is no peace created by paint in Homer's groups of girls on grass or boys in fields. Conflict and disharmony are invoked by that same black glitter we have come to know and love in movies, a drama that leaps out of the screen from the perpetual collision of brilliance and pitch black, whatever the color of the clothes, trees, or teacups, and that keeps things moving, suggesting what we haven't yet seen.

Homer was an early glorifier of the American Girl, that same Girl who was so prominent in James novels as a foil to European sexual assumptions and who later was the heroine of so many movies proceeding from the new American sexual assumptions that James helped define. Her own consciousness is the focal point of the story, not her effect on male sensibility; her moral being is the battleground, her sense of her own possible changes, her successes and failures; and we are watching. Later she became the characters played by Katharine Hepburn, Ginger Rogers, and Doris Day in the virtuous mode, by Joan Crawford and Barbara Stanwyck in the wicked one, by Bette Davis in both, still later by Natalie Wood and Angie Dickinson—all American girls trying to keep their personal honor whatever the sexual stakes, half-consciously struggling with the problematic meanings attached to the beautiful clothes their own beauty has demanded from the production designer, insisting on independence of spirit even while maintaining perfect grooming, active and passive at once, real and unreal, walking contradictions.

There are many such girls in Homer's art, girls exquisitely and confidently dressed but brooding or bursting with imperfect thought and feeling at odds with their select finery. When Homer shows such a girl alone, a story seems to rise around her; she refuses to be part of the pleasing land-scape, as she is in paintings by William Merritt Chase, for example. Simi-larly, these girls are emphatically different from Tissot's French and English much-dressed girls from the same period, all of whom are Objects with a vengeance. Nothing is happening to the women in Tissot's pictures; they are quite inert. Their sulky or dreamy looks are part of their costume, and emotional importance is allowed only to the ones who observe them—us, or the man in the picture, if there is one. The lady has no comprehensi-ble existence except to be observed; her inner world will not come to life or budge outside the frame; she is seen as a generic Mystery (13.19, 13.20).

13.19 JAMES TISSOT, *Portrait of Miss Lloyd*

13.20 JAMES TISSOT, *The Gallery of H.M.S. "Calcutta"*

But a Homer-like sort of girl was a cinematic given for several American movie generations—the perfect-looking Girl, cast and presented in the same visual style, whether she was playing a marine biologist or an international spy, a sour-minded poor man's daughter or a burdened suburban housewife, a spunky librarian or a honky-tonk dancer. She was someone with strong feelings and an active part to play in the drama, someone whose thoughts and actions mattered when you couldn't actually see her; but she was housed in incongruously passive-seeming fashion-model looks. And just as in Homer, these very looks were themselves important in the American romantic scheme, some invocation to the commercial muse in the midst of the most serious romantic-realistic projections, some daring connection made between the independent spirit of American women and their skill as consumers. Henry James has an older lady in *Daisy Miller,* someone who lives in Europe, say first of Daisy, "Of course she is pretty. But she is very common." And then later, unbelievingly, "She has that charming look they all have. I can't think where they pick it up; and she dresses in perfection—no, you don't know how well she dresses. I can't think where they get their taste." James only developed the American Girl; Homer had invented her. Her "taste" was some stroke of New World genius, the sounding of a new creative female note.

Homer's near contemporary Thomas Eakins had a different but no less acute emotional view of women's trappings. In line with his devotion to the meaning in what the camera reveals, his ardent religion of Realism, Eakins stresses the wrinkles and displacements of the perfect feminine costume rather than its first fresh and ideal moment. He dwells on how it looks in wear rather than when put on before the mirror, and especially how it looks in wear under spiritual or physical stress. The best examples of this are in the two pictures of women singing, *The Concert Singer* and *The Pathetic Song,* painted about ten years apart (13.21, 13.22). In each of these the singing lady's dress is completely detailed, without generalizations that might suggest the unimportance of finery to the serious performance of music. Like other cinematic artists, Eakins does not retreat from understanding the minutiae of fashion, respecting them as carriers of the same emotional current borne by music itself. With all his interest in the actual, he never sneers at ruching. His singers produce Mendelssohn from within their trimmed and stiffened taffeta as naturally as they might speak or sigh at some pointed moment; the seams and frills are a little displaced by the action of breathing, and show the slight stress under the light; and the earnest faces are supported rather than mocked by the earnest elaborateness of the dresses. In each picture the music, with its power over everyone's soul, pours through the lady and through the potted palm, through the setting and the supporting players, through the shiny fabric and its tailoring.

Keeping to the tonal center, Eakins' realism is not the sort that scorns elegance as if it were falsity. He turns the same intent eye on the bloodied hand of the surgeon as he does on the fashionable singer, and neither loses to the other as each performs with a wholly American seriousness. The women in his portraits wear finery or nudity with the same earnestness, shared in turn with that of men in official robes or dusty jackets or nakedness as required. What makes Eakins cinematic is his insistence on the music of the person as the channel of drama and importance, the absolute sovereignty of individual experience as the core of any interesting image. The faces flicker with their inner orchestration and the clothes shift and stretch to match, whether they are boxing gear or an embroidered bodice or bare skin. And to authenticate the inner moment, absolute fidelity to perspective and lighting is brought to bear; you "know what o'clock it is," as Eakins famously said, and that optical exactness naturally makes any inward reality sharper. In the cinematic mode of realism, an over-Baroque distortion of ordinary things would diminish rather than intensify feeling. But the apparently unnoticed droop of an otherwise puffed sleeve, the slight unconscious tilt of a normally upright neck, or the suggestion of a frown only barely brought out by the light from the window gives great resonance to the cinematic view of an ordinary person in a prosaic moment.

13.21 THOMAS EAKINS, *The Concert Singer*

13.22 THOMAS EAKINS, *The Pathetic Song*

Eakins doesn't go in for detached pictorial clarity or dazzle; and the suppression of color is one of the signals of his insistence on engagement. It doesn't mean that only the grim and ugly facts of living are truthful, the ones without the caress of chromatic beauty, but that light suffices to concentrate the curious mobility of emotional truth, and that color, which deals in pleasure, is something of an irrelevancy. There is no fun in Eakins' work; he never has a good time, pleasure is strangled; but there is movement, the haunting flow of unspecified feeling, and consequently the hope and possibility of eventual fulfillment and future pleasure, perhaps not now but soon or sometime. His pictures are dim but never gloomy, only provisionally at rest in some evaded cadence before the next phrase or after the last tonic resolution. They, too, participate in the American romance of perpetual aspiration couched in documentary terms.

The camera was a constant presence in Eakins' artistic life, and it is clear that it served him as a marvelous new medium for emotion rather than any sort of distancing mechanism. He knew the famous Muybridge motion studies, and made many of his own; for him photography was a key to making things move, not a way of holding them still. Eakins was able to trans-

13.23 THOMAS EAKINS,
Portrait of Mrs. Eakins

late camera habits into paint (as Degas was also able to do) so as to record not merely the right looks of legs or wheels in motion but the persistent movement behind still faces and motionless figures, even behind quiet spaces and still objects. Thus he could show the influence of those inward tides for which music so often stands, and which it so often accompanies in movies themselves.

The movement of eroticism in Eakins' work is all the more volatile for being somewhat submerged, compressed into the intensifying channel of homoeroticism, and keeping clear of any expression of simple pleasure. There is no simplicity in the world of Eakins. Everyone and everything is complicated—as in the work of Henry James, whose novels are full of private moments like those being lived through by Eakins' pensive subjects. They gaze out of the frame, wondering about their feelings and others', about the difficulties and distortions that accompany the appropriate management of the more awkward passions. Mrs. Eakins in particular looks like someone exercising huge patience, burdened with understanding (13.23). The listening tilt of these heads is to that inner music, which it is a blessing not everyone can hear.

Eakins' ungainly naked youths in water and sunlight are clothed in swirls of complex feeling—partly theirs, partly ours, and partly the painter's, everyone's unfixed and unsimple, caught in a sequence rather than a composition. The thick emotional texture of *The Swimming Hole* was built up by Eakins through various kinds of study for it, which included photographs, models in wax, and oil sketches, a whole array of possible approaches to these boys he finally swims toward, out of the brown corner into which he has painted himself (13.24). The restrained delicacy of feeling with which he approached female nudity also has a Jamesian respect for women in it, a cautious, ambivalent, and very American mindfulness of a female strength of mind and perception that is powered rather than opposed by the force of sex.

Eakins' landscapes share with Homer's the flavor of being settings. They have the subjective look of personal atmosphere, whether people are actually present in them or not. When they are present, moreover, they are often seen from a certain distance with their faces in shadow, as they are in Homer, inviting our empathy, drawing us by the unfocused, self-absorbed postures of their bodies. *Starting Out After Rail* and *Sailing* are two frames from the same shot; and both could almost be by Homer, using the encompassing sea to cradle the actionless scene in total motion (13.25, 13.26). In the second version, *Sailing,* the horizontal format is more cinematically successful and permits the broadening of the water, the raising of the horizon, and the cropping of the sail, devices that suggest we are floating to-

13.24 THOMAS EAKINS, *The Swimming Hole*

ward the men in the boat as they move slowly out of reach, while the sea
that floods both sides of the frame surrounds us along with them on their
quiet venture. It has that Friedrich look of investigation, of a search with
an outward excuse and an unformed inward goal. So do all the Homers.

   The third in this group of Jamesian, proto-cinematic American painters
is Sargent. He, too, was a solitary inward struggler, a character like the
eponymous hero of James' "The Pupil" with expatriated nomadic parents,
one who learned early, for reasons quite different from those of Homer and
Eakins, to fortify himself inside a citadel even while happily moving among
rich and social people. You can see it in his self-portrait, the lifted chin and
distancing gaze that correspond to Eakins' stiff tilt in his (13.27, 13.28).
Both these painters learned portraiture from the Dutch and Spaniards,
even though both studied art in France; and the lesson of combining inwardness with a strict rendering of phenomena was well absorbed by each

13.25 **THOMAS EAKINS,** *Sailing*

13.26 **THOMAS EAKINS,** *Starting Out After Rail*

13.27 THOMAS EAKINS,
Self-Portrait

13.28 JOHN SINGER SARGENT,
Self-Portrait

—the way to show a face as if it were the scene of private activity
intuitively perceived, not a stage on which private feelings are skillfully arranged in a bouquet prepared for our detached appreciation.

Sargent's affinity with Eakins and Homer shows up in his works that
deal with children, notably in the great *Daughters of Edward Boit* and in
such public-seeming portraits as *Mrs. Davis and Her Son Livingston* and
Mrs. Carl Meyer and Her Children (see 13.32). James lurks in these works,
too, as he does in the Eakins scenes with one or two or three people,
whether or not they are family portraits (13.29, 13.30). There is a strong
resonance in Eakins' *Home Scene,* showing two sisters, one an adult and
one a child, that resembles that in Sargent's Boit and Meyer paintings,
done more than twenty years later but following a similar track, a track
that starts in the seventeenth century (13.31).

The looks of children, presented as a reminder of free and unlimited responses to life and consequently as a foil to the compromised feelings and
limiting pretensions of adults, is a strong theme in art. It seems to have
begun with Velázquez. The great Dutch painters, especially De Hooch, separately developed the theme a generation later, incorporating it into a general view of their urban, Protestant milieu, where family intimacy was

prized in a way now familiar to middle-class viewers accustomed to believing in the feelings of children. Children in Renaissance art have the look of half-formed adults, sometimes of malformed ones, and they rarely seem independently conscious. But by the 1630's Velázquez was able to present the royal children of an austere, Catholic, and almost feudal court in the same psychologically telling aspect arrived at only later in the century by De Hooch in visual art, and only in the nineteenth century by writers of fiction.

Velázquez, especially in the irresistible *Las Meninas,* rendered the royal offspring as true centers of sensibility, both their own, which radiates from them, and the sensibility so immensely projected onto them by attentive adults. He thus provided a perfect model for a painter like Sargent, who served both real and pseudo aristocrats, and who could find in Velázquez a key to making his clients and their children look both imposing and natu-

13.29　JOHN SINGER SARGENT, *The Daughters of Edward Boit*

13.30 JOHN SINGER SARGENT, *Mrs. Davis and Her Son Livingston*

13.31 THOMAS EAKINS, *Home Scene*

ral, refined and direct, possessed not only of riches and status but of imagination and personal feeling, like the characters in James' fiction. Certainly
in James, fiction caught up with Velázquez at last, and Sargent was able to
make the connection manifest.

Eakins and Homer investigated the intensifying value of children in an
analogous way without needing quasi-royal pomp. Their pictorial method
has more of the Dutch stamp—the look of light rendered as a psychological
ambience that leaks into every corner of life with the same equalizing insis-

13.32 JOHN SINGER SARGENT,
Mrs. Carl Meyer and Her Children

tence, whatever generations are represented; relations among children and their elders share in the atmosphere that gives rise to poignant suggestion; and details are sharpened into meaning by its effects, not by any special pleading they do on their own.

Sargent instead uses the example of Velázquez, to create the individual glitter sharply worked up against a dim interior that made the Spanish painter's grandees seem to shine with myriad fleeting psychic reflections, not just silver braid and cosmetics. Velázquez' serious children especially lend themselves to Sargent's emulation (13.33). The stiffly clad royal infants with their steady gazes and well-brushed little scalps resurface in the Boit front hall, the Meyer drawing room, and the Sears parlor, where the same ambiguous murk threatens to swallow them up. They, too, hold gallantly still, fighting back with their own concentrated light all the complex forces of parental pride.

Homer, Eakins, and Sargent share a confrontational emotional style, an illustrative mode that is very American, despite the differences among their lives, their subjects, and their sources, a style linked to the movies of the future even more than to the paintings of the past. It is very insistent in the Meyer portrait, for example, composed as if the lady were being loomed over by a viewer, a painter, a movie camera (13.32). As we come near and look down at her, we see her quickly enfold her son's fingers in her own, so that the book drops, and he cannot get away; we see how his sister holds him, too, as she peers from behind. Her face is full of acceptance and some ruthlessness, his of doubt and some fear. Mother's face is tense and cordial at once; she looks as if she were in the middle of speaking—she would like the children to come around and put in a proper appearance next to her for the picture, but of course without lolling and crushing her perfect skirt. All three exude conscious beauty in their sumptuous clothes and brunette looks; but we are moving in on this family group before it is quite ready for scrutiny. It is a *scene*—as *Las Meninas* is and as James said the Boit painting is; but it is an even more movielike and less painterly scene than either of those, since the action seems to be the process of preparation for action. In a moment, the book will be put away, the kids suitably settled, and Mother sitting back with her face, skirt, and fan composed; and then the painter will be allowed to back up and begin.

Velázquez could not approach his noble sitters from above like this, or appear to move toward them as they arranged themselves. Eakins also takes great liberties, so that we even see the baby on the flagstones as if we had crawled on our stomachs to get a view of her, and we seem nearer to his female subjects than they ought to let us come, as if we were a movie camera spying on their state of mind. Homer keeps a physical distance, but he also views his characters from unexpected points of vantage, showing them in the middle of something without waiting for their permission to start.

In twentieth-century American painting these cinematic ways of using old themes were continued in the work of artists like Edward Hopper, who were unquestionably influenced by cinema itself. Hopper is the heir of Homer and Eakins, and more indirectly of Sargent, whose watercolors resemble both Homer's and Hopper's: the same white light, sharp tonality, and odd viewpoints are there, and in works with visible characters, the

13.33 DIEGO VELÁZQUEZ, *Las Meninas*

same movielike sense of psychological action. But in Hopper are also the modern clothes and rooms and corners of buildings once artlessly apparent in films of the 1930's and 1940's, the offices and hotel rooms and lunch counters that formed the settings of much unpretentious film.

Only in the last decade has this kind of material in Hopper been retrieved and reprocessed in current films, as if to elevate them through association with Fine Art, like references to Hogarth and Bruegel. In fact Hopper made the references himself in the first place, deliberately displaying his sympathy for the emotional potential of the ordinary film-set (13.34). He did it even more in his magazine illustrations. In the paintings and illustrations, the Hollywood-style hair, shoes, and makeup reinforce the impression that we are watching some inconsequential frames between action shots in an old George Raft movie, those parts of the sequence which forge an enduring visual fantasy about urban locales apart from any tangle in the plot, and which linger in the memory after the story is forgotten.

At the same time these works looks like references to Homer, with his similar sense of the neutral but charged setting in its rural form. Some of

13.34 EDWARD HOPPER, *Room in New York*

Hopper's are also in country surroundings: the two women on the upstairs porch of a white house, seen from a distance, are like Homer's milkmaids, schoolteachers, or hikers, visibly partaking in some private course of life as we stare at them from way over here (13.35). Their inwardness registers all the better across distance and with minimal facial detail.

The graphic works of Hopper are especially American despite all Hopper's French affiliations, and linked to the Northern tradition. Such images as *Night Shadows* and *The Balcony* may owe much to Degas and perhaps to Caillebotte and Charles Meryon; but Hopper admired the directness of Dutch graphic art, and the graphic character of these two pictures is more illustrative and cinematic, more engaged, like Rembrandt, than detached in the usual French style (13.36). Since Hopper, like Homer, had been a commercial illustrator, his later career is similarly viewed as an escape from all that. But again the appeal of his later works lies in an emotional flavor that seems to have seeped into them in spite of his desire for neutrality and reticence. The force of drama thrusts itself into the picture without a text or a product to sell. The dramatic character of phenomena

13.35 EDWARD HOPPER, *Second Story Sunlight*

13.36 EDWARD HOPPER, *Night Shadows*. Etching

themselves, especially human ones, forces the image into an illustrative shape as if it were a movie frame.

Hopper's graphic work for magazines was done in the early years of this century, in the period when Hopper (who died in 1967) overlapped Homer (d. 1910), Eakins (d. 1916, the same year as Henry James), and Sargent (d. 1925). Gail Levin has shown that they are clearly connected both to his own later etchings and paintings and to a vivid tradition of magazine art (13.37, 13.38). This was already in place in Homer's youth in the 1860's in England and America (with precedents in Menzel's Germany in the 1840's) and was itself an eventual source for cinema. Hopper is an artistic figure in whom traditional European painting, modern French painting, popular illustration, and modern American movies legitimately meet. His references, echoes, and allusions to all of them come from direct experience, synthesized by a uniquely American romantic temper, something puritanical and self-testing and aspiring. Although his strongest New York teacher was Robert Henri, these three earlier Americans—Homer, Eakins, and Sargent—were unquestionably his forerunners, with their similar combinations of solitary independent effort, private way with European conventions, and instinctive illustrative genius that moves toward the masterpieces of cinema rather than along the path to abstraction, past or future.

Sargent did several street scenes and interiors in Venice in the 1880's after he had visited Spain and absorbed the Velázquez viewpoint (13.39).

13.37 E D W A R D   H O P P E R , "He did it just on purpose to frighten me ..." Illustration in *Farmer's Wife,* March 1919

13.38 E D W A R D   H O P P E R , *Summer Evening.* 1947

13.39 JOHN SINGER SARGENT, *Venetian Bead Stringers*

These share in the same American ability to adapt Dutch and Spanish ways of managing color and using light to create feeling out of nothing, just as movies do, rather than using it chiefly for widening painterly scope, as French artists were doing; and they have a marked affinity with the Homers of the same date and the Hoppers of much later.

Eastman Johnson (1824–1906) was a largely sentimental American genre painter who had studied in both Düsseldorf and Paris before the Civil War, and who had seen the Dutch art in The Hague. He did at least one painting that further suggests, like Sargent's, the way American artists might use European realism to prefigure the future of American cinematic romance. *Not at Home,* from the mid-1870's, has the flavor of a Vrel or Boursse domestic scene coupled with the same emotional currents present in the works of both Degas and Hopper. They arise from the way he uses light and framing to show nothing happening as if it were something significant (13.40).

When he had no portrait subject to confine him, Sargent also produced suggestive little oils of dim rooms lit like the chamber in *Las Meninas* by a

13.40 EASTMAN JOHNSON, *Not at Home*

remote door and invisible windows, inhabited by inexplicable and transient characters. He also did sections of streets very like Hopper's pregnant urban glances that echo Berckheyde and De Witte even while they seem to fit into films.

Some recent heirs to the American psychological style are Richard Diebenkorn and Fairfield Porter and lately Eric Fischl, all three of whom, like Eakins and Homer, show their closer links to the North European and cinematic idea of drama than to France or to Velázquez (13.41). Fischl, however, shows how Velázquez dwarfs and idiots, stuck in their courtly garb and role, may be translated across time and society into modern citizens stuck in modern life, grinning and fumbling and hopelessly distorted as they appear to take their ease and enjoy their privileges (13.42). In keeping with current fashions in feeling, Fischl also adjusts his psychological register to the very young, as De Hooch and Velázquez both knew how to do, and as Homer so often did; but for Fischl it is a device to keep the erotic and emotional pitch up without resorting to cacophony of the Expressionist kind. In some harmony with Eakins, he also shows the debt such vision pays to the old North European artistic *sympathy* with what is sexually questionable, grotesque, or ridiculous. Such sympathy operates in contrast to the classical horror that requires an exaggeratedly *theatrical* and therefore subtly ameliorative rendering. Porter and Diebenkorn follow Homer, Sargent, and Hopper, however, and keep things nicely ambiguous instead

13.41 FAIRFIELD PORTER, *A Short Walk*

13.42 ERIC FISCHL, *Daddy's Girl*

of straightforwardly unbearable. Fischl's divergent style may represent the difference, increasingly vivid, between film and the cruder realistic romanticism of television.

It is noteworthy that Velázquez became a favorite with nineteenth-century painters on both sides of the Atlantic and both sides of the Channel. His peerless technique, original vision, and absolute unbombastic confidence gave modern painters renewed belief in the autonomy and sovereignty of art itself. If painting for its own sake could so obviously transcend the grim demands of an archaic Spanish court on a captive artist, it might well be trusted to prevail against modern forces—social, commercial, or artistic—and, especially, technological. The camera haunted all realistic art after the middle of the nineteenth century; it was necessary to fight or flee, or come to terms. The glorious painterly uses to which Velázquez put his naked eye and non-classic spirit, heroically forming his unique style of realism against a fixed religious and aristocratic background, gave nineteenth-century painters fresh hope. Velázquez certainly provided the historic proof that any painter may feel superior to society; but he also showed painters how they might feel superior to the camera, without having to forsake the endless treasure-house of natural appearances that heartless and vulgar photography seemed to be swallowing up.

FOURTEEN

France in the
Nineteenth Century

AMERICAN painters studied in Germany during the first half of the nineteenth century, but by the second half they had to go to France. Homer, Eakins, Sargent, and Hopper all had distinct affinities with the North European tradition, but they all went to Paris for training. They also went there perhaps for deeper ratification of their choice of profession than private conviction could sustain, because only in Paris was painting then taken as seriously as an aspiring talent could wish, as a natural *métier* for a serious man.

The pre-eminence of France as a training ground for artists was due to centuries of French official acknowledgment that art had primary importance, and that talent and originality had primary importance for art. By the nineteenth century, there was not only a state-supported Academy— such a thing existed elsewhere—but also a government prepared to supplement and even oppose its own Academy in order to support and exhibit divergent and diverse artistic effort; and there was an established profession of art criticism, to keep the reading public awake and engaged by the enterprise, and to produce an intellectual milieu for artists themselves. All this was true during a century of political upheaval when republics, monarchies, and empires followed one another, during which the city of Paris was transformed. The condition of painting was a clouded mirror of such turbulence, since, whatever the regime and the condition of society, French art was constantly acknowledged to be important to French life and national awareness, and control of it mattered enormously. Students and patrons from other places had to come and see it to believe it.

The spirit of revolt was built into the ideals of French art after the Revolution, the idea that enlightened French civilization would always stand for Liberté, Egalité, and Fraternité in its cultural endeavors, however these might be interpreted. The drama of French art in the last century has in consequence been perceived in this one as the perpetual triumph of freedom over tyranny, partly because the style of French self-perception seemed to demand it. After the triumph of classic simplicity over Rococo frivolity came the triumph of Romantic painters like Delacroix over the chilly rigidities of Neoclassicism, then that of earthy Realists like Courbet over the high-flown nonsense of Romanticism, then the triumph of Impressionism over the literal-minded and sentimental purveyors of conventional subject matter, and finally the triumph of form over content and the alleged liberation of painting from the ancient grip of natural appearances. Only in France did so much esthetic battle seem to be taking place and such continuous revolution in process.

Recent study of nineteenth-century art has resulted in a more complicated account of French artistic circumstances during the period, but their general commitment to mobility is unmistakable. Stasis was never the prevailing disposition. Throughout the century, as brisk new styles and flavors emerged, the prestige of the Académie gradually declined, and dissatisfaction grew with the educational aims and methods of the Ecole des Beaux-Arts. These institutions, founded in the seventeenth and eighteenth centuries under the terms of absolute monarchy, had undergone considerable later modification without ever going out of existence. By the middle of the nineteenth century, however, the future of painters trained in the strict methods of the Ecole was no longer secure in view of changes in public taste, which were being fostered by some of the same institutions that supported the continuation of the old scheme. Tension and conflict were inevitable in such a complex administrative tangle, since the future of French art was seen by everyone as an important issue, and lack of originality was generally deplored, even while the academic education of painters virtually ensured it.

In this creative tension and conflict, independent artists steadily flourished. There was a public for them and a market as well, and state commissions to be had that did not necessarily go to Académie-trained painters. The state-supported Salon was open to all artists, and seen by thousands of viewers daily, although the decisions and indeed the composition of its jury and hanging committee were always matters of dispute. As in any situation where a great deal of art is produced, most of what was done was bad, and much of what was bad was popular and sold well; so the question of what the Salon jury rejected or rewarded was fraught. The idea of art as public entertainment was also entrenched, and soon became part of the general expansion of Parisian life, contributing to the sense so well expounded by T. J. Clark that the city—that France altogether—had an Image, and needed to have one. The image it had by the middle of the century was fluid, diverse, and fast becoming uncontrollable—the image of a mixed, corruptible, and unaccountable society.

It was also a romantic image. The blunt Realist vision of Courbet and Manet no less than the smoother one of Fantin-Latour and Degas has the flavor of a search and a quest, especially a search inward, a longing to go beyond the boundaries not only of former artistic practice but of legitimate subjects for the attention of art, to find the key to the moving modern soul. Means for realizing such romantic aims in art naturally lay in the possibilities of re-vision, of finding a way to overstep the boundaries of fundamental visual custom in art, in order to illustrate appropriately the new escape from the old Hierarchy of the Genres and the tyranny of pictorial "finish" established in Napoleonic times. Not just startling themes and a mobile surface rendering, but flexible ways of framing and composing the contents of pictures were required, to match the constant reorganization of reality that was going on in France at the middle of the century. Modern Life had to yield up its own romantic core; the essence of modern longing had to be found and represented in new visual terms. The powerful romanticism of the Revolutionary period, conceived in Neoclassic visual syntax, had lost its force. The vigorous beauty of Delacroix' work, with its reference to the painterly freedom of the Baroque, had a movement unrelated to the harsh thrust of later days.

Ever since the seventeenth century, French visual custom for serious history paintings had been founded on Italian principles. Antique references had remained appropriate for figures and drapery, supplemented by modern references derived from an array of Renaissance masters, and Claudian and Poussinesque arrangements of space remained correct for exterior views. Before the Revolution, genre works such as those of Chardin had been exempt from such principles, and so were *fêtes galantes,* portraits, and rural landscapes, all of which were considered comparatively unserious even though delightful, and which therefore could show the influence of Dutch vision without compromising their integrity.

Under the academic system established after the Revolution, the quest was not for delight but for perfection, following the Italian Renaissance notion of an antique standard that claimed to raise the artist to the level of ideal visionary, and keep him out of the gutter of mindless craft or slavish adherence to visual fact. Lofty French national themes seemed to require a purified style with such an idea behind it. The frivolity and elegance of pre-Revolutionary styles seemed to debase them, and at the same time condemned their North European reliance on actuality, on the flow of light and air that suggests the free play of private feeling and an individual viewpoint.

Ever since the founding of the French Fine Arts Academy in Rome during the reign of Louis XIV, successful students in the academic system in Paris might win the coveted Prix de Rome and seek Classical perfection at the imperial source. Academic training led specifically to that goal; and the system was continued through the eighteenth and most of the nineteenth centuries, with prize winners duly spending several years in Rome and sending work home. The copying of antique masterpieces and the imitation of an idealizing style were basic requirements, and history painting was necessary to display them, even after Delacroix, Chassériau, and others had broken free of its classic strictures in the 1820's and gone back to Rubens and Tintoretto for models.

In the 1830's Paul Delaroche began sentimentalizing the flavor of history painting to suit the taste of the July Monarchy, toning down the painterly freedom propounded by the Romantics while at the same time injecting some show business into the dignified Neoclassic program, and dealing with costumed history instead of draped legend. By 1850 Courbet was undertaking his own personal overthrow of old painterly aims, methods, and subjects, magnifying the crudity and awkwardness of the contemporary poor, eschewing history, operating an atelier without a strict hierarchy, rendering nudes with all their bulges and rural life with all its mud. But through it all, the Prix de Rome winners' paintings from 1800 to 1865 look very much the same—clear-edged, bright-colored, smooth, and perfectly static.

Nevertheless originality was officially fostered by the Académie, and eye-training was encouraged. Students in the Ecole des Beaux-Arts were expected to make quick oil sketches recording the effects of light and color in natural scenery, as well as on-the-spot drawings of street life, and to create fresh, inventive compositional sketches of imagined subjects in the studio. But a serious academic painting would have to be "finished" before it could do honor to art and fully reveal the artist's skill as well as his gifts, even though movement and spontaneity were refined away during the process. Training for that result still consisted of learning to draw from casts of Classical sculpture, and adapting drawings of the live model to fit the Classical ideal. The quick personal rendering, however, was admired as the test of talent; and at the Salon, the public was responding to its immediate appeal, since the non-academic, independent painters of France were exploring its possibilities, especially its suitability for modern themes.

Albert Boime has described a gradual rise throughout the nineteenth century in the officially acknowledged value of the spontaneous oil sketch, and a corresponding decline in the prestige of highly finished academic works and of academic training. A significant change was also occurring in the medium used for academic life-drawing itself: fine pencil was being replaced by soft charcoal, the better to emphasize broad tonal values rather than sharp outlines shaded with painstaking cross-hatching. Amazingly informal, "Impressionist" works survive by many academic painters who would not have considered them fit to show, despite the eye, verve, and invention they display. At the same time, critics and the public were admiring independent painters' works, exhibited as finished, which by strict academic standards could only be called preparatory sketches. This volatile situation was already in place long before the Impressionists' great revolt, initiated by their first exhibit in 1874. At least a generation before that, the desire for a more unmediated painterly vision was replacing the old respect for the maintenance of noble standards. The public needed a shiftier image, one with more movement, more ambiguity, and more range.

For some independent painters during the early nineteenth century, such as those of the Barbizon school and Corot, landscape had offered an excellent way out of the academic mold, and for the Barbizon painters the Dutch models might be learned from with profit. The Impressionists later took the same path. For them, landscape stood for the non-illustrative aspects of painting, for pure actuality without anecdote, for pure movement—nature keeps moving, light is never still, color vibrates—and for the limitless possibilities of pure paint, in direct opposition to the history-bound scope of the classical figure.

Landscape had long been a source of painterly exercise, offering a way to train in comfort outdoors, to stretch the artistic muscles during the long, confining task of creating historical works in the studio. What more radical way to elevate pure painting than to glorify such fundamental material, such a basic relation between the artist and his art? Well before Impressionism, the great Dutch landscape-painters of the past and the great English artists in the genre were being honored by French landscape-painters. It was apparent that French landscape-art might strengthen itself by encompassing the vital art of other modern nations, with no apologies to ancient Greece and Rome. Landscapes are also easy to like and easy to sell; they can provide pleasure without making demands. Throughout the century, landscapes did well at the Salon and among dealers.

But landscape in nineteenth-century France was increasingly anti-Romantic, more and more committed to detachment and withdrawal into neutral painterly territory, to a search in the opposite direction. It could not satisfy the desire for illustrative imagery, fanciful or real, that a painter like Delaroche had supplied at the Salon, or a cartoonist like Daumier in the newspaper. It had no power to slake the thirst for mirrors. Delaroche, whose *Execution of Lady Jane Grey* and *Princes in the Tower* remain thrilling to this day, and later his pupil Gérôme, with his Oriental slave-markets and Classical incidents, were adept at maintaining an operettalike pictorial tone for historical genre, something entertaining and sumptuous, something exotic and remote, something provisionally serious but also guaranteed to be quite undisturbing, and something at the same time firmly *artistic,* comfortably in line with academic assumptions.

But Thomas Couture, another pupil of Delaroche who became a nonacademic painter and teacher, made a great splash in 1847 with his *Romans of the Decadence.* He favored a rough-surfaced, harshly lighted style that suggested an uncomfortable modernity, a relation between his ancient revelers and modern living people—the painting makes it easy to believe that he was Manet's teacher (14.1). Couture's personnel were still firmly ancient, however, in trappings and attributes; and it was not until Manet presented his *Olympia* in 1865 that Parisians were brought face to face with themselves minus all disguises, and Delaroche's legacy announced itself as virtually spent. During the 1860's Manet, Fantin, Whistler, and Degas were seeking other resources.

For representing modern human life in a new visual style, old and rich sources could be tapped, and known themes revived. Once free of the dominance of classical forms, French modern painters looked with fresh eyes not only on their own Rococo predecessors but on still earlier models in Dutch art. The development of the camera and the revival of interest in Vermeer and his colleagues seem to go together as avenues of discovery for Parisian artists in the 1860's. Optical reality was an appropriate metaphor for the new social reality; and Dutch bourgeois imagery, rendered in terms of light, lent itself admirably to the new French bourgeois world in its new Ville de Lumière.

The newest mirror of the newest mode of living was the city itself, the metropolitan mirror of universal life. The village was no longer the world, as it might seem to be when Courbet painted *Burial at Ornans* in 1850; it wasn't artificial enough, ephemeral enough, variable enough, deceptive enough. The new Haussmannized Paris of the 1860's—with its old *quartiers* destroyed, along with their old social and commercial arrangements, and a new public street life created, mixing all classes, especially for entertainments—was a new metaphor for the panorama of humanity. As such, Paris far outclassed even a busy Dutch townscape; but the point could be made by using other old artistic material, especially the graphic renderings of specialized *métiers* and *figures diverses* that had had a vogue in the chic

14.1 THOMAS COUTURE, *Romans of the Decadence* (detail)

urban life of the eighteenth century—single-sheet prints of kitchen maids, hat vendors, scissors grinders, and the like. These were taken up and modified by mid-century artists, and they stand behind Degas' laundresses and Manet's ragpickers, and eventually behind Lautrec's prostitutes and entertainers.

Such new urban paintings founded on old prints reveal the painters' knowledge that commercial graphic art, which is devoted to meaning rather than beauty and is aimed at everybody, has current importance to any city's image. The new French painting that dealt with the new world of the city had to take account of graphic tradition, especially in its popular mode, where images gather and disperse, come and go, form and re-form in comic, mawkish, or stark visions in a continuum of black and white. Despite its appeal, the crisply polychromed and stagy look of paintings on the Neo-classic formula, even when it was used for contemporary genre themes, could not suffice for the representation of mixed city feelings: some kind of graphic projection, some kind of mixture of the vulgar and the hopeful, some fusion of the ironic and the romantic, some kind of *cinema* was called for to create the Painting of Modern Life.

The serious stage was not a proper model for this, and painting that suggested it directly failed of its eventual effect. What worked wonderfully

was the other kind of show business, the crude and sexy, the wordlessly romantic or satiric, and the traditionally popular—anything that conveyed
the idea of seriousness portrayed in ephemeral terms. Suggestions of the
cabaret stage, the opera ballet, and the street performer therefore abound
in the works of Manet and Degas, and they did in those of Daumier, an artist who also used the graphic medium to satirize serious, literary theater
while creating his own form of draftsmanly show business, a new comic theater of the world. Baudelaire's essay on Constantin Guys, "The Painter of
Modern Life," was written at the beginning of the 1860's as if to articulate
the need for someone to transcend Daumier, to do the same thing, only to
take the theme of modern absurdity beyond journalistic satire, to illustrate
the new life of Paris—and therefore of the world—even more accurately,
and bring it home at the highest level.

Manet and Degas both answered this need; and one measure of their success is how much abuse was heaped on their efforts between the 1860's and

14.2 EDGAR DEGAS, *Woman Ironing, Seen*
Against the Light

14.3 EDGAR DEGAS, *Dancers Climbing a Stair*

the 1880's. They were trying to do what Guys and Daumier had done, only they were doing it in the sphere of serious painting, as contenders with David and Ingres in the use of respected prototypes. But to do it they had to use a broader range of prototypes, raiding the works of Goya and Velázquez and the non-classical Dutch to render the world anew.

When it was in fact rendered by them, it was initially unrecognizable, partly perhaps because it was rendered in paint, the customary medium of idealization, rather than in popular graphic media. Daumier's ridicule had met no resistance. But Manet's *Olympia* and Degas' later beach scenes and laundrywomen, his oblique and ironic views of stage performance, were railed at for their grubbiness, the harsh dirty look not of the depicted *métier* but of the artist's means, the dark shadows and dim planes in which arms and faces were made out, the unpleasing foreshortening and smudginess of the figures—the kind of effect that the modern camera, still and moving, has so well encompassed and elevated (14.2, 14.3).

The twentieth-century world, accustomed to modern painting that celebrates detached painterly concerns, has found these painters both prophetic and acutely of their time; but that is also largely because it has absorbed the transcendent graphic medium of cinema, and can see these washerwomen and prostitutes and derelicts, these racetrack patrons and café sitters as rightly reflected by an art that suits them, not just an art of

14.4 EDOUARD MANET, "Open here I flung
the Shutter." Illustration for Poe's *The Raven*

painting but a new kind of graphic-cum-painterly representation, an exalt-
edly realistic, mobile "graphic" art.

Both Degas and Manet used actual graphic expression to keep their eyes
and thoughts afloat, experimenting with extant techniques, sometimes with
a straight illustrative purpose such as Manet's lithographs for Poe's
Raven, sometimes for private effort such as Degas' monotypes of whores
off-duty (14.4). Degas indeed used his own monotypes as foundations for
pastels or oils, in that same undifferentiated use of different media that
began with Rembrandt. And Degas, inevitably, experimented with the camera, too. In the work of Manet and Degas, the superimposition of the
graphic and the painterly was a stamp of their new vision, something Daumier could not yet achieve. Daumier's paintings tended to depart from
graphic speed and optical irreverence, and partake more purely of painterly history. It was, moreover, a program different from the one the Impressionists wished to establish, through which paint could leave the
graphic field altogether, and cease to act as a mirror for the viewer.

The famous Degas *Interior* (1868–9) has defied attempts to attach it to a specific scene in a specific play or novel, although it has all the uncanny instantaneous look of a very particular moment (14.5). But it might well be from Zola's *Thérèse Raquin* or any of the other novels that have been proposed, even if it does not match the written descriptions, because it represents a new kind of illustration—or, rather, an old/new kind, derived from Dutch art and prefiguring the movies. The scene is not made to delineate a written passage. By now, illustrators were no longer in such a business, supplying a visual line-for-line accompaniment to fiction to fill it out. Writers were supplying their own visual details; not only Dickens but the Goncourt brothers and Zola were already writing the equivalent of screenplays. Illustrators had a new freedom to fasten on psychological tension, suggestion, atmosphere, and visual details of their own choosing that emphasized such elements, as Menzel had prophetically done for the Frederick biography and as the English were doing in magazines. Degas knew and admired Menzel's work and copied one of his teeming genre paintings—the

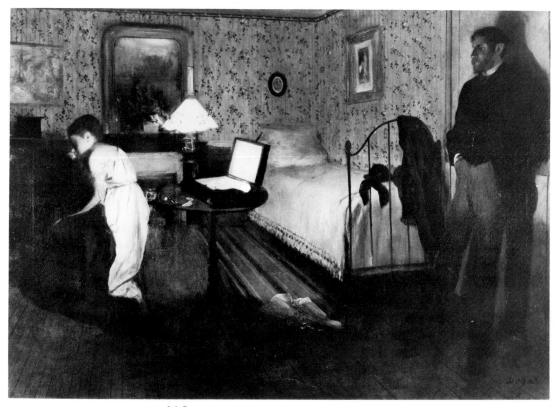

14.5 EDGAR DEGAS, *Interior (Le Viol)*

two artists shared the cinematic eye. Like a film-maker, Degas has recon-
structed a whole scene from scratch for *Interior,* imagining it completely as
if he were making a movie of a novel and adjusting it to suit his own medium. It may well represent a scene from *Thérèse;* but it is his own *Thérèse.*
Zola only wrote the story; Degas shot the scene.

Degas arrived at such an activity by stages, having begun by creating
straight old-fashioned history-painting (*Jephthah's Daughter* and *Semir-
amis Founding a Town*) and then moving further into modern terms by
painting theatrical representations of legendary scenes (*Mlle. Fiocre in . . .
"La Source"*), and then ending with present history itself, modern drama in
the manner of the realistic novel. The earlier works on ancient topics—the
sort of theme Gleyre or Gérôme might have chosen—have an uncomfortable
look, as if the painter could not fit these harsh human moments into the
correctly distanced anecdotal style. They look like blurred photographs of
posed models dressed to act the parts, and the surroundings fail to jell into
something convincing, again as if Degas could not believe in the painterly
reality of medieval Orléans or ancient Sparta. But the modern scene has
total conviction, partly because it has no anecdote. The painter has found
the confrontational mode that really suits him; but in so doing, he has kept
faithfully to the solid principles of drawing he admired in Ingres, refusing
to abandon past realities but insisting on expanding them, so as to be a
truer mirror of the way life really is.

Composed, like some of his early historical pictures, with the provok-
ingly vulnerable female on the left and the anxiously embattled male on the
right, the *Interior* nevertheless changes the unwieldy elements of the history paintings into new harmony and real mystery. Degas fixes the bond
between the man and woman with a lamplit room that is itself a character in
the scene, a room jammed with poignant glinting surfaces and breathing
shadow. This room has been carefully built to show that modern drama is
never a neat fable; it is a constant flow of interlocking personal experiences, as Zola was showing it in his Rougon-Macquart series of interlocking
novels. In a picture suited to it, true modern drama is shown to dwell in casually grouped components seen as if by chance and stirred into an emotional atmosphere created by light. We see everything and identify
instantly with this fraught sexual moment, and yet we can actually know
nothing until the next thing happens, someone moves or someone speaks.
We are urged to project what we know of men, women, underwear, and bed-
rooms, what we feel about such juxtapositions, into this incomplete visual
situation. The scene is like a movie frame; it is also like the Vermeer and De
Witte harpsichord scenes, with similar reliance on lighted interior space
and arresting domestic objects to set up emotional terms.

Another scene much like it but without a sexual component is the *Milliner's Shop,* with the mute standing mirror blocking our view of the mute standing shopgirl, while at the same time reflecting the florid customer with its surface turned from us, so that the mirror's responses are just as hidden as the girl's (14.6). This again is an example of specifically cinematic drama, not derived from the stage or the history of anecdotal painting. The camera is, as it were, in motion around the group, offering this passing view as itself integral to the situation that connects these two women, this mirror, and these hats. Again attempts have been made to connect the painting to a Zola novel. The narrative flavor is all the stronger for the absence of old narrative methods, and for its faint look of current magazine illustration, which the *Interior* also has—the latter could be a Millais, if it were a wood engraving.

By the time the *Milliner's Shop* was painted in the 1880's Degas had long abandoned full-scale genre painting; *Interior* was the only one of its kind. Instead he had become the cruising seeker of framable moments in a floating world, in places where repetition is a constant theme: the laundry,

14.6　EDGAR DEGAS, *The Milliner's Shop*

where the most ephemeral of ordinary tasks is done and done again and again, as it is in the ballet and as it is in the whorehouse. He seized on bathing, too, that act which is repeated and repeated, never finished for good. He seems to have been obsessed with mutable female living, its endless pulse that continues whether anyone is watching or not.

Vermeer had painted women in a similar way, as conductors of change and flow, balancers of scales, pourers of milk, players of music, readers and writers of letters, containers of recurrent ambiguity. Other Dutch artists had done the same; the theme included prostitution, as it did for both Manet and Degas, in that same self-absorbed mode that makes the Dutch harlots and the Degas bathers, who are probably French harlots, and Manet's Olympia seem entirely to transcend the role of conventional pleasure-machine. Each is shown primarily as a private person, whatever she does; the subjective mode, the theme of personal experience, connects all these works. In Manet and Degas, it sets in motion the quest for a new illustration that would suit modern fantasy, and produce a romance of the actual, the optical, the personal, and eventually of the repeatable. The new romanticism was concerned with the psyche, not with expressive overflow; recurrence is one of its essential themes.

The camera entered the stream of artistic consciousness fairly early in the century, having been invented in the late 1820's and patented in 1839. Photography was at the outset yet another interesting graphic technique, and quickly recognized for its capacities to reproduce pictures along with other phenomena. By the crucial 1860's, photographs of paintings and graphic works were available to the public and to artists, and the process of perceiving art was undergoing radical change through the camera's capacity to offer direct views unmediated by engraving styles. At that same time, shutter speed became almost instantaneous, and often produced odd visions of people and objects in motion, figures with strangely bent legs or cabs vanishing out of the frame, so that artists saw a new way to render visual fact, and new reasons to reconsider the old ways.

Soon informal portraiture was taken over by the camera, the miniature portrait painters were driven out of business, and portraitists began to rely on photographs for preliminary studies. Painters also hired photographers to record their works, to provide pictures that might offer basic material, and to provide reproductions of others' works. Many creative and advanced nineteenth-century artists did their own photography, sometimes painting right over the results, or just plain stealing from them.

In general, Impressionist painters were not interested in the camera, but those devoted to drama and atmosphere were—beginning with Delacroix, the great Romantic, who made wide use of photographs near the beginning of their history, modifying their elements when he painted from them. Turner, that other great Romantic, was also entranced by the possibilities of luminousness he saw in landscape photographs during the late 1840's. Before photography became a great commercial venture, before it seemed to forfeit its claim on the imagination, it gave to these discerning eyes an idea of its scope. Later painters, who had to abandon human situations tainted by sentiment or embalmed in formulas in favor of situations generated only by color and shape, or ones who wished to create worlds far from ours, like Puvis de Chavannes, were not prepared to participate in the serious romanticism of the future, the romanticism of the camera that would depend on real men and women, moving through the here and now to create their myths.

But the camera was ahead of its time and did not become a romantic tool in France until this century. It was used far more poetically in England and Scotland during its first two decades, where more purely Northern sensibilities could perhaps make better use of it than hard-headed French artisans. It was the French painters and graphic artists, however, who transmuted camera vision into romantic terms, using the odd angles and cut-off shapes as well as the strange blurry and unrecognizable form things took—the clothes overhead in a Degas laundry, for example—and the harsh darks and lights in which they were made to appear. In order to make a vital new illustrative art for France, however, it was necessary not just to copy Dutch pictures and old prints, or to copy photographs, although these were receiving close attention, but to use them as starting points.

French nineteenth-century artists were in fact developing the poetry of other graphic techniques at the same time that photography was becoming an established fact of artistic life. Manet and Degas, Whistler and Fantin created sharply dramatic black-and-white imagery, often suggestive both of Rembrandt or Goya and of film, and quite unlike old-fashioned steel engravings. Degas' smudgy whorehouse monotypes are emphatically movie-like, flickering with subfusc reality and motion; so are Manet's crisp lithographs (14.7–14.9). A revived admiration for Piranesi occurred at about the same period; the new romance of chiaroscuro was gathering momentum. Etching was undertaken with new enthusiasm by painters and written about by critics; and the graphic artist Charles Meryon had a brilliant impact with architectural fantasies that derived from Dutch prints but displayed a wholly modern preoccupation with city demons, a truly *film noir* temperament.

Meryon had a short career, and his best work was done in the 1850's, but

Left: 14.7 EDGAR DEGAS,
Resting on the Bed. Monotype.
Below: 14.8 EDGAR DEGAS,
Getting Out of the Bath. Monotype.
Opposite: 14.9 EDGAR DEGAS,
*The Cardinal Sisters Talking to
Admirers.* Monotype, illustration
for a novel by Halèvy

he did more than any other nineteenth-century artist to suggest the romantic dread that can be generated in modern city imagery simply by recording in black and white the way the buildings look. His was a realistic romanticism, achieving keen emotional effects without manufacturing artificially sinister gloom. Facts in crude light are sinister enough. In the tradition of Piranesi, his views are both perfectly straight and obliquely suggestive. They have an individual personality that seems partly projected into them by our responses to their flavor. It is also brought about by small details that pose nasty questions and set up trains of uneasy thought, and occasionally by what appear to be dream phenomena, also offered without fanfare. His Paris scenes have the look of nineteenth-century photographic topography, which was a thriving business by the 1850's, pushed several steps further toward cinematographic expression.

One reason for this is that Meryon was color-blind; he was forced into black and white. His etchings do not have the quality of a minor art pur-

14.10 CHARLES MERYON, *The Morgue*. Etching, 1854

sued occasionally by a major painter in an investigative spirit, or of a minor art pursued by a modest talent, but of fiercely condensed high artistic effort. He had the kind of vision that overloads the black-and-white medium so as to wrench unforeseen color out of it, in ferocious despite of the ordinary spectrum. Such a quality is what makes the great black-and-white movies so compelling, especially the ones with urban settings. Both the drama and the visual charm of such films are forced into a tonal vocabulary; they show a universe of chromatic diversity channeled sharply into a colorlessness that nevertheless seems complete. The colors are there; we can almost see them, because of the intense pressure on the medium to be universal.

Baudelaire admired Meryon's etchings and wrote eloquently about their modern romantic mode that made use of scaffolding and smoke as well as ancient monuments, their paradoxical bitter beauty that matched the modern city. Meryon showed a Paris not yet transformed, still punctuated by its Gothic buildings and small streets, not yet defined by the huge boulevards and broad spaces that were soon to come; but he makes no effort at picturesqueness. This Paris is current; and so are the flying monsters in the sky, the anthropomorphic clouds, the mysteriously drowning man, the balloon, the threatening birds. These are modern fantasies, similar to Goya's, devoid of formal reference to storybook horrors of the Gothic kind, visions almost unnoticeable but spine-chilling.

Meryon's morgue is a matter-of-fact structure, with a plain modern chimney and drainpipe, and washing on a line alongside it; the tension of the scene in which it figures is created by the harsh shapes of plain buildings in a flat light that casts black shadows (14.10). For a moment these are all you see. Then the sense of horror is fed as you gradually notice the small agitated crowd, the men carrying the corpse while the woman and child lament and the police direct proceedings. The personality is entirely of the scene, not the artist; we are drawn to it, not his vision of it. The graphic hand has been withheld, and the glaring light, the anxious eye, and the infinite city have conspired to produce this momentary shudder. Something similar might be said of Degas' brothel scenes with scratching women unmodified by graphic elegance. Degas, too, like Meryon and Manet, kept out of the way to let the view speak and move if it would.

Death and imminent death certainly compel attention, and a new corpse or a drowning man is a natural excitement; but what about the monsters in the sky over the Ministry of Marine (14.11)? Again the scene is topographical, and the armed flying fish are offered as phenomena just like the building; it looks like documentary-style footage from a science-fiction film. The curiously movielike quality of Meryon's Paris is confirmed by a look at his

14.11 CHARLES MERYON, *The Ministry of Marine*. Etching

bizarre working methods. The etching of the *Pont-au-Change* went through eleven states, and each has a different sky, as if a movie camera had been trained on the view while the balloon rose and vanished, the clouds shifted and re-formed into figures, and the horrible Hitchcock birds swept in and away as the moon emerged—all while the wretched man floundered in the water, and those in the boat failed to rescue him, and the crowd milled on the bridge. Each repeated take is slightly different (14.12–14.15).

Meryon worked from camera views, like so many of his painter contemporaries. He clearly saw what the camera could do with urban sites if it had the means to move; and as a graphic artist, he did not need to filter such insight through painterly conventions established by Velázquez or Vermeer. Meryon went beyond painting and into graphic motion; he had the topographical past with which to make cinematic poetry out of modern Paris, a Paris packed with dramas, both inward and external, none of which stops or may be stopped for. Degas and Whistler, arriving on the graphic scene about a decade later, tended to rely on Rembrandt for their etching style, and to keep graphic media allied to the painterly frame of mind; they had a disposition to use drawing and etching or monotype and lithograph as if they were kinds of paint, and paint a kind of graphic material. But the sense of city living is the same, and the aim to illuminate it in the harsh new kind of romantic idiom in which recurrence plays a part.

Whistler, having been ahead of Degas in illustrating modern living in a modern way early in the 1860's, gave it up for art's sake, moved to England, and largely withdrew from any dramatic situations that might occur inside pictures. His famous confrontation with Ruskin in 1877 still reverberates in this century as the moment when subject matter ceased to be important for serious art and all who cared about it in the English-speaking world. Whistler did much in that world to separate the illustrative impulse from the proper sphere of painting, and thus to focus later attention on the formal qualities of past art, especially in England and consequently in America. In both nations he figures as the spokesman of French theories of modern painting, making them comprehensible and demonstrating their importance.

At the same time, he helped to discredit the effectiveness of illustration and any direct play on emotional responses through conventional subject matter. Consequently, partly because of Whistler's influence, the camera and all careful painting that might suggest its more rigid or banal forms of realism were usually lined up in opposition to high esthetic considerations. The narrative capacities that might be released by the camera stayed obscure, the property of painters and graphic artists who embraced a sort of underground romanticism waiting for its day. Meanwhile Whistler helped

14.12 CHARLES MERYON, *The Pont-au-Change*. Etching, fifth state

14.13 CHARLES MERYON, *The Pont-au-Change*. Etching, seventh state

people in this century to find Impressionist paintings beautiful, to see a new classicism in them, a new unromantic universality that forever canceled the opinions of their own time, when they had seemed incoherent, discordant, and ugly.

Portraiture remained in the sphere of painting, despite the commercial production of *carte de visite* photographs both public and domestic, and of portrait photography. But portraiture, too, became a form of illustration in the hands of Degas and Fantin and others after the 1860's, breaking bounds, coming closer to genre painting, making gestures toward cinema.

14.14 CHARLES MERYON, *The Pont-au-Change*. Etching, tenth state

14.15 CHARLES MERYON, *The Pont-au-Change*. Etching, eleventh state

While the stiff style of camera portraiture continued, the animated sort of painted portrait that is itself a whole scene became possible. We have seen how Sargent managed it, using references to Velázquez; but when he was still in Paris, his *Madame X* had already gone well beyond old limits into uncharted visual territory, had become illustrative and photographic in unheard-of ways (see 1.8).

Madame X has the look of a Degas or a Manet, the air of unmediated confrontation without any softening drawn from familiar anecdote or classical sources. It is a modern Parisian picture, an erotic vision impossible in

England or America at the moment, but very similar to Manet's pictures of women—not exactly portraits—reading journals or sitting in cafés and conservatories, wearing cosmetics and chic frills at the neck, conscious of sexuality and reflecting its pulse and flow, breathing faster as they sit (14.16). Or Madame X might be the girl in *Interior* at a later stage in her career, once again looking away. The arm bent back on the little table, the tilted body and turned head, the graphic black and white—all these elements set the image in motion, so that it seems part of an encounter, a scene in a story; the audaciously vulval pink ear and the stark lack of gloves or jewelry especially make the woman look undressed, even though her shoulder strap is now back in place. With it fallen, she must have looked much more like a later version of Degas' smock-clad, bare-shouldered girl. The camera lurks in this picture, as it does in Degas' haunting portrait of Henri De Gas and his little niece (14.17), or in Fantin's portrait of his two sisters in black dresses; but it is the camera of the future rather than the moment, the romantic narrative camera of the next century (14.18). By

14.16 EDOUARD MANET, *Reading "l'Illustré"*

14.17 EDGAR DEGAS, *Henri De Gas and His Niece*

contrast, Corot's dark women sit in their frames with an ancient painterly confidence, free of all time and all movement, participating in art alone, anticipating only further degrees of abstraction as a possible fate.

Caillebotte is a compelling painter of cinematic romanticism, an admirer of Impressionist themes and achievements who nevertheless remained firmly within the world of contingency and feeling. Kirk Varnedoe has compared him to Eakins for the contemplative look of his indoor figures, whose thick thoughts are washed by thin city light as they stand at the window. But Caillebotte, unlike Eakins, did not try for the distinctive rural note; the city made a new nature for his eye. Unlike Degas, he was deeply interested in the way buildings, streets, and parts of buildings interact with people's lives in towns, producing moving views of the corners where people meet and part, setting up temporary viewpoints from which to gaze and think, making environments for passing human moments as if they had no other function. His works dare to leave space blank, to keep naked the pavement or the carpet where the characters have just walked, or will walk

14.20　GUSTAVE CAILLEBOTTE, *The Luncheon*

cially the tradition of reticent artists such as Janssens Elinga, Boursse, and Vrel, who so unassumingly offered their visual sympathy to people moving through rooms and things, or streets and light.

Nothing is stated in the lunch painting about the young man who ducks his head to cut his meat and the old woman being served by the old butler, or about us sitting in our place and feeling all the obscure violence of quiet family meals. But just as in movies, the shot begins to tell the story while the people in it and those watching are still unaware there is one. The laden but austere black table, the bright daylight kept at bay by curtains and the rituals of food, the few silent dim persons, and the eloquent company of shiny objects are being *discovered* to have meaning as we watch, neither arranged to fit an idea nor allowed to mean nothing.

The awkward perspective, here used indoors instead of in the street, further shows how Caillebotte brought phenomena created by the camera to bear directly on the creation of atmosphere. The optical imbalance that feeds the mood of family anxiety and sadness in this picture is like the kind later produced by camera motion for the same purpose—the distant lady seems to pull farther back, the crystal to march forward and keep us from her, the carafe to swell as it guards the nearby youth from our interfering interest. It is like a scene from a Bergman movie. The stretch of floor to the right shows the path the butler always takes; there is none on the left, and so we know he will not walk around that way.

There is a certain stiffness and simplicity in Caillebotte's painting technique that keeps him well away from the brilliant sketchiness of the Impressionists and from the visibly brushed structures of Cézanne. He goes against the modernity of The Sketch as the new conveyor of painterly genius, in which the paint shows its sovereignty. The painterly means by which the image has taken shape have been tamed and flattened, subdued as if the artist kept from showing off with either an old-fashioned high "finish" or a modish brushy style. Caillebotte insists on keeping the paint itself neutral and merely useful for filtering the precise quality of the image he wants to summon.

This method gives his work the uneven texture so common in many cinematic paintings, as if the artist ignored the demands of the surface so as to plunge straight past it. Degas did the same thing, using a variety of media that all produce fluctuations of the rough and smooth across the picture, which in turn is held together only by the exact magic of its fragmented and tantalizing subject. Fantin, another camera-struck painter, adopted a great modesty of surface for his flower paintings and portraits, in both of which he managed a transcendent cinematographic presence—the flowers visibly breathe and wilt, the people brood and wait (14.21–14.23). For his Wagnerian fantasies, however, Fantin did take up the painterly sketch, staying on the surface and quite abandoning the depths of the mirror. These "illustrations" therefore are far less illustrative than the portraits and still-lifes.

We can see how cinematic painters by the late 1870's in France had finally come under the influence of actual photography, besides learning from Goya and Vermeer and Chardin. They had begun to foreshadow film explicitly by making use of resources the camera had revealed that were not of value to the new practitioners of commercial portraiture and topography, and that were also not interesting to the French architects of modern painting: Monet and Renoir, Van Gogh, Gauguin, and Cézanne. Unlike these artists, they were early pioneers of an illustrative form yet to come, which would hang on the unpainterly modernity of the camera, the handless eye.

The romantic quest for some unattainably true mirror of common fantasy could be fully satisfied only after actual cinema had passed through its introductory stages and manifested its visual power over modern life.

14.21   HENRI FANTIN-LATOUR, *Portrait of Mr. and Mrs. Edwin Edwards*

Only then might the works of Manet, Degas, and Caillebotte retrospectively look like real and natural visions of Parisian life, recognizably charged with ambiguous modern narrative, illustrations of the highest order. Their strangeness in their own time, which came from their unlikeness to familiar painting, has now been washed away by our informed movie-vision, as well as by a schooled understanding of modern art that has also taught us to view them as examples of detached painterly achievement.

Far to the north, the use of light characteristic of traditional Northern painting had continued in the work of nineteenth-century Scandinavian

14.22 HENRI FANTIN-LATOUR, *Spring Flowers, Apples and Pears*

14.23 HENRI FANTIN-LATOUR, *Still Life, Corner of the Table*

painters, several of whom produced startlingly cinematic images without benefit of the Parisian milieu and its critics or its search for new illuminations. These Scandinavian artists have been judged according to their proximity to Impressionism, Symbolism, or Expressionism, since they could not claim a central contribution to nineteenth-century imagery, and many of them did travel and study in other parts of Europe; but one or two seemed to leap effortlessly into the modern movie mode on their own.

Among these, the Danish artist Vilhelm Hammershoi, who was a student at the Copenhagen Academy, just as Friedrich had been a century earlier, seems to have swallowed whole the German Romantic aims of 1800, and translated them directly into film without consciousness of intervening artistic stages. His views of spare interior spaces with an occasional female figure seen from the back sharply recall similar Friedrich themes—too sharply, perhaps; they look quite contrived in their studied melancholy (14.24). They lack the diurnal quality of the sadness in Fantin or Caillebotte, or indeed in Friedrich; but they do seem to foreshadow the Nordic cinema, with its slow-moving revelations of existential despair. Similarly,

14.24 VILHELM HAMMERSHOI, *Interior with Seated Woman*

14.25 VILHELM HAMMERSHOI, *Five Portraits*

the huge *Five Portraits* with its grim group of men around a candlelit table resembles nothing in art so much as it looks ahead to murky rooms in Dreyer films (14.25). Scandinavian movies continue another theme explored by the painters of these regions, that of moving water. Many canvases contain nothing but the mesmerizing ripples of a stream or fjord, occasionally interrupted by one stone or thin branch, a surging flood ready to drown us if we want.

The Scandinavian nineteenth-century realist painters have had to wait for Scandinavian cinema to claim them and set them in motion, to show the world what they could have done if film-making had been open to them, to put them on the international artistic map. The paintings themselves are often purely depressing, unlit by any hope of futurity despite all their unearthly winter light.

FIFTEEN
Twentieth-Century
Graphics; Movies

T H E   M O V I E S began nearly simultaneously in several countries during the last decade of the nineteenth century. Their abrupt rise suggests that the need to invent them was universally felt at the same moment, and it is not hard to see why. Between the 1840's and the 1890's, while two generations of the public had been getting used to camera vision, they were also getting used to greater naturalism and more sensation in stage productions, and to a fresh abundance of printed illustrative material. This was also increasingly realistic and increasingly dependent on camera conventions for reality, especially in America. Longing for the next step was inevitable, the desire to see illuminated by camera magic what now appeared on the stage or the page, to see romanticized even further both the new documentary mode in pictures and the new drama of visual fantasy. In Europe, the decline of romanticism in art increased the need to find new media for a realism suitable to ambiguous modern feelings.

In France, long before painters like Degas took on photography's challenges and appeared to move in cinematic directions, early connections were made between the camera, the stage, and traditional Romantic painting. These links, too, suggest an emergent need for cinema—which, like the camera, was officially born in France, although its early life occurred in several places. The early impulse to invent movies is embodied in the person of Daguerre, one of the inventors of photography during the late 1820's and 1830's, who was famous not only as a Romantic landscape-painter but as a stage designer and as the creator, in 1822, of the celebrated diorama. This last was the same one that appeared a year later in

London, pirating the works of John Martin and causing a great sensation with its "dissolving views."

Daguerre was clearly interested in harnessing the emotional impact of light in some way beyond the reach of contemporary art and theater. His settings and paintings are charged with drama in much the same way as those of Schinkel and other Germans, with towers silhouetted against moonlight and many eerie shadows; but he seems to have needed actual illumination—real light, first manufactured on the stage or in the diorama, and finally seized from the sun itself by the camera. Except for the shifting scenes of the diorama, actual movement was beyond his reach; he had to settle for the motion that the clever use of light can set up in the viewer's responses (15.1).

All this represents a romantic sort of wish that cinema might exist, when it was still only being approximated in pictures or stage pictures. In the field of nineteenth-century French popular graphics, the figure most associated with cinematic fantasy is Gustave Doré, who was born after Daguerre's invention of the early Romantic camera, and so already several

15.1 LOUIS DAGUERRE, *The Ruins of Holyrood Chapel*

steps nearer to the realizations movies could offer. Although it was Meryon who grasped what cinema might be like, in his peculiar graphic renderings of ordinary urban atmosphere, Doré invented an everyday brand of fantasy as effective as Disney's, and rather similar. His contribution lay in the realm of book illustration; and by the time he died in the 1880's he had produced a whole storehouse of imagery for the later cinema to tap. His visualizations of fairy-tale characters, of Don Quixote, the Ancient Mariner, and scenes from Milton and Dante are still relied on by production designers, although his artistic talent is usually held in rather low esteem. His paintings are uninteresting; but he had a magnificent gift for sensational composition in black and white, based on spatial depth and light rather than on detail and line or abstract surface interest, as if he were conceiving film frames. And like the old illuminations, Doré's pictures were offered in books, personally aimed at each viewer. What they lack in action they make up for in satisfying stolid realism—visions and monsters look feasible, as if designed so that a studio workshop could handle them (15.2, 15.3).

15.2 GUSTAVE DORÉ, "The Gnarled Monster."
Illustration for *The Legend of Croquemitaine*

15.3 GUSTAVE DORÉ, "The Fall of Satan."
1866. Illustration for Milton's *Paradise Lost*

Doré was greatly loved for generations—people felt comfortable visualizing fantastic things in his essentially undisturbing style. It was family entertainment; and Doré certainly made an important and liberating contribution to the movies of later days, including animated cartoons. His other interesting influence was upon Van Gogh, a Northern graphic genius who could grasp the true core of feeling in Doré's scenes of the London poor. They, too, are cinematic, relying on chiaroscuro for emotional effect and otherwise allowing sober fact to speak for itself. Doré cannot qualify as a great artist, but he was a French proto-film-maker, a proleptic genius who could suggest the right graphic future for Romantic art.

The very earliest French experiments with actual cinema were far from romantic. The Lumière brothers, taking off from Edison's inventions of a few years before, invented the Cinématographe in the mid-1890's, a sort of camera and projector in one. Not having anything to do with art or theater, they made short films of ordinary events and showed them in theaters as a novelty, to increasingly large audiences. Their greatest contribution was in distributing knowledge and experience of their enterprise to the general public, not just in Paris but in many countries. Creative drama and fantastic imagery were first undertaken only a year or two later by Georges Méliès, who made comic fictions based on entirely invented scenery and situations celebrating the capacities of cinema to do the impossible and be like dreams. Using painted fantasy sets and trick photography, Méliès began the deliberate control of the photographed environment that was later developed in Germany for *The Cabinet of Dr. Caligari* and other films, a movement that paralleled the Surrealist and Expressionist impulses arising in other European visual art, more and more at odds with straightforward naturalism and old-fashioned romanticism.

Early European film continued to be allied to movements in art more than any American productions were. Following the example of European avant-garde theater and painting, film-making first appealed as a new esthetic departure in the general modern tradition of innovation, as photography had done decades before, and appealed to educated audiences. But since American movie-making began firmly as a part of the popular-entertainment business, it rightly continued to rely on old successful formulas drawn from theater and illustration rather than joining the European pictorial avant-garde. Only somewhat later, after Griffith had demonstrated how ordinary popular melodrama could be made into great romantic art through the alchemy of cinema, could European movies return to realism for expressive purposes, and French film begin to recover the romantic spirit of Daguerre and Doré. Similarly, after certain ambitious European movies appeared in this country, American movies began to expand their visual and emotional flavors.

But American movies were romantic to begin with, although the earliest films were also essentially documentaries: short records of arriving boats or departing trains demonstrating the magic of the moving picture in everyday terms. The romance of the ordinary was built into the American painterly tradition already, and into its pictorial fantasy, so much of which had come into existence via the empirical German brand of Romanticism. The earliest American film narratives were also naturalistic episodes, comic or thrilling or sentimental, enhancing the documentary style with fictional excess.

The famous *Great Train Robbery* of 1903 was the first in a still-endless series founded on amazing adventures that erupt in banal and boring surroundings. Westerns are only one variation of the theme; it is a constant in American fiction and certainly in such American paintings as Homer's *The Life Line,* for example. In American movies, essentially uninteresting urban and rural life has been the background for violent dramas of crime and disaster, and of both comic and tragic madness; cinema became the best vehicle for such fictions, since it could carry ordinary visual realism so much further than stage designers, or the most skillful illustrator of the everyday—further than anyone, that is, except a great painter.

But the example set by painters could be followed only much later in the history of American film, after lessons in psychological atmosphere had been learned from more sophisticated film-makers in Europe, Russia, and Japan, and after American geniuses with the stature of Griffith (Orson Welles being the prime example) had helped to push the cinematic medium itself toward greatness along American paths. Paintings, the "cinematic" kind that I have been tracking, were already a source for illustrators; but only when American movies began to outstrip illustration did they find themselves right back in painterly territory, confronting the same problems of how to render continuing drama inside a frame in terms of immediate phenomena. Such a similarity between painters' and film-makers' problems was not recognizable, however, in the context of American popular show business.

The movies were nevertheless bound to be an American specialty because of the very nature of American romantic visualization, not just because of the American talent for commercial production and distribution or the American need for widespread popular entertainment. At the turn of the century, David Belasco had done in the United States what Irving had been doing in London, creating sensationally detailed and thrilling stage presentations at vast expense, with strong reliance on known illustrative material. But his themes, in the American mode, included modern situations and mundane settings, waterfronts and mine shafts, sleazy streetcorners and saloons, besides legendary temples and medieval tombs. And he set a standard for stage realism in America that was very hard to meet for the traveling companies that specialized in bringing realistic melodrama to provincial communities—the sort of group for which Griffith had originally worked.

A. Nicholas Vardac has described how many elaborate productions, made famous in cities, were severely reduced and mutilated by the limitations of provincial stages, where old-fashioned suspension of disbelief was still required. What could not be done in the way of sensational illusion by a theatrical road company could be done in a movie, however; and the film could offer an even better version of the mine, the saloon, the windswept cliff, the daring rescue. It is easy to see how movies followed neatly in the footsteps of popular theater all over the country. It is less easy, perhaps, to see their visual antecedents in the sorts of illustration that were inspiring the stage, and which could inspire film even more, eventually leading it further into the domain of painting than the stage could ever go.

The very realism of much pictorial material in turn-of-the-century Amer-

15.4 KENYON COX, "Lodgers in a crowded Bayard Street tenement—
'Five Cents a Spot.' " 1889. Illustration in *Scribner's Monthly Magazine*,
after a photograph from Jacob Riis' *How the Other Half Lives.*

ican papers and magazines makes it seem unremarkable, and not especially
painterly. It looks more like failed photography, even though the basic
methods derive from Northern "photo-graphic" painting. Illustrations
were printed in conjunction with actual photographs and with the same reproductive techniques; and many documentary drawings were made directly from photographs, using their casual groupings and lighting (15.4).
But at the same time the illustrations of Charles Dana Gibson and Howard
Chandler Christy, for example, seem like animated Sargent portraits, still
carrying his debt to Velázquez and Manet and ultimately to Rembrandt's
dramatic chiaroscuro (15.5). The placement of figures, many seen from the
back, and the light source inside the composition share with the Paget
"Sherlock Holmes" illustrations a resemblance to Menzel's Frederick
series from fifty years before, which in turn derive ultimately from Rembrandt even while they resemble storyboards, or frames from movie melodrama (15.6, 15.7).

The debt owed to serious painting by popular illustration, and by the
film that stemmed from it, is in fact hard to see at first glance, because the
chiaroscuro mode of realism *modernizes* as it goes along. The same atmospheric, emotional arrangements created by light and shade and deep focus

will render up-to-date, current dress and detail as realistically as Biblical or medieval costume and circumstance (15.8). The style of art is intended primarily to suggest the actual experience of the passing moment, and so the style itself is not formally archaized or classicized. Therefore a magazine ad or a film frame resembling a Rembrandt may show a hotel lobby in 1924, with no references to the seventeenth century, just as Menzel's illustrations for Frederick's life make no effort to suggest eighteenth-century Rococo art and also resemble Rembrandt. And Rembrandt, for his part, made Biblical costume take the same shapes and fill up space the same way as his modern dress, just as the movie camera does.

The alternative decorative and calligraphic mode in illustration, the one that derives from Botticelli, Greek vases, and other exquisite linear models, did appear in equal profusion in advertising and poster art at the turn of the century, wrought into the fashionable Art Nouveau forms that were even more current in Europe. This illustrative style relies on classicizing and archaizing, and on the use of *stylistic* allusion to past art. In magazine art, such a style was rarely used for fiction and satire, which demanded the realism of the immediate moment rather than a precise modishness of shape and line. Pictures that told a story or suggested a tense or comic situation held to the chiaroscuro method of rendering and to the deep-focus Dutch style of composition, often complete with the window,

15.5 HOWARD CHANDLER CHRISTY, "Her husband and I turned on her together." Illustration in *Scribner's Monthly Magazine,* December 1900

15.6 CHARLES DANA GIBSON, "Stage-Struck." Illustration in *Collier's
Weekly,* March 1905

15.7 Still from *You and Me,* 1938

15.8 J . H E N R Y , "You nervy little devil, you!"
Illustration for Edna Ferber's *Fanny Herself,* 1917

the table, the character seen from the rear, the dramatic *repoussoir,* and
the play of light on mobile fabric. And all this material found its way naturally into the movies, where the camera could do it by nature.

And so American commercial movies, although they were not competing
with the high artistic standards set in Europe early in cinematic history,
nevertheless followed in a respectable graphic path, with august if unnoticeable painterly antecedents. Many Hollywood productions were indeed

admired in art-conscious Europe for the way they looked, much more than they were respected in the United States; and American movie-goers, thinking of foreign films as artistic and their own as purely commercial, never got to see the huge amount of bad commercial cinema turned out in other countries in imitation of ours and not exported. Hindsight has lately recaptured the Hollywood corpus and now permits us to make every kind of distinction among its works; and to compare them appropriately with foreign material, old and new.

It was in fact the esthetically alert French who first convincingly pointed out to Americans that their popular films could be seriously considered as works of art, that they were poetic and suggestive, with mythic overtones conveyed in their own stylized format, which had an undeniable graphic authenticity: American *film noir* is, after all, a French invention of the Second World War. Only since then has The Whole Art of Film, defined by a new criticism that submits movies to one comprehensive set of standards, come gradually into existence. We are, in fact, returning to the very earliest and truly international conditions of film-making.

Against the present background of enlarged awareness, we can see the purely pictorial sources of American Hollywood movies, along with those

15.9 FREDERIC REMINGTON, "Long sat waiting for an answer." Photogravure from a monochrome painting. 1892. Illustration for Longfellow's *The Song of Hiawatha*

much more overtly and consciously tapped by film-makers in other countries, who felt more allied with artistic aims. One important source for Westerns, for example, has been the paintings and illustrations of Frederic Remington, who in himself bridged the gap between serious painting and commercial art. He represents the means by which movies were able to use painterly convention without seeming to.

Remington was born in 1861 in upstate New York, the son of a Civil War cavalry officer who later became a newspaper publisher, and he was trained at the Yale Art School. He went out west after his father's death to seek his fortune as a sheep farmer and only gradually abandoned farming for a career as a pictorial journalist devoted to the romantic, vanishing Old West. His early sketches were awkward, and redrawn by more skillful artists to prepare them for reproduction. But he undertook more training at the Art Students League in New York after returning east, having shipped home quantities of Western gear and paraphernalia to furnish him with further details for the "Western" pictures and sculptures that he had managed to make a successful specialty.

Remington was a thorough Easterner who deliberately mythologized the West in the new documentary tradition now deemed necessary for visual fiction, showing a real Hollywood spirit before the fact. Eventually, by the 1890's, he was making use of Muybridge's motion studies of the horse, translating them into illustrative language and making horses familiar to everyone in the Romantic-Realist, cinematic terms that replaced the old idealized engraved style, in which the "flying gallop" had figured. Estelle Jussim has described how pictures based on photographic renderings gradually replaced these conventions everywhere in the documentary-illustration business, because new processes made a printed and reproduced photograph look very much like a printed and reproduced *painting* that had been specially done to look like a photograph. The technologies of reproduction made painting and photography into a single illustrative enterprise (15.9, 15.10).

The camera had become the desirable vehicle of truth by 1880; all printed illustrations pretending to show what anything was really like—whether imagined historical moments or current events—could be convincing only if they appeared in the sort of rendering that resembled printed photographs. Remington did scores of such pictures of the Old West, some based on actual photographs, some invented; and many of his paintings were done in monochrome to begin with, to aid the reproducing process. Some of his imagined renderings of various current events, such as Teddy Roosevelt's campaigns in Cuba, were printed side by side with photographs; and one can see a new world of documentary-romantic visualization

15.10 FREDERIC REMINGTON, "Branding a Calf." Process-engraving
from an ink drawing based on a photograph by Theodore Roosevelt.
Illustration in *Century Magazine,* April 1888

15.11 FREDERIC REMINGTON, *The Sentinel*

15.12   H O W A R D   P Y L E ,   "In the Presence of Washington."
Illustration in *Century Magazine,* April 1897

gradually taking shape in American popular magazines, during the same decades when movies began (15.11).

Facial types, bodily attitudes, groupings, and lighting might thus be created by an academically trained artist such as Remington or his contemporary Howard Pyle, who would have absorbed the lessons of Gérôme and Meissonier as well as those of Velázquez and Goya, and translated them into the new, popular graphic camera language to match real photographs (15.12).

Glossy, decorative illustration was a somewhat different matter, more self-evidently connected to artistic sources; but when realism was the mode, as with Gibson or Christy or James Montgomery Flagg, the effect was similar. Cinema simply took over the conventions and set them in motion. This couldn't have been done with direct references to Vermeer or Goya, because such allusions would either not register or seem ludicrous; but indirectly, the basic ways to fill a frame with action and feeling came from such early inventors of the cinematic method, filtered through their interpreters in the illustration business.

It is very important to note that during these same decades the great and not-so-great art of the past also came to be generally available through *photographic* reproduction. Therefore it, too, entered the general pictorial theater of popular life in the same photo-graphic medium that was slowly taking over the representation of ordinary reality. The history of art eventually "got into the movies" because the reproductive still camera encompassed it first, forcing past art to share in the documentary spirit of the new photographic romanticism. Instead of being reproduced in the form of engraved "fine prints," of which the technical finish could be admired for itself and form a mediating veil between the original picture and the connoisseur, paintings came straight at the ordinary viewer from the pages of a book or magazine as if untranslated. They were, of course, reduced in scale, cut down to size, forced into submission in a different way; but that put them into new competition with camera-based popular graphics; and it put those popular graphics into competition with them.

Paintings were also naturally offered in black and white, like so much other illustrative material, and thus joined with the rest of it to create the visual matrix for the cinema. They helped to set the standard for how to show a cavalry charge, how to dress a Byzantine empress, or how to decorate the interior of an eighteenth-century boudoir, how to show terror and pity or spiritual aspiration with gesture and facial expression—all without color. Conscious borrowing straight from theatrical convention for many such elements was clearly necessary to the success of early movies, since they arose in competition with the stage; but the resources of the camera soon made unconscious borrowings from art even more necessary, as film more and more transcended all stage visualizations *except* for their color. And the camera, now rendering past art into terms of modern black-and-white graphic technology, was soon making it available to further graphic development in movie terms—the terms of pure light and shade.

Thus a resemblance between a frame from an ordinary commercial American film and a Vermeer may be understood neither as a coincidence nor as a conscious imitation, but as an example of cultural continuity, of

15.13 Still from *The Man Who Came to Dinner*, 1941

15.14 JAN VERMEER, *Officer and Laughing Girl*

15.15 Still from *The Great Lie,* 1941

15.16 JAN VERMEER, *The Loveletter* (detail)

pictorial tradition becoming internalized and naturalized, as it always has, only this time by means of the great leaps made by phototechnology at the turn of the century. Such a correspondence between a modern film-frame and an old painting might be called an indirect quote, an unconscious allusion like a Latin tag or a Shakespearean phrase. It would arise from the effect on visual consciousness of many photographic reproductions of Vermeer, overlaid and confirmed by reproductions of works by all artists influenced by him. So that a view of a man and woman at a table by a window, facing the woman from behind the man's shoulder, would seem like the most natural, the most effective, the most "realistic" representational device to use in a movie, chiefly because it would have the support of such mingled generations of illustrative genius behind it—not just current illustrations, but all their great sources (15.13–15.16).

The specific tradition behind it all was the North European one, devoted to the casual fall of light on phenomena and the apparently artless dip into the flow of passing experience, rather than to the visibly composed, controlled rendering of groups in significant poses, harmonized by a unifying style. Dramatic and unstable angles from which to see things, with looming figures in front partially blotting the source of light, or lighted distant views through doors and windows of ambiguous action at odds with the dim foreground, or scenes observed as if from the viewpoint of a marginal bystander—all these effects had been developed by Northern artists of the past and confirmed by popular modern illustrators under their influence; and they lay at hand for movie-makers, as soon as the camera itself could move and the shot became the unit of film narrative. Howard Pyle's well-known picture of Jefferson writing the Declaration of Independence, for example, derives directly from Honthorst, with its lighted tabletop and figure seen from the knees up; but it could well be a frame from a very recent historical film, with careful period details well subdued to the general atmosphere (15.17, 15.18).

The pernicious split between "artist" and "illustrator" seems to have become most pronounced in America, as opposed to France, and to have been linked with the dissemination of the camera-bound material in magazines. The widespread use for illustration of photography and pseudo photography and doctored photography put real art in another category, even when many fine illustrators did have highly developed personal styles. For a century we have insisted on a gulf between art intended for commercial reproduction and any other kind; and movies, being in the former camp, were not considered to have any connection with what real artists had ever done. Both Homer and Hopper, for example, apparently felt that their popular illustrations and their paintings were incompatible, and they had to

15.17 H O W A R D   P Y L E ,
Thomas Jefferson (detail)

15.18 G E R R I T   V A N   H O N T H O R S T ,
Christ before the High Priest

desert the one for the other. Art, once embraced, precluded illustration. When the current Wyeth is disparaged, he is called an illustrator. Printmaking, on the other hand, became a more and more elevated and prestigious branch of fine art separate from commercial graphics, and it still is.

The more photomechanical reproduction was perfected, the less prestige attached to the camera as an esthetic medium, and the more it was purely associated with documentary illustration. Movies thus arose in this country just when the camera itself had become somewhat debased, even though certain successful illustrators were greatly admired. Serious artistic photography was also pushed into an embattled position as an avant-garde mode of art, carefully at odds with bastard commercial productions.

In Europe during the same period the camera remained a legitimate esthetic medium, and so did commercial graphic art; with the result that European posters and postage stamps and advertisements displayed a high, advanced standard of pure design, and so did European movies when they first appeared. But narrative, creative ones tended not to be *documentary* in spirit, and had much less reason to stay with romantic realism. Abstract design and formal innovation were far more fruitful fields, and so were experiments in psychological flavor such as Symbolist painters were attempting.

What American film managed was to mythologize the old, realistic modes of art without appearing to do so, and to allow them to penetrate the whole consciousness of the nation through the intensely romantic medium of film. The Garbo spell, for example, is a matter of light and shade creating an emotional atmosphere analogous to the spell of Vermeer's women, an uncanny evocation of female inwardness conveyed in a picture that seems to show a sequence of important moments without showing any action. A fashionably dressed woman is in a room—we see her from the knees up. Perhaps a man has just left, or is just coming, or is on the other side of the world. She is aware and full of feeling, but her face is still and her hands quiet. She holds something, a vessel or a hairbrush, a letter or the window frame; meanwhile we look at her and feel that the scene is momentous, she is heartbreaking, the image is unforgettable. Garbo could never create such effects on a theatrically lighted stage; and it wasn't acting. She (and we) needed the "realistic" film-lighting, the film setting, and the creative camera "loving" her as it moved in to regard her, just as Vermeer seems to have "loved" the lady with the scale, the glass, or the guitar.

Instead of becoming outmoded, as it was fast doing in Europe, realism was first carried further here by painters such as Homer and Hopper, then shifted (partly with their help) into the realm of popular documentary graphics, and finally reconstituted and irradiated on the screen. The *film noir* is an example of this eventual romanticization of documentary realism; and as a genre, it demonstrates how the old Northern pictorial methods were needed for the process. German immigrant directors such as Fritz Lang could instinctively follow old German artistic habits of manipulating light and shade for emotional purposes, just as Friedrich and long before him Altdorfer had done, and as Rembrandt did. They also employed the Northern Renaissance trick of using old myths in new, realistic guise. In film, folklore and conventional Romantic themes gain power when seen as actualities.

Movies may indeed have owed a measure of their powerful effect to their participation in the satisfying old tradition of Rembrandt; but first, cinema had to develop its method. And even there the techniques of montage and cross-cutting, of close-up and long shot, tracking, dissolve—all the ways of using the moving picture to move the feelings—were founded on earlier methods for doing the same thing with still pictures. The more refined cinematic methods became, the nearer they approached what certain earlier painters suggested. European film-frames finally began to resemble Degas paintings or Goya lithographs or Dutch genre works, rather than bleached stage productions, when the camera began to move and the close-up began to record the new art of film acting—this was well on in the third decade of film history. Between about 1910 and 1920, the screen picture really came to life, as much life as still pictures long since had.

At that time film was still truly international, because it had no audible dialogue. Film captions could be translated into any language and run with the action so as to be perfectly convincing to native speakers, without the incongruities of dubbed speech or incomplete and intrusive subtitling. Film-makers pooled their visual resources very quickly, borrowing each other's effects and tapping pictorial sources, knowingly or not, that became common to all movies within a very few years. The *wordlessness* of cinema was essential to its speedy start as a visual medium and its use of painterly precedents: captions were already familiar in illustrations and reproductions since the Renaissance. Unlike the stage, where convincing drama depends on language, the realistic and romantic screen began with pure picture-making, to which utterance was an appendage. Situations and scenic effects resembled those in known pictures in order to deliver their message inside the familiar frame.

National characteristics affected the early movie style in Europe, as they had informed the flavor of artistic tradition, and the early style of film acting, too. Early Danish and Swedish films were atmospheric and subtly acted rather than spectacular, following the North European talent for using light and facial expression to convey meaning and importance, as in Scandinavian painting of the preceding period. The Italians tended toward stylish line and shape and strong architectural settings, using classical material—Troy and Carthage, or stories in Dante and Tasso, the stuff of the classical opera rather than political or psychological themes.

But what united all movies was the romanticism of their medium, its commitment not just to feeling but to the emotional foundations of living —unconscious fantasy and wish, the desire for something beyond immediate knowledge even if the content ostensibly made an appeal to the intellect. This was the point first grasped and made use of by Eisenstein and the other Russians. The very use of light to make each picture, combined with the illustrative purpose to make all the pictures carry a narrative directly by emotional means, relying only on fragmentary captions, prevents any detachment on the viewer's part. His contribution is ensured, his own psychological history engaged. Film shots took on the emotional freight borne by family snapshots, for example, which in the years between 1890 and 1910 had a great poignancy unmatched by the usual posed studio portraits or landscape studies. The look of people caught off-guard and in motion, or posed against their will in the full grip of some intractable mood —the artless drama of life relentlessly illuminated by the camera—lends a prophetic, movielike look to such early amateur pictures (15.19). They may have seemed unpicturesque at the time; but now they show what the camera was then already able to do with raw human material. Clever movie-makers took it up; and then the editorial skill that makes one particular image succeed another became the new art of the cinema romanticist, who could string together such gripping visions, intersperse them with stirring spectacle and excruciating detail, add music, and so weave a tale guaranteed to keep a total hold on anyone's emotional attention.

Like painting in the Northern tradition, the film aim is unmediated vision; and one of its strongest assistants has always been music, the sort of sound that requires no actual language, and forms a touchstone for romantic expression. It was a fundamental nineteenth-century Romantic idea that music is the ultimate art, the purest vessel; and movies were never silent, in that they were always underscored, sometimes with elaborate orchestral arrangements. Originally this was live music, and it was indispensable for carrying the sequence of visions along on a wave that swept the spectator into the realm of association and fantasy. It was partly the music that turned movies into dreams—and that signaled such an intention by its very presence.

15.19 Family photograph, c. 1905

In some way the music stood for the kind of pictures movies were, and indicated the right way to take them. In the old Dutch paintings, music is often made *in* the picture to give the same message. Perpetually underscored, early cinema thus displayed the affinity of film not with plays but with opera. In opera, narrative proceeds in a sequence, not of incidents and confrontations expounded in comprehensible dialogue, but through translation into the larger irrational terms of music, so that getting the whole meaning at any moment means responding to the music and the story *as one.* Listening to the music alone may render the story ridiculous and therefore remove much of the point of the whole work; trying to follow the story without listening to the music makes the music seem obtrusive and irrelevant and thus cancels the point altogether. The story must be perceived only through the music, and the music may be rightly understood only as it tells the story. In such a situation, although the plot may seem bald and stupid or strange and unbelievable if given in synopsis, the tale itself becomes significant, moving, and emotionally comprehensible when it is offered and received on music's terms. Analogously in film, the impact of a dramatic moment is made by its entire visual frame and ground and its score, too, not just by the situation.

It is a feature of some movies that their visual flavor seems at odds with the flavor of their story, that beautiful cinematography and settings may be conveying a chilling tale otherwise rendered with great detachment. In a bad movie, overdressing a modest story creates a silly imbalance; but in the hands of a serious movie-maker like Stanley Kubrick, for example with *Barry Lyndon,* the tension between the benign beauty of its eighteenth-century mise-en-scène and its harsh story of spiritual poverty functions as a sort of constant ironic pedal-point, giving the movie its unforgettable bite. The rather formal, tragic sound of the eighteenth-century music in the score intensifies the effect. As in a Mozart opera, the story is full of humiliation, folly, and callous betrayal, but the music is ravishing; and the total effect is the result of their interplay and interdependence.

Such an effect is difficult to achieve; the connection must not break between the style and meaning of the moving picture. If cinematic beauty is developed independently of the point being made by the action, the movie is pretty but crippled, and the audience is being seduced by a lovely face so it won't notice the limp. Bad operas at one time were put together in the same way, with no connection between the narrative theme and the music, so that the public would applaud the stars and the beauty of the arias and not care what they meant. In the case of both opera and cinema, the power of the medium is so strong, its direct effect on the feelings so intense, that controlled artistry is not at all necessary for crude success.

Because of how much psychological material loads each film shot, much of it elicited from the viewer, they are heavy with suggestion, indirect reference, multiple possibilities for meaning depending on the next shot, and the next. A great deal of visual matter is thrown away, having raised expectations it cannot meet in the next and next, because of what the director wants and the editor does. Some of this excess content may be so dazzling, however, so full of undifferentiated emotional power, that it functions like a compelling melody, defining the character of the movie even if it makes no immediate sense. If it makes no sense ever, the movie can still appeal and make money; but it will be a failure.

Best is if such visual dazzle *creates* the film's sense, however, and manages to carry all other meanings, as in most of Kubrick's movies. The visual glamour and clarity of the boot-camp sequences in *Full Metal Jacket,* for instance, emphasize the beauty of the applied order in that ferocious artificial existence. The extreme elegance of the cinematography creates the sense of it as a perverse, polished treasure to be laid up for the future—especially the future of actual war, when the chaotic, absurd elements in real life—the slackness and disorder and uncertainty and ridiculousness, the small hilarities and senseless brutalities in normal existence—are intensified. The second half of the movie has that haphazard and ragged visual flavor—with modern rubble and ancient temples, heavy artillery and personal vanity, blood and bureaucracy, mess and horror and silliness all mixed, colors all melted and blurred, localities indefinite, and no point made by anything. A killer is crisply and systematically created in the first half, as intended; in the second, no such outcome, only a sort of chronic, low-level dementia, is produced by war.

In all this, as in most movies, the score works as if it were operatic. Kubrick knows how to make the music help to create the meaning of the action, sometimes to make its point while appearing to go against it. Most other movies, on the other hand, in the past have tended to follow Wagner's method, whereby the music is composed to match the action closely, including the inner action of characters' memories and wishes—the *leitmotif* idea. Lately the habit of embedding a whole film inside a constant, independent performance by one group doing one kind of music has taught us to think of life as a movie underscored by the comforting sound of our favorite performers; but it has further taught us to notice how the visual elements in films are similar to music, in the way they transmit emotive material without calling attention to it, spread suggestions that are responded to personally by the viewer but not by the actors, and fill a rich emotional bath for each viewer, in the depths of which he may get the other material as it can best reach him, with or against the current.

In this way a lot of visual movie material has been swallowed whole, seen without being remarked, responded to without consciousness. Many visual movie myths have seeped unnoticed into the culture and lodged there, along with the stories and situations and famous faces that make up the known legend. Camera angles, spatial relations, relations of lighting and texture have made up more of it than have the details of material life, which tend to catch the conscious eye. And just these basic elements, the background-musical ones, are the ancient legacy of the cinematic painters. Such painterly effects had made their mark on the public eye long before, mostly through being reproduced; and in their emotional, musical, unnoticeable way had long since prepared the modern eye for film language.

THE MOVIES' debt to painting has often been left-handedly acknowledged during their history, with many art-historical quotations occasionally punctuating the flow of historical films. The more sophisticated the lighting in modern movies, as I have suggested, the better this works; but it was already being managed in black-and-white movies fairly early, especially when graphic artists were being quoted. Two German films about Frederick the Great, one silent in 1921 and one with spoken dialogue in 1931, made ample use of Menzel's famous illustrations, as if to show what those had been intended for. Similarly and even more acutely, Alexander Korda's biographical *Rembrandt* of 1936 emulates Rembrandt etchings and chiaroscuro Biblical scenes with great success, even though some

15.20 Still from *Rembrandt,* 1936

15.21   PIETER SAENREDAM, *The Old Town Hall of
Amsterdam*

of the costume details are slightly wrong. The movie offers a Dutch world
through the eyes of Rembrandt's contemporaries as well; Steen and Saenredam supply the neutral interiors and exteriors, as if we were seeing life
through the ordinary representational conventions of Rembrandt's milieu,
and only perceiving private emotional moments in his distinctive mode
(15.20, 15.21). At the very end of the film, as old, dying Rembrandt gazes
at his mirror and prepares his last self-portrait on the easel, the camera
stops contemplating him and rises to seek the universal source, the incoming light. Korda seems to have got the point about Rembrandt, despite the
oversimplified view the film gives of his life.

Carl Dreyer inevitably used Dutch art in 1943 for *Day of Wrath,* set in
seventeenth-century Denmark (15.22, 15.23). A preponderance of stiff
black clothing with white neckwear set against dimly lit and austerely furnished interiors makes the moments featuring flames or outdoor sunlight
all the more startling, and the texture of skin almost unbearably telling, as
they are in the Northern painting tradition. The theme of this grim tale is
God's mysterious will, visually conveyed as His conquering way with light,
whether cruel and lurid or tender and comforting. Its penetrating force is
unrelieved by color or pleasant surfaces, its ultimate reach is unaffected by
men's zealous wish for mastery. Fire and sun outwit the smallness of windows, the dimness of garments, and show up the blackness of souls.

15.22 Still from *Day of Wrath*, 1943

15.23 REMBRANDT, *Syndics of the Drapers' Guild*

15.24 Still from *The Front Page*, 1931. Dutch style in modern dress

Quoting from the multicolored works of the Pre-Raphaelite school has become more accurate since the control of light has increased for film-makers using color. The pale flattening of the detailed imagery has been successfully imitated for English historical themes during the last twenty years, in sharp contrast to the easier deep chiaroscuro effects achieved much earlier in black and white. Pre-Raphaelite imitations, notably in Tony Richardson's *The Charge of the Light Brigade* (1968), and more recently *The French Lieutenant's Woman* (1981), for example, are deliberate visual embodiments of mid-nineteenth-century attitudes, highly suitable to the films' subjects and recognizable to audiences as characteristic *painterly* visualizations of the period. So are many of Korda's in *Rembrandt*. But unlike those early black-and-white ones, which tap the graphic elements in Dutch painting, Pre-Raphaelite references are to an extremely static, non-cinematic kind of art; and so they are used to point up the *difference* between film and painting, not to demonstrate the continuity between them. They are pointed quotes, not assimilations. Interwoven with the texture of the cinematography, they naturally enrich the films enormously, as sensitive period stage designs based on painting enrich plays and operas; but they are not examples of the connection I am trying to make, precisely because such quoting is confined to "period" movies, to make the "period"

15.25 JACQUES CALLOT, *Combat with Swords.* Etching, 1632

15.26 Still from *Alexander Nevsky,* 1938

point. *Rembrandt* and *Day of Wrath,* on the other hand, seamlessly look both period and modern, since the chiaroscuro mode fits both (15.24).

Occasionally even more deliberate spot-quotes will occur in a movie about a painter, like the living Toulouse-Lautrecs momentarily imposed on the otherwise very un-Lautrec-like color cinematography of *Moulin Rouge,* for example, or Van Gogh's Crows in the Wheatfield suddenly attacking Kirk Douglas in *Lust for Life,* or the hilarious Creation-of-Adam cloud formations inspiring Charlton Heston in *The Agony and the Ecstasy.* That last movie was otherwise filmed as if it were a Western, in the style which turns out to be the most generally suitable for any "period" material, after all, since it was invented for such a favorite "period" genre: Porter and Griffith started it, and no amount of quotations from paintings can keep historical movies from quoting themselves to much greater advantage. But when they do it, they are also unwittingly quoting not only Remington but Callot, with his streams of extras pouring over the hills, no matter what artist the movie may be about (15.25–15.28).

One excellent small example in recent times of the perfectly integrated *Rembrandt* kind of film about an artist was a short film made for British television of the Sheridan Le Fanu story entitled "Schalcken." The story is a Romantic tale published in 1851, full of the supernatural effects characteristic of the Irish author; but the subject was the real late-seventeenth-century Dutch painter, who specialized in ambiguously erotic scenes usually lighted with a single candle. The movie successfully combines both late-Baroque Dutch art and nineteenth-century Romanticism in every one of its scenes, many of which had to be invented, since the Le Fanu story is rather sparse. Schalcken's own style of painting is perpetually invoked, in scenes combining candlelit brothel settings and views of the painter's studio with prostitutes as models, all of which are well fitted into the latter part of Le Fanu's story, even though he did not specify them; and scenes early in the story display the style of Gerard Dou, who was in fact the painter's teacher, and whose meek and pretty daughter Le Fanu invented for the young apprentice to adore from a hopeless distance. The faintly sinister look of Schalcken's mature works, overlaid on their sexual content, were romantically expounded by Le Fanu in his tale, which tells how the young girl is virtually sold by her greedy father, as the student looks on in helpless horror, to a mysterious, ancient, deathly bridegroom bearing a coffer of gold coins. She is spirited away, seems to die or merely vanish, and then reappears to the young painter as a seductive, demonic apparition; and so the red glow and enticing smiles of Schalcken's obsessively repeated views of single female figures are accounted for. The movie accounts for both painter and writer, giving the Dutch details an English

15.27 JACQUES CALLOT, "The Conversion of St. Paul," from *The New Testament*. Published posthumously, 1635

15.28 Still from *Stagecoach*, 1939

Romantic cast, even flavoring the girl's seventeenth-century costumes with nineteenth-century details. The lighting follows both Schalcken and certain Romantic gestures seen in Danby, Wilkie, and early Windus—the quaint supernatural cast of the story precludes referring to Turner, but permits allusion to English genre artists of the first half of the century, who often used historic dress and setting. This small effort is an example of what can be done in historical movies if the right understanding is reached about their relation to historical paintings and historical tales. Twentieth-century cinematic romanticism was put to the very best creative use in this neat small synthesis of nineteenth-century English (actually Irish) and seventeenth-century Dutch fictions.

The essentially romantic character of the film medium makes neutral historical chronicle almost impossible in movie form. No matter how much research is done on pots and pans, on private motivation and social forces, on dialect or custom, and how much historical expertise is brought to bear even on the actual shooting, a movie like *The Return of Martin Guerre* ends up a poetic romance. Efforts to reproduce Bruegel paintings fail of their effect, since Bruegel himself was a highly detached, "modern" sort of painter—although highly cinematic in his compositional methods. In his treatment of subject matter, he was an ironic, not a romantic realist. He won't translate very well into the romantic terms of a film like this, which builds a modern romantic French story on an original real-life romantic plot from southern Renaissance France—which was indeed an original home of literary Romance. Bruegel, with his slightly grotesque Northern style, could only be stuck onto the surface of *Martin Guerre* as a necessary allusion, to make a flattering reference to what we are all supposed to know from him about the look of European rural life in the sixteenth century. It might have been better to use the manuscript illuminations for the Romantic epic poems from sixteenth-century France itself, which have the right emotional flavor even if they haven't as many well-known picturesque peasants. An avowedly romantic film-maker like Visconti can very smoothly translate historic painting into historical film by adapting only works of art that depend, like his camera, on the romantic use of light to convey romantic themes; and so he can make the past come alive in *The Leopard*, for example, as it fails to do in *Martin Guerre*.

The visual sequences in that movie carry a message not so much of sixteenth-century rural life as of the romantic conventions of twentieth-century French film-making, in the familiar style of the poignant bittersweet love stories of the 1940's. The historical films of that period, such as *Les Enfants du Paradis* and *Les Visiteurs du Soir,* used to have perfectly acceptable somewhat *incorrect* period costumes, to support the ahistorical, romantic spirit of the films. No pointed references to paintings were attempted; it was pure French movie-making, melodrama made transcendent by the chiaroscuro mode in motion. *Martin Guerre* is actually very similar, and all the expensive historical accuracy is wasted and irrelevant. The stars' amorous relation is the real subject of the movie, and the greatest care and finesse are expended on the modern emotional accuracy of the sequences depicting it—not on a true rendering of French Renaissance peasant life.

By contrast, the quality of Italian peasant existence—its tedium, its weight; the way delicate feelings seek expression in obscure physical terms; how relationships become muffled by circumstance and vulnerable to crude chance—all this itself constitutes the romance in Olmi's *The Tree of Wooden Clogs*. That film is altogether a good example of documentary pictorial romanticism. Emotional response to its situations is drawn from the viewer directly by the muted color, the composition, lighting, and editing of the action that renders it apparently *artless*—just as in the cinematic Realist paintings of peasants by Courbet and Millet (or again by Rembrandt)—and not by rendering "moving" scenes with theatrical pointedness, or by giving youthful characters an attractive gloss—as in *Martin Guerre,* or in the sentimental Realist peasant paintings by Jules Breton.

It should be mentioned here that the Japanese movie-making enterprise has naturally had the advantage of the extraordinary traditions of Japanese graphic art, both in ink and brush and in prints. A graphic history of surpassing sophistication may well have put Japanese film-making ahead of the West in finding ways to show experience as part of a "floating world" that can only be made even more explicit in movies. The influence of the West on Japanese film was large and deep; but the fundamental cinematic narrative conceptions explored and abstracted by Harunobu and Hiroshige, who were inevitably admired by cinematic painters like Degas, show a comparatively advanced understanding for their time. Such a past has undoubtedly given Japanese movie-makers something of an edge, even when they are not treating historical material in historical ways.

Quotation in movies from movie history itself has become the true sign that film has allied itself with the other arts that have built on their own past, forming traditions based on what has worked, making a community of fellow strugglers out of the roster of past practitioners, raiding the entire canon, as Shakespeare and everybody else has done, for whatever earlier discoveries will best serve the turn of present talent. Only the temporary power of rigid academies, rigid regimes, or both, has ever stopped this natural artistic process, and only the failure of present talent has ever made it dangerous or reprehensible.

When American movies were supposed to be not art but entertainment, critical disapprobation used to be expressed of movies that quoted other movies, as if to say that performers should never hope to succeed by stealing tricks from their predecessors—even, or perhaps especially, if it pays off. More recently such obvious use of past greatness was called "homage" to whoever did it first; and most recently it is perceived as right and customary, appreciated if a real talent like Woody Allen plainly builds on the accomplishments of the cinematic past, and censured only if he and his associates steal for lack of natural gifts or good ideas.

By encompassing its own history, film has thus openly acknowledged and encompassed the whole history of visual art: just as Manet stole from both Goya and Velázquez, so a movie-maker can steal from both Manet and Hitchcock. The future of cinema can only be richer if such acknowledgment is more thoroughly internalized and at the same time more consciously understood. Although theater, opera, and all the old poetic and musical and more recent novelistic traditions have fed the movies, they were in fact born of printed graphic art and sired by a certain tradition in great painting. Their noble lineage shows more and more, as maturity has begun to overtake and affect them. As with any career, their future is full of forward movement inspired by hope and daring, and possible enlightenment through the lessons of the past.

SOURCES FOR
ILLUSTRATIONS

SELECT BIBLIOGRAPHY
AND NOTES

INDEX

SOURCES FOR ILLUSTRATIONS

1 MOVING PICTURES

1.1 Jan Vermeer, *Woman Pouring Milk*. Amsterdam, Rijksmuseum. Marburg/Art Resource.

1.2 Rembrandt van Rijn, *The Conspiracy of Claudius Civilis*. Stockholm, Nationalmuseum. Marburg/Art Resource.

1.3 Rembrandt van Rijn, *The Adoration of the Shepherds*. Munich, Alte Pinakothek. Giraudon/Art Resource.

1.4 Sandro Botticelli, *The Birth of Venus*. Florence, Uffizi. Alinari/Art Resource.

1.5 Hendrick Goltzius, *The Farnese Hercules*. Engraving. New York, The Metropolitan Museum of Art.

1.6 Karl Friedrich Schinkel, *Gothic Cathedral by a River*. Berlin, Nationalgalerie. Marburg/Art Resource.

1.7 Edouard Manet, *Olympia*. Paris, Musée d'Orsay.

1.8 John Singer Sargent, *Madame X*. New York, The Metropolitan Museum of Art.

1.9 Edouard Manet, *Au Paradis*. Lithograph. Philadelphia Museum of Art.

1.10 William Cameron Menzies, continuity sketch for *Gone With the Wind*, 1939.

1.11 Anthonie van Dyck, *Christ Carrying The Cross*. Sketch. Bremen, Kunsthalle.

1.12 Sidney Paget, "His eyes fell upon the stick in Holmes' hand." Illustration for Conan Doyle's *The Hound of the Baskervilles*. *The Strand Magazine,* August 1901.

1.13 Francisco Goya, *Mala Noche*. Aquatint from *Los Caprichos*, 1799.

2 THE FIFTEENTH CENTURY

2.1 Jan van Eyck, *The Madonna in the Church*. Berlin, Museum Dahlem.

2.2 Hugo van der Goes, *Monforte Altar*, central panel. Berlin, Museum Dahlem. Marburg/Art Resource.

2.3 Piero della Francesca, *The Baptism of Christ*. London, The National Gallery.

2.4 Cima da Conegliano, *The Virgin and Child*. London, The National Gallery.

2.5 *The Baptism of Christ*. Detail of illumination from *The Turin-Milan Hours*. Turin, Museo Civico. Marburg/Art Resource.

2.6 Gerard David, *The Baptism of Christ*, central panel. Bruges Museum. Marburg/Art Resource.

2.7 *The Massacre of the Innocents*. Illumination, South Netherlands; folio 146v from *The Book of Hours of Isabel la Católica*. The Cleveland Museum of Art.

2.8 Simon Bening, *Winter Evening*. Illumination from *The Da Costa Hours*. New York, Morgan Library.

2.9 Simon Bening, *June*. Detached leaf. Munich, Bayerische Staatsbibliothek.

3 THE SIXTEENTH CENTURY

3.1 *The Impatience of the Sick Man*. Engraving from "*L'art au Morier*" (*Ars Moriendi*).

3.2 Albrecht Dürer, *The Resurrected Christ*. Woodcut from *The Small Passion*. Marburg/Art Resource.

3.3-6 Hans Holbein, *The Merchant, The Duchess, The Ploughman, The Child*. Four woodcuts from *The Dance of Death*.

3.7 Geertgen tot Sint Jans, *The Nativity at Night*. London, The National Gallery.

3.8 Hans Baldung-Grien, *Christ Carried to Heaven by Angels*. Engraving. Karlsruhe, Staatliche Kunsthalle.

3.9 Hans Baldung-Grien, *The Elevation of Mary Magdalen*. Engraving. Basel, Kunstmuseum.

3.10 Albrecht Altdorfer, *The Regensburg Synagogue*. Etching. New York, The Metropolitan Museum of Art.

3.11 Albrecht Altdorfer, *The Danube Valley*. Etching. The Art Institute of Chicago.

3.12 Albrecht Dürer, *The Lake in the Woods*. London, British Museum. Bridgeman/Art Resource.

3.13 Pieter Bruegel the Elder, *The Fall of Icarus*. Brussels, Musée des Beaux Arts. Scala/Art Resource.

3.14 Pieter Bruegel the Elder, *The Return of the Herd*. Vienna, Kunsthistorisches Museum. Marburg/Art Resource.

4 THE EARLY BAROQUE

4.1 Hercules Seghers, *The Mossy Tree*. Monotype. Amsterdam, Rijksmuseum.

4.2 Hercules Seghers, *Distant View with Branch of Pine Tree*. Monotype. Amsterdam, Rijksmuseum.

4.3 Adam Elsheimer, *Jupiter and Mercury in the House of Baucis and Philemon*. Dresden, Gemäldegalerie. Marburg/Art Resource.

4.4 Adam Elsheimer, *The Stoning of St. Stephen*. Edinburgh, National Gallery of Scotland.

4.5 Adam Elsheimer, *The Flight into Egypt*. Munich, Alte Pinakothek.

4.6 Adam Elsheimer, *The Mocking of Ceres* (copy). Madrid, Prado.

4.7 Caravaggio, *The Martyrdom of St. Peter*. Rome, Sta. Maria del Popolo.

4.8 Jacques Callot, *The Opening of the Red Sea*. Etching, 1629.

4.9 Jacques Callot, *Carrying of the Cross*. Etching, c. 1620.

4.10 Georges de la Tour, *The Angel Appearing to St. Joseph*. Nantes, Musée des Beaux Arts. Marburg/Art Resource.

4.11 Georges de la Tour, *A Woman Searching for Fleas*. Nancy, Musée Historique de Lorraine. Giraudon/Art Resource.

5 DUTCH GENRE

5.1 Hendrick Terbrugghen, *The Calling of St. Matthew*. Utrecht, Centraal Museum.

5.2 Still from *Perfect Understanding*, 1933.

5.3 Theodor van Baburen, *The Procuress*. Museum of Fine Arts, Boston.

5.4 Georges de la Tour, *The Payment of Dues*. Lvov, Museum.

5.5 Shot from *The Breaking Point*, 1950.

5.6 Gerard David, *The Virgin and Child*. Brussels, Musée des Beaux Arts. Giraudon/Art Resource.

5.7 Adriaen van Ostade, *Cottage Dooryard*. Washington, D.C., National Gallery of Art, Widener Collection.

5.8 Jan Steen, *The Doctor's Visit*. Philadelphia Museum of Art.

5.9 Gabriel Metsu, *The Musical Party*. New York, The Metropolitan Museum of Art.

5.10 Pieter de Hooch, *Mother Lacing Her Bodice*. Berlin, Museum Dahlem. Marburg/Art Resource.

5.11 Gerard Dou, *Mother and Child*. Berlin, Museum Dahlem.

5.12 Pieter de Hooch, *Child and Mother in a Bedroom*. Washington, D.C., National Gallery of Art, Widener Collection.

5.13 Pieter de Hooch, *The Kolf Players*. National Trust, Polesden Lacey.

5.14 Pieter de Hooch, *Mother Delousing a Child*. Amsterdam, Rijksmuseum. Alinari/Art Resource.

5.15 Pieter de Hooch, *Couple in a Bedroom with a Dog*. New York, The Metropolitan Museum of Art.

5.16 Gerard Terborch, *Woman Peeling Fruit*. Vienna, Kunsthistorisches Museum. Bridgeman/Art Resource.

5.17 Gerard Terborch, *Soldier and Girl*. Paris, Louvre. Alinari/Art Resource.

5.18 Emanuel de Witte, *Interior with Woman at a Clavichord*. State-owned Art Collections, The Hague. Museum Boymans–van Beuningen, Rotterdam.

5.19 Jan Vermeer, *A Man and Woman at the Virginals*. London, Collection of Her Majesty Queen Elizabeth II. Marburg/Art Resource.

5.20 Pieter de Hooch, *Interior of the New Town Hall in Amsterdam*. Lugano, Thyssen-Bornemisza Collection.

5.21 Jacobus Vrel, *Woman at a Window*. Vienna, Kunsthistorisches Museum.

5.22 Pieter Janssens Elinga, *Woman Reading*. Munich, Alte Pinakothek. Marburg/Art Resource.

5.23 Esaias Boursse, *Interior with a Woman Spinning*. Amsterdam, Rijksmuseum.

5.24 Jan Vermeer, *Officer and Laughing Girl*. New York, The Frick Collection.

5.25 Willem Duyster, *Soldiers by a Fireplace*. Philadelphia Museum of Art.

5.26 Gerard Terborch, *Officer and Trumpeter (The Dispatch)*. Philadelphia Museum of Art.

5.27 Jan Vermeer, *Woman Writing a Letter, with her Maid*. Blessington, Ireland, Alfred Beit Collection. Giraudon/Art Resource.

5.28 Pieter Codde, *Young Man with a Pipe*. Lille, Musée des Beaux Arts.

5.29 Gabriel Metsu, *Interior of a Smithy*. London, The National Gallery.

6 LANDSCAPE; PRINTS; REMBRANDT

6.1 Aelbert Cuyp, *Cavaliers Watering Their Horses*. Amsterdam, Rijksmuseum.

6.2 Philips Koninck, *View of Fields*. Amsterdam, Rijksmuseum.

6.3 Rembrandt van Rijn, *Joseph Accused by Potiphar's Wife*. Washington, D.C., National Gallery of Art, Andrew W. Mellon Collection.

6.4 Aert de Gelder, *The Way to Golgotha*. Munich, Galerie Aschaffenburg.

6.5 Jacob Hogers, *The Dance of Salome*. Amsterdam, Rijksmuseum.

6.6 Nicholas van Galen, *The Judgment of Count William the Good*. Hasselt, Province of Overijssel, Town Hall.

6.7 Abraham Bloemaert, *The Marriage of Peleus and Thetis*. Munich, Alte Pinakothek.

6.8 Eglon van der Neer, *Portrait of a Man and a Woman in an Interior*. Seth K. Sweetser Fund. Courtesy Museum of Fine Arts, Boston.

6.9 Jan Vermeer, *View of Delft*. The Hague, Mauritshuis. Giraudon/Art Resource.

6.10 Emanuel de Witte, *A Market in a Port*. Moscow, Pushkin Museum of Fine Arts.

6.11 Gerrit Berckheyde, *The Marketplace at Haarlem*. London, The National Gallery.

6.12 Rembrandt van Rijn, *The Entombment*. Etching, first state.

6.13 Rembrandt van Rijn, *The Entombment*. Etching, fourth state.

6.14 Rembrandt van Rijn, *The Holy Family with a Cat*. Etching.

6.15 Andrea Mantegna, *The Virgin of Humility*. Engraving.

6.16 Rembrandt van Rijn, *Christ Presented to the People*. Etching, seventh state.

6.17 Rembrandt van Rijn, *The Descent from the Cross*. Munich, Alte Pinakothek. Giraudon/Art Resource.

6.18 Rembrandt van Rijn, *The Blinding of Samson*. Frankfurt, Städelsches Kunst-institut. Marburg/Art Resource.

6.19 Rembrandt van Rijn, *Joseph and Potiphar's Wife*. Etching.

6.20 Rembrandt van Rijn, *The Raising of Lazarus*. Los Angeles County Museum. Giraudon/Art Resource.

6.21 Rembrandt van Rijn, *The Raising of Lazarus*. Etching. Giraudon/Art Resource.

6.22 Rembrandt van Rijn, *The Artist in His Studio*. Zoe Oliver Sherman Collection. Given in memory of Lillie Oliver Poor. Courtesy Museum of Fine Arts, Boston.

6.23 Rembrandt van Rijn, *Jan Six Reading*. Etching.

6.24 Rembrandt van Rijn, *Jan Six with a Dog*. Drawing. Amsterdam, Six Collection.

7 FRENCH PRINTS; WATTEAU, CHARDIN

7.1 Jan Verkolje, *An Elegant Couple in an Interior*. Private collection.

7.2 Gotfried Schalcken, *The Doctor's Visit*. Private collection.

7.3 Gotfried Schalcken, *Lady with a Candle*. Florence, Pitti. Giraudon/Art Resource.

7.4 J. D. de St.-Jean, *Suit Worn with a Sword*. Fashion print, 1670's.

7.5 J. D. de St.-Jean, *Lady Walking in the Country*. Fashion print, 1670's.

7.6 J. D. de St.-Jean, *Gentleman of Quality*. Fashion print, 1690's.

7.7 Jacques Callot, figure of a nobleman from *La Noblesse lorraine*, 1624.

7.8 Abraham Bosse, *Shops under the Law Courts*. Etching, c. 1640.

7.9 Antoine Watteau, *Man Walking, Seen in Profile*. Etching, second state. Paris, Bibliothèque Nationale.

7.10 Antoine Watteau, *Peaceful Love*. Berlin, Schloss Charlottenburg. Marburg/Art Resource.

7.11 J.-B.-S. Chardin, *The Return from Market*. Paris, Louvre. Alinari/Art Resource.

7.12 J.-B.-S. Chardin, *The Diligent Mother*. Paris, Louvre. Giraudon/Art Resource.

7.13 J.-B.-S. Chardin, *Little Girl with a Shuttlecock*. Florence, Uffizi. Giraudon/Art Resource.

7.14 J.-B.-S. Chardin, *Self-Portrait*. Paris, Louvre. Giraudon/Art Resource.

7.15 J.-B.-S. Chardin, *The Governess*. Engraving from the painting. Paris, Bibliothèque Nationale. Giraudon/Art Resource.

7.16 J.-B.-S. Chardin, *Glass of Water and Coffeepot, with Onions*. The Carnegie Museum of Art, Pittsburgh, Howard A. Noble Collection, 1966.

8 TIEPOLO, PIRANESI, CANALETTO

8.1 G. B. Tiepolo, *Apotheosis of the Pisani Family*. Strà, Villa Pisani. Alinari/Art Resource.

8.2 G. B. Tiepolo, *La Fortuna* (detail). Venice, Palazzo Labia. Alinari/Art Resource.

8.3 G. B. Tiepolo, *The Sacrifice of Iphigenia*. Vicenza, Villa Valmarana.

8.4 G. B. Tiepolo, *Death Gives Audience*. Etching.

8.5 G. B. Tiepolo, *Two Magicians with Punchinello*. Etching.

8.6 Giuseppe Galli-Bibiena, *scena per angolo* for a *Theatrum Sacrum*.

8.7 Giuseppe Galli-Bibiena, illustration from *Architetture e Prospettive*, 1740.

8.8 Still from Leopoldo Carlucci's *Teodora*, 1919.

8.9 G. B. Piranesi, prison view. No. 15 from *Carceri d' Invenzione*, 1745.

8.10 Canaletto, *The Portico with a Lantern*. Etching.

8.11 Canaletto, *The Thames and London from Richmond House*. Goodwood, Sussex, the Duke of Richmond and Gordon.

8.12 Esaias van de Velde, *View of the Zierickzee*. Berlin, Dahlem Museum. Giraudon/Art Resource.

8.13 Canaletto, *Capriccio: Palace with Clock Tower*. Arundel, Sussex, the Duke of Norfolk.

8.14 Canaletto, *View of the Bacino with the Bucintoro Arriving* (detail). Alinari/Art Resource.

9 HOGARTH, GREUZE, GOYA

9.1 Joseph Highmore, *Mr. Oldham and His Friends*. London, Tate Gallery.

9.2 William Hogarth, *A Midnight Modern Conversation*. New Haven, Yale Center for British Art.

9.3 Joseph Highmore, *The Harlowe Family*. New Haven, Yale Center for British Art.

9.4 J.-B.Greuze, *The Chastised Son*. Paris, Louvre. Alinari/Art Resource.

9.5 Daniel Chodowiecki, two pages from *The Progress of Virtue and Vice*, 1778.

9.6 Daniel Chodowiecki, *Thirst for Knowledge of the World*. Scene from *The Life of a Rake,* 1774.

9.7 Daniel Chodowiecki, *Usual Refuge*. Scene from *The Life of an Ill-educated Girl,* 1780.

9.8 Francisco Goya, "Wait till you've been anointed." No. 67 of *Los Caprichos*, 1799.

9.9 Francisco Goya, "All this and more." No. 22 from *Los Desastres de la Guerra*.

9.10 Francisco Goya, "One cannot look at this." No. 26 from *Los Desastres de la Guerra*.

9.11 Francisco Goya, *Portrait of the Marquesa de Pontejos*. Washington, D.C., National Gallery of Art, Andrew W. Mellon Collection.

10 WATERCOLOR; TURNER, MARTIN

10.1 John Sell Cotman, *Shady Pool*. Edinburgh, National Gallery of Scotland.

10.2 J. M. W. Turner, *Interior at Petworth*. London, British Museum.

10.3 J. M. W. Turner, *Two Women with a Letter*. London, Tate Gallery.

10.4 J. M. W. Turner, *Hannibal Crossing the Alps*. London, Tate Gallery.

10.5 J. M. W. Turner, *Messieurs les Voyageurs on Their Return from Italy (par la Diligence) in a Snow Drift upon Mount Tarrar—22nd of January, 1829*. Reproduced by Courtesy of the Trustees of the British Museum, London.

10.6 J. M. W. Turner, *George IV at the Provost's Banquet*. London, Tate Gallery.

10.7 Francisco Goya, *The Fire*. San Sebastian, Collection José Barez.

10.8 J. M. W. Turner, *Avalanche in the Grisons*. London, Tate Gallery.

10.9 J. M. W. Turner, *The Battle of Fort Rock, Val d'Aouste, Piedmont, 1796*. London, Tate Gallery.

10.10 J. M. W. Turner, *Paestum*. Mezzotint from the *Little Liber*. New Haven, Yale Center for British Art.

10.11 John Ward, *Gordale Scar*. London, Tate Gallery.

10.12 John Martin, *Belshazzar's Feast*. New Haven, Yale Center for British Art.

10.13-14 John Martin, *The Bridge of Chaos* and *Pandemonium*. Engraved illustrations for Milton's *Paradise Lost,* 1827.

10.15 Architectural vision from Lang's *Metropolis,* 1927.

10.16 John Martin, *The Great Day of His Wrath*. London, Tate Gallery.

10.17 John Martin, *The Destruction of Tyre*. The Toledo Museum of Art. Gift of Edward Drummond Libbey.

10.18 Shot from *Samson and Delilah,* 1947.

10.19 John Martin, *The Fall of Nineveh*. Tinted mezzotint. London, Victoria and Albert Museum. Bridgeman/Art Resource.

11 FRIEDRICH, SCHWIND; MENZEL AND HIS INFLUENCE

11.1 J. M. W. Turner, *Peace: Burial at Sea*. London, Tate Gallery.

11.2 C. D. Friedrich, *The Cross in the Mountains*. Dresden, Neue Meister Gemäldegalerie. Marburg/Art Resource.

11.3 Still from *Jesus Christ Superstar,* 1973.

11.4 C. D. Friedrich, *The Cross by the Baltic*. Cologne, Wallraff-Richartz Museum.

11.5 C. D. Friedrich, *Two Men at Moonrise by the Sea*. Chalk and sepia drawing. Moscow, Museum of Fine Art.

11.6 C. D. Friedrich, *The Solitary Tree*. Berlin, Nationalgalerie.

11.7 C. D. Friedrich, *Couple Looking at the Moon*. Berlin, Nationalgalerie.

11.8 Still from *Evangeline,* 1929.

11.9 Still from *Tom Sawyer,* 1938.

11.10 C. D. Friedrich, *Early Snow; Entrance into a Wood*. Hamburg, Kunsthalle. Marburg/Art Resource.

11.11 Still from *Modern Times*, 1936.

11.12 C. D. Friedrich, *View from the Studio Window, left*. Sepia. Vienna, Kunsthistorisches Museum.

11.13 C. D. Friedrich, *View from the Studio Window, right*. Sepia. Vienna, Kunsthistorisches Museum.

11.14 Moritz von Schwind, *The Morning Hour*. Munich, Schackgalerie. Marburg/Art Resource.

11.15 Moritz von Schwind, *Apparition in a Forest*. Munich, Schackgalerie.

11.16 Moritz von Schwind, *Departure in the Early Morning*. Berlin, Nationalgalerie. Marburg/Art Resource.

11.17 Alfred Rethel, *The Visit of Otto III to the Crypt*. Düsseldorf, Kunstmuseum.

11.18 Karl Spitzweg, *The Widower*. Munich, Neue Pinakothek. Marburg/Art Resource. Adolph Menzel, scenes from *The Life of Frederick the Great:*

11.19 Frederick by a river in consultation about improvements.

11.20 Frederick with his minister Cocceji.

11.21 Armed farmers.

11.22 Frederick observes the enemy position at Kollin from an upstairs window.

11.23 Frederick exercises his troops in the rain.

11.24 Adolph Menzel, *A Room with the Artist's Sister*. Munich, Bayerische Staatsgemäldesammlungen. Marburg/Art Resource.

11.25 Adolph Menzel, *The Interruption*. Karlsruhe, Staatliche Kunsthalle.

11.26 Adolph Menzel, *Frederick at Hochkirk*. Berlin, Nationalgalerie.

11.27 Still from *The Horse Soldiers*, 1959.

11.28 John Everett Millais, *Accepted*. Sepia. New Haven, Yale Center for British Art.

11.29 Charles Keene, "Hard Lines." Illustration in *Punch's Almanack*, 1869.

11.30 Still from *Marty*, 1955.

12 ENGLISH ART AND ILLUSTRATION; WHISTLER

12.1 Abraham Solomon, *Waiting for the Verdict*. London, British Museum. Bridgeman/Art Resource.

12.2 H. K. Browne, "Mr. Pinch is amazed by an unexpected apparition." Illustration for Dickens' *Martin Chuzzlewit*, 1843.

12.3 William Powell Frith, "The Arrest." No. 3 from *The Road to Ruin*. Etching by Leopold Flameng from the 1878 painting.

12.4 Arthur Hughes, *The Eve of St. Agnes*. London, Tate Gallery.

12.5 William Holman Hunt, *The Hireling Shepherd*. Manchester City Art Gallery.

12.6 Laurence Alma-Tadema, *Sappho*. Baltimore, The Walters Art Gallery.

12.7 Sidney Paget, "Really, sir, this is a very extraordinary question." Illustration for Conan Doyle's *The Hound of the Baskervilles*, from *The Strand Magazine*, January 1902.

12.8 Frank Holl, *Newgate: Committed for Trial*. Egham, Surrey, Royal Holloway College. Bridgeman/Art Resource.

12.9 Frank Bramley, *A Hopeless Dawn*. London, Tate Gallery.

12.10 Gustave Caillebotte, *The Floor Scrapers*. Paris Musée d'Orsay. Giraudon/Art Resource.

12.11 Lovis Corinth, *Salome*. Leipzig, Museum der Bildenden Kunst. Marburg/Art Resource.

12.12 Atkinson Grimshaw, *View of Liverpool Quay by Moonlight*. London, Tate Gallery.

12.13 J. A. McN. Whistler, *Nocturne in Black and Gold: The Falling Rocket*. Detroit Institute of the Arts. Marburg/Art Resource.

12.14 J. A. McN. Whistler, *Study in Flesh Tones and Black: Portrait of Theodore Duret*.

12.15 J. A. McN. Whistler, *Rotherhithe*. Etching, 1860.

12.16 J. A. McN. Whistler, *Wapping on Thames*. Private collection.

13 AMERICA

13.1 John Singleton Copley, *Watson and the Shark*. Gift of Mrs. George von Lengerke Meyer. Courtesy Museum of Fine Arts, Boston.

13.2 M. J. Heade, *Sunrise on the Marshes*. Michigan, Flint Institute of the Arts.

13.3 Fitz Hugh Lane, *Brace's Rock, Brace's Cove*. The Lano Collection.

13.4 Thomas Cole, *The Expulsion from the Garden of Eden*. Gift of Mrs. Maxim Karolik for the Karolik Collection of American Paintings, 1815–1865. Courtesy Museum of Fine Arts, Boston.

13.5 Thomas Cole, *The Waters Receding After the Deluge*. Washington, D.C., National Museum of American Art, Smithsonian Institution. Gift of Mrs. Katie Dean, in memory of Minnibel S. and James Wallace Dean, and Museum Purchase through Major Acquisitions Fund, Smithsonian Institution.

13.6 Albert Bierstadt, *Mount Adams, Washington*. The Art Museum, Princeton University. Gift of Mrs. Jacob N. Beam.

13.7 Albert Bierstadt, *The Rocky Mountains*. New York, The Metropolitan Museum of Art.

13.8 Winslow Homer, *West Point, Prout's Neck*. Williamstown, Mass., Sterling and Francine Clark Art Institute.

13.9 Winslow Homer, *The Croquet Game*, 1866. Friends of American Art Collection, The Art Institute of Chicago.

13.10 Claude Monet, *Women in the Garden*. Paris, Musée d'Orsay. Giraudon/Art Resource.

13.11 Winslow Homer, *Croquet Player*. New York, National Academy of Design.

13.12–15 Winslow Homer, magazine illustrations. From *Harper's Weekly:* 13.12 "Winter—A Skating Scene," 1868. 13.13 "Our National Winter Exercise — Skating," 1866. From *The Galaxy:* 13.14 "She turned her face to the window," 1868. 13.15 "Weary and dissatisfied with everything," 1869.

13.16 Winslow Homer, *Boys in a Pasture*. The Haydon Collection. Courtesy Museum of Fine Arts, Boston.

13.17 Winslow Homer, *Undertow*. Williamstown, Mass., Sterling and Francine Clark Art Institute.

13.18 Winslow Homer, *The Life Line*. Philadelphia Museum of Art.

13.19 James Tissot, *Portrait of Miss Lloyd*. London, Tate Gallery.

13.20 James Tissot, *The Gallery of H.M.S. "Calcutta."* London, Tate Gallery.

13.21 Thomas Eakins, *The Concert Singer*. Philadelphia Museum of Art.

13.22 Thomas Eakins, *The Pathetic Song*. Washington, D.C., The Corcoran Gallery of Art.

13.23 Thomas Eakins, *Portrait of Mrs. Eakins*. Washington, D.C., Hirshhorn Museum and Sculpture Garden, Smithsonian Institution. Gift of Joseph H. Hirshhorn, 1966.

13.24 Thomas Eakins, *The Swimming Hole*. Collection Modern Museum of Fort Worth. Purchased by the Friends of Art.

13.25 Thomas Eakins, *Sailing*. Philadelphia Museum of Art.

13.26 Thomas Eakins, *Starting Out After Rail*. The Haydon Collection. Courtesy Museum of Fine Arts, Boston.

13.27 Thomas Eakins, *Self-Portrait*. New York, National Academy of Design.

13.28 John Singer Sargent, *Self-Portrait*. Florence, Uffizi.

13.29 John Singer Sargent, *The Daughters of Edward Boit*. Gift of Mary Louisa Boit, Jane Hubbard Boit, and Julia Overing Boit, in memory of their father, Edward Darley Boit. Courtesy Museum of Fine Arts, Boston.

13.30 John Singer Sargent, *Portrait of Mrs. Edward L. Davis and Her Son Livingston Davis*. Los Angeles County Museum of Art.

13.31 Thomas Eakins, *Home Scene*. The Brooklyn Museum. Gift of George A. Hearn, Frederick Loeser Art Fund, Dick S. Ramsay Fund, Gift of Charles A. Schieren.

13.32 Diego Velázquez, *Las Meninas*. Madrid, Prado.

13.33 John Singer Sargent, *Mrs. Carl Meyer and Her Children*. Surringdale, Berkshire, Sir Anthony Meyer. Marburg/Art Resource.

13.34 Edward Hopper, *Room in New York*. University of Nebraska at Lincoln, Sheldon Memorial Art Gallery.

13.35 Edward Hopper, *Second Story Sunlight*. New York, Collection Whitney Museum of American Art.

13.36 Edward Hopper, *Night Shadows*. Etching. New York, Collection Whitney Museum of American Art.

13.37 Edward Hopper, "He did it just on purpose to frighten me . . ." Illustration in *Farmer's Wife,* March 1919.

13.38 Edward Hopper, *Summer Evening*, 1947. Private collection.

13.39 John Singer Sargent, *Venetian Bead Stringers*. Buffalo, N.Y., Albright-Knox Art Gallery.

13.40 Eastman Johnson, *Not at Home*. The Brooklyn Museum. Gift of Miss Gwendolyn O. L. Conkling.

13.41 Fairfield Porter, *A Short Walk*.

13.42 Eric Fischl, *Daddy's Girl*. London, Saatchi Collection.

14 FRANCE IN THE NINETEENTH CENTURY

14.1 Thomas Couture, *Romans of the Decadence* (detail). Paris, Musée d'Orsay. Alinari/Art Resource.

14.2 Edgar Degas, *Woman Ironing, Seen Against the Light*. Washington, D.C., National Gallery of Art.

14.3 Edgar Degas, *Dancers Climbing a Stair*. Paris, Musée d'Orsay. Giraudon/Art Resource.

14.4 Edouard Manet, "Open here I flung the Shutter." Illustration for Poe's *The Raven*. Alinari/Art Resource.

14.5 Edgar Degas, *Interior (Le Viol)*. Philadelphia, Macilhenny Collection.

14.6 Edgar Degas, *The Milliner's Shop*. New York, The Metropolitan Museum of Art.

14.7 Edgar Degas, *Resting on the Bed*. Monotype. Paris, Madame Le Garrec Collection.

14.8 Edgar Degas, *Getting Out of the Bath*. Monotype. Paris, Bibliothèque Nationale.

14.9 Edgar Degas, *The Cardinal Sisters Talking to Admirers*. Monotype, illustration for a novel by Halèvy.

14.10 Charles Meryon, *The Morgue*. Etching, 1854. London, British Museum.

14.11 Charles Meryon, *The Ministry of Marine*. Etching. Philadelphia Museum of Art.

14.12 Charles Meryon, *The Pont-au-Change*. Etching, fifth state. The Saint Louis Art Museum.

14.13 Charles Meryon, *The Pont-au-Change*. Etching, seventh state. New York, The Metropolitan Museum of Art.

14.14 Charles Meryon, *The Pont-au-Change*. Etching, tenth state. Minneapolis Institute of Arts.

14.15 Charles Meryon, *The Pont-au-Change*. Etching, eleventh state. Philadelphia Museum of Art.

14.16 Edouard Manet, *Reading "l'Illustré,"* c. 1878–79. Mr. and Mrs. Lewis Larned Coburn Memorial Collection, The Art Institute of Chicago.

14.17 Edgar Degas, *Henri De Gas and His Niece, Lucie De Gas*, 1875–78. Mr. and Mrs. Lewis Larned Coburn Memorial Collection, The Art Institute of Chicago.

14.18 Henri Fantin-Latour, *The Two Sisters*, 1859. The Saint Louis Art Museum.

14.19 Gustave Caillebotte, *Paris Street; Rainy Weather*, 1876–77. Charles H. and Mary F. S. Worcester Fund, The Art Institute of Chicago. All Rights Reserved.

14.20 Gustave Caillebotte, *The Luncheon*. Paris, private collection.

14.21 Henri Fantin-Latour, *Portrait of Mr. and Mrs. Edwin Edwards*. London, Tate Gallery.

14.22 Henri Fantin-Latour, *Spring Flowers, Apples and Pears*. New York, The Metropolitan Museum of Art.

14.23 Henri Fantin-Latour, *Still Life, Corner of the Table*, 1873. Ada Turnbull Hertle Fund. The Art Institute of Chicago.

14.24 Vilhelm Hammershoi, *Interior with Seated Woman*. Aarhus Kunstmuseum.

14.25 Vilhelm Hammershoi, *Five Portraits*. Stockholm, Thielska Galleriet.

15 TWENTIETH-CENTURY GRAPHICS; MOVIES

15.1 Louis Daguerre, *The Ruins of Holyrood Chapel*. Liverpool, Walker Art Gallery.

15.2 Gustave Doré, "The Gnarled Monster." Illustration for *The Legend of Croquemitaine*.

15.3 Gustave Doré, "The Fall of Satan," 1866. Illustration for Milton's *Paradise Lost*.

15.4 Kenyon Cox, "Lodgers in a crowded Bayard Street tenement—Five Cents a Spot," 1889. Illustration in *Scribner's Monthly Magazine*, after a photograph from Jacob Riis' *How the Other Half Lives*.

15.5 Howard Chandler Christy, "Her husband and I turned on her together." Illustration in *Scribner's Monthly Magazine*, December 1900.

15.6 Charles Dana Gibson, "Stage-Struck." Illustration in *Collier's Weekly*, March 1905.

15.7 Still from *You and Me*, 1938.

15.8 J. Henry, "You nervy little devil, you!" Illustration for Edna Ferber's *Fanny Herself*, 1917.

15.9 Frederic Remington, "Long sat waiting for an answer." Photogravure from a monochrome painting, 1892. Illustration for Longfellow's *The Song of Hiawatha*.

15.10 Frederic Remington, *The Sentinel*. All Rights Reserved. Courtesy Frederic Remington Art Museum, Ogdensburg, N.Y.

15.11 Frederic Remington, "Branding a Calf." Process-engraving from an ink drawing based on a photograph by Theodore Roosevelt. Illustration in *Century Magazine*, April 1888.

15.12 Howard Pyle, "In the Presence of Washington." Illustration in *Century Magazine*, April 1897.

15.13 Still from *The Man Who Came to Dinner*, 1941.

15.14 Jan Vermeer, *Officer and Laughing Girl*. New York, The Frick Collection.

15.15 Still from *The Great Lie*, 1941.

15.16 Jań Vermeer, *The Loveletter* (detail). Amsterdam, Rijksmuseum.

15.17 Howard Pyle, *Thomas Jefferson* (detail).

15.18 Gerrit van Honthorst, *Christ before the High Priest*. London, The National Gallery.

15.19 Family photograph, c. 1905.

15.20 Still from *Rembrandt*, 1936.

15.21 Pieter Saenredam, *The Old Town Hall of Amsterdam*. Amsterdam, Rijksmuseum.

15.22 Still from *Day of Wrath*, 1937.

15.23 Rembrandt, *Syndics of the Drapers' Guild*. Amsterdam, Rijksmuseum. Marburg/Art Resource.

15.24 Still from *The Front Page*, 1931.

15.25 Jacques Callot, *Combat with Swords*. Etching, 1632.

15.26 Still from *Alexander Nevsky*, 1938.

15.27 Jacques Callot, "The Conversion of St. Paul," from *The New Testament*. Published posthumously, 1635.

15.28 Still from *Stagecoach*, 1939.

SELECT BIBLIOGRAPHY
AND NOTES

PAINTING

Alpers, Svetlana. *The Art of Describing*. Chicago, 1983.

Andrews, Keith. *Adam Elsheimer*. New York, 1977.

Banks, Oliver. *Watteau and the North: Studies in the Dutch and Flemish Influence on French Rococo Painting*. New York, 1977.

Benesch, Otto. *The Art of the Renaissance in Northern Europe: Its Relation to the Contemporary Spiritual and Intellectual Movements*. Cambridge, 1947.

Bicknell, Peter. *Beauty, Horror and Immensity: Picturesque Landscape in Britain, 1750–1850* (catalogue). Fitzwilliam Museum, Cambridge, 1981.

Blankert, Albert, et al. *Gods, Saints and Heroes: Dutch Painting in the Age of Rembrandt* (catalogue). Washington, D.C., 1980.

Boime, Albert. *The Academy and French Painting in the 19th Century*. New Haven, 1986.

Börsch-Supan, Helmut. *Casper David Friedrich* (trans. Sarah Twohig). New York, 1974.

Boyle, Richard J. *American Impressionism*. Boston, 1974.

Brett, Bernard. *A History of Watercolor*. New York, 1984.

Brion, Marcel. *Art of the Romantic Era*. New York, 1966.

Brown, Jonathan. *Velázquez, Painter and Courtier*. New Haven and London, 1986.

Clarke, Kenneth. *Landscape into Art* (1949). Boston, 1961.

———. *The Romantic Rebellion*. New York, 1973.

Clark, T. J. *The Absolute Bourgeois*. London, 1973.

———. *The Painting of Modern Life*. Princeton, 1984.

DeWinter, Patrick M. "A Book of Hours of Queen Isabel La Católica." *The Bulletin of the Cleveland Museum of Art*, Vol. 67, No. 10, December 1981.

Foucart, Bruno. *Courbet*. New York, 1977.

Fried, Michael. *Absorption and Theatricality: Painting and Beholder in the Age of Diderot*. Berkeley and Los Angeles, 1980.

———. "Manet's Sources; Aspects of his Art, 1859–1865." *ArtForum*, March 1969.

———. "Thomas Couture and the Theatricalization of Action in 19th-Century French Painting." *ArtForum*, June 1970, pp. 42–46.

Fromentin, Eugène. *The Masters of Past Time* (1876). Oxford, 1948.

Fuchs, R. H. *Dutch Painting*. New York and London, 1978.

———. *Rembrandt in Amsterdam*. New York Graphic Society, 1969.

Gassier, Pierre. *Goya: A Witness of His Time*. Fribourg, 1983.

Gerson, Horst. *Rembrandt Paintings*. Amsterdam, 1968.

Gombrich, E. H. *Art and Illusion*. Princeton, 1960.

──────. "Moment and Movement in Art." *Journal of the Warburg and Courtauld Institutes*, No. 27 (1964), pp. 293–306.

──────. *The Heritage of Apelles*. Oxford, 1976.

Goodrich, Lloyd. *Edward Hopper*. New York, 1976.

Gowing, Lawrence. *Turner, Imagination and Reality*. New York, 1966.

──────. *Vermeer* (1952). New York, 1970.

Hanson, Anne Coffin. *Manet and the Modern Tradition*. New Haven and London, 1977.

Hendricks, Gordon. *Albert Bierstadt*. New York, 1974.

──────. *The Life and Work of Thomas Eakins*. New York, 1974.

Hofmann, Werner. *Art in the Nineteenth Century*. London, 1960.

Honour, Hugh. *Romanticism*. London, 1979.

James, Henry. "The Painter's Eye," in John C. Sweeney (ed.), *Notes and Essays on the Pictorial Arts*. Cambridge, 1956.

Jensen, Jens Christian. *Adolph Menzel*. Cologne, 1982.

Johnstone, Christopher. *John Martin*. London, 1974.

Kren, Thomas, ed. *Renaissance Painting in Manuscripts*. New York, 1983.

Levey, Michael. *Painting in XVIII Century Venice*. London, 1959.

Licht, Fred. *Goya: The Origins of the Modern Temper in Art*. New York, 1979.

Maas, Jeremy. *Victorian Painters*. New York, 1967.

Meisel, Martin. *Realizations: Narrative, Pictorial and Theatrical Arts in nineteenth century England*. Princeton, 1983.

McShine, Kynaston, ed. *The Natural Paradise* (essays by Barbara Novak, Robert Rosenblum, and John Wilmerding). New York, 1976.

Nochlin, Linda. *Realism*. New York, 1971.

──────. "The Realist Criminal and the Abstract Law." *Art in America*, September–October 1973.

Novak, Barbara. *American Painting of the 19th Century*. New York, 1969.

──────. "Landscape Permuted: From Painting to Photography." *ArtForum*, October 1975.

──────. *Nature and Culture*. New York, 1980.

Olson, Stanley. *John Singer Sargent, His Portrait*. New York, 1986.

Panofsky, Erwin. *Early Netherlandish Painting*. Cambridge, 1953.

Paulson, Ronald. *Hogarth, His Life, Art and Times*. New Haven, 1974.

Ratcliff, Carter. *John Singer Sargent*. New York, 1982.

Reff, Theodore. *Degas: The Artist's Mind*. New York, 1976.

──────. *Manet: Olympia*. New York, 1977.

Reiss, Stephen. *Aelbert Cuyp*. Boston, 1975.

Rewald, John. *History of Impressionism* (fourth rev. ed.). New York, 1973.

Reynolds, Graham. *A Concise History of Watercolors*. London, 1971.

Rosen, Charles, and Henri Zerner. *Romanticism and Realism*. New York, 1984.

Rosenberg, Pierre, and Margaret Morgan Grasselli. *Chardin* (catalogue). Cleveland, 1979.

──────. *Watteau* (catalogue). Washington, D.C., 1984.

Rosenblum, Robert. *Modern Painting and the Northern Romantic Tradition*. New York, 1975.

──────, and H. W. Janson. *19th Century Art*. New York, 1984.

Schapiro, Meyer. "Courbet and Popular Imagery" (1941) and "The Introduction of Modern Art in America: The Armory Show" (1952), both reprinted in *Modern Art*, New York, 1978.

Schiff, Gert, et al. *German Masters of the Nineteenth Century* (catalogue). New York, 1981.

Schiff, Richard, "The End of Impressionism." *Art Quarterly*, Vol. 1, No. 4, Autumn 1978.

Schwartz, Gary. *Rembrandt: His Life, His Paintings*. New York, 1985.

Sewell, Darrel. *Thomas Eakins, Artist of Philadelphia*. Philadelphia, 1982.

Seznec, Jean. *John Martin en France*. London, 1964.

Stokes, Adrian. *Painting and the Inner World* (1963) and *The Invitation in Art* (1965), both in Vol. 3; *The Quattro Cento* (1932), in Vol. 2 of *The Critical Writings of Adrian Stokes*, London, 1978.

Strong, Roy. *"And when did you last see your father?"* London, 1978.

Sutton, Peter. *Pieter de Hooch*. Oxford, 1980.

————, et al. *Masters of Seventeenth Century Dutch Genre Painting* (catalogue). Philadelphia, 1984.

Swanson, Vern G. *Alma-Tadema*. New York, 1977.

Ten-Doesschate Chu, Petra. *French Realism and the Dutch Masters*. Utrecht, 1974.

Varnedoe, Kirk. "Caillebotte: An Evolving Perspective," in *Gustave Caillebotte, a Retrospective Exhibition* (catalogue). Houston, 1976.

————. *Gustave Caillebotte*. New Haven and London, 1987.

Vaughan, William. *German Romantic Painting*. New Haven, 1980.

Waterhouse, Ellis. *Painting in Britain, 1530–1790* (fourth ed.). New York, 1978.

Weelen, Guy. *Turner*. New York, 1982.

Weisberg, Gabriel P. *The Realist Tradition: French Painting and Drawing, 1830–1900* (catalogue). Cleveland, 1980.

Wilmerding, John. *American Light: The Luminist Movement 1850–1875* (catalogue). Washington, D.C., 1980.

Wilton, Andrew. *J. M.W. Turner: His Art and Life*. Fribourg, 1979.

————. *Turner and the Sublime*. Chicago, 1980.

Wind, Edgar. "The Revolution of History Painting." *The Journal of the Warburg Institute*, Vol. 2 (1938–39), p. 116.

GRAPHIC ART

Adhémar, Jean, and Françoise Cachin. *Degas: The Complete Etchings, Lithographs and Monotypes*. Paris, 1973.

Boon, K. G. *Rembrandt: The Complete Etchings*. New York, n.d.

Burke, James D. *Charles Meryon Prints and Drawings* (catalogue). New Haven, 1974.

Clark, James M., ed. *Dance of Death by Hans Holbein*. Oxford, 1947.

Daniel, Howard. *Callot's Etchings: 338 Prints*. New York, 1974.

Davis, Natalie Zemon. "Printing and the People," in *Society and Culture in Early Modern France*. Palo Alto, 1975.

Eisenstein, Elizabeth L. *The Printing Press as an Agent of Change*. Cambridge, Eng., 1979.

Hofer, Philip, ed. *The Disasters of War, Francisco Goya*. Mineola, N.Y., 1967.

————, ed. *Los Caprichos, Francisco Goya*. Mineola, N.Y., 1969.

Ivins, William M. *How Prints Look*. Boston, 1943.

———. *Notes on Prints* (1930). New York, 1967.

———. *Prints and Visual Communication*. Cambridge, 1953.

Jussim, Estelle. *Visual Communication and the Graphic Arts*. New York, 1974.

Kunzle, David. *The Early Comic Strip*. Berkeley, 1973.

Marrow, James H., and Alan Shestack, eds. *Hans Baldung Grien, Prints and Drawings* (catalogue). New Haven, 1981.

Mayor, A. Hyatt. *Prints and People*. Princeton, 1971.

McLuhan, Marshall. *The Gutenberg Galaxy*. Toronto, 1962.

Mélot, Michel, et al. *Prints: History of an Art*. New York, 1981.

Panofsky, Erwin. *Albrecht Dürer* (third ed.). Princeton, 1948.

Rowlands, John. *Hercules Segers*. New York, 1979.

Wilton-Ely, John. *The Mind and Art of Giovanni Battista Piranesi*. London, 1978.

Zigrosser, Earl. *Prints and Their Creators* (1937). New York, 1979.

ILLUSTRATION

Beam, Philip. *Winslow Homer's Magazine Engravings*. New York, 1979.

Benesch, Otto. *Artistic and Intellectual Trends from Rubens to Daumier as Shown in Book Illustration*. New York, 1969.

Finley, Gerald. *Landscapes of Memory: Turner as Illustrator to Scott*. Berkeley and Los Angeles, 1980.

Gosling, Nigel. *Gustave Doré*. New York, 1974.

Harvey, John. *Victorian Novelists and Their Illustrators*. New York, 1971.

Hunnisett, Basil. *Steel Engraved Book Illustration in England*. Boston, 1980.

Larkin, Oliver. *Art and Life in America*. New York, 1949.

Levin, Gail. *Edward Hopper as Illustrator*. New York, 1979.

———. *Edward Hopper: The Complete Prints*. New York, 1979.

Reid, Forrest. *Illustrators of the Eighteen-sixties* (1928). Mineola, N.Y., 1975.

PHOTOGRAPHY

Coke, Van Deren. *The Painter and the Photograph*. Albuquerque, N.M., 1964.

Galassi, Peter. *Before Photography: Painting and the Invention of Photography*. New York, 1981.

Gernsheim, Helmut. *A Concise History of Photography* (third rev. ed.). New York, 1986.

Gosling, Nigel. *Nadar*. New York, 1976.

Ivins, William M. "Photography and the Modern Point of View: A Speculation in the History of Taste." *Metropolitan Museum Studies,* Vol. 1 (1928–29), pp. 16–24.

Malcolm, Janet. *Diana and Nikon*. Boston, 1980.

Needham, Gerald. "Manet, Olympia and Pornographic Photography," in Thomas Hess and Linda Nochlin (eds.), *Woman as Sex Object*. New York, 1972.

Newhall, Beaumont. *History of Photography* (1949). New York, 1964.

Scharf, Aaron. *Art and Photography*. London, 1968.

———. "Painting, Photography and the Image of Movement." *Burlington Magazine*, May 1962, pp. 186–95.

Sontag, Susan. *On Photography*. New York, 1977.

Terrasse, Antoine. *Degas et la photographie*. Paris, 1983.

Thomas, Alan. *Time in a Frame*. New York, 1977.

MOVIES

Andrew, Dudley. *Concepts in Film Theory*. Oxford, 1984.

――――. *The Major Film Theories*. Oxford, 1976.

Arnheim, Rudolf. *Film as Art*. Berkeley and Los Angeles, 1957.

Barsacq, Leon. *Caligari's Cabinet and Other Grand Illusions: A History of Film Design*. Boston, 1975.

Bazin, André. *What Is Cinema?* Berkeley, 1967.

Braudy, Leo. *The World in a Frame*. New York, 1976.

Cavell, Stanley. *The World Viewed*. New York, 1971.

Corliss, Mary, and Carlos Clarens. "Designed for Film: The Hollywood Art Director." *Film Comment*, May–June 1978.

Eisner, Lotte. *L'Ecran demoniaque*. Paris, 1965.

Gambill, Norman. "Harry Horner's Design Program for *The Heiress*." *Art Journal*, Vol. 43, No. 3, Fall 1983.

Harbison, Robert. *Eccentric Spaces*. New York, 1977.

Jacobs, Lewis. *The Emergence of Film Art* (anthology). New York, 1969.

Krakauer, Siegfried. *Theory of Film: The Redemption of Physical Reality*. Oxford, 1960.

Mast, Gerald. *A Short History of the Movies* (fourth ed.). New York, 1986.

――――, and Marshall Cohen. *Film Theory and Criticism* (second ed.; anthology). New York, 1979.

Ross, T. J. *Film and the Liberal Arts* (anthology). New York, 1970.

Sarris, Andrew. *The American Cinema*. New York, 1968.

Schickel, Richard. *D.W. Griffith, An American Life*. New York, 1984.

Schrader, Paul. *The Transcendental Style in Film: Ozu, Bresson, Dreyer*. Berkeley and Los Angeles, 1972.

Truffaut, François. *Hitchcock*. New York, 1985.

Tyler, Parker. *Classics of the Foreign Film*. New York, 1962.

Vardac, A. Nicolas. *Stage to Screen: Theatrical Method from Garrick to Griffith*. Cambridge, 1949.

SOCIETY, HISTORY, AND ART

Baudelaire, Charles. *The Painter of Modern Life and Other Essays* (trans. and ed. Jonathan Mayne). London, 1964.

Becker, George J., and Edith Philips, trans. and eds. *Paris and the Arts, 1851–1896: From the Goncourt Journal*. Ithaca, N.Y., 1971.

Berger, John. *Ways of Seeing*. London, 1972.

Burke, Peter. *Popular Culture in Early Modern Europe*. New York, 1978.

Cardinal, Roger. *German Romantics in Context*. London, 1975.

Focillon, Henri. *The Life of Forms in Art* (1936). Second English ed., New York, 1948.

Gay, Peter. *Art and Act: On Causes in History—Manet, Gropius, Mondrian*. New York, 1976.

Holt, Elizabeth G., ed. *The Triumph of Art for the Public: The Emerging Role of Exhibitions and Critics*. New York, 1979.

Klingender, Francis D. *Art and the Industrial Revolution* (ed. Arthur Elton). New York, 1968.

Kubler, George. *The Shape of Time: Remarks on the History of Things.* New Haven, 1982.

Podro, Michael. *The Critical Historians of Art.* New Haven, 1982.

Schama, Simon. "The Unruly Realm: Appetite and Restraint." *Daedalus,* Vol. 108, No. 3 (1971), pp. 103–23.

———. "Wives and Wantons: Versions of Womanhood." *Oxford Art Journal*, April 1980, pp. 5–13.

Williams, Raymond. "Advertising: The Magic System," in *Problems in Material Culture.* London, 1980.

Wind, Edgar. *Art and Anarchy.* New York, 1964.

NOTES ON SOURCES OF QUOTATIONS IN THE TEXT

page 15 "a handless eye": Focillon, p. 73.

  51 "integral . . . being": Fried, *Absorption,* p. 91.

  61 ". . . *in* the landscape": Clark, *Landscape*, p. 17.

  68 ". . . infinitely large": Panofsky, *Early Netherlandish Painting*, p. 3.

  77 "sadism . . . seemingly strong" and "unstylized reality": Panofsky, "Style and Medium," in Mast and Cohen, p. 263.

  86 "the Northern day": Stokes, *Writings*, Vol. 1, p. 39.

 183 "the upward look": Mayor, p. 490.

    "He suddenly puts . . .": Mayor, p. 489.

 253 ". . . no need for color . . .": Goya quoted in Hofer, *Disasters*, p. 20.

 262 "Nature wants cooking": Varley quoted in Reynolds, p. 102.

 279 "the first chaos": Hazlitt quoted in Stokes, *Writings*, Vol. 3, p. 251.

 284 "towered structures": Lamb quoted in Johnstone, p. 16

 298 "the search . . .": Rosenblum, *Modern Painting*, p. 218.

 346 "You behave . . .": Reff, *Degas*, p. 18

 370 "She has . . .": "Daisy Miller," *Henry James Selected Short Stories,* Penguin Modern Classics, p. 143.

 371 "what o'clock": Eakins quoted in Sewell, p. 15.

INDEX

Note: Page numbers in *italics* refer to illustrations.

A NOTE ABOUT THE AUTHOR

Anne Hollander was born in Cleveland and educated at Barnard College
in New York City. An art historian with a special interest in the
representation of dress in art, she is the author of *Seeing Through Clothes*
(1978) and has frequently contributed to *The Times Literary Supplement,*
The New York Review of Books, The New York Times Magazine, The New
Republic, and other magazines. She lives in New York City.

A NOTE ON THE TYPE

This book was set in a digitized version of DeVinne, an American typeface that is actually a recutting by Gustav Schroeder of French Elzevir. It was introduced by the Central Type Foundry of St. Louis in 1889. Named in honor of Theodore Low DeVinne, whose nine-story plant, called the Fortress, was the first building in New York City erected expressly for printing, the type has a delicate quality obtained by the contrast between the thick and thin parts of letters. An enormously popular type during the early part of this century, DeVinne combines easy readability with a nostalgically atmospheric feeling.

Composed by New England Typographic Service, Inc.,
Bloomfield, Connecticut
Printed and bound by Halliday Lithographers,
West Hanover, Massachusetts
Designed by Iris Weinstein